T0212351

Undergraduate Topics in Computer Science

'Undergraduate Topics in Computer Science' (UTiCS) delivers high-quality instructional content for undergraduates studying in all areas of computing and information science. From core foundational and theoretical material to final-year topics and applications, UTiCS books take a fresh, concise, and modern approach and are ideal for self-study or for a one- or two-semester course. The texts are all authored by established experts in their fields, reviewed by an international advisory board, and contain numerous examples and problems, many of which include fully worked solutions.

The UTiCS concept relies on high-quality, concise books in softback format, and generally a maximum of 275–300 pages. For undergraduate textbooks that are likely to be longer, more expository, Springer continues to offer the highly regarded Texts in Computer Science series, to which we refer potential authors.

Vicenç Torra

Guide to Data Privacy

Models, Technologies, Solutions

 Springer

Vicenç Torra
Department of Computing Science
Umeå University
Umeå, Sweden

ISSN 1863-7310   ISSN 2197-1781   (electronic)
Undergraduate Topics in Computer Science
ISBN 978-3-031-12836-3   ISBN 978-3-031-12837-0   (eBook)
https://doi.org/10.1007/978-3-031-12837-0

This Springer imprint is published by the registered company Springer Nature Switzerland AG
The registered company address is: Gewerbestrasse 11, 6330 Cham, Switzerland

To my parents

Preface

Data privacy is now a hot topic. Big data have increased its importance. Nevertheless, computational methods for data privacy have been studied and developed since the 70s, at least.

I would say that there are three different communities that work on data privacy from a technological perspective. One is the statistical disclosure control (people with a statistical background), another is the privacy-preserving data mining (people that proceed from databases and data mining), and finally the privacy-enhancing technologies (people that proceed from communications and security).

This book tries to give a general perspective of the field of data privacy in a unified way and cover at least partially some of the problems and solutions studied by these three communities. The goal is not to present all methods and algorithms for all types of problems, nor the latest algorithms and results. I think that this is an almost impossible task. The goal is to give a broad view of the field and present the different approaches (some of them in their basic form), so that the reader can then deepen in their field of interest.

In this way, the book differs from others that focus on only one of the areas of data privacy. For example, we find the reference books on statistical disclosure control [520, 156, 239, 467] and privacy-preserving data mining ([18], edited book), [194], [505] (focusing on computation-driven/cryptographic approaches). We also edited [346] a book that presents the research on privacy in the ARES project. In addition, there are other books that focus on a specific type of data protection approach or type of problem (e.g., association rule hiding [118], data outsourcing [189], synthetic data generators [152, 467], differential privacy [289, 541], and databases and microaggregation [140, 467]). A book that gives a broad picture of privacy for big data is the one by Lane et al. [276] but, in contrast to the others, it does not include details on data privacy technologies.

I have been working on data privacy for more than 20 years. My research has mainly focused on topics related to privacy for databases, and disclosure risk measurement. Because of that, the book is biased toward data protection mechanisms for databases.

The book is partially based on the lectures I have given at Universitat Autònoma de Barcelona, University of Linköping, Maynooth University, University of

Skövde, and Umeå University and using material from the one I published in 2017 [483]. While some text is kept from this previous text, the structure has been revised and changed, and some new chapters are included, others removed.

The book is written for the last courses of undergraduate studies or at the master level in computer engineering, statistics, data science, and related fields. It contains bibliographical notes and references to help deepening in the area. The book is expected to be self-contained.

Privacy Models

I understand privacy models as computational definitions of privacy. Then, privacy mechanisms are to ensure that the requirements associated to the definitions hold. Different definitions focus on different understandings or requirements of privacy. I also understand that privacy is not only a security problem, e.g. someone has unauthorized access to some data or information. I expect that intruders do some kind of inference, because data has been protected in a way.

The boundaries of privacy and, e.g. security are vague. In this book, I leave access control outside the area of privacy technologies. The same applies to encryption for databases. They are, of course, a basic component of any current information system. Nevertheless, I consider that they are not key privacy technologies. In contrast, I include as privacy models secure multiparty computation and homomorphic encryption and present an example of secure multiparty computation for a particular function (adding a few numbers in a distributed setting).

I think that designing and implementing an information system in a way that satisfies privacy by design usually require a variety of tools. Some applications need homomorphic encryption and secure multiparty computation. We therefore need to understand when they can be useful from a privacy perspective, and this means to understand what type of privacy they are providing. In other words, we need to know which privacy model they satisfy.

Organization

The structure of the book is as follows. Chapter 1 gives an introduction to the field, reviewing the main terminology. Chapter 2 is a brief summary of techniques in the machine and statistical learning, and cryptography. I focus on the tools we need or mention later.

Chapter 3 defines disclosure and presents privacy models. Among others, we review privacy from reidentification, k-anonymity, and differential privacy. Privacy models related to cryptography are also included. So, we include homomorphic encryption and secure multiparty computation. The chapter finishes with a road-map of data protection procedures. This last part is a classification of protection procedures from different perspectives.

Then, Chap. 4 focuses on methods for user privacy. I discuss methods for communication and information retrieval. I present tools to protect the identity and the data of users.

Chapter 5 is about privacy for computations. This includes tools to achieve differential privacy, as well as tools for secure multiparty computation.

The following chapter (Chap. 6) is about privacy for data. In this chapter, we describe the major families of masking methods and include some algorithms of these families. For example, noise addition, microaggregation, rank swapping, and PRAM. I make connections of some of these methods with k-anonymity and differential privacy. I also describe some tools for synthetic data generation including model-based methods and generative adversarial networks (GANs). Selection has been based on the simplicity of the algorithm, well-knownness, and personal bias.

Chapter 7 is about the selection of data protection mechanisms. I mainly discuss information loss measures and R-U maps as a tool to visualize the trade-off between information loss and disclosure risk. The chapter finishes on the problem of method selection in machine learning and, more particularly, federated learning.

Chapter 8 is about the protection of other types of data. I provide an overview of mechanisms for result privacy and for protecting tabular data.

The book finishes with some conclusions and guidelines for data privacy (Chap. 9).

How to Use This Book

The book can be used to give a general introduction to data privacy to engineers and statisticians. We would describe the different types of problems and solutions using privacy technologies. For this, the course would start with the first and third chapters of the book. Then, if the course is expected to be technical, we would use most of the material in the remaining chapters (probably excluding Chap. 8). Only the most relevant algorithms in Chap. 6 would be explained.

Alternatively, it can be used focusing on masking methods and differential privacy. In this case, the emphasis would be given to Chap. 6 and to differential privacy in Chap. 5. We would add an overview of Chaps. 3 and 7. For an audience in statistics, tabular data protection methods in Chap. 8 would be included.

The book can also be used focusing on data privacy for big data. It contains a description of data privacy methods for big data. In Chap. 6 (on masking methods) there is for each family of methods a section focusing on big data, and Sect. 6.6, at the end of the chapter, wraps up all these partial discussions. The sections on each family of methods and their use for big data are as follows. Section 6.1.1 is on rank swapping, Sect. 6.1.2 on microaggregation, Sect. 6.1.3 on additive and multiplicative noise, Sect. 6.1.4 on PRAM, Sect. 6.1.5 on lossy compression, and Sect. 6.4.3 on algorithms for k-anonymity for big data. Then, we also discuss disclosure risk and information loss for big data in the corresponding chapters. That is, Sect. 3.3.2 is on disclosure risk (including a subsection on guidelines and research issues) and Sect. 7.1.5 is on information loss.

I used parts of this book in courses on data privacy with 6 and 12 hours of lectures, plus additional work. The course of 12 hours described the main concepts of data privacy, the classification of methods, a high-level description of disclosure risk and information loss, and a summary of masking methods. A course syllabus for 8 lectures of 2 hours follows. The structure maps the chapters of this book.

- L1. Introduction to data privacy.
- L2. Basic concepts on machine learning and cryptography.
- L3. Privacy models.
- L4. Differential privacy.
- L5. Differential privacy and Secure multiparty computation.
- L6. Masking methods.
- L7. Masking methods and method selection.
- L8. Tabular data protection.

For experimentation, open software such as the sdcMicro package [466] in R can be used. I used this in my courses. Another open-source software for data anonymization is ARX [543]. To generate synthetic data, we have synthpop [363], also in R.

Acknowledgements

I was introduced to this field by Josep Domingo-Ferrer when we met in Tarragona, at the Universitat Rovira i Virgili, at the end of the 1990s. We have worked together on national and international projects. So, my first acknowledgment goes to him. Second, special thanks go to former and present (PhD) students and postdocs of my research group with whom we have researched in different areas of data privacy. A significant amount of my research has been done in collaboration with Guillermo Navarro-Arribas and Julián Salas. Guillermo has read and commented on parts of this manuscript. A big thanks to them.

My research in this area has been funded by Catalan, Spanish, Swedish, and EU funding bodies. In the period 2008–2014, most of our research on data privacy was funded by the Spanish CONSOLIDER research project titled ARES. Since 2020 I am funded by the WASP initiative. So, this work is partially supported by the Wallenberg AI, Autonomous Systems and Software Program (WASP) funded by the Knut and Alice Wallenberg Foundation. My research has also been benefited by unfunded projects and rejection decisions.

Last but not least, thanks to my family for their support, and particularly to Klara for the long discussions on privacy-related issues.

Naturally, all errors in the book (except the ones to avoid disclosure) are mine.

Umeå, Sweden   Vicenç Torra
June 2022

Contents

Introduction

Abstract

Large amounts of data are collected and processed nowadays. Sensitive information is present in these data, or can be inferred from them. Data privacy is to ensure that disclosure of sensitive information does not take place. In this chapter we give an introduction to the field. We describe the motivations for data privacy, underline the links between data privacy and the society, and review terminology and concepts.

Neuk ere izan nuen ezkutuko maite bat

K. Uribe, Bitartean heldu eskutik, 2001,
p. 46 [505]

Data is nowadays gathered in large amounts by companies and governmental offices. This data is often analyzed using statistical and data mining methods. When these methods are applied within the walls of the company that has gathered the data, the danger of disclosure of sensitive information might be limited. In this case it is mainly an issue of technologies for ensuring security. In contrast, when the analysis has to be performed by third parties, privacy becomes a much more relevant issue. Similar problems arise when other actors not directly related to the data analysis enter into the scene (e.g., software developers who need to develop and test procedures on data they are not allowed to see).

To make matters worst, it is not uncommon the scenario where an analysis does not only require data from a single data source, but from several ones. This is the case of banks tracking fraud detection and hospitals analyzing diseases and treatments. In the first case, data from several banks might help in fraud detection. Similarly, data from different hospitals might help in the process of finding the causes of a bad

© The Author(s), under exclusive license to Springer Nature Switzerland AG 2022
V. Torra, *Guide to Data Privacy*, Undergraduate Topics in Computer Science,
https://doi.org/10.1007/978-3-031-12837-0_1

clinical response to a given treatment, or the causes of a given disease; and data from
the pharmaceutical industry to help on drug discovery.

Privacy enhancing technologies (PET), Privacy-Preserving Data Mining [18]
(PPDM), and Statistical Disclosure Control [143,521] (SDC) are related fields with
a similar interest on ensuring data privacy. Their goal is to avoid the disclosure of
sensitive or proprietary information to third parties.

Privacy appeared first within the statistical community in relation to the publication of data from census. For example, Dalenius work [110] dates back to 1977. In
order to avoid the disclosure of sensitive data from respondents, tools and methodologies were developed. Research mainly focuses on statistical databases, and users
typically are decision makers and social scientists. Later the computer science community became also interested in this topic, involving people working on database
and data mining on the one hand, and people working on data communications on
the other hand. In databases and data mining, researchers faced problems similar to
the ones of the statistical community but in this case issues are related to the exploitation of data from companies. In this area, it is common to use proprietary databases
(e.g., data from banks, hospitals, economic transactions) for building data-driven
models using data mining and machine learning. Accordingly, the focus, the type of
data and the data uses are slightly different. First papers appeared in late 1990s. In
data communications, researchers studied privacy and security with respect to data
tranmission (see e.g., Chaum's work [89] published in 1981). Anonymous communication falls in this area. In both fields, several methods have been proposed for
processing and analysing data without compromising privacy, and for releasing data
ensuring some levels of data privacy.

Privacy models have been defined to establish when data and computation do not
lead to disclosure and, thus, can be safely shared or released. Measures and indices
have been defined for evaluating disclosure risk (that is, to what extent data and
computation satisfy the privacy constraints), and for evaluating utility or information
loss (that is, to what extent protection causes some harm in the results). In addition,
tools have been proposed to visualize and compare different approaches for data
protection. All these elements will be presented in this book.

In this chapter we discuss why methods for data privacy are required, we underline
some links between data privacy and society, and conclude with a review of the
terminology related to data privacy. This will include concepts such as anonymity,
unlinkability, disclosure, transparency, and privacy by design.

1.1 Motivations for Data Privacy

We can distinguish three main motivations for companies to apply data privacy procedures. They are legislation, companies own interest, and avoiding privacy breaches.
Let us look into these three motivations in more details.

Legislation

Nowadays privacy is a fundamental right that is protected at different levels. The Universal Declaration of Human Rights states in its Article 12 the following.

Article 12. No one shall be subjected to arbitrary interference with his privacy, family, home or correspondence, nor to attacks upon his honour and reputation. Everyone has the right to the protection of the law against such interference or attacks. (Universal Declaration of Human Rights [562], 10 December 1948, UN General Assembly)

In Europe, the Council of Europe entered into force in 1953 the European Convention on Human Rights (ECHR). This convention contains the following article focusing on privacy.

Article 8. Right to respect for private and family life.

1. Everyone has the right to respect for his private and family life, his home and his correspondence.

2. There shall be no interference by a public authority with the exercise of this right except such as is in accordance with the law and is necessary in a democratic society in the interests of national security, public safety or the economic wellbeing of the country, for the prevention of disorder or crime, for the protection of health or morals, or for the protection of the rights and freedoms of others.

(European Convention on Human Rights [558], November 1950, Council of Europe)

State-members of the Council of Europe have the international obligation [107] to comply with the convention. There are 46 member states in May 2022.

In the European Union, the General Data Protection Regulation (GDPR) is the law enforced from 2018 on data protection and privacy. The regulation consolidates some rights related to privacy, as the right to erasure and the right to rectification. The regulation also establishes that data breaches need to be reported, and there are fines in case of violation of the GDPR.

In USA, the most relevant laws are probably the Health Insurance Portability and Accountability Act (HIPAA, 1996), the Patriot Act (2001), the Homeland Security Act (2002), and the Children's Online Privacy Protection Act (COPPA, effective 2000). In California, there is the Californian Consumer Privacy Act (CCPA). There are other states with their own regulations.

Several countries include similar rights in their constitutions, and laws have been approved to guarantee these rights. Information of national level legislation in Europe can be found in the Handbook on European data protection law [107] and within the European Union in a dedicated web [546]. The Chap. 2 of the Handbook [107] includes a dicussion on the data protection terminology.

Companies Own Interest

Companies and organizations need to define protocols and practices so that their activities with data are compliant with the laws. In addition to that, companies are often interested in protecting their own data because of their own interest (data releases can lead to the disclosure of information that can be used by competitors for their own profit), and there may also be intellectual property rights to protect. Holder privacy (see Sect. 3.5.1) focus on this particular problem.

Avoiding Privacy Breaches

There are several cases of privacy breaches that have been reported in the media. Some of them are due to a bad understanding of data privacy fundamentals, and a lack of application of appropriate technologies. Others (a large majority) are due to security breaches (the most extreme being non-encrypted data forgotten in public transport and, probably, the most typically being unauthorized internet access to the data).

Two well known examples of voluntary data releases that lead to privacy issues are the AOL [41] and the Netflix [342] cases. Besides the unintended damages to users, and reputation damages for companies, privacy breaches may represent direct financial losses due to fines as with the GDPR.

In the AOL case (August/September 2006), queries submitted to AOL by 650,000 users within a period of three months were released for research purposes. Only queries from AOL registered users were released. Numerical identifiers were published instead of real names and login information. Nevertheless, from the terms in the queries a set of queries was linked to people.

In the NETFLIX case, a database with the ratings to films of about 500,000 subscribers of Netflix was published in 2006 to foster research in recommender systems. About 100 milion film ratings were included in the database. Narayanan and Shmatikov [342] used the Internet Movie Database as background knowledge to link some of the records in the database to known users.

1.1.1 Privacy, Security and Inference

Privacy technologies are developed and applied to avoid disclosure. Privacy leaks can be due to multiple factors. For example, transmission of unencrypted e-mails can allow intruders to access the names of senders and receivers, as well as to e-mail content. Unauthorized access to an account or service can also imply leakage of sensitive information. In some occasions, intruders need further work than just accessing the data. The AOL and NETFLIX case above required appropriate inferences. For example, in the AOL case, all queries from the same person had to be linked, and used to find a user's profile. This was due to the fact that user information was not present in the database. There were no names or addresses from users. Nevertheless, there was enough information in a profile to narrow the search, and identify a few people as the actual author of the query, from this small set the user was identified.

We want to stress this need for inference. This inference process is what makes the difference between privacy and security, and what distinguishes the core privacy technologies from the ones on data security. The latter include access control and other countermeasures for security breaches. They are, of course, relevant and important for avoiding privacy breaches, but they are often not enough.

As we will show in two motivating examples later, we may allow a user to access some data, i.e., to grant access control to these data, but at the same time we want to avoid some *unexpected* inferences from this data that can imply disclosure. In other words, someone needs to access to data to perform an authorized analysis, but access to the data and the result of this analysis should avoid disclosure of other analysis.

1.2 Two Motivating Examples

There have been a significant number of data leakages in which sensitive information has been released inadvertently, or has been acquired taking advantage of security flows. Nevertheless, as we have mentioned above, we consider that the main focus of data privacy is on inferences from releases of information that are provided on purpose. In order to make things clear we provide two canonical scenarios that can lead to disclosure of sensitive information. The first one is about sharing or releasing a database. The second one is about sharing or releasing a computation from a database.

1.2.1 Sharing a Database

Most organizations need to share databases to either their own employees or to third parties to take full advantage of the data they have stored. For this purpose, access control permits to reduce the view of the database to those elements (e.g., records or attributes) that seem to be required for e.g. a particular data analysis. Nevertheless, restricting the database to a few records and a few features may no avoid the disclosure of sensitive information.

Let us consider the following example. A hospital of Castelló de la Plana (300 km south of Barcelona and 100 km north of València) is planning to study the average hospital length of stay for children. They want to consider how different children ages and diagnoses affect this length. They also want to study if the average length of stay is decreasing in the last years due to new hospital policies. For this purpose they want to use their existing database with all previous admissions in the years 2010–2019. To avoid disclosure they provide a view of their database restricting records to belong to children born before 2019 and only providing for these records year of birth, town, year of admission, illness, and length of stay.

Table 1.1 Table for the hospital at Castelló with information about children and average length of stay. Only a restricted view of the database is published with a few attributes

Year of birth	Year of admission	Town	Illness	Length of stay (in days)
2017	2019	Castelló	a	3
2015	2020	Castelló	b	2
2011	2020	Vila-real	c	5
2017	2019	Vila-real	a	2
2016	2020	Llucena	b	4
2016	2020	La Foia	d	2
2015	2019	Figueroles	e	4
2015	2019	Figueroles	e	4
2015	2018	Figueroles	e	4
2015	2018	Figueroles	e	4

So, they produce a database as the one in Table 1.1. At a first glance the table seems to be safe. No personal information is given about the children. Nevertheless, this is not so. The region served by the hospital includes several towns with small villages (La Foia has about 150 inhabitants, Figueroles a little more than 500) with only a few children born each year. Because of that, the information in the table will lead to disclosure. Anyone in the town will be able to identify who is the one born in 2016 in La Foia or in 2015 in Figueroles.

Naturally, the fact that we are able to identify a record can led to additional disclosure. E.g., we can learn about the illness of this child and the length of stay at the hospital. Also, we can even learn that a child has been multiple times admitted to the hospital.

This example shows that a *naif* protection (e.g., restriction to a particular view) does not ensure privacy. Note that we can even remove some additional information and this does not need to avoid complete disclosure. Consider the case of replacing (year of birth, year of admission) by a single attribute (age at time of admission). This latter attribute computed as the difference of the former two can still lead to disclosure if it happens that we know that our little neighbor was admitted at the age of 4.

We can provide a large number of examples of the same type. For example, a university wants to study how student's stress is influenced by studies and commuting distance. So, they provide a researcher with records of the following form:

(town, degree, stress leave?)

This again seems not to contain personal information. Nevertheless, if there is a town with only one person studying a certain degree, this will lead to disclosure. We can surely identify the record and deduce whether the person was on leave because of stress.

In these examples we have one or a few attributes that can help us to find a person in the database. In some cases, we need a large number of attributes, but the identification can also be made. For example, if we consider data from stores, the shopping cart will probably made us unique. Similarly, if we consider the products we buy with a credit card, the films we watch in a video streaming service, our rating to films, our preferences on books, etc. it is not a single item that makes us singular, it is a set of them that makes us singular.

As a summary, in database releases there are two main situations that makes us possible to find someone in the database. The first one is when a few attributes can cause disclosure because they make a person highly unique. The first examples follow this pattern. We have one or two attributes that provide all the information necessary to identify a child or a student at the university. Another typical example of this situation is location data. For example, when we have location data from mobile phones. In most of the cases, just two locations (e.g., location at 23:50 and at 11:00 am) give enough information to identify a person. That is, for most of us there is probably only one person leaving at our home and working in our workplace. The other situation is when there is no such good attributes for finding someone in the database but the information is so rich that we can find a person anyway. Data from online services are usually in this second type of scenario.

1.2.2 Sharing a Computation

When we consider a database and compute a value from this database, we expect that this value is safe from a privacy perspective. Specially, we would expect that this is indeed the case if this computation is a summary. E.g. the mean of an attribute. Nevertheless, this is not necessarily so, as we will now illustrate.

Consider the problem of computing the mean income of those admitted to a hospital unit for a given town. E.g., to the psychiatric unit. We access the database and compute the mean of those attending the unit and are from Bunyola (Majorca). Note that no one accessed the raw data, and only the summary (i.e., the mean) is delivered as output.

Assuming that the income of those from Bunyola attending the psychiatric unit are (in Euros):

$$1000, 2000, 3000, 2000, 1000, 6000, 2000, 10000, 2000, 4000$$

we obtain as the mean income: 3300 Euros.

This mean income, which seems to be slightly larger than the mean salary in Majorca in 2021, does not seems to give us any insight on who is attending the unit, or providing us with any sensitive information. Nevertheless, this is not the full picture. Consider now that Dona Obdúlia de Montcada, landlord of Bearn, has in fact attended the psychiatric unit. Then, her income would be also taken into consideration when computing the summary. That is, when we compute the average income we are computing the mean of

$$1000, 2000, 3000, 2000, 1000, 6000, 2000, 10000, 2000, 4000, 100000.$$

That is, previous incomes plus the income of Dona Obdúlia (i.e., 100000 Euros). This leads to a mean income of 12090.90 !

Naturally, in this case, knowing that Dona Obdúlia is the only rich landlord in the town, we can easily infer from the mean salary that she is in the database and that her salary was used to compute the mean. Subsequently, we can infer that she has been attending the psychiatric unit.

So, in the latter case we infer that she was attending the unit. Nevertheless, it is important to note that if the mean were 3300 Euros, we would also infer about Dona Obdúlia. In that case, the inference is that she was not attending the unit.

As a summary, this example shows that a computation can lead to disclosure, and the cause of disclosure can be due to a simple summary. In fact, disclosure can appear also in case of building more complex structures from data. This is the case of machine and statistical learning models. Such models can also provide us with traces of the data used and lead to disclosure. The so-called membership inference attacks are an example of exploitation of a data-driven model to learn about the data used to identify the model.

We will illustrate this problem with a simple example of regression. It is known that linear regression can be influenced by an outlier. That is, for a regression of an attribute y with respect to x, adding a single pair (x_0, y_0) can have a large influence in the regression line.

Let us consider again the same people from Bunyola from the previous example, and let us now consider also their age. The information available (i.e., age and income) is represented in Table 1.2. Then, we build a linear regression model of income with respect to age. We have in Fig. 1.1 (left) the case without including the record associated to Dona Obdúlia and (right) the case considering this record. We can observe the important change in the regression line. Being the income of this record so high, and having an age that is larger than the one of the other records, we have that the impact of the record in the model is large.

As we have explained above, we are only releasing the output of the computation, but not the original data. So, adversaries, researchers and data analysts have only access to the regression model but not the data themselves. Nevertheless, it is clear analyzing the model that Dona Obdúlias data is present in the dataset, and that her data has been used to build the model. Therefore, the publication of this model leads to disclosure.

Table 1.2 Records used to build a linear regression model for income with respect to age. The record (65, 100000) corresponds to Dona Obdúlia

Age	Income	Age	Income
24	1000	40	6000
30	2000	50	2000
40	3000	55	10000
33	2000	37	2000
26	1000	42	4000
65	100000		

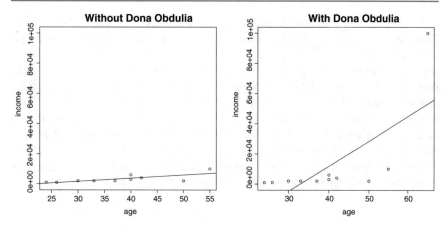

Fig. 1.1 Regression of income with respect to age with (right) and without (left) the record of Dona Obdúlia

1.2.3   Privacy Leakages and Risk

There is a discussion on whether information leakages, as in the two cases described above, should prevent the publication of information that is useful to people, and, in general, to what extent some risk should be tolerated.

Some researchers [123, 245] state that privacy is "impossible" because either the disclosure risk is too high or the modifications we need to apply to the data to make them safe are too large (and, thus, resulting data are useless). There are other researchers [38, 421] arguing that it is possible to find a good balance, and others stating that even if the risk exists, this should not be overemphasized. For example, Yakowitz [532] states that "there is only a single known instance of de-anonymization for a purpose other than the demonstration of privacy". Then, she adds that "this is not surprising, because the marginal value of the information in a public dataset is usually too low to justify the effort for an intruder. The quantity of information available in the data commons is outpaced by the growth in information self-publicized on the Internet or collected for commercially available consumer data". In a later work, Bambauer [36] compares the chance of breaking disclosure in the 2009 ONC Study [274] which is 0.013% (2 over 15,000 HIPAA-compliant records) and the chance of dying from a motor vehicle accident that year in USA, which is 0.018% (18 over 100,000 licensed drivers in 2008 in USA [556]). Thus, the probability of reidentification in the 2009 ONC Study is smaller than the one of dying from a motor vehicle accident. For the AOL case, the proportion of actual reidentified users is even smaller.

It is true that for high dimensional data (e.g. records with a large number of attributes) it is in general difficult to make data safe without compromising their quality. This can also be the case of some small datasets. That is why privacy is a challenging area of research.

In any case, any release of sensitive data needs to evaluate the risk of disclosure. Data has to be correctly protected so that the risk is low, and this requires an accurate evaluation of the risk. Experience and literature show that risk is not always estimated appropriately (see e.g. the discussion by Muralidhar [339]). A data set well protected may have a low risk, as the computations by Bambauer above show, but conversely, no protection (or a bad protection) may lead to a high risk. For comparison, Sweeney reports [459] a set of experiments and show that "87.1% (216 million of 248 million) of the population in the United States had characteristics that were likely made them unique based only on *5-digit ZIP, gender, date of birth*", and that "3.7% of the population in the United States had characteristics that were likely made them unique based only on *5-digit ZIP, gender, Month and year of birth*".

1.3 Privacy and Society

It is well known that privacy is not only a technical problem but that has social roots as well. Schoeman edited a book [426] which reproduces a few articles devoted to social, legal, and philosophical questions related to privacy, and also wrote a book [427] that analyzes and summarizes some of the main issues on these topics. In the introduction [425] of the former book [426], the author gives classifications and definitions of these topics. In particular, it discusses the nature of privacy (their definitions and whether it is a moral right even if there is no associated legal right) and whether it is culturally relative.

About the nature of privacy, Shoeman claims ([425], p. 2) that privacy has been defined according to different perspectives and distinguishes the following ones.

- Privacy as a claim, entitlement, or right of an individual to determine what information about himself or herself may be communicated to others.
- Privacy as the measure of control an individual has over: information about himself; intimacies of personal identity; or who has sensory access to him.
- Privacy as a state or condition of limited access to a person. People have privacy to the extent that others have limited access to information about them.

Cultural relativeness makes us wonder whether the importance of privacy is the same among all people, if privacy is superfluous and dispensable as a social value. Another question is whether there are aspects of life which are inherently private or just conventionally so.

From a historical perspective, the first explicit discussion of privacy as a legal right is attributed to Warren and Brandeis in their paper [516] published in 1890. Nevertheless, privacy issues were already considered before (see e.g. Stephen's paper in 1873 [445]). Warren and Brandeis argue that the right to privacy is the *next step which must be taken for the protection of the person, and for securing to the individual what Judge Cooley calls the right "to be let alone"*.

The causes of needing this right are, according to Warren and Brandeis, related to the inventions and business methods of the time (i.e., circa 1890).

Instantaneous photographs and newspaper enterprise have invaded the sacred precincts of private and domestic life; and numerous mechanical devices threaten to make good the prediction that "what is whispered in the closet shall be proclaimed from the house-tops."
(...)
Gossip is no longer the resource of the idle and of the vicious, but has become a trade, which is pursued with industry as well as effrontery (...) To occupy the indolent, column upon column is filled with idle gossip, which can only be procured by intrusion upon the domestic circle.
(S. D. Warren and L. D. Brandeis, 1890 [516])

Computers, massive storage, the internet, and online social networks have made the right to privacy even more relevant. The persistence and easy access to data caused the need for other related rights such as the right to rectification and the right to erasure (right to be forgotten) as in e.g. articles 16 and 17 of the General Data Protection Regulation (GDPR) in the European Union.

The relationship between privacy, freedom, and respect for people has been discussed in the literature, among others by Benn in 1971 [45] in a paper reproduced in Schoeman's book [426]. See, for example:

Anyone who wants to remain unobserved and unidentified, it might be said, should stay at home or go out only in disguise. Yet there is a difference between happening to be seen and having someone closely observe, and perhaps record, what one is doing, even in a public place. (...) Furthermore, what is resented is not being watched *tout court*, but being watched without leave. (S. I. Benn, 1971 [45], p. 225 in [426])

The dangers, and misuse, of this being watched without leave quickly relates the lack of privacy to Orwellian states [369] (and to the Panopticon). See e.g. the poem by the Galician poet Celso Emilio Ferreiro.

Un grande telescopio nos vixía
coma un ollo de Cíclope
que sigue os nosos pasos
e fita sin acougo o noso rumbo,
dende tódalas fiestras,
dende tódalas torres,
dende tódalas voces que nos falan.
(Celso Emilio Ferreiro, Longa noite de pedra, 1962 [187])

We finish this section with another quotation of S. I. Benn that expresses the relationship between privacy and autonomy. Note that there are other connections between privacy and autonomy in e.g. relationship to voting [326,363].

This last stage of my argument brings me back to the grounds for the general principle of privacy, to which I devoted the first half of this paper. I argued that respect for someone as a person, as a chooser, implied respect for him as one engaged on a kind of self-creative enterprise, which could be disrupted, distorted, or frustrated even by so limited an intrusion as watching. A man's view of what he does may be radically altered by having to see it, as it were, through another man's eyes. Now a man has attained a measure of success in his

enterprise to the degree that he has achieved autonomy. To the same degree, the importance
to him of protection from eavesdropping and Peeping Toms diminishes as he becomes less
vulnerable to the judgements of others, more reliant on his own (though he will still need
privacy for personal relations, and protection from the grosser kinds of persecution). (S. I.
Benn, 1971 [45], p. 242 in [426])

1.4 Terminology

In this section we give a few definitions of concepts related to privacy. The main
concepts we review are anonymity, linkability, disclosure, and pseudonyms. For these
and related definitions, we refer the reader to the document written by Pfitzmann and
Hansen [382] with the goal of fixing a common terminology in the area of privacy
and privacy enhancement technologies, and to the glossary of Statistical Disclosure
Control terms [551]. Both documents include a larger number of definitions than the
ones included here. We focus on the ones that are directly related to the content of
this book.

1.4.1 The Framework

Following Pfitzmann and Hansen [382] and most literature on information security,
let us consider a system in which there are senders and recipients which communicate
through a communication network through messages (see Fig. 1.2). The senders are
also called the actors, and the receivers the actees. There is no distinction on whether
the senders (or the receivers) are human or not. That is, the same context applies
when a user or a software agent queries a database.

The terms attacker, adversary, and intruder are used to refer to the set of entities
working against some protection goal. Pfitzmann and Hansen [382] consider the
terms attacker and adversary as synonyms, attacker being of older use and adversary is
more recently used in information security research. Privacy preserving data mining
uses the terms adversary and adversarial attacks (see e.g. their use in the book edited
by Aggarwal and Yu [18]). Intruder is the most used term in statistical disclosure
control.

The goal of adversaries are to increase their knowledge on the items of interest.
These items of interest can be any type of objects or people involved in the communication as senders, receivers, messages, and actions. Knowledge can be described
in terms of probabilities on these items. So, we can represent adversaries increasing
their knowledge on who sent a particular message, or on what is described in a message. Naturally, the more knowledge an intruder has, the more the probabilities are
closer to the true probabilities.

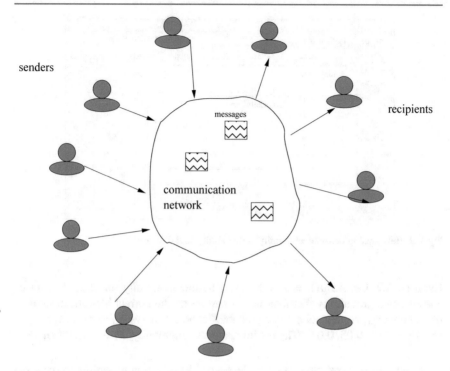

senders

recipients

messages

communication
network

Fig. 1.2 Privacy setting in a communication network

1.4.2 Anonymity and Unlinkability

In our framework, anonymity and anonymity set are defined as follows.

Definition 1.1 [382] Anonymity of a subject means that the subject is not identifiable within a set of subjects, the anonymity set.

In communications, we may have e.g. sender anonymity when it is not possible to link a certain message to the sender. We have an anonymity set for a message on the possible senders of this message. Similarly, we have recipient anonymity when adversaries cannot link a message to the one that receives the message.

In this definition not identifiable means that the subject is not distinguishable (in any way) from the other subjects within the anonymity set. Note that this definition implicitly quantifies anonymity: different sizes of the anonymity set may imply different levels of anonymity. For example, s_1 and s_2 have different levels of anonymity if the anonymity set of s_1 has only three subjects and the one of s_2 has ten subjects. Naturally, the anonymity of s_2 is better than the one of s_1.

Even in the case of two subjects with anonymity sets of the same cardinality, we may have different levels of identification. We illustrate this with the following example.

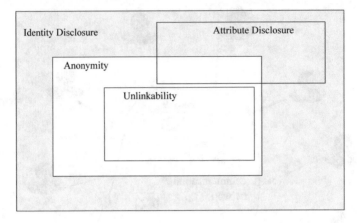

Fig. 1.3 Relationship between anonymity, unlinkability, and disclosure

Example 1.1 Let $AS(s_1) = \{s_{11}, s_{12}, s_{13}\}$ be the anonymity set of s_1, and let us consider two probability distributions P_1 and P_2 on the correct identification of s_1 being either s_{11}, s_{12} or s_{13}. Let these probabilities be as follows: $P_1 = (1/3, 1/3, 1/3)$ and $P_2 = (0.9, 0.05, 0.05)$. Then, with respect to anonymity, P_1 is better than P_2.

Because of that, we have different levels of identification according to the sizes of the anonymity set and to the shape of the probability distributions. We can then discuss and compare [452] different distributions with respect to disclosure risk. We revise below the previous definition of anonymity making explicit the level of identification.

Definition 1.2 From an adversary's persective, anonymity of a subject s means that the adversary cannot achieve a certain level of identification for the subject s within the anonymity set.

Linkability is an important concept in privacy as its negation, unlinkability, implies anonymity. For example, when the interest of the adversary is to know which is the sender of a message, unlinkability with the sender implies anonymity of the sender. We define unlinkability below.

Definition 1.3 [382] Unlinkability of two or more items of interest (IOI) from the perspective of an adversary means that within the system (comprising these IOIs and possibly other items), the adversary cannot distinguish sufficiently whether these IOIs are related or not.

Pfitzmann and Hansen [382] point out that unlinkability is a sufficient condition of anonymity but not a necessary condition. That is, unlinkability implies anonymity. We represent graphically in Fig. 1.3, the concepts introduced in this section as well as their relationships. The property that unlinkability implies anonymity is represented in Fig. 1.3 with the box of unlinkability inside the box of anonymity. On the contrary, we might have a case where linkability is possible but that anonymity is not compromised. As an example of the later case consider when an intruder can link all messages of a transaction, due to timing, nevertheless if all of them are encrypted and no information can be obtained about the subjects in the transactions, then anonymity is not compromised [382]. In Fig. 1.3 this example belongs to the region of the anonymity box outside the unlinkability box.

1.4.3 Disclosure

Another important concept related to privacy is the one of disclosure. It is mainly used within the statistical disclosure control and privacy preserving data mining communities. Note that this concept does not appear in the report by Pfitzmann and Hansen [382]. In data privacy we understand disclosure with respect to some data or model. We define it as follows.

Definition 1.4 Disclosure takes place when intruders take advantage of the observation and analysis of a release to improve their knowledge on some item of interest.

Thus, disclosure is defined in terms of the additional information or knowledge that an adversary can acquire from observing the system. When data is shared, the adversary typically observes a protected file or database. Then, disclosure is about improving the knowledge of a particular subject whose data is in the database. According to the terminology we introduce in Sect. 3.5.1, this subject is known as the respondent of the database. Alternatively, the release can be a data aggregate, a statistic, or a machine learning model.

Most disclosures can be classified as one of the following types [275,371]:

- **Identity disclosure.** This type of disclosure takes place when the adversary can correctly link a respondent to a particular item on the release. Typically, this applies to data releases and the adversary identifies a record. Only respondents whose data have been published can be identified. According to Lambert [275], even if "the intruder learns nothing sensitive from the identification, the re-identification itself may compromise the security of the data file". Identity disclosure is also known as entity disclosure. It corresponds to the concept of linkability discussed above.
- **Attribute disclosure.** This type of disclosure takes place when the adversary can learn something new about an attribute of a respondent, even when no relationship can be established between the individual and a release. For example, if data is released, disclosure takes place when adversaries increase their accuracy on an attribute of the respondent.
  Attribute disclosure is not only about attributes present in the database. It can be about an attribute not present in the database, when we infer its value from the data. For example, observance of religious holidays from electrical consumption.

Table 1.3 Table that permits an adversary to achieve identity disclosure and attribute disclosure. Only attributes City, Age, and Illness are published

Respondent	City	Age	Illness
ABD	Barcelona	30	Cancer
COL	Barcelona	30	Cancer
GHE	Tarragona	60	AIDS
CIO	Tarragona	60	AIDS
HYU	Tarragona	58	Heart attack

We can also classify as attribute disclosure determining that friend's data is in a protected database (even without knowing which is our friend's record) or determining that friend's data has been used to build a data-driven model. The latter is called membership inference attack and this is relevant in both disclosure risk assessment and forensics.

For data publishing, identity disclosure is neither stronger nor weaker than attribute disclosure. Nevertheless, the most common implication is that identity disclosure implies attribute disclosure. This is the case when we identify one of the records in the protected data set using a subset of the attributes. In this case, after identification, we learn about the values of the other attributes.

To illustrate this case, let us consider a data release and an adversary. The later has a friend from Tarragona who is 58 years old. Let us summarize this information with the record: $(HYU, Tarragona, 58)$. The data release consists of patients' data from a hospital with attributes City, Age, and Illness as in Table 1.3 (i.e., names in the first column are not published). Then, the adversary can link the record $(HYU, Tarragona, 58)$ to the last row of the table and this results into identity disclosure. This disclosure implies attribute disclosure, as the adversary learns that HYU has had a heart attack.

However, in general we might have all possible cases.

- Neither identity nor attribute disclosure
- Identity disclosure and attribute disclosure
- No identity disclosure but attribute disclosure
- Identity disclosure but not attribute disclosure

We have discussed the second case. We illustrate below two other cases. Note that the last case is the one that makes the implication "identity disclosure implies attribute disclosure" fail.

- **Attribute disclosure without identity disclosure.** This case applies when we have sets of indistinguishable records, for example, due to k-anonymity (see Sects. 3.4.2

Table 1.4 Table that permits an adversary to achieve attribute disclosure without identity disclosure. Only attributes City, Age, and Illness are published

Respondent	City	Age	Illness
ABD	Barcelona	30	Cancer
COL	Barcelona	30	Cancer
GHE	Tarragona	60	AIDS
CIO	Tarragona	60	AIDS

Table 1.5 Table that permits an adversary to achieve identity disclosure without attribute disclosure. Only attributes City, Age, and Illness are published

Respondent	City	Age	Illness
TTY	Manresa	60	AIDS
GTJ	Manresa	60	Heart attack
FER	Manresa	30	Heart attack
DRR	Barcelona	30	Heart attack
ABD	Barcelona	30	Cancer
COL	Barcelona	30	Cancer
GHE	Tarragona	60	AIDS
CIO	Tarragona	60	AIDS
HYU	Tarragona	60	Heart attack

and 6.4). When all indistinguishable records for an intruder have the same value for a confidential attribute, we have attribute disclosure for this confidential attribute. The data release in Table 1.4 illustrates this case. Again, only attributes City, Age and Illness are published. If the information of the intruder is *(ABD, Barcelona, 30)*, identity disclosure cannot take place because there are two indistinguishable records, but as both records has illness associated to cancer, the attribute can be learned for *(ABD, Barcelona, 30)* and, thus, attribute disclosure takes place. In other words, we have an anonymity set of two people *ABD* and *COL* but this does not avoid disclosure.

This problem motivated the definition of *l*-diversity, as we discuss in Sect. 3.4.2.

- **Identity disclosure without attribute disclosure.** This applies when all attributes are needed for reidentification, or when the attributes not used for reidentification do not cause disclosure.

To illustrate this case, let us consider the publication of attributes City, Age and Illness in Table 1.5 when the intruder has the following information *(HYU, Tarragona, 60, Heart attack)*. In this case reidentification is possible, as the only possible record is the last one, but as all the attributes are used in the reidentification, no attribute disclosure takes place.

We want to underline that identity disclosure and anonymity are exclusive. That is, identity disclosure implies non-anonymity, and anonymity implies no identity disclosure. Nevertheless, as we have shown in the example above we may have attribute disclosure. In general, when all items in an anonymity set satisfy a property p, the adversary can infer this property p for the items of interest.

The relationship between all these terms is represented graphically in Fig. 1.3. Note that the region of identity disclosure (colored region) is the one outside the region of anonymity because they are exclusive.

The literature also discusses as a separate type of disclosure inferential disclosure. The difference is whether the information is obtained directly from the protected data set, or whether it is inferred from this data set. We do not make this distinction here. We consider that from the perspective of risk analysis, what is relevant is to determine which are the attributes that are sensitive, and this is more relevant than how the value is inferred. For illustration, we include an example of attribute disclosure for an attribute not present in a released database.

The following example illustrates inferential disclosure. The example is taken from the term Inferential Disclosure in the Glossary of Statistical terms [551].

Example 1.2 The data may show a high correlation between income and purchase price of a home. As the purchase price of a home is typically public information, a third party might use this information to infer the income of a data subject.

Disclosure and time

Anonymity and disclosure cannot decrease. Once some information has been released, this information can be used to compute an anonymity set and have some level of disclosure. Any additional information released later will eventually reduce the anonymity set and increase the disclosure. Similarly, if we have some knowledge on an item of interest additional releases would permit to increase our knowledge. For example, narrowing the interval of possible values.

1.4.4 Dalenius' Definitions for Attribute and Identity Disclosure

One of the first detailed discussions on disclosure (statistical disclosure) is due to Dalenius [110]. He points out the different sets of data that are relevant when evaluating disclosure risk, and presents a classification of the types of disclosure. Figure 1.4 gives an overview of Dalenius dimensions for disclosure risk assessment.

Let x be a particular individual of a population $\{O\}_T$. Let A be a characteristic (an attribute), either one present in the data set (or survey following Dalenius) or not present in the set. Let $A(x)$ denote the value of this characteristic for x. Then, Dalenius defines disclosure as follows.

Definition 1.5 [110] (p. 433) If the release of the statistics S makes it possible to determine the value $A(x)$ more accurately than is possible without access to S, a disclosure has taken place.

Dalenius (1977) classifies disclosure according to the following dimensions. The definition uses D to denote a characteristic, and D_K to denote the characteristic for the kth record. Here we use A to denote an attribute as used elsewhere in this text, and $A(x_k)$ to denote the value of A for the kth record x_k. We will use A' to denote the attribute of a protected file, and A^* to denote the estimation of A using the published dataset. In most cases $A^* = A'$ but in some cases, this is not the case. Inference procedures can be used and then the equality does not necessarily apply.

1. Kinds of statistics released. Two cases are considered: statistics for sets of objects (macro-statistics) and statistics for individual objects (micro-statistics). The former corresponds to tabular data and the latter to microdata.
2. The measurement scale used to express the data. Two main cases are considered: scales yielding attribute/counts (binary data i.e., A is either 0 or 1 for record x_k) and yielding magnitudes (Dalenius considers A measured in a ratio scale).
3. Accessibility of disclosure. Direct and indirect disclosure are distinguished. The former corresponds to the case that A is included in the published dataset, and the latter to the case that A is computed from the published dataset. That is, attribute disclosure and inferential disclosure.
4. Accuracy of disclosure. Exact and approximate disclosure are distinguished. We have *exact disclosure* when the published data corresponds to the original data. In contrast, we have *approximate disclosure* when this is not the case and there is some imprecision or uncertainty in the disclosure. Two types of approximate disclosure are considered: approximation of the true value by means of an interval $[A_L, A_U]$ (i.e., $A_L \leq A^*(x_k) \leq A_U$) and approximation in terms of a category (i.e., a boolean value $A^*(x_k) \in \{0, 1\}$). Dalenius further considers that an approximation can be *certain* or *uncertain*. The former corresponds to the case that the object belongs to the interval or category involved, the latter when this is not always the case and, therefore, there is some uncertainty. Probabilities are considered to model this latter case.
5. External versus internal disclosure. We have external disclosure when disclosure for record x_k takes place without information about other objects x_j in the released dataset. Internal disclosure takes place when disclosure for x_k takes advantage of information about other records x_j with $j \neq k$. We might have both external and internal disclosure. Let $A^*(x_k)$ be the best approximation of $A(x_k)$ obtained using only data from x_k, and $A^{**}(x_k)$ the best approximation obtained using data from other records x_j with $j \neq k$. Then, if $A^{**}(x_k)$ is a better approximation to $A(x_k)$ than $A^*(x_k)$, we have internal disclosure. Note that we have interval disclosure when a collusion of individuals use their information to discover information about another one.
6. The disclosing entities. S-based disclosure and $S \times E$-based disclosure. Here E, which denotes the term extra-objective data, corresponds to any kind of additional data. These data are not part of the objective of the survey. Naturally, we have S-based disclosure when only the information of the released data set is used, and $S \times E$-based disclosure when additional information is used to have better approximations A^* of A.

Fig. 1.4 Statistical disclosure according to Dalenius [110]

This definition corresponds to what we have defined as attribute disclosure.

Dalenius, in a latter paper [111], also considered what we call identity disclosure. He considered the case that a set of attributes makes a record unique (he calls a certain combination of values/attributes a P-set of data) or almost unique (less than k individuals with $k = 2$ or 3 for a given combination of values/attributes). In the latter case, Dalenius discusses about the possibility that a collusion of the $k - 1$ individuals permit them to identify the other one.

1.4.5   Plausible Deniability

An important concept related to privacy is the one of plausible deniability. In relation to any release of information, can I state that I have nothing to do with the information being released? If this is so, and such statement is credible, then we have plausible deniability. Definitions will differ according to the type of data release. For example, we may have plausible deniability with respect to a data-driven model and with respect to a database release. In the former case, we have plausible deniability if we can state, with credibility!, that our data has not been used to train the model. Similar definition applies for data releases. In this case, we can define it

- at record level (i.e., "This record is not mine"), but also
- at the database level (i.e., "I am not in this database").

The following example satisfies plausible deniability at record level.

Example 1.3 Let us consider a sample from a population publishing only a few attributes. For each record in the file there are several individuals in the population. This sample satisfies plausible deniability at record level for all individuals in the sample.

For example, in Table 1.4, HYU can deny the ownership of the corresponding record if there is someone else in Tarragona with the same attributes *(Tarragona, 60, Heart attack)*.

A relationship can be built between plausible deniability and anonymity sets: When for an individual, we have an anonymity set larger than one, plausible deniability holds at record level. E.g., respondents ABD and COL both can deny their association to any of the records *(Barcelona, 30, Cancer)*.

Plausible deniability and anonymity sets can be seen as related ideas but from different perspectives. When we define anonymity set we take the perspective of the intruder. That is, given some information at intruder's hand, we consider the set of items of interest consistent with this information. In contrast, plausible deniability focuses on individuals, and individuals know all their information and whether this information makes them unique.

1.4.6   Undetectability and Unobservability

The concepts of undetectability and unobservability are also related to data privacy. We begin defining undetectability.

Definition 1.6 [382] Undetectability of an item of interest (IOI) from adversary's perspective means that this adversary cannot distinguish sufficiently whether it exists or not.

For example, if adversaries are interested in messages, undetectability holds when they cannot distinguish the messages in the system from random noise. Steganography [321,518] gives tools to embed undetectable messages in other physical or digital objects for their transmission. In computer science, messages are often embedded in images but also in other objects such as databases [61].

Having said that, there are approaches to counter attack steganographic systems. This area of research is known as steganalysis. For example, Westfeld and Pfitzman [519] describe visual and statistical attacks for steganographic images.

Undetectability is not directly related to anonymity or privacy, but it is clear that an undetected message will not raise the interest of the adversary.

Unobservability is a related term where anonymity, and, thus, privacy, has a role. It is defined as follows.

Definition 1.7 [382] Unobservability of an item of interest means

- undetectability of the IOI against all subjects uninvolved in it, and
- anonymity of the subject(s) involved in the IOI even against the other subject(s) involved in that IOI.

So, unobservability pressumes undetectability but at the same time it also pressumes anonymity in case the items are detected by the subjects involved in the system. From this definition, it is clear that unobservability implies anonymity and undetectability.

1.4.7 Pseudonyms and Identity

The origin of pseudonyms is well known to be previous to computers and internet, and in some cases they were already used to avoid the disclosure of sensitive information, such as gender. This is the case of Amandine Aurore Lucile Dupin (Paris, 1804–Nohant-Vic, 1876) who used the pen name George Sand, and of Caterina Albert (L'Escala, 1869–L'Escala, 1966) who used the pen name Víctor Català. Similar uses are found nowadays in information systems and internet.

Definition 1.8 [382] A pseudonym is an identifier of a subject other than one of the subject's real names.

Definition 1.9 Pseudonymising is defined as the replacing of the name or other identifiers by a number in order to make the identification of the data subject impossible or substantially more difficult. (Federal Data Protection Act, Germany, 2001; in Korff (2010) [267] p. 4)

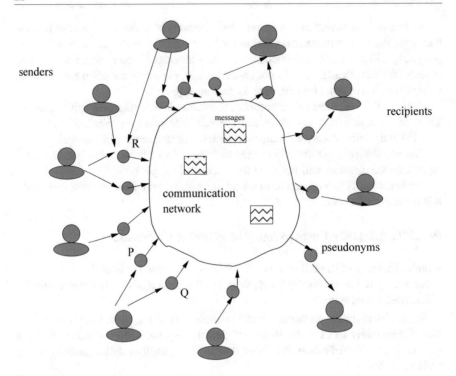

senders

recipients

messages

communication
network

pseudonyms

R

P

Q

Fig. 1.5 Pseudonyms in a communication network

The holder of a pseudonym corresponds to the subject to which the pseudonym refers to. Several pseudonyms may correspond to the same subject. See pseudonyms *P* and *Q* in Fig. 1.5. In addition, it is also possible that several subjects share the same pseudonym (a group pseudonym). In this latter case, the subjects may define an anonymity set. See pseudonym *R* in Fig. 1.5.

Pseudonyms may permit us to cover the range between anonymity (no linkability) to accountability (maximum linkability). They permit us to avoid the one-to-one correspondence between individuals and system access. An individual can have a set of pseudonyms to avoid linkability.

Nevertheless, in some systems it is easy to establish links between a pseudonym and its holder. See e.g. the case of user names in email accounts and social networks, access logs (as the case of AOL, see Sect. 1.1), and unique identifier number in software and services (e.g., the unique ID of the Chrome browser).

To complete this section we review the concept of identity, from the computer science perspective, and then some additional related concepts such as role and partial identity.

Definition 1.10 [382] An identity is any subset of attribute values of an individual person which sufficiently identifies this individual person within any set of people. So usually there is no such thing as "the identity", but several of them.

Definition 1.11 Roles are defined as the set of actions that users (people) are allowed to perform.

For example, in a university, there are individuals who work as professors or members of the administration, and others who study. Therefore, there are people with the role of a professor, an official, or a student. In an information system for universities we implement these three roles. Roles are not exclusive as we may have e.g. professors who are registered and studying (hopefully not the subjects of their own professorship) and, because of that, information systems permit a user to login using different roles.

Definition 1.12 [382] Each partial identity represents the person in a specific context or role.

Then, the terms virtual (partial) identity and digital (partial) identity are used interchangeably to refer to the data stored by a computer-based application. Virtual identities can correspond to subjects' login information into computer-based application. Systems can then have profiles for each virtual (partial) identity. That is, the data for such identities.

Identity management focuses on creating, storing and processing the identities of users in an information system. This includes, authentication of a user, assigning roles to users so that they can only perform authorized actions, managing stored information about users and their logged activities.

1.4.8 Transparency

> Il faut qu'il n'exige pas le secret, et qu'il puisse sans inconvénient tomber entre les mains de l'ennemi
>
> A. Kerckhoffs, La cryptographie militaire, 1883 [259]

When data is published, it is a good practice to give details on how data has been produced. This naturally includes a description of any data protection process applied to the data as well as any parameter of the methods. The same applies to privacy-preserving data-driven models.

Transparency has a positive effect on utility. For example, if we consider protected data, researchers can take advantage of the information about how protection took place in their analysis. As we will see in Sect. 6.1.3, in the case that masking is done by adding noise, information on the type of the added noise can be used to compute the exact values of the mean and variance of the original data.

Nevertheless, the information published can also be used by intruders to attack the release. For example, effective attacks can be defined for rank swapping and some implementations of microaggregation, two protection mechanisms for data sharing. We will discuss them in Sects. 6.1.1 and 6.1.2, respectively. They use information on how data has been protected (both the method and its parameters). We call this type of attacks transparency attacks.

A good protection method is resilient to attacks even in the case of transparency. That is, a good data protection method is the one that cannot be attacked even in case an intruder has all the information about how data has been protected. We call them transparency aware methods.

This approach to privacy is similar to the Kerckhoffs's principle [259] in cryptography. The principle states that a cryptosystem should be secure even if everything about the system is public knowledge, except the key. We can formulate this principle for masking methods as follows.

Principle 1 Given a privacy model, a masking method should be compliant with this privacy model even if everything about the method is public knowledge.

Transparency attacks look for vulnerabilities of masking methods when the transparency principle is applied.

1.5 Privacy and Disclosure

From a computational perspective, privacy breaches represent disclosure. In this case, identity disclosure is the strongest disclosure and it is related to data sharing and data releases.

Under the identity disclosure perspective, privacy problems appear when information about individuals make them unique. However, as we have already reported above, in general, only a few attributes (e.g., *zip code, gender and date of birth*) are enough to make individuals unique. In a more general context, individuals are multifaceted and each of their faces (or interests) do not lead to uniqueness (e.g., opera or rock listener, F.C. Barcelona or Skövde IK supporter, vegetarian or beef lover). It is the intersection of their interests that make people unique. We will further discuss this fact in Sect. 4.2.2.2.

Building large enough anonymity sets permits us to ensure appropriate privacy levels with respect to identity disclosure. Data protection procedures correspond to different approaches of achieving this.

The role of attribute disclosure in data privacy when identity disclosure does not take place is not so clear. Attribute disclosure can appear on any type of release (e.g., data or data-driven models). This is so because attribute disclosure is often the fundamental reason for building statistical and data mining models or, even, for releasing data. Nevertheless, some protection procedures have been developed specifically to avoid or reduce this type of disclosure.

1.6   Privacy by Design

Software needs to be developed so that privacy requirements are satisfied. "Privacy by design" was introduced by Ann Cavoukian to stress the fact that privacy "must ideally become an organization's default mode of operation" [85] and thus, not something to be considered a posteriori. In this way, privacy requirements need to be specified, and then software and systems need to be engineered from the beginning[1] taking these requirements into account.

Cavoukian established seven principles that may permit to fulfill the objectives of privacy by design. The principles are listed below.

1. Proactive not reactive; Preventative not remedial.
2. Privacy as the default setting.
3. Privacy embedded into design.
4. Full functionality—positive-sum, not zero-sum.
5. End-to-end security—full lifecycle protection.
6. Visibility and transparency—keep it open.
7. Respect for user privacy—keep it user-centric.

There is discussion on how privacy by design has to be put into practice, or, in other words, which are the design strategies that permit us to build systems that are compliant with our privacy requirements. Engineering strategies for implementing privacy by design have been discussed in the literature [108,117,209,210,228].

Data minimization is a cornerstone for privacy. Gurses et al. [210] state that a key strategy for achieving privacy is data minimization, and then establish some strategies based on minimization (minimize collection, minimize disclosure, minimize replication, minimize centralization, minimize linkability, and minimize retention). See the following quotation.

> After further examination of existing privacy preserving system designs, it became evident that a whole family of design principles are lumped under the term 'data minimization'. The term conceals a number of design strategies that experts apply intuitively when developing privacy preserving systems. A number of these are constraints on information flows like minimizing collection, disclosure, linkability, replication, retention and centrality. Systems engineered by applying these constraints intend to 'minimize risk' by avoiding a single point of failure, and minimize the need to trust data collectors and processors by putting data under the user's control. (S. Gürses et al., 2015 [210])

Hoepman [228] defines eight design strategies for privacy by design. Data minimization is also one of them. This is the full list of strategies: minimize, separate,

---

[1] See e.g. "In the context of developing IT systems, this implies that privacy protection is a system requirement that must be treated like any other functional requirement. In particular, privacy protection (together with all other requirements) will determine the design and implementation of the system" in (Hoepman, 2014 [228].)

aggregate, hide, inform, control, enforce, and demonstrate. The author discusses how these design strategies cover the privacy principles of the ISO 29100 Privacy framework: (i) consent and choice, (ii) purpose legitimacy and specification, (iii) collection limitation, (iv) data minimisation, (v) use, retention and disclosure limitation, (vi) accuracy and quality, (vii) openness, transparency and notice, (viii) individual participation and access, (ix) accountability, (x) information security, and (xi) privacy compliance.

In this book we will not discuss (software) strategies and methodologies to satisfy these strategies and principles. We will focus on the technologies that permit us to build systems that satisfy the privacy by design requirements.

1.7 Bibliographical Notes

1. **First results and definitions.** Most seminal works in the statistical disclosure control, communications, and data mining communities are from late 1970s, 1980s and 2000s. First research in the statistical disclosure control include the work of Dalenius [110] (published in 1977). Later Chaum [89] (1981) worked on privacy for communications. Finally, we have the works by Estivill, Agrawal, Samarati and Sweeney [24,176,419,463] in the turn of the century.
2. **Disclosure.** Both identity and attribute disclosure are discussed by Dalenius [110]. Other relevant references on identity disclosure include Lambert [275] and a paper by Dalenius focusing on identification on anonymous census records [111]; on attribute disclosure include the work by Duncan and Lambert [159,160]. Pfitzmann and Hansen [382] discuss repeatedly that anonymity cannot increase. As we have stated in this chapter, the same happens with disclosure.
3. **Measurement theory and scales.** It is usual to distinguish numerical and categorical attributes. Measurement theory studies the type of scales according to permissible transformations. The most relevant ones are absolute, ratio, interval, ordinal, and nominal scales. The books [270,308,406,458] by Krantz, Luce, Suppes, Tversky, and Roberts provide a good insight of the theory.
4. **Transparency.** Effective attacks for rank swapping [354] and microaggregation [356,361,524] are based on intersection attacks and re-identification. The first explicit mention of the term transparency in data privacy was due to Karr [255], although the transparency attacks precede the use of this term. First transparency aware data protection methods were for microaggregation [147,148] and rank swapping [354].
   There is a current trend to stress the need for transparency. Transparency is also a key point in artificial intelligence, trustworthy AI, and is mentioned in GDPR. Transparency in this book stands for all processes related to data processing and transformation, and, particularly, to privacy technologies affecting the data. Transparency also applies to how models are built, models make decisions, and how human decision makers use these decisions in their daily work.

Machine and Statistical Learning, and Cryptography

2

Abstract

This chapter reviews main concepts on machine and statistical learning, as well on cryptography that are needed in the rest of the book. Algorithms for supervised and unsupervised learning are described. They include regression, clustering, and association rule mining. Some additional tools as indices to compare indices are also described. A summary of most important cryptographic concepts is also included. For example, private-key and public-key cryptography as well as homomorphic encryption is described.

> It may be summed up in one short sentence:
> 'Advise your son not to purchase your wine in Cambridge'
>
> C. Babbage, Passage from the life of a philosopher, 1864, p. 25 [31]

This chapter reviews some of the tools that we need in this book. We divide it in two parts. The first one is about machine and statistical learning. The second part is about cryptography.

2.1 Machine and Statistical Learning

In this chapter we will review some tools in machine and statistical learning that we need in the rest of the book. These techniques are used later for two different

© The Author(s), under exclusive license to Springer Nature Switzerland AG 2022
V. Torra, *Guide to Data Privacy*, Undergraduate Topics in Computer Science,
https://doi.org/10.1007/978-3-031-12837-0_2

Fig. 2.1 Notation for
supervised machine learning

$$
\begin{array}{c|ccc|c}
 & A_1 & \cdots & A_M & A_y \\
\hline
x_1 & A_1(x_1) & \cdots & A_M(x_1) & y_1 = A_y(x_1) \\
\vdots & \vdots & & \vdots & \vdots \\
x_N & A_1(x_N) & \cdots & A_M(x_N) & y_N = A_y(x_N)
\end{array}
$$

purposes. Some data protection mechanisms use techniques based or similar to some machine learning techniques. We will see, for example, that microaggregation, one masking method, is based on clustering. In addition, data is to be used, and typical uses require to apply, of course, machine learning and statistics. Therefore, we need these techniques as a tool when analyzing the effects of data protection mechanisms.

In the literature there is some discussion on similarities and differences between machine learning and statistics [62,191,545,549,552,553]. We do not make any distinction here. In order to present the different tools, we will mainly follow the terminology of Hastie, Tibshirani, and Friedman [221].

2.2 Classification of Techniques

Methods and techniques in machine learning are typically classified into three large classes according to the type of information available. They are supervised learning, unsupervised learning, and reinforcement learning. We discuss them below. All of them presume a set of labeled examples X used in the learning process. We will also presume that each example x_i in X is described in terms of a set of attributes $A_1, \ldots, A_M$. We will use $A_j(x_i)$ to denote the value of the attribute A_j for example x_i. That is, x_i is a vector in a M-dimensional space.

- **Supervised learning.** In this case, it is presumed that for each example in X there is a distinguished attribute A_y. The goal of supervised learning algorithms is to build a model of this attribute with respect to the other attributes. For example, if the attributes $A_1 \ldots A_M$ are numerical and the distinguished attribute A_y is also numerical, the goal of the supervised learning algorithm might be to express A_y as a linear regression of $A_1, \ldots, A_k$ for $k \leq M$. In general, A_y is expressed as a function of $A_1, \ldots, A_k$. When A_y is categorical, we call this attribute the class. Figure 2.1 summarizes the notation for supervised learning.
  For the sake of simplicity, it is usual to use x_i to denote $A(x_i)$, X to denote the full matrix (or just the full matrix without the attribute A_y), and Y to denote the column A_y. In some applications we need some training sets C that are subsets of X. That is, $C \subseteq X$. Then, we denote by M_C that we have a model learnt from C.
  Formally, let us consider a training set C defined in terms of the examples X where for each example x_i in X, we have its known label (outcome or class label) y. Then,

we presume that we can express y in terms of a function f of x_i and some error. That is, $y = f(x_i) + \epsilon$. With this notation we can say that the goal is to build a model M_C that depends on the training set C such that $M_C(x_i)$ approximates $f(x_i)$ for all x_i in the training set. This model is then used to classify unseen instances. Within supervised learning algorithms we investigate regression problems and classification problems. They are described further below.

- **Regression problems.** They correspond to the case in which A_y is numerical. Models include linear regression (i.e., models of the form $A_y = \sum_{i=1}^{k} a_i A_i + a_0$ for real numbers a_i), non-linear regression, and neural networks.
- **Classification problems.** They correspond to the case in which A_y is categorical. Models include logistic regression, decision trees, and different types of rule based systems.
- **Search problems.** They correspond to the problems in artificial intelligence to speed up search algorithms. However, this type of problems are of no interest in this book.

- **Unsupervised learning.** In this case, all the attributes are equal with respect to the learning process, and there is no such a distinguishable attribute. In this case, algorithms try to discover patterns or relationships in the data that can be of interest. Unsupervised learning includes clustering and association rules mining. The former discovers partitions in the data and the latter discovers rules between the attributes.
- **Reinforcement learning.** In this case we presume that there is already a system (or model) that approximates the data. When the model is used, the system receives a reward if the outcome of the model is successful and a penalty if the outcome is incorrect. These rewards are used to update the model and increase its perfomance.

2.3 Supervised Learning

A large number of algorithms for supervised machine learning have been developed. We give a brief overview of a few of them.

2.3.1 Classification

We explain superficially decision trees and the nearest neighbor.

Decision Trees

A decision tree classifies an element x by means of a chain of (usually binary) questions. These questions are organized as a tree with the first question in the top (the root) and classes in the leaves.

Machine learning algorithms build decision trees from data. The goal is to classify new elements correctly, and minimize the height of the tree (i.e., minimize the number of questions to be asked when a new element arrives).

Nearest Neighbor

Classification of a new example x is based on finding the nearest record from a set of stored records (the training set C). The class of this record is returned. Formally,

$$class(x) = class(arg \min_{x' \in C} d(x', x))$$

where $class(x) = A_y(x)$ using the notation given above.

An alternative is to consider the k nearest records and then return the class of the majority of these k records. This approach corresponds to the k-nearest neighbor.

2.3.2 Regression

There are different approaches to build models for regression. In this section we only review the expressions for linear regression models. There are, however, alternatives. For example, we have non-linear regression models and we can use k-nearest neighbor for regression. The k-nearest neighbor for regression follows the approach of the k-nearest neighbor explained above but instead of returning the class of the majority, the mean of the output of the majority is used.

Let us now focus on linear regression. We will give the expressions in matrix form. For details on regression see e.g. Ryan's book [414].

We denote the data (the training set) by the pair X, Y where Y corresponds to the attribute to be modeled (the dependent attribute) and X corresponds to the attributes of the model (the independent or explanatory attributes). In linear regression the model has the following form

$$y_i = \beta_0 + \beta_1 x_{i1} + \beta_2 x_{i2} + \cdots + \beta_M x_{iM} + \epsilon_i.$$

In matrix form, using

$$Y^T = (y_1 y_2 \ldots y_N)$$

$$\beta^T = (\beta_0 \beta_1 \beta_2 \ldots \beta_M)$$

and

$$X = \begin{pmatrix} 1 & x_{11} & x_{12} & \ldots & x_{1M} \\ 1 & x_{21} & x_{22} & \ldots & x_{2M} \\ \vdots & \vdots & \vdots & & \vdots \\ 1 & x_{N1} & x_{N2} & \ldots & x_{NM} \end{pmatrix} \tag{2.1}$$

we have that the model has this form:

$$Y = X\beta + \epsilon.$$

Then, the ordinary least squares (OLS) method estimates the parameters β of the model computing

$$\beta = [X^T X]^{-1} X^T Y.$$

Statistical properties of this methods (as e.g. the Gauss-Markov theorem) can be found in Ryan's book [414].

2.3.3 Validation of Results: k-fold Cross-validation

This is one of the most used approaches to evaluate the performance of a model. The approach is based on having a data set Z and then building several pairs of *(training, testing)* sets from this single data set. For each pair we can compute a model using the training set and evaluate its performance with the test set.

For a given parameter k, we divide the set Z into k subsets of equal size. Let

$$Z = (Z_1, Z_2, \ldots, Z_k)$$

be these sets. Then, we define for $i = 1, \ldots, k$ the pair of training and test sets (C_i^{Tr}, C_i^{Ts}) as follows:

$$C_i^{Tr} = \cup_{j \neq i} Z_j$$

$$C_i^{Ts} = Z_i.$$

Given these sets, we can compute the accuracy of any machine learning algorithm that when applied to the training set C returns the model M_C using the following expression:

$$accuracy = \frac{\sum_{i=1}^k |\{x | M_c(x) = A_y(x), x \in C_i^{Ts}\}|}{\sum |C_i^{Ts}|}.$$

Note that accuracy is not the only way to evaluate the performance of a classifier. Nevertheless, we will not discuss alternatives here. Cross-validation can also be used to evaluate regression.

2.4 Unsupervised Learning

The area of unsupervised learning has developed several families of methods to extract information from unclassified raw data. In this section we will focus on methods for clustering, for association rule mining, and on the expectation-maximization algorithm. They are the ones that will be used later in this book.

2.4.1 Clustering

> The objective is not to choose a 'best' clustering
> technique or program. Such a task would be
> fruitless and contrary to the very nature of
> clustering.
>
> R. Dubes and A. K. Jain, 1976 [155], p. 247

The goal of clustering, also known as cluster analysis, is to detect the similarities between the data in a set of examples. Different cluster methods differ on the type of data considered and on the way used to express the similarities.

For example, most clustering methods are applicable to numerical data. Nevertheless, other methods can be used on categorical data, time series, search logs, or even on nodes in social networks. With respect to the way used to express the similarities between the data, some clustering methods build partitions of the data objects, others build fuzzy partitions of these data, fuzzy relationships between the objects, and hierarchical structures (dendrograms).

In all cases, the goal of a clustering method is to put similar objects together in the same group or cluster, and put dissimilar ones in different clusters. For achieving this, a crucial point is how to measure the similarity between objects. Different definitions of similarity and distance lead to different clusters.

Methods and algorithms for clustering can be classified according to several dimensions. As expressed above, one is the type of data being clustered, another is about the type of structure built around the data. Hastie et al. [221] (page 507) consider another dimension that refers to our assumptions on data. The following classes of clustering algorithms are considered: combinatorial algorithms, algorithms for mixture modeling, and algorithms that are mode seekers. See the outline in Fig. 2.2. We briefly describe these classes below.

- **Combinatorial algorithms.** They do not presume any underlying probability distribution. They directly work on the data.
- **Mixture modeling algorithms.** They presume an underlying probability density function. Assuming a parametric approach, clustering consists of finding the parameters of the model (a mixture of density functions). E.g., two Gaussian distributions are fitted to a set of points.
- **Mode seeker algorithms.** They also presume an underlying probability density function but in this case the perspective is nonparametric. So, there is no such a prior assumption that data follows a particular model.

In the rest of this section we review some methods for clustering. We focus on methods for numerical data that lead to crisp and fuzzy partitions. These algorithms belong to the family of combinatorial algorithms. Both type of methods are *partitive*, this means that we have initially a single set of data (a single cluster) and then we

Clustering methods

- Combinatorial methods.

    - Partitive methods (top-down): c-means, fuzzy c-means.
    - Agglomerative methods (bottom-up): single linkage.

- Mixture modeling methods.
- Mode seeker methods.

Fig. 2.2 A classification of some clustering methods

partition this cluster into a set of other clusters. In contrast, we find in the literature agglomerative methods that start with as many clusters as data, and then merge some of these clusters to build new ones. Agglomerative methods can be seen as bottom-up methods, and partitive methods as top-down.

Following Dubes and Jain [155,242], we can distinguish between clustering methods (or techniques) and clustering algorithms (or programs). A clustering method is to specify the general strategy for defining the clusters. In contrast, a clustering algorithm implements the strategy and might use some heuristics. This difference will be further stressed below when describing the k-means.

Crisp Clustering

Given a data set X a crisp clustering algorithm builds a partition of the objects in X. Formally, $\Pi = \{\pi_1, \ldots, \pi_c\}$ is a partition of X if $\cup \pi_i = X$ and for all $i \neq j$ we have $\pi_i \cap \pi_j = \emptyset$.

For any set of n objects, given c, the number of possible partitions of c clusters is the Stirling number of the second kind [242] (p. 91) [221] (Sect. 14.30):

$$S(n, c) = \frac{1}{c!} \sum_{k=1}^{c} (-1)^{c-k} \binom{c}{k} k^n.$$

When c is not known and any number of clusters of $c = 1, \ldots, n$ is possible, the number of possible partitions of a set with n elements is the Bell number.

$$B_n = \sum_{k=1}^{n} S(n, c).$$

It is known [46] that for $n \in \mathbb{N}^n$

$$\left(\frac{n}{e \ln n} \right)^n < B_n < \left(\frac{0.792n}{\ln(n+1)} \right)^n.$$

Different methods exist for selecting or constructing one of these partitions. In optimal clustering, the partition is selected as the one that minimizes an objective function. That is, given an objective function OF, and a space of solutions S, select Π as the solution s that minimizes OF. Formally,

$$\Pi = \arg \min_{s \in S} OF(s).$$

One of the most used methods for clustering is k-means, also known as crisp c-means in the community of fuzzy clustering. This algorithm uses as inputs the data set X and also the number of clusters c. This method is defined as an optimal clustering with the following objective function.

$$OF(\Pi) = \sum_{k=1}^{c} \sum_{x \in \pi_k} ||A(x) - p_k||^2 \tag{2.2}$$

Here, π_k, which is a part of partition Π, corresponds to a cluster and p_k is the centroid or prototype of this cluster. $||u||$ is the norm of the vector u. That is, $||u|| = \sqrt{u_1^2 + \dots u_M^2}$.

Expression 2.2 can be rewritten in terms of characteristic functions χ_k of sets π_k. That is, for each set π_k we have a characteristic function $\chi_k : X \rightarrow \{0, 1\}$ such that $\chi_k(x) = 1$ if and only if $x \in \pi_k$. Using this notation, the goal of the clustering algorithm is to determine the set of characteristic functions $\chi = \{\chi_1, \dots, \chi_c\}$ as well as the cluster centroids $P = \{p_1, \dots, p_c\}$.

The characteristic functions define a partition. Because of that we require χ to satisfy

- $\chi_k(x) \in \{0, 1\}$ for all $k = 1, \dots, c$ and $x \in X$, and that
- for all $x \in X$ there is exactly one k_0 such that $\chi_{k_0}(x) = 1$.

The last condition can be equivalently expressed as $\sum_{k=1}^{c} \chi_k(x) = 1$ for all $x \in X$.

Taking all this into account, we formalize the c-means problem as follows:

Minimize
$$OF(\chi, P) = \sum_{k=1}^{c} \sum_{x \in X} \chi_k(x) ||A(x) - p_k||^2$$
subject to
$$\chi \in M_c = \left\{ \chi_k(x) | \chi_k(x) \in \{0, 1\}, \sum_{k=1}^{c} \chi_k(x) = 1 \text{ for all } x \in X \right\} \tag{2.3}$$

This optimization problem is usually solved by means of an iterative algorithm that interleaves two steps. In the first step, we presume that P is known and determines the partition χ that minimizes the objective function $OF(\chi, P)$ given P. In the second step, we presume that the partition χ is known and we determine the cluster centers P that minimize the objective function $OF(\chi, P)$ given χ. This process is repeated until convergence.

To bootstrap the process, we select at random a set of objects from X and define them as centroids, or we can define an initial partition and compute its set of centroids P. The former is usually a better strategy.

This algorithm does not ensure a global minimum, but ensures convergence to a local minimum. We discuss this in more detail later.

Let us now formalize the steps above and give expressions for their calculation. The steps are as follows.

Step 1.   Define an initial set of centroids P.
Step 2.   Solve $min_{\chi \in M_c} OF(\chi, P)$.
Step 3.   Solve $min_P OF(\chi, P)$.
Step 4.   Repeat steps 2 and 3 till convergence.

The solution of Step 2 consists of assigning each object in X to the nearest cluster. Formally, for all $x \in X$ use the following assignments.

- $k_0 := \arg \min_i ||A(x) - p_i||^2$
- $\chi_{k_0}(x) := 1$
- $\chi_j(x) := 0$ for all $j \neq k_0$

Note that in this definition k_0 depends on $x \in X$.

To prove that this is the optimal solution of the problem stated in Step 2, let us consider the objetive function

$$OF(\chi, P) = \sum_{k=1}^{c} \sum_{x \in X} \chi_k(x) ||A(x) - p_k||^2.$$

Naturally, we have that for a given x and $p_1, \ldots, p_c$, it holds

$$||A(x) - p_k|| \geq ||A(x) - p_{k_0}||$$

for all $k \in \{1, \ldots, c\}$, when k_0 is the index $k_0 = \arg \min_i ||A(x) - p_i||^2$. Therefore, the assignment $\chi_{k_0}(x) = 1$ and $\chi_j(x) = 0$ for all $j \neq k_0$ minimizes

$$\sum_{x \in X} \chi_k(x) ||A(x) - p_k||^2$$

for all $k \in \{1, \ldots, c\}$, and thus the objective function.

The solution of Step 3 consists in computing for all $k = 1, \ldots, c$.

$$p_k = \frac{\sum_{x \in X} \chi_k(x) A(x)}{\sum_{x \in X} \chi_k(x)} \tag{2.4}$$

To prove that this is the optimal centroid we consider again the objective function $OF(\chi, P)$ and derive it with respect to p_k. Taking into account that $\frac{\partial OF}{\partial p_k} = 0$, we obtain an expression for p_k. Note that

$$0 = \frac{\partial OF}{\partial p_k} = 2 \sum_{x \in X} \chi_k(x)(A(x) - p_k)(-1),$$

and, therefore, we get the equation

$$-2 \sum_{x \in X} \chi_k(x) A(x) + \sum_{x \in X} \chi_k(x) p_k = 0,$$

that leads to Eq. 2.4.

Algorithm 1: Clustering: c-means.

Step 1.　　Define an initial set of centroids P.

Step 2.　　Solve $min_{\chi \in M_c} OF(\chi, P)$ as follows:

- For all $x \in X$,
    - $k_0 := \arg\min_i ||A(x) - p_i||^2$
    - $\chi_{k_0}(x) := 1$
    - $\chi_j(x) := 0$ for all $j \in \{1, \ldots, c\}$ s.t. $j \neq k_0$

Step 3.　　Solve $min_P OF(\chi, P)$ as follows:

- for all $k \in \{1, \ldots, c\}$,

    - $p_k := \dfrac{\sum_{x \in X} \chi_k(x) A(x)}{\sum_{x \in X} \chi_k(x)}$

Step 4.　　Repeat steps 2 and 3 till convergence

If we put all the items together, we get Algorithm 1.

As stated above, there is no guarantee that this algorithm leads to the global optimal solution. However, it can be proven that it converges to a local optimal one. Note that at each step the objective function is reduced. In Step 2, with fixed centroids P, the objective function is reduced changing χ. Then, in Step 3, with fixed χ, the objective function is reduced changing P. As the objective function is always positive, convergence is ensured.

Different executions of this algorithm using the same initialization lead to the same results. Nevertheless, due to the fact that the algorithm does not ensure a global minimum but a local one, we have the situation where different initializations can lead to different local minima. This fact is very important when we need to compare clusters obtained from the application of this algorithm.

To partially solve this problem, we can use some of the existing methods for selecting a good initialization [258] for a dataset X. Another option is to apply the same algorithm several times to the same data set X, but with different initializations. Then, each application will lead to a partition with its corresponding value for the objective function. Let $r = 1, \ldots, R$ denote the rth application, Π_r the partition obtained and OF_r its corresponding objective function. All partitions Π_r are local optima of the same objective function OF. Then, we select the partition Π_r with minimum OF_r. That is, we select the partition [488,489]

$$r_0 = \arg \min OF_r.$$

This approach does not ensure finding the global optimum, it can still lead to a local optimum. Nevertheless it gives us more chances of finding it.

The outcome of c-means permits us to define classification rules for any element d in the same domain D of the elements in X. That is, not only the elements x can be classified but any $d \in D$ can be classified to one of the clusters $\pi_1, \ldots, \pi_c$. The classification rule is:

$$cluster(d) = \arg \min_{k=1}^{c} ||d - p_k||^2.$$

The application of this classification rule in a domain D results into a Voronoi diagram described by the centers P and the Euclidean distance. Recall that the Voronoi diagram of a domain D divides D into a set of regions. Here, the regions are $(R_k)_{k \in \{1,\ldots,c\}}$, where

$$R_k = \{d \in D| \ ||d - p_k|| \leq ||d - p_j|| \text{ for all } j \neq k\}.$$

Fuzzy Clustering

Fuzzy clustering algorithms return a fuzzy partition instead of a crisp partition. In fuzzy partitions, clusters typically overlap. This causes elements $x \in X$ to have partial membership to different clusters. Partial membership is represented by a value in the [0, 1] interval.

In this section we review some of the algorithms that lead to fuzzy partitions. We begin by reviewing the notion of membership function used to define fuzzy sets [538], and then the notion of fuzzy partition. Bezdek [50] provided some discussion and examples on the difference between fuzzy and probabilistic uncertainty (from a *fuzzy* point of view).

Definition 2.1 [538] Let X be a reference set. Then $\mu : X \rightarrow [0, 1]$ is a membership function.

Definition 2.2 [412] Let X be a reference set. Then, a set of membership functions $\mathcal{M} = \{\mu_1, \ldots, \mu_c\}$ is a fuzzy partition of X if for all $x \in X$ we have

$$\sum_{i=1}^{c} \mu_i(x) = 1$$

Fuzzy c-means (FCM) [49] is one of the most used algorithms for fuzzy clustering. It can be seen as a generalization of crisp c-means that has a similar objective function. The solution of the problem is a fuzzy partition. That is, given a value c, the algorithm returns c membership functions $\mu_1, \ldots, \mu_c$ that define a fuzzy partition of the elements of the domain X. Figure 2.3 discusses a naive fuzzification of c-means.

Naive fuzzy c-means. A naive fuzzification of the c-means algorithm is to replace the constraint of χ in $\{0, 1\}$ in Equation 2.3 by another requiring χ to be a value in $[0, 1]$. Nevertheless, this fuzzification has no practical effect. It does not lead to fuzzy solutions. In other words, all solutions of this alternative problem are crisp partitions. That is, although χ is permitted to take values different to 0 and 1, all solutions have values of χ in the extremes of the interval $[0,1]$.

Fig. 2.3 Remark on a naive fuzzy c-means

The notation follows the one of c-means. X is the set of records, $P = \{p_1, \ldots, p_c\}$ representing the cluster centers or centroids, μ_i is the membership function of the ith cluster and, then, $\mu_i(x_k)$ is the membership of the kth record to the ith cluster. μ_{ik} is also used as an expression equivalent to $\mu_i(x_k)$.

Fuzzy c-means has two parameters. One is the number of clusters c, as in the c-means. Another is a value m that measures the degree of fuzziness of the solution. The value m should be larger than or equal to one. When $m = 1$, the problem to optimize corresponds to the c-means and the algorithm returns a crisp partition. Then, the larger the m, the fuzzier is the solution. In particular, for large values of m, we have that the solutions are completely fuzzy and memberships in all clusters are $\mu_i(x_k) = 1/c$ for all i and $x_k \in X$.

The optimization problem follows.

Minimize
$$OF_{FCM}(\mu, P) = \sum_{i=1}^{c} \sum_{x \in X} (\mu_i(x))^m \|x - p_i\|^2$$
subject to   (2.5)
$$\mu_i(x) \in [0, 1] \text{ for all } i \in \{1, \ldots, c\} \text{ and } x \in X$$
$$\sum_{i=1}^{c} \mu_i(x) = 1 \text{ for all } x \in X.$$

This problem is usually solved using Algorithm 2. The algorithm is an iterative process similar to the one of c-means. It iterates two steps. One step estimates the membership functions of elements to clusters (taking centroids as fixed). The other step estimates the centroids for each cluster (taking membership functions as fixed). The algorithm converges but as in the case of c-means the solution can be a local optimum. The algorithm [231,322,323] does not discuss the case of denominators equal to zero. This is solved with adhoc definitions for μ. The method needs to be bootstraped, this can be done selecting a random set of centroids from the data set X.

Expressions for $\mu_i(x)$ and p_i in Steps 2 and 3 are determined using Lagrange multipliers [49]. The expression to minimize includes the objective function OF_{FCM} as well as the constraints $\sum_{i=1}^{c} \mu_i(x) = 1$ for all $x \in X$. Each constraint is multiplied by the corresponding Lagrange multiplier λ_k (for $k = 1, \ldots, N$).

$$L = OF_{FCM}(\mu, P) + \sum_{k=1}^{N} \lambda_k \left(\sum_{i=1}^{c} \mu_i(x_k) - 1 \right)$$
$$= \sum_{i=1}^{c} \sum_{k=1}^{N} (\mu_i(x_k))^m \|x_k - p_i\|^2 + \sum_{k=1}^{N} \lambda_k \left(\sum_{i=1}^{c} \mu_i(x_k) - 1 \right)$$ (2.6)

Algorithm 2: Clustering: fuzzy c-means.

Step 1.   Generate initial P.

Step 2.   Solve $min_{\mu \in M} OF_{FCM}(\mu, P)$ by computing for all $i \in \{1, \ldots, c\}$ and $x \in X$:

$$\mu_i(x) := \left(\sum_{j=1}^{c} \left(\frac{||x - p_i||^2}{||x - p_j||^2} \right)^{\frac{1}{m-1}} \right)^{-1}$$

Step 3.   Solve $min_P OF_{FCM}(\mu, P)$ by computing for all $i \in \{1, \ldots, c\}$:

$$p_i := \frac{\sum_{x \in X} (\mu_i(x))^m x}{\sum_{x \in X} (\mu_i(x))^m}$$

Step 4.   If the solution does not converge, go to Step 2; otherwise, stop.

Now, in order to find the expression for $\mu_i(x_k)$, we consider the partial derivatives of L with respect to $\mu_i(x_k)$, that need to be zero. These partial derivatives are

$$\frac{\partial L}{\partial \mu_i(x_k)} = m(\mu_i(x_k))^{m-1} ||A(x_k) - p_i||^2 + \lambda_k = 0$$

Therefore, we have the following expression for $\mu_i(x_k)$

$$\mu_i(x_k) = \left(\frac{-\lambda_k}{m ||A(x_k) - p_i||^2} \right)^{\frac{1}{m-1}}$$

Now, taking advantage of the fact that $\sum_{i=1}^{c} \mu_i(x) = 1$ for all $x \in X$, we get rid of λ_k and obtain the expression for $\mu_i(x_k)$ in Step 2.

Similarly, in order to find the expression for p_i, we proceed with the partial derivative of L with respect to p_i. That is,

$$\frac{\partial L}{\partial p_i} = \sum_{k=1}^{N} (\mu_i(x_k))^m 2 (A(x_k) - p_i) (-1) = 0.$$

From this expression we get the expression for p_i in Step 3.

Comparison of Cluster Results

The need to compare different sets of clusters on the same data set appears naturally when we want to analyse the result of clustering algorithms. We can either need to compare the results of the clustering algorithm with respect to a known set of clusters (a reference partition), or to compare different executions of the same clustering algorithm.

Rand [393] (1971, Sect. 3), Hubert and Arabie [235], and Anderson et al. [28] mention the following applications related to clustering where functions to compare clusters are needed.

- **Comparison with a reference partition or golden standard.** This golden standard are the "natural" clusters using Rand's terminology. The results of a clustering algorithm are compared with the reference partition.
- **Comparison with noisy data.** The results of clustering the original data and the perturbed data permits us to measure the sensitivity of an algorithm to noisy data.
- **Comparison with supressed data (to missing individuals).** Comparison of an original data set X and the same data set after suppression measures the sensitivity of an algorithm to missing data.
- **Comparison of two algorithms.** The results of two different algorithms applied to the same data are compared.
- **Comparison of two successive partitions given by the same algorithm.** This is useful for defining stopping criteria in iterative algorithms.
- **Comparison for prediction.** This is about using one of the partitions to predict the other.

In the remaining part of this section we discuss some of the distances and similarity measures for clusters that can be found in the literature. In our definitions we use Π and Π' to denote two partitions of a data set X. We presume that both partitions have the same number of parts, and that this number is n. Then, let $\Pi = \{\pi_1, \ldots, \pi_n\}$ and $\Pi' = \{\pi'_1, \ldots, \pi'_n\}$, that is, π_i and π'_i denote. A part of Π and $\Pi+$, and, therefore, $\pi_i \subseteq X$ and $\pi'_i \subseteq X$ for all $i = 1, \ldots, n$.

Let $I_\Pi(x)$ denote the cluster of x in the partition Π. Then, let us define $r, s, t,$ and u as follows:

- r is the number of pairs (x_1, x_2), with x_1 and x_2 elements of X, and both in the same cluster in Π and also both in the same cluster in Π'. That is, r is the cardinality of the set
$$\{(x_1, x_2) \text{ with } x_1 \in X, x_2 \in X, \text{ and } x_1 \neq x_2 | I_\Pi(x_1) = I_\Pi(x_2) \text{ and } I_{\Pi'}(x_1) = I_{\Pi'}(x_2)\};$$
- s is the number of pairs (x_1, x_2) where x_1 and x_2 are in the same cluster in Π but not in Π'. That is,
$$\{(x_1, x_2) \text{ with } x_1 \in X, x_2 \in X, \text{ and } x_1 \neq x_2 | I_\Pi(x_1) = I_\Pi(x_2) \text{ and } I_{\Pi'}(x_1) \neq I_{\Pi'}(x_2)\};$$
- t is the number of pairs where x_1 and x_2 are in the same cluster in Π' but not in Π. That is,
$$\{(x_1, x_2) \text{ with } x_1 \in X, x_2 \in X, \text{ and } x_1 \neq x_2 | I_\Pi(x_1) \neq I_\Pi(x_2) \text{ and } I_{\Pi'}(x_1) = I_{\Pi'}(x_2)\};$$
- u is the number of pairs where x_1 and x_2 are in different clusters in both partitions.

In addition, we denote $np(\Pi)$ as the number of pairs within clusters in the partition Π. That is
$$np(\Pi) = |\{(x_1, x_2) | x_1 \in X, x_2 \in X, x_1 \neq x_2, I_{\Pi(x_1)} = I_{\Pi(x_2)}\}|$$
where $|\cdot|$ is the cardinality of the set.

Note that using the notation above, $np(\Pi) = r + s$ and $np(\Pi') = r + t$. Table 2.1 presents a summary of these definitions.

Table 2.1 Definitions for comparing two partitions Π and Π'

	$I_\Pi(x_1) = I_\Pi(x_2)$	$I_\Pi(x_1) \neq I_\Pi(x_2)$	Total
$I_{\Pi'}(x_1) = I_{\Pi'}(x_2)$	r	t	$r + t = np(\Pi')$
$I_{\Pi'}(x_1) = I_{\Pi'}(x_2)$	s	u	$s + u$
	$r + s = np(\Pi)$	$t + u$	$\binom{|X|}{2}$

The literature presents a large number of indices and distances [26,28] to compare (crisp) partitions. The most well known are the Rand, the Jaccard and the Adjusted Rand index. We present these three and a few other ones.

- **Rand index.** Defined by Rand [393], this index is defined as follows:
$$RI(\Pi, \Pi') = (r + u)/(r + s + t + u)$$
For any Π and Π', we have $RI(\Pi, \Pi') \in [0, 1]$, with $RI(\Pi, \Pi) = 1$.
- **Jaccard Index.** It is defined as follows:
$$JI(\Pi, \Pi') = r/(r + s + t)$$
For any Π and Π', we have $JI(\Pi, \Pi') \in [0, 1]$, with $RI(\Pi, \Pi) = 1$.
- **Adjusted Rand Index.** This is a correction of the Rand index so that the expectation of the index for partitions with equal number of objects is 0. This adjustment was done assuming generalized hypergeometric distribution as the model of randomness. That is, if we consider a random generation of two partitions so that they have both n sets, the adjusted Rand index is zero. The definition of the index is as follows.
$$ARI(\Pi, \Pi') = \frac{r - exp}{max - exp}$$
where
$$exp = (np(\Pi)np(\Pi'))/(n(n-1)/2)$$
and where
$$max = 0.5(np(\Pi) + np(\Pi')).$$
First discussion of the adjusted Rand index is due to Morey and Agresti [329] and current expression is due to Hubert and Arabie [235].
- **Wallace Index.** This index is defined in terms of the following expression.
$$WI(\Pi, \Pi') = r/\sqrt{np(\Pi)np(\Pi')}$$
- **Mántaras distance.** This distance [312] is defined for two partitions by
$$MD(\Pi, \Pi') = \frac{I(\Pi/\Pi') + I(\Pi'/\Pi)}{I(\Pi' \cap \Pi)}$$
where
$$I(\Pi/\Pi') = -\sum_{i=1}^{n} P(\pi_i') \sum_{j=1}^{n} P(\pi_j/\pi_i') \log P(\pi_j/\pi_i')$$

Transaction number	Itemsets purchased	Items (only first letter)
x_1	{apple, biscuits, chocolate, doughnut, ensaïmada, flour}	{a, b, c, d, e, f}
x_2	{apple, biscuits, chocolate}	{a, b, c}
x_3	{chocolate, doughnut, ensaïmada}	{c, d, e}
x_4	{biscuits}	{b}
x_5	{chocolate, doughnut, ensaïmada, flour}	{c, d, e, f}
x_6	{biscuits, chocolate, doughnout}	{b, c, d}
x_7	{ensaïmada}	{e}
x_8	{chocolate, flour}	{c, f}

Fig. 2.4 Database $\mathscr{D}$ with 8 transactions for the itemset I={apple, biscuits, chocolate, doughnut, ensaïmada, flour, grapes}

$$I(\Pi' \cap \Pi) = -\sum_{i=1}^{n} \sum_{j=1}^{n} P(\pi_i' \cap \pi_j) \log P(\pi_i' \cap \pi_j)$$

and where $P(A)$ is the probability of A estimated as $P(A) = |A|/|X|$.

In the case of fuzzy clusters, a comparison can be done through α-cuts. That is, all those elements with a membership larger than α have their membership assigned to the value 1, others assigned to zero. Nevertheless, this process does not generate in general partitions and the above expressions cannot be used. Instead, we can compute the absolute distance between memberships. For binary memberships, this distance corresponds to the Hamming distance.

Alternatively, there are a few definitions [28,63,236,237] to generalize some of the existing distances for crisp partitions to the case of fuzzy partitions.

2.4.2 Association Rules Mining

Association rules establish relationships between attributes or items in a database. Association rule learning algorithms try to find relevant rules in a given database. A typical application of these algorithms is market basket analysis. A market basket is the set of items a costumer buys in a single purchase. Then, a rule relates a set of some items that can be purchased with some other items that consumers usually buy at the same time.

Formally, a database $\mathscr{D} = \{x_1, \ldots, x_N\}$ has N transactions (or records) consisting each one in a subset of a predefined set of items. Let $I = \{I_1, \ldots, I_m\}$ be the set of items. Then, $x_i \subset I$ for all $i \in 1, \ldots, N$. We call itemset any subset of I. Thus, x_i are itemsets.

In order to simplify the algorithms, it is usual to presume that the items in I are ordered in a particular preestablished order, and that the itemsets are not empty (i.e., $|x_i| \geq 1$).

An association rule is an implication of the form

$$X \Rightarrow Y$$

where X and Y are nonempty itemsets with no common items. Formally, $X, Y \subseteq I$ such that $|X| \geq 1$, $|Y| \geq 1$, and $X \cap Y = \emptyset$. X is called the antecedent and Y the consequent of the rule.

We review now some definitions that are needed later. We give examples for each definition based on the database $\mathcal{D}$ in Fig. 2.4.

- **Matching.** An itemset S *matches* a transaction T if $S \subseteq T$. For example, $S_1 = \{chocolate, doughnut\}$ matches transactions x_1, x_3, x_5, x_6, $S_2 = \{flour\}$ matches transactions x_1, x_5, and x_8, and there is no transaction matching $S_3 = \{grapes\}$.
- **Support count.** The support count of an itemset S, expressed by *Count(S)*, is the number of transactions (or records) that match S in the database $\mathcal{D}$. For example, $Count_{\mathcal{D}}(S_1) = 4$, $Count_{\mathcal{D}}(S_2) = 3$, and $Count_{\mathcal{D}}(S_3) = 0$.
- **Support.** The support of an itemset S, expressed by *Support(S)* is the proportion of transactions that contain all items in S in the database $\mathcal{D}$. That is, $Support_{\mathcal{D}}(S) = Count_{\mathcal{D}}(S)/|\mathcal{D}|$. For example,

$$Support_{\mathcal{D}}(S_1) = 4/8, \ Support_{\mathcal{D}}(S_2) = 3/8, \ \text{and} \ Support_{\mathcal{D}}(S_2) = 0/8.$$

When the context makes clear the database used, we will simply use $Count(s)$ and $Support(s)$ instead of $Count_{\mathcal{D}}(s)$ and $Support_{\mathcal{D}}(s)$.

Lemma 2.1 *Let I_1 and I_2 be two itemsets; then if $I_1 \subseteq I_2$ then*

$$Support(I_1) \geq Support(I_2).$$

Note that this holds because I_1 matches more itemsets in the database (because has less requirements) than I_2.

Given a rule of the form $R = (X \Rightarrow Y)$, its support will be the proportion of transactions in which both X and Y hold. This is computed defining the support of the rule as the support of the union of the two itemsets that define the rule.

- **Support of a rule.** The support of the rule $R = (X \Rightarrow Y)$ is the support of $X \cup Y$. I.e.,

$$Support(R) = Support(X \cup Y).$$

For example, the support of the rule

$$R_0 = (X \Rightarrow Y)$$

with $X = \{chocolate, doughnut\}$ and $Y = \{ensaïmada\}$ is

$$Support(X \Rightarrow Y) = Support(X \cup Y) = Support(\{chocolate,$$
$$doughnut, ensaïmada\}) = 3$$

because $\{chocolate, doughnut, ensaïmada\}$ matches x_1, x_3, and x_5.

Note that the rule R_0 in the last example does not hold for all the transactions in the database. Although the support of $X = \{$chocolate, doughnut$\}$ includes x_1, x_3, x_5, x_6, we have that x_6 does not include ensaïmada. Therefore, the rule does not hold for this transaction. In general, rules do not hold 100% of the time.

In order for a rule to be interesting, it should

- apply to a large proportion of records in the database, and
- have a large prediction capability.

For measuring the first aspect we can use the support. Note that support precisely measures the proportion of itemsets where the rule is applicable and holds. For the example above R_0 applies to

$$Support(R_0) = 3/8$$

of the transactions in $\mathscr{D}$.

For measuring the second aspect, we need to estimate the predictive accuracy of a rule. This is measured by the *confidence* of a rule, which is defined in terms of the support of the rule with respect to the support of the antecedent of the rule. In other words, the confidence states how many times the rule leads to a correct conclusion.

- **Confidence of a rule.** The confidence of the rule $R = (X \Rightarrow Y)$ is the support of the rule divided by the support of X. That is,

$$Confidence(R) = Support(X \cup Y)/Support(X).$$

Or, equivalently, using *Count*:

$$Confidence(R) = Count(X \cup Y)/Count(X).$$

As stated above, it is usual that rules are not exact. That is, $Confidence(R) < 1$ because for Lemma 2.1, $Support(X \cup Y) \leq Support(X)$.

As an example, the confidence of the rule $R_0 = (X \Rightarrow Y)$ is

$$\begin{aligned} Confidence(X \Rightarrow Y) &= Support(X \cup Y)/Support(X) \\ &= Support(\{c, d, e\})/Support(\{c, d\}) = 3/4. \end{aligned} \tag{2.7}$$

In order to filter the rules that are not interesting, we will reject all the rules that have a support below a certain threshold. That is, we reject all the rules that only apply to a small set of transactions. For example, the rules with a support less than 0.01. Given a threshold for the support $thr - s$, we say that an itemset I_0 is supported when $Support(I_0) \geq thr - s$.

For supported itemsets, the following holds.

Lemma 2.2 *Let I_0 be a supported itemset. Then, any non empty subset I_0' of I_0 (i.e., $I_0' \subseteq I_0$ such that $|I_0'| \geq 1$) is also supported* □

Algorithm 3: Association Rule Generation: Simple algorithm.

Step 1.	$R := \emptyset$
Step 2.	L be the set of supported itemsets with cardinality larger than 2 $(thr - s)$
Step 3.	for all $l \in L$
Step 4.	for all $X \subset l$ with $X \neq \emptyset$ (generate all possible rules from l)
Step 5.	if $(Confidence(X \Rightarrow (l \setminus X)) \geq thr - c$ then
Step 6.	$R := R \cup (X \Rightarrow (l \setminus X))$
Step 7.	end if
Step 8.	end for
Step 9.	end for
Step 10.	return R

Proof From Lemma 2.1 and the fact that I_0 is supported, it follows

$$Support(I_0') \geq Support(I_0) \geq thr - s.$$

So, I_0' is also supported. $\qquad\qquad\qquad\qquad\qquad\qquad\qquad\qquad\qquad\qquad\square$

In addition we will also reject the rules below a certain confidence level. That is, the rules that fail too often. For example, rules that apply correctly less than 75% of the times are not valid. We will denote this threshold by $thr - c$.

So as a summary, we are interested in finding rules R such that

$$Support(R) \geq thr - s \tag{2.8}$$

and

$$Confidence(R) \geq thr - c. \tag{2.9}$$

Algorithms to find such rules are known by rule mining algorithms. Algorithm 3 is a simple algorithm for rule mining. The algorithm first considers all supported itemsets. That is, it selects all itemsets with a support larger than $thr - s$. Then, for each of these itemsets, it generates all possible rules, and all those rules with enough confidence are returned.

The cost of this algorithm is very large. If the number of items in the itemset I is m, there are 2^m subsets of I. Of these, $2^m - m - 1$ are the number of subsets of I with cardinality larger than or equal to 2. With small m, the cost becomes unfeasible. For example for the cardinalities (number of different products in the supermarket) $m = 10, 20$, and 100 we have $2^{10} = 1024$, $2^{20} \approx 10^6$, and $2^{100} \approx 10^{30}$. Because of this, more efficient and heuristic methods have been defined to find relevant and interesting rules.

Support and confidence can be understood as probabilities. In particular, the support of an itemset X can be understood as the probability that X occurs. Therefore, we can estimate $P(X)$ as follows:

$$P(X) = Support(X) = \frac{\text{transactions satisfying X}}{\text{number of transactions}}.$$

Algorithm 4: Association Rule Generation: Apriori algorithm.

Step 1.	L_1 be the set of supported itemsets of cardinality one$(thr - s)$.
Step 2.	Set $k := 2$
Step 3.	while $(L_{k-1} \neq \emptyset)$
Step 4.	$C_k :=$ new candidate set (L_{k-1})
Step 5.	$L_k :=$ remove non supported itemsets in $C_k(thr - s)$
Step 6.	$k := k + 1$
Step 7.	end while
Step 8.	return $L_1 \cup L_2 \cup \cdots \cup L_k$

Then, the confidence of rule $R = (X \Rightarrow Y)$ can be understood as the conditional probability of $X \cup Y$ given X. So, we can estimate the probability for this rule $P(Y|X)$ as

$$P(Y|X) = \frac{P(X \cup Y)}{P(X)}.$$

Apriori Algorithm

The Apriori algorithm [23] is a well known algorithm for association rule learning. The algorithm incrementally defines candidate itemsets of length k from itemsets of length $k - 1$. This process is based on the following lemma, which is known as the *downward closure lemma*.

Lemma 2.3 *[22] Let L_k be all itemsets with cardinality k. That is,*

$$L_k = \{S| \, |S| \geq k, \, Support(K) \geq thr - s\}.$$

Then, if L_k is empty, $L_{k'}$ is empty for all $k' > k$.

Proof Let us presume that L_k is empty but $L_{k'}$ is not for $k' = k + 1 > k$. This means that there exists a supported itemset I_0 of cardinality $k + 1$. Let i_0 be an item in I_0. Then, $I_0 \setminus \{i_0\}$ is also supported by Lemma 2.2. As I_0 has cardinality k, we have a contradiction and the proposition is proved. □

This result permits us to define an algorithm that considers supported itemsets of increasing cardinality. For each itemset L_{k-1} of cardinality $k - 1$ we will define a candidate set for the itemsets of cardinality k and then prune all those that are not sufficiently supported. The supported ones will define L_k. Algorithm 4 describes this process.

The process of constructing the new candidate set is given in Algorithm 5 [23, 310]. For each pair of itemsets J_1 and J_2 that share all items except one we compute the union that will have exactly k items. The union will be in C_k. Formally,

$$C_k = \{J_1 \cup J_2 | J_1, J_2 \in L_{k-1} and | J_1 \cap J_2| = k - 2\}.$$

Algorithm 5: Association Rule Generation: Apriori algorithm. Computation of the new candidate set from L_{k-1}. If the elements in the itemsets J_1 and J_2 are ordered, this order can be exploited to speed up the procedure.

Step 1.	$C_k := \emptyset$
Step 2.	for each pair J_1, J_2 in L_{k-1}
Step 3.	if (J_1 and J_2 share $k-2$ items) then
Step 4.	$C_k := C_k \cup \{J_1 \cup J_2\}$
Step 5.	end if
Step 6.	end for
Step 7.	return C_k

Algorithm 6: Association Rule Generation: Apriori algorithm. Removal of non supported itemsets in $C_k(thr - s)$ to compute L_k.

Step 1.	for all c in C_k
Step 2.	for all subsets c' of c with $k-1$ elements
Step 3.	remove c from C_k if c' is not in L_{k-1}
Step 4.	end for
Step 5.	end for
Step 6.	for all c in C_k
Step 7.	if ($Support(c) < thr - s$) then remove c from C_k
Step 8.	end for
Step 9.	return C_k

For example, let us consider $k = 5$ and $L_{k-1} = L_4$ including, among others, $J_1 = \{a, b, c, d\}$ and $J_2 = \{a, b, c, e\}$. Then, as J_1 and J_2 share $k - 2 = 5 - 2 = 3$ items, we will include in C_5 the itemset $J_1 \cup J_2 = \{a, b, c, d, e\}$.

In order to know if an itemset $c \in C_k$ should be in L_k or not, we first check whether its subsets of cardinality $k - 1$ are in L_{k-1}. If one fails to be in L_{k-1}, then c should not be in L_k. However, this is not enough to ensure that the support of c is larger than the threshold. This has to be checked also. Algorithm 6 describes this process.

In the remaining part of this section we consider the application of the Apriori algorithm (Algorithm 4) to the database in Table 2.2. This example is from Agrawal and Srikant [23]. We will use a threshold of $thr - s = 2/4$. For the sake of simplicity we will work with the count instead of the support, so, we will use a threshold of 2.

The algorithm starts with the definition of supported itemsets of cardinality one. These itemsets define L_1. Using the database in Table 2.2, we compute the following count values:

- Count({1})=2
- Count({2})=3
- Count({3})=3

Table 2.2 Database [23] for the example of the Apriori algorithm

Transaction number	Itemsets
x_1	$\{1, 3, 4\}$
x_2	$\{2, 3, 5\}$
x_3	$\{1, 2, 3, 5\}$
x_4	$\{2, 5\}$

- Count($\{4\}$)=1
- Count($\{5\}$)=3

Therefore, L_1 consists of all items except 4. That is,

$$L_1 = \{\{1\}, \{2\}, \{3\}, \{5\}\}.$$

The next step (Step 4) is to compute C_2, the candidate set of itemsets with cardinality 2. This is computed from L_1 using Algorithm 5. This consists in combining itemsets from L_1 such that they have all elements except one in common. In the case of C_2 this corresponds to the pairs J_1 and J_2 from L_1. Therefore, we get

$$C_2 = \{\{1, 2\}, \{1, 3\}, \{1, 5\}, \{2, 3\}, \{2, 5\}, \{3, 5\}\}.$$

Let us now apply Step 5, which consists in removing all non supported itemsets from C_2 to define L_2. To do so we apply Algorithm 6. So, first we have to remove all elements in C_2 with subsets not in L_1. In our case, there is no such set as all subsets of itemsets in C_2 are in L_1. Then, we have to check in the database if itemsets in C_2 are supported. The following counts are found:

- $Count(\{1, 2\}) = 1$
- $Count(\{1, 3\}) = 2$
- $Count(\{1, 5\}) = 1$
- $Count(\{2, 3\}) = 2$
- $Count(\{2, 5\}) = 3$
- $Count(\{3, 5\}) = 2$

As $thr - s = 2$, we have

$$L_2 = \{\{1, 3\}, \{2, 3\}, \{2, 5\}, \{3, 5\}\}.$$

From this set, we compute C_3 obtaining

$$C_3 = \{\{1, 2, 3\}, \{1, 2, 5\}, \{1, 3, 5\}, \{2, 3, 5\}\}.$$

Then, L_3 will contain only the itemsets from C_3 that are supported using Algorithm 6. Step 3 in this algorithm removes $\{1, 2, 3\}$ and $\{1, 2, 5\}$ as $\{1, 2\}$ is not supported, $\{1, 3, 5\}$ as $\{1, 5\}$ is not supported and only $\{2, 3, 5\}$ remains. Then, in Step 7 we check in the database if $\{2, 3, 5\}$ is supported and as this is so ($Count(\{2, 3, 5\}) = 2$) we get

$$L_3 = \{2, 3, 5\}.$$

Then, in the next step we compute C_4, but this is empty, so the algorithm finishes and we have obtained the following sets:

- $L_1 = \{\{1\}, \{2\}, \{3\}, \{5\}\}$,
- $L_2 = \{\{1, 3\}, \{2, 3\}, \{2, 5\}, \{3, 5\}\}$,
- $L_3 = \{\{2, 3, 5\}\}$.

Therefore, the algorithm returns these sets from which rules will be generated.

2.4.3   Expectation-Maximization Algorithm

In this section we describe the EM algorithm, where EM stands for expectation-maximization. The algorithm looks for maximum likelihood estimates. We define in this section first likelihood estimate and then the EM algorithm.

Likelihood Function and Maximum Likelihood

The *maximum likelihood* is a method for estimating the parameters of a given probability density. Let us consider a probability density $f(z|\theta)$. That is, f is a parametric model of the random variable z with parameter θ (or, parameters, because θ can be a vector). Let $\mathbf{z} = \{z_1, \ldots, z_e\}$ be a sample of the variable z. Then, the *likelihood* of z under a particular model $f(z|\theta)$ is expressed by:

$$f(\mathbf{z} = (z_1, \ldots, z_e)|\theta) = \prod_{i=1}^{e} f(z_i|\theta)$$

That is, $f(\mathbf{z}|\theta)$ is the probability of the sample $\mathbf{z}$ under the particular model $f(z_i|\theta)$ with a particular parameter θ. The likelihood function is the function above when the sample is taken as constant and θ is the variable. This is denoted by $L(\theta|\mathbf{z})$. Thus,

$$L(\theta|\mathbf{z}) = \prod_{i=1}^{e} f(z_i|\theta)$$

Often, the *log-likelihood* function is used instead of the likelihood function. The former is the logarithm of the latter and is denoted by $l(\theta|\mathbf{z})$ or, sometimes, by $l(\theta)$. Therefore,

$$l(\theta|\mathbf{z}) = \log L(\theta|\mathbf{z}) = \log \prod_{i=1}^{e} f(z_i|\theta) = \sum_{i=1}^{e} \log f(z_i|\theta)$$

Given a sample $\mathbf{z}$ and a model $f(\mathbf{z}|\theta)$, the maximum likelihood estimate of the parameter θ is the $\hat{\theta}$ that maximizes $l(\theta|\mathbf{z})$. Equivalently, the estimate is $\hat{\theta}$ such that

$$l(\theta|\mathbf{z}) \leq l(\hat{\theta}|\mathbf{z})$$

for all θ.

EM Algorithm

The EM algorithm [128] (where EM stands for *Expectation-Maximization*) is an iterative process for the computation of maximum likelihood estimates. The method starts with an initial estimation of the parameters and then in a sequence of two step iterations builds more accurate estimations. The two steps considered are the so-called Expectation step and Maximization step.

The algorithm is based on the consideration of two sample spaces $\mathcal{Y}$ and $\mathcal{X}$ and a many-to-one mapping from $\mathcal{X}$ to $\mathcal{Y}$. We use y to denote this mapping, and $X(y)$ to denote the set $\{x|y = y(x)\}$. Only data y in $\mathcal{Y}$ are observed, and data x in $\mathcal{X}$ are only observed indirectly through y. Due to this, x are referred to as complete data and y as the observed data.

Let $f(x|\theta)$ be a family of sampling densities for x with parameter θ, it is clear that the corresponding family of sampling densities $g(y|\theta)$ can be computed from $f(x|\theta)$ as follows:

$$g(y|\theta) = \int_{X(y)} f(x|\theta)dx$$

Now, roughly speaking, the expectation step consists on estimating the complete data x and the maximization step consists on finding a new estimation of the parameters θ by maximum likelihood. In this way, the EM algorithm tries to find the value θ that maximizes $g(y|\theta)$ given an observation y. However, the method also uses $f(x|\theta)$.

2.5 Cryptography

Cryptography provides tools that are fundamental to implement privacy technologies. In this section we review the most relevant ones, but we do not go into the details of the algorithms.

2.5.1 Symmetric Cryptography

We have symmetric-key or private-key algorithms when there is a single key, which is a shared secret between parties, and that permits encryption and decryption of a text. That is, the same key is for both encryption of the text and for its decryption. This key is, of course, private.

There are different algorithms for this purpose. Two examples are DES and AES. DES stands for the Data Encryption Standard, and uses a key of 56 bits. This is nowadays too short and insecure for applications. AES stands for Advanced Encryption Standard, and is currently extensively used. Other algorithms exist as well.

2.5.2 Public-key Cryptography

We have public-key or asymmetric-key cryptography when two separate keys are used. One is private and only known by the agent (e.g., user) and another that is public which the agent shares. One of the keys is used for encryption and the other is used for decryption. We denote the private key by SK and, if there are multiple agents, the one of agent A by SK_A. The public key is denoted by PK and, similarly, PK_A the one of agent A. Encryption of text m using a key K_A is denoted by $E_K(m)$ and decription of a text m by $D_K(m)$.

Depending on the usage of keys for encryption and decryption we can provide digital signature or public-key encryption, or both.

- Digital signature. Agent A signs a message or document m by means of encrypting it by its own private key. Then, any other agent can know that the document has been generated by A decrypting it using the public key. That is, A produces $m' = E_{SK_A}(m)$ and shares this value m' together with m. Any other agent can decrypt m', obtain $m'' = D_{PK_A}(m')$, and compare with the original m. With high probability, only A can have produced m' using its own private key.
- Public encryption. Agent A wants to send a message m to B so that only B can read it. Then, A encrypts m with the public key of B. This produces $m' = E_{PK_B}(m)$. Only B can decrypt m' to obtain m. That is, $m'' = D_{SK_B}(m')$ will produce m.

A combination of both digital signature and public encryption procedures (using private key of agent A and public key of agent B) will permit agent A to sign a message m only readable for B.

There are several algorithms that provide public-key cryptography. RSA is one of them. Other examples are Diffie-Hellman key exchange, and ElGamal encryption.

In general, public-key algorithms are more computationally costly than secret-key ones. In practice, some systems combine both to be computationally efficient. For example, TLS uses first asymmetric encryption to exchange the private key between two parties, and then uses private-key algorithms once this private key is shared. Same applies to SSH. Systems of this type are called hybrid cryptosystems.

A fundamental issue in public-key cryptography is that agents need to know that the public key really belongs to the agent.

2.5.3 Homomorphic Encryption

Mathematically, an homomorphism is a map between two algebraic structures of the same type that preserve operations. An example is the exponential function, $f(x) = e^x$. As $(\mathbb{R}, +)$ and $(\mathbb{R}^+, \cdot)$ are groups, and $e^{x+y} = e^x \cdot e^y$. We have homomorphism between the two groups.

That is, we can move back and forth from $(\mathbb{R}, +)$ and $(\mathbb{R}^+, \cdot)$ using the exponential function e^x and its inverse the logarithm $f^{-1}(y) = \ln(y)$. So, we can transform the numbers with function f, operate them with multiplication, and, then, once we have the result, return to the original group with its inverse f^{-1}. Such operations are equivalent to just adding them.

The same idea applies to encryption. Let us consider that we want to operate elements in a group (e.g., $\mathbb{Z}_N$ integers module N) with some operations $+$ and $\cdot$. Then, we have an encryption mechanism E that encrypts a number m (e.g., $m \in \mathbb{Z}_N$) producing $m' = E(m)$, and a decryption mechanism that permits to decrypt $E(m')$ and obtain m. That is, $D(E(m)) = m$. The goal of homomorphic encryption is that we have some operators on the encrypted numbers that correspond to addition $+$ and multiplication $\cdot$ on the original numbers. Let us call them, $\oplus$ and $\odot$. Formally, $\oplus$ is a homomorphic addition for $+$, and $\odot$ is a homomorphic multiplication for $\cdot$. That is, the following equations hold:

$$D(E(m_1) \oplus E(m_2)) = m_1 + m_2$$

$$D(E(m_1) \odot E(m_2)) = m_1 \cdot m_2$$

If such operators exist, then, we can encrypt all our data using the encryption mechanism, implement algorithms on the encrypted data using the operations $\oplus$ and $\odot$ and, when all is computed, decrypt the result. Using homomorphic encryption this would be just equivalent to operate with the original numbers. Properly encrypted data would not allow their access without the decryption procedure.

We have partially homomorphic encryption when only one operation is available, and fully homomorphic encryption when we have several operations. ElGamal, mentioned above, is an example of partially homomorphic cryptosystem. The NTRU-based scheme is an example of fully homomorphic cryptosystems.

2.6 Bibliographical Notes

1. **Machine and statistical learning.** For details and further algorithms the reader is referred to reference books [221,528].
2. **Cryptography.** For details on cryptography, the reader is referred to books on cryptography, as the one by Katz and Lindell [257].

Disclosure, Privacy Models, and Privacy Mechanisms

3

Abstract

This chapter describes the different types of disclosure that can take place in data and data-driven model releases. They are, mainly, of two types: identity and attribute disclosure. Then, we formalize privacy models. That is, computational definitions of privacy. These privacy models include, among others, k-anonymity, differential privacy, and secure multiparty computation. Finally, we give a roadmap of the privacy mechanisms and relate them with the privacy models.

Jo vinc d'un silenci
antic i molt llarg,
de gent sense místics
ni grans capitans,
que viuen i moren
en l'anonimat.

Raimon, Jo vinc d'un silenci, 1975.

In order to define and implement privacy mechanisms, and know that algorithms provide privacy preserving solutions, we need a clear understanding of what type of disclosure can take place in our problem. We also need to decide on how we define privacy. The Merriam-Webster defines "disclosure" as to make known or public, to expose to view. From a data privacy perspective, disclosure takes place when this exposure is unintended and it is a consequence of a data or computation release.

V. Torra, *Guide to Data Privacy*, Undergraduate Topics in Computer Science,
https://doi.org/10.1007/978-3-031-12837-0_3

Disclosure risk measures are ways to assess this risk. That is, they give a numerical evaluation of the extent of disclosure. Different understandings of what disclosure is lead to different measures.

Privacy models are computational definitions of privacy. That is, they are a formalization of what privacy is. To define privacy preserving solutions we need a precise description to later validate that such solutions are compliant with it.

In addition to these three terms (disclosure, disclosure risk, and privacy model), there is another one that has an important role: privacy attacks. We find in the literature of our field different types of attacks, most of them with the objective to show that a method or an approach is not effective enough in providing a certain privacy guarantee. That is, the goal of an attack is to show a vulnerability of a (privacy) mechanism. Naturally, a vulnerability in the context of data privacy is that the mechanism still allows for some type of unintended inference or disclosure.

These four concepts are closely related. In particular, the motivation for defining privacy models are the different ways of understanding disclosure and of measuring disclosure risk. Privacy models focus on a particular type of disclosure and attacks for one such model usually show a vulnerability with respect to another type of disclosure. Then, the study of attacks have lead to either more stringent privacy models or to the use of disclosure risk measures to evaluate the extent in which this other disclosure takes place.

In this chapter we begin reviewing the definition of disclosure. Then, we introduce disclosure risk measures, and define privacy models. In this way, we consider that some of the components that privacy models need are seen first. Nevertheless, we could have started with the privacy models and then proceed with the measures, or even described them in parallel together with attacks. All these elements are intertwined.

We end the chapter with a classification of privacy mechanisms. We will present them organized according to several dimensions. This will provide a road map to help us to navigate among them. Privacy mechanisms are implemented to provide privacy. As we will see, the way we classify the procedures link with our definitions of disclosure, and with the privacy models.

3.1 Disclosure: Definition and Controversies

We have already provided in Sect. 1.4.3, Definition 1.4 for disclosure. Let us recall it here.

Definition 3.1 In data privacy, disclosure takes place when intruders take advantage of the observation and analysis of a release to improve their knowledge on some item of interest.

In other words, and in line with the Merriam-Webster definition above, disclosure is to make known or to expose to view information that was not intended to be released or shared.

Releases can take different forms, it can be a data file but also a complex data-driven machine learning model. Then, disclosure is not just about what is being released, but also about inferences that can be computed from the release. For example, we can learn about Mr. Scrooge fortune from a database release, but other questions can also be relevant: can we infer that a database release includes a record corresponding to Mr. Scrooge? or, can we infer that a bank has used data associated to Mr. Scrooge to build a loan prediction model? Our concern on the inferences intruders can do from a release is what distinguishes privacy from the typical concerns in security and data access control. In access control, concern is only about accessing a particular object, not on what an intruder can do or infer from the object once acquired.

We will describe later with more detail the two essential types of disclosure: identity disclosure and attribute disclosure. The former is about identifying an item of interest in a release (e.g., finding Mr. Scrooge or our friend Alice in a database) and the later is about increasing our knowledge on an item based on the information in the release (e.g., learning about Mr. Scrooge fortune or increase our knowledge on Alice's salary). We have already discussed, and provided examples, in Sect. 1.4.3 that while identity disclosure usually leads to attribute disclosure, this is not always the case. In general, any combination of presence and absence of identity and attribute disclosure is possible.

3.1.1 A Boolean or Measurable Condition

Disclosure can be seen as a Boolean condition or as a measurable one. As we will see, differential privacy and k-anonymity are two examples of Boolean conditions. They define a formal requirement that, when satisfied, implies that our privacy standards are met and, thus, disclosure is assumed not to take place. In contrast, privacy from re-identification is an example of a measurable condition. It estimates the probability of finding a particular record.

In general, the definition of disclosure as a Boolean condition permits us to focus on how the privacy mechanisms affect utility. Utility can take different forms according to what is released and what this released object is used for. For example, we can focus on usefulness of data, accuracy of machine learning models, or even execution time of the privacy mechanism. This is so because once the Boolean condition is met, we take for granted the privacy guarantees.

In contrast, when we consider disclosure risk as a measurable condition, we need disclosure risk measures to evaluate in what extent disclosure takes place. Then, the definition of a privacy mechanism focuses not only on utility, performance and so on, but also on the disclosure risk.

In other words, for Boolean disclosure, the problem of selecting a privacy mechanism corresponds to the maximization problem of finding the best solution for a

privacy guarantee (or a minimization problem with respect to information loss or distortion). In contrast, for measurable quantitative disclosure, we have a multi-objective
optimization problem where we need to cope with both the quality of the solution
but also its disclosure risk. So, in the latter case we need to find a good balance or
trade-off between both components risk and e.g. utility.

3.1.2 Identity Disclosure

We formally define this type of disclosure as follows.

Definition 3.2 Identity disclosure takes place when intruders are able to identify in
a release some information related to an item of interest (usually an individual or an
entity).

In this context, the release is typically a data file and the intruder links a record
with a particular person. E.g., an intruder finds the record corresponding to Alice in
a released database.

We discuss measures to assess identity disclosure in Sect. 3.3. Privacy models
that focus on identity disclosure can be found in Sect. 3.4.

3.1.3 Attribute Disclosure

We consider the following definition for attribute disclosure.

Definition 3.3 Attribute disclosure takes place when intruders increase their knowledge related to an item of interest.

Typically, this is about knowledge on an attribute or property of a particular
individual. So, we can learn the actual value, or just narrow significantly the possible
values for this attribute.

Here, attribute and property are understood in a broad sense. Let us consider
a hospital publishing a database. Then, the most straightforward case is when the
attribute is in this database. E.g., illness. However, the attribute can also be a property
not directly listed in the schema of the database and, thus, not explicitly released.
For example, consider a database about patients of the psychiatric unit. Then, even
if illness or health condition is not an explicitly stated attribute, an intruder may
infer that Alice has been attending the unit from the information in the database.
Then, this is understood as attribute disclosure. Observe that this disclosure can take
place even in the case that no record is linked to Alice. Similarly, it is also attribute
disclosure learning that data from an individual has been used to train a certain model.
Membership attacks for deep learning models have precisely this goal.

Attribute disclosure has to be defined with caution. Note that it is often inevitable
(and probably useful) that releases of both data and models lead to attribute disclosure

in some extent. Otherwise, the utility of such releases might be too low and releases useless. Consider the case of releasing a dataset with information on age, gender, profession, and salaries. We expect this data to be useful if it permits us to have good prediction for salaries. As a consequence, if we build a model on salaries from this dataset, and apply this model to predict Alice's salary (using Alice's information), we expect to increase our knowledge on Alice's salary. So, in short, any data release is expected to improve our knowledge with respect to, at least, the relationship between the attributes in the release. Similarly, when we publish a model concluding on attribute V, we expect to increase our knowledge on V. Vaidya, Clifton, and Zhu [506] also discussed this issue in the following terms:

> At the other extreme, any improvement in our knowledge about an individual could be considered an intrusion. The latter is particularly likely to cause a problem for data mining, as the goal is to improve our knowledge. (J. Vaidya et al., 2006, p. 7 [506])

The definition of attribute disclosure is very general, and because of that there have been different ways to measure this risk as well as different privacy models focusing on this type of disclosure.

We will discuss measures related to attribute disclosure in Sect. 3.2. Privacy models that take into account attribute disclosure are introduced in Sect. 3.4.

3.1.4   Attribute Disclosure in Clusters and Cells

Our motivating example in Sect. 1.2.2 about computing the mean of salaries shows that data aggregates do not avoid disclosure. This naturally means that grouping individuals or entities, and providing summaries is often not enough to guarantee their privacy. In particular, attribute disclosure is still possible.

Inferences will depend on the type of summaries provided. Examples of summaries are counts (e.g., number of people with certain characteristics), sums or averages (e.g., of income), frequencies or distributions of values (e.g., frequencies of different illnesses and probability distribution of salaries). A very simple example of attribute disclosure is when we learn that Mr. Scrooge has a money disorder when all the individuals associated to the cell have this money disorder. We can distinguish two types of attacks for clusters and cells. We illustrate them with the example of the mean salary.

- **External attack.** That is, we consider that the intruder is external to the cell or cluster and the information is extracted from the analysis of the aggregate. This is the case of learning the disorder of Mr. Scrooge. This is also the case of an intruder inspecting the mean of salaries of all individuals attending the psychiatric unit (for Bunyola) learns that Dona Obdúlia was there. So, we acquire some information on her.
- **Internal attack.** In this case, the leakage is caused by intruders (a single one or a coalition of them) that use their own information to learn about the others in the

cluster. Any coalition of intruders can subtract their own salary to the total salary and have a better estimation of the salary of the others. Internal attacks can be quite effective if the contribution of one of the intruders is too dominant in the cell. E.g., if we consider that the total salary for people in the cell is 363, and one of the people has a salary of 350, this person can infer that the total of the others is 13. This type of inference is known as internal attack with dominance. Let us consider a similar case. All in a cell but Mr. Scrooge have eating disorders, then it is clear that Mr. Scrooge knows with certainty the disorder of the other people.

Anonymization methods that avoid identity disclosure and re-identification by means of clustering (e.g. microaggregation) or generalization may suffer for this type of attacks. The same applies to tabular data. Tabular data typically consists on aggregates with respect to a few attributes. Anonymization methods based on clustering are described in Sect. 6.1.2, methods for achieving k-anonymity are described in Sect. 6.4, and methods for tabular data are in Sect. 8.2.

To solve the problems outlined here, we may require the values associated to clusters or cells to satisfy certain privacy constraints. Some privacy models specifically address this type of problem. Some variants of k-anonymity deal with this situation when we consider sets of records. They are, for example, the case of the following privacy models: l-diversity, p-sensitive k-anonymity, and t-closeness. We review them in Sect. 3.4.4. In contrast, tabular data (see Sect. 8.2) provides methods to detect sensitive cells and then procedures to remove them. Detection is done by means of the rule (n, k)-dominance, rule pq, and rule $p\%$.

3.1.5 Discussion

As we have seen, the two main types of disclosure are identity and attribute disclosure. None of them is stronger than the other one. E.g., we can learn that Dona Obdúlia is in the database, even if we don't find her record, or we can find Alice in the database without learning anything about Alice. See the discussion in Sect. 1.4. Nevertheless, in a database release, one expects that identity disclosure leads to attribute disclosure. I.e., when we find Alice's record in a database, we find information we didn't know about Alice.

There is discussion in the literature on the significance of both identity and attribute disclosure, and whether they need to be avoided or not.

With respect to identity disclosure, we have already underlined in Sect. 1.1, the discussion [36, 532] on the importance of re-identification and identity disclosure in real data and whether re-identification risk should prevent data dissemination. Discussion is based on the following facts:

- only a few cases of re-identifications are known, and most privacy breaches are due to causes (i.e., security breaches) other than to a bad use of data privacy techniques;
- re-identification algorithms are not straightforward to use and the gain an intruder can obtain from analysing a data set may be very low.

In addition to this, as Polonetsky et al. [386] underline, re-identification can only be done when the adversary has some additional information on the person being re-identified. So, the release of a data set with a certain disclosure risk does not imply that a bunch of intruders will have the time and interest to try to deindentify the data set. It is also relevant to underline that possible re-identification does not mean an actual risk. This is discussed in Section 3.3.2. For example, can intruders distinguish correct links? Muralidhar [339] discusses this problem in a real data release.

A related fact we have discussed in Sect. 3.1.3 is that attribute disclosure is, to some extent, always expected. Any data release keeps information on the relationship between attributes, and data-driven models built from these data are expected to have good accuracy. That is, inferences from the model are accurate. Otherwise, the interest of the release will be, at most, extremely limited. In this sense, attribute disclosure (or at least some attribute disclosure) without identity disclosure can be considered an optimal goal for any database release. From a machine and statistical learning perspective, high values of attribute disclosure (i.e., good accuracy) imply that classifiers are quite robust to the noise introduced by the masking method. A more detailed discussion of this point of view is given by Herranz et al. [224]. The authors show that some data protection mechanisms have low identity disclosure risk with high accuracy (high attribute disclosure!).

Arguments stating that risk should not be overestimated can be seen as at one extreme of the spectrum of controversies. On the other, we have those that state that privacy is impossible because disclosure risk cannot be avoided unless data become useless. This position has been supported by e.g. de Montjoye et al. [123] and Jandel [245]. The later underlines the difficulties of protecting data correctly, the data releases that lead to disclosure due to insufficient protection (e.g. the AOL and the Netflix cases) and the fact that high dimensional data may need a large perturbation to make them safe.

More particularly, de Montjoye et al. [123] discuss the difficulty of avoiding disclosure. They focus on the risk of deidentified credit card data. This paper was replied [38,421] (which lead to a subsequent answer from the authors [124,125]). Replies point out that uniqueness in a sample does not imply uniqueness in the population (we discuss uniqueness in Sect. 3.3.1) and that data masking methods used in the experiments were not effective (i.e., appropriate).

All these arguments on the difficulties of data privacy are partially true but this does not mean that privacy is impossible. The difficulty and success of privacy protection mechanisms will depend on the type of data or model we have and the level of protection we want to achieve. The selection of an appropriate protection mechanism is essential to have an outcome that does not lead to disclosure.

All these discussions only point out the importance of defining correctly disclosure risk, the need of accurate ways of measuring disclosure risk and well-defined privacy models. This is all essential to implement mechanisms that guarantee our privacy requirements. The measures permit us to evaluate and compare privacy mechanisms (e.g., masking methods and privacy-preserving machine learning algorithms) as well as different instantiations of these mechanisms using different parameters. The measures will be used by decisors to make informed decisions.

To summarize this discussion, we give in Fig. 3.1 an outline of privacy models and disclosure risk assessment approaches reviewed in this book.

- Types of disclosure according to what is disclosed.

    1. Attribute disclosure (Section 3.1.3)
    2. Identity disclosure (Section 3.1.2)

- Privacy models and measures of disclosure.

    1. Measures for attribute disclosure (Section 3.2)
    2. Measures for identity disclosure (Section 3.3)
    3. Privacy as a measurable condition
        a. Uniqueness (Section 3.3.1)
        b. Re-identification (Section 3.3.2)
            i. Data integration: schema and data matching
            ii. Record linkage algorithms: distance-based and probabilistic RL
            iii. Generic vs. specific record linkage algorithms
    4. Privacy as a Boolean condition
        a. k-Anonymity (Section 3.4.2)
        b. Differential privacy (Section 3.4.6)
        c. Secure multiparty computation (Section 3.4.10)
        d. Interval disclosure (Section 3.2.1)

Fig. 3.1 Outline of privacy models and disclosure risk measures

3.2 Measures for Attribute Disclosure

The definition of attribute disclosure is very general. It depends on the type of release (e.g., data, models) and what is considered sensitive and private information. We have already discussed in Sect. 3.1.3 the difficulty of assessing attribute disclosure in a machine learning and statistical environment. We have seen the intrinsic difficulties of attribute disclosure. In short, this can be stated as follows:

> For a data-driven model it is difficult to know in what extent we are measuring attribute disclosure and in what extent we are discussing about the quality of the model. The same applies to data releases. Are we producing data of good quality or are we causing attribute disclosure?

Ideally, let M be a data-driven model for attribute A with an excellent generalization capability and no overfitting. Then, the replacement of values $A(x)$ by $M(x)$ does not imply attribute disclosure.

In this section we discuss some measures for assessing attribute disclosure. In applications, it is a critical issue to determine which attributes need to be considered and whose disclosure measured.

For data releases and given an attribute, we can define attribute disclosure risk in terms of the divergence between the original values and the protected ones. In the following sections we introduce attribute disclosure measures of both numerical and nominal (categorical) data releases. We will use X to denote an original database, X' to denote the released protected dataset, and ρ the data protection mechanism (e.g.,

---

Algorithm 7: Rank-based interval disclosure: $rid(X, V, V', x, p)$.

Data: X: Original file; V: Original attribute; V': Masked attribute; x: record; p: percentage
Result: Attribute disclosure for attribute V' of record x
1 **begin**
2      $R(V) :=$ Rank data for attribute V'
3      $i :=$ position of $V'(x)$ in $R(V)$
4      $w := p \cdot |X|/2/100$ (establish the width of the interval)
5      $I(x) = [R[\min(i - w, 0)], R[\max(i + w, |X| - 1)]]$ (definition of the interval for record x)
6      $rid := V(x) \in I(x)$
7   **return** rid
8 **end**

---

a masking method) that produces X' from X. That is, $X' = \rho(X)$. We will denote a particular attribute by V and for a record $x \in X$, $V(x)$ is the value of this record for attribute V, and $V'(x)$ is the value of the corresponding protected record in X'.

3.2.1 Attribute Disclosure for Numerical Data Releases

Our way to measure attribute disclosure for a database release is to determine if the protected version of an attribute is too similar to the original one. Let us consider some of the existing definitions.

Rank-based interval disclosure [139, 144] is detected for a record x when the value $V(x)$ is within an interval defined from ranked values and a width based on the p percent of the records. Here p is a given parameter. To compute this measure of disclosure for record x, first, the attribute is ranked. Then, we locate the value $V(x)$ in this rank obtaining its position. This is the *center* of the interval. Then, we select the limits of the interval from the ranked values using the p percent. I.e., $p/2$ percent of the values will be smaller than the *center* and $p/2$ percent of the values will be larger than the *center*. Algorithm 7 describes this process for a given attribute and record. Observe that the larger p we select, the more records we mark as risky. In particular, a selection of $p = 100\%$ results into a situation of full risk because the value of the record will be always within the interval. That is, the intruder is completely sure that the original value lies in the interval around the protected value. I.e., there is interval disclosure. Naturally, the smaller the p, the smaller the number of records marked as risky. We can also observe that the interval is not balanced around the *center*. That is why we have used italics. Observe that the algorithm takes w positions in each side of position i. As the value selected is from the ranked values we may have some dense regions in one side of the *center* and not so dense regions in the other side.

A variation exists [317] in which intervals are based on a percentage of the standard deviation of the attribute. This definition is called $SDID$, for standard deviation-based interval disclosure. See Algorithm 8. Observe that in this case, p is also the parameter that establishes the amount of risk that we can assume. Observe that

---

Algorithm 8: Standard deviation-based interval disclosure
: $sdid(X, V, V', x, p)$.

Data: X: Original file; V: Original attribute; V': Masked attribute; x: record; p: percentage
Result: Attribute disclosure for attribute V' of record x

1 **begin**
2     $sd(V) :=$ standard deviation of V
3     $sdid := |V(x) - V'(x)| \leq p \cdot sd(V)/100$
4   **return** $sdid$
5 **end**

---

in this measure the interval is balanced as both limits of the interval are at the same distance from the original value $V(x)$. More concretely, the algorithm uses the interval $[V(x) - p \cdot sd(V)/100, V(x) + p \cdot sd(V)/100]$.

The R package sdcMicro [467] includes a multivariate version of this latter definition. The function $dRiskRMD$ defines the center of the interval in terms of the original value and checks whether the masked value is within a certain distance computed using the robust Mahalanobis distance. Note that this is to replace $|V(x) - V'(x)|$ by an appropriate distance in Algorithm 8, that does not depend on attribute V but on a set of attributes. When all attributes in X are used, this would mean $d(x, x')$ where x' represents the masked version of x.

Alternatively, we can define attribute disclosure risk using a model built for the given attribute as a function of the other attributes. That is, given the original database X, the masked database $X' = \rho(X)$, and a given attribute V, we build a model for V using the other attributes in X'. Let us denote by $X' \setminus V$ the set X' without the attribute V and let us denote the model of V in terms of $X' \setminus V$ by $m_{X' \setminus V}$. Then, we can consider whether $m_{X' \setminus V}(x)$ is too similar to $V(x)$. For this we can use both Rank-based interval disclosure and Standard deviation-based interval disclosure. This approach was introduced [358] for categorical data. We will see its definition for categorical data below. We call it model-based attribute disclosure. See Sect. 3.2.3.

3.2.2 Attribute Disclosure for Categorical Data Releases

Categorical attributes are typically classified between ordinal and nominal ones. We have an ordinal attribute when there is a natural order (usually expressed by $<$ between categories). For this type of attributes, the rank-based interval disclosure defined for numerical attributes can be used. Note that as the set of different categorical values is usually much smaller than the set of different numerical values, the risk can be overestimated. For example, if all records have the same value, (i.e., there is a v_0 such that for all $x \in X$, $V(x) = v_0$), rank-based interval disclosure will assess that we have maximum risk. Therefore, this definition should be used with care.

As the number of different categories can be very low, we can define a risk measure for an attribute V just checking whether the original and the protected values are the same. The proportion of records in X with this property is a measure of disclosure.

We call it, simple attribute disclosure risk (*SADR*). That is, the risk is the cardinality of the set $\{x \in X | V(x) = V'(x)\}$ divided by the number of records of X (i.e., $|X|$):

$$SADR(X, X') = \frac{|\{x \in X | V(x) = V'(x)\}|}{|X|}.$$

In short, this definition means that we prefer protection mechanisms that change the values of individual records, and any change is equally acceptable. This definition does not take into account that maybe all other attributes different to V have been modified, so, equality between V and V' is not so relevant.

As an alternative, we can consider record coincidences based on several attributes. More concretely, we consider the set of records x' in the masked file $X' = \rho(X)$ that have (at least) t attributes in common with x. Let $V(X', x, t)$ be the multiset of values of attribute V for these records. Then, we can consider that there is risk if the majority of these values correspond to $V(x)$. In this definition, we are considering inference from similar records (where similar records are the ones with at least t coincident values). We call this definition, t-similarity-based attribute disclosure. This definition means that we prefer to avoid having combinations of t or more values in a protected record that also appear in the original database. Using this definition, a large t may imply that there is only a record in the set. This means that the file will be safe if and only if a value associated to this only record in the protected set is different from the original one.

A more sophisticated approach is to consider machine learning models (i.e., classifiers) built for a given categorical attribute. Then, we compare the values in the original data and the predictions obtained by the model, the percentage of correct predictions is a measure of the risk. This approach [358] is called model-based attribute disclosure.

3.2.3   Model-Based Attribute Disclosure

For model-based attribute disclosure we need to establish first the particular model. Let us consider a classifier. For illustration, we use the nearest neighbor model (see Sect. 2.3.1). In other words, the adversary uses the most similar record among the masked data set to guess the value of the attribute V. Then, for a given record x the adversary selects the most similar record in the released data set $X' \setminus V$ (excluding attribute V). Let use x' to denote this record. Therefore, $x' = \arg\min_{x_i \in X' \setminus V} s(x, x_i)$, for a given similarity function s. Then the adversary uses the attribute V' (e.g., illness) of x' to estimate V (the illness) of x. The percentage of times that this approach succeeds is a measure of attribute disclosure risk. In general, we have a model $m_{X' \setminus V}$ and compare $m_{X' \setminus V}(x)$ with $V(x)$.

In order to have a more systematic way to assess risk when we use machine learning models, we can explicitly consider the algorithms and the training sets needed to build the models. Let us consider a training set C_{tr} to learn a model using algorithm A. Then, we can consider the value inferred from such model. If this value corresponds to the original value, we have attribute disclosure.

Algorithm 9: Model-based attribute disclosure: $mbd(C_{tr}, A, V, V', x)$.

Data: C_{tr}: training set; A: algorithm to build a classification model; V: original attribute; V':
   masked attribute; x: an example

Result: attribute disclosure for x

1 **begin**

2   Take the dataset C_{tr} as input and construct a model of the attribute V using the
   algorithm A. Let this model be denoted by $M_{C_{tr},A}$

3     $V'(x) := M_{C_{tr},A}(x)$. That is, the application of the classifier $M_{C_{tr},A}$ to the data x

4     $ad := (V'(x) = V(x))$

5   **return** ad

6 **end**

This model-based disclosure is described in Algorithm 9. The computation of
the percentage of records that are risky, as described in [358], is inspired in k-fold
cross validation. Using the notation in Sect. 2.3.3, we have k training sets C_i^{Tr} for
$i = 1, \ldots, k$. Then, we build k different models $M_{C_i^{Tr},A}$ for $i = 1, \ldots, k$ each one in
terms of the set C_i^{Tr} using algorithm A. Finally, attribute disclosure corresponds to
the proportion of correct answers. This is computed taking into account for each x in
C_i the outcome of the model $M_{C_i^{Tr},A}$ for such x and comparing with the true value of
$V(x)$ that can be found in X. Algorithm 10 details this process. It uses Algorithm 9.

As a summary, attribute disclosure for attribute V is estimated for a pair of files
X and X' as the proportion of correct answers of records in X using the information
in X' estimated using the algorithm A. In this way, simple attribute disclosure and
t-similarity-based attribute disclosure can be seen as particular cases of model-based
disclosure.

Now, let use consider the case of regression instead of classification. Then, we can
either (i) redefine Algorithm 10 using rank-based attribute disclosure, or (ii) leave
Algorithm 10 without modification and redefine the condition of attribute disclosure
ad in Algorithm 9. For the latter case we can replace Line 3 by

$$ad := |V(x) - V'(x)| \leq p \cdot sd(V)/100$$

as in Algorithm 8.

Model-based attribute disclosure as defined here can be used for any type of data
and any type of inference. For example, we can use it to assess risk of a sensitive
attribute associated to nodes in social networks. In this case, we build a model to
infer this attribute from a protected version of the network.

3.2.4 Attribute Disclosure for Absent Attributes

Our discussion above has been focused on attributes that are present in the database
being released. Nevertheless, the whole discussion also applies to attributes that are

---

Algorithm 10: Attribute disclosure for attribute V and data sets X, X' according to the algorithm A: $adr(X, X', A)$.

Data: X: original set; X': masked data set; A: algorithm to build a classification model
Result: attribute disclosure risk

1 **begin**
2 $\quad$ Define C_i^{Tr} a partition of X as in Sect. 2.3.3 (cross-validation)
3 $\quad$ Compute attribute disclosure risk as follows

$$adr_{A,C,X} := \frac{\sum_{i=1}^{k} |\{x \,|\, x \in C_i \text{ and } mbd(C_i^{Tr}, A, V, V', x)\}|}{|X|}.$$

$\quad$ Note that here $V(x)$ refers to the true value of attribute V of x (i.e., according to the original data set)

4 $\quad$ **return** $adr_{A,C,X}$
5 **end**

---

not present in the database but that can be inferred from them. In other words, we may have attribute disclosure on attributes that are absent in the database.

Let V represent a sensitive attribute neither present in X nor in X' but sensitive, and that can be inferred from the data on X. Inference can be due to the presence of a proxy attribute (i.e., an attribute V_0 in X that is highly correlated with V) or to complex inferences from the data in X (e.g., because we can build a rather accurate model of V from X). Observe that data mining and machine learning have proven in different contexts to be able to build effective estimators [269] of sensitive attributes (e.g., predict sexual and political orientation, parental separation and religious views from data in social networks). Data-driven models have been built for these inferences.

Let us describe an attribute risk measure in this context. Let V denote the sensitive attribute not present in X. E.g., V stands for political orientation. Then, we can use a model-based attribute disclosure for V in terms of a model of V using X. If the model is good (e.g., if the political orientation is predicted with good accuracy) we have that $V(x)$ is a good estimate of V for x and, thus, V can be considered the ground truth. Then, we build another model for the same attribute from X'. Let us call this alternative model V'. Then, there is attribute disclosure for x if $V'(x')$ is equal to $V(x)$. That is, the estimation using the model inferred from the protected file using the protected version of x equals the original estimation (i.e., the ground truth). We call this risk data-driven model-based attribute disclosure. Algorithm 11 describes the computation of the measure. In general, the risk will be associated to a particular algorithm to compute the model. We use A in the algorithm. Naturally, different algorithms may produce different levels of risk. Also, different types of databases may require different types of algorithms A (e.g., evaluating the release of social networks data will require different types of data mining algorithms than release of smart grid data).

Algorithm 11: Data-driven model-based attribute disclosure for attribute V and data sets X, X' according to the algorithm A: $ddmbar(X, X', A)$.

Data: X: original set; X': masked data set; A: data mining algorithm
Result: attribute disclosure risk in [0,1]

1 **begin**
2 | Build a data-driven model V from X using algorithm A
3 | Build a data-driven model V' from X' using algorithm A
4 | Compute attribute disclosure as follows

$$DDMBAR_A = \frac{|\{x|V(x) = V'(x')\}|}{|X|}$$

   | where x' is the protected version of x
5 | **return** $DDMBAR_A$
6 **end**

3.2.5 Discussion on Attribute Disclosure

We have already underlined above the difficulty of assessing attribute disclosure for data releases. The boundaries between attribute disclosure and data of good quality are difficult to define. Some hints that can be useful are given below:

- Given an attribute V, a good estimate requiring a large number of input attributes (from the database) may be ok, while a good estimate from a few of them can be problematic from a privacy point of view. In this sense, good inferences from small t, where t is the number of attributes, should be probably avoided. In other words, we may use attribute disclosure with small values of t.
- Not all attributes are equally important when analysing attribute disclosure risk. Confidential and sensitive attributes need to be identified and used for attribute disclosure risk analysis.
- Not all the information is always directly available in a database. It may be the case that sensitive information can be inferred from the database but it is not present there. E.g., observance of religious holidays or political orientation may not be an attribute in the database, but the database may contain enough information to estimate these attributes with good accuracy. Attribute disclosure analysis needs to consider whether these cases are relevant.

The difficulty of establishing a boundary between attribute disclosure and good data quality can be seen from a different perspective. In machine and statistical learning, models are expected to generalize data and avoid over-fitting. When a model generalizes correctly and there is no over-fitting, any inference for a particular individual x is due to general properties and not to its particularities. In contrast, bad generalization and over-fitting may imply that inferences are due to memorization and to learning particular features of certain records. When we require good data utility from a machine learning perspective, attribute disclosure should avoid detecting general information found in the data and focus on detecting these particular features of individuals. This has connections with membership attacks, that, in short, try to detect records that are known to have been used in training a model, and they are detected because they are somehow distinguishable from more common ones.

Exercise 3.1 Discuss attribute disclosure, and, particularly, model-based one for grid data electric.

3.2.6   Attribute Disclosure Through Membership Inference Attacks

For data-driven models, it can be sensitive to know which records have been used in training. Consider, for example, developing data-driven models for estimating the average length of hospital stay for cancer patients at admission. Knowing that data from patient x has been used is sensitive, as it implies that x is a cancer patient.

Given a data-driven model m, membership inference attacks try to determine with good accuracy whether a given record x was in the training set of m. This can be formulated in terms of a classifier mia. This model mia is applied to x (and some additional information) and returns true if x belongs to the training set of m, and false otherwise. There are alternative ways to build this membership inference attack classifier.

We consider the attack given by Shokri et al. [436] in which m is a classifier and each record x can be classified into c different classes.

A key concept to build the classifier mia is the construction of shallow models. They are models learnt using the same premises used to build the model m but using other, but similar, data. Let k be the number of shallow models to be built. Then, we need datasets D_i for $i = 1, \ldots, k$. It is assumed that each D_i follows the same distribution as X but that $D_i \cap X = \emptyset$. That is, these sets are similar to the ones used to train the model m but they are disjoint. In other words, no record of the original data set appears in D_i. Then, we use each D_i to build a shallow model sm_i, using the same learning algorithm used for building m. For this, we split D_i into training and test sets as usual in machine learning. Let D_i^{tr} and D_i^{te} be the training and test sets, respectively, to train sm_i.

These models will be classifiers, as it is m. The output of both sm_i and m is a probability distribution on the set of c classes. That is $m, sm_i : S \to [0, 1]^c$ where S is the input space. In this way, for each $x \in D_i$ we can compute its output $y = sm_i(x)$, where y is a c-dimensional vector. With these data we can train the mia classifier. The data to train mia is composed by records each one with the following components: (i) a vector that represents a possible input of m (i.e., $x \in D_i$), (ii) the output of the corresponding shallow model (i.e., $y = sm_i(x)$ with $y \in [0, 1]^c$), and (iii) the information on whether the vector x is in the training set of sm_i or not. So, to train mia we have something like $(x, y = sm_i(x), used\ Yes)$. The classifier, once trained, uses (i) and (ii) to infer (iii). That is, we will call this classifier with $mia((x, y))$ and obtain whether x is in the training set or not. The construction of mia is described in Algorithm 12.

Algorithm 12: Model for membership inference attack: $mia(C_{tr}, A)$.

Data: D^i: data sets for building shallow models (each D^i partitioned into training and testing
  D_i^{tr}, D_i^{te}); A: algorithm to build shallow models
Result: Classifier for membership inference attack

1 **begin**
2 | $sm_i = A(S_i^{tr})$ for all $i = 1, \ldots, k$
3 | $tuples = \emptyset$
4 | **for** $i = 1, \ldots, k$ **do**
5 | | **forall** $x \in D_i^{tr}$ **do**
6 | | | $tuples = tuples \cup \{(x, sm_i(x), training)\}$
7 | | **end**
8 | | **forall** $x \in D_i^{te}$ **do**
9 | | | $tuples = tuples \cup \{(x, sm_i(x), no - training)\}$
10 | | **end**
11 | **end**
12 | $mia = $ build-classifier($tuples$)
13 | **return** mia
14 **end**

Once we have the mia classifier there are different ways to evaluate risk. If we are the researchers producing m, we will have at our disposal the training set X and we can count the proportion of records of X correctly identified as members of the training dataset. That is,

$$mia AR = \frac{|\{x | mia(x) = training\}|}{|X|}.$$

We can use usual mechanisms in classification (recall, precision, F1-score) for assessing the effectiveness of the attacks.

In practice, to build the models we need the sets D^i. One option is to partition X into two parts, one for building the model (i.e., for training and testing it), and the other to build the shallow models.

3.3 Measures for Identity Disclosure

Identity disclosure applies to data releases, as it is about finding an entity (typically a person) in a database. We can use re-identification and uniqueness to assess this risk. Following the notation used above, we consider in this section a data base X and a protected version $X' = \rho(X)$ computed from X using a protection mechanism ρ.

- **Re-identification.** Risk is defined as an estimation of the number of correct re-identifications that an intruder can attain. We can estimate this number theoretically or empirically.

The usual process for an empirical analysis of risk is as follows. We model the information of the intruder in terms of a database, and then establish links between intruder's database and the protected database X'. That is, we establish which records refer to the same items or individuals. For this purpose we use record linkage algorithms. In this way we find correct and incorrect associations between the two databases. A correct association is when a record is actually linked with its protected version. The success rate of this linkage process is an estimation of risk.

- **Uniqueness.** Risk is defined as the probability that rare combinations of attribute values in the protected data set are rare in the original population. This approach is typically used when data is protected using sampling [521] (i.e., X' is just a subset of X). Note that with perturbative methods it makes no sense to investigate the probability that a rare combination of protected values is rare in the original data set, because *that* combination is most probably *not found* in the original data set.

We describe uniqueness and re-identification below in Sects. 3.3.1 and 3.3.2, respectively.

A problem related to identity disclosure is to find minimal uniqueness within a database. This means finding a record and a subset of attributes that makes the record unique in the database. As expressed in [311] "every superset of a unique attribute set is itself unique". So, only minimal sets of attributes are of interest. The uniques are called MSU, for minimal sample uniques. SUDA [171] and SUDA2 [311] are algorithms to search for these uniques up to a user-specified size in discrete datasets. The limitation of up to a user-specified size can be linked to the concept of computational anonymity. We define it in Sect. 3.4.5.

3.3.1 Uniqueness

Given no other background knowledge, given a data base DB, the risk of a record $x \in DB$ being re-identified depends on whether this record is unique or not. In general, DB is only a view of a sample from a whole population P. That is, we are not considering all attributes that apply to x but only a set of them. In addition, we are not considering the whole population but a subset of, probably relevant, individuals of the whole population. Recall that this applies when we are considering the release of a sample of a population.

From this perspective, two types of disclosure risk measures based on uniqueness can be distinguished: file-level and record-level. File-level uniqueness provides a single measure for the whole file (i.e., an average measure) and record-level uniqueness provides a value for each record in the file. We describe both of them below.

- **File-level uniqueness.** Disclosure risk is defined as the probability that a sample unique (SU) is a population unique (PU) [170]. This probability can be expressed [168] as

$$P(PU|SU) = \frac{P(PU, SU)}{P(SU)} = \frac{\left|\{x_j^u | F_P(x_j^u) = 1, F_{DB}(x_j^u) = 1\}\right|}{\left|\{x_j^u | F_P(x_j^u) = 1\}\right|}$$

where x_j^u denotes all possible different values in the sample, $F_P(x_j^u)$ denotes the number of records in the population P with value x_j^u and $F_{DB}(x_j^u)$ the number of records in the sample DB with this same value. Unless the sample size is much smaller than the population size, $P(PU|SU)$ can be dangerously high; in that case, an intruder who locates a unique value in the released sample can be almost certain that there is a single individual in the population with that value, which is very likely to lead to that individual's identification.

Note that for numerical attributes where the values are almost always unique, the uniqueness is very high.

- **Record-level risk uniqueness.** This is an individual risk measure. The key point [169] of this definition is that risk is not homogeneous for all records in a database. So, we may need to evaluate it at record-level. Then, risk is defined as the probability that a particular sample record is re-identified.

  If we have a record x with values equal to x_j^u. Then the risk associated to this record is $1/F_P(x_j^u)$. The frequencies $F_P(x_j^u)$ are usually not known, and instead the frequencies of the sample $F_{DB}(x_j^u)$ are known. Franconi and Polettini [190] describe how to estimate the record-level risk with this information.

Some data protection procedures transforms X into X' making some records indistinguishable. This means that the number of different records in X' is reduced with respect to the ones in X. This can be evaluated using the *real anonymity measure*:

$$k' = \frac{|X|}{|\{x'|x' \in X'\}|}. \tag{3.1}$$

This measure, that can also be understood as the average indistinguishability of X' with respect to X is the ratio between the total number of records in the original file and the number of protected records. The inverse of this expression gives also an estimation of risk for X' with respect to X. We call it indistinguishability-based re-identification risk, and, therefore, corresponds to:

$$iReid = 1/k' = \frac{|\{x'|x' \in X'\}|}{|X|}.$$

3.3.2 Re-Identification for Identity Disclosure

We have described above that re-identification risk can be estimated empirically by means of record linkage. It corresponds to the number or proportion of records in intruder's database that are correctly linked to a protected database. In this section we describe the scenario and give an overview of the measures.

An scenario for identity disclosure

We consider a protected data set X' and an intruder having some partial information about the individuals in the published data set. The protected data set is assumed to be a data file or, more generally, a database. It is usual to consider that intruder's information can be represented in the same way. That is, in terms of a file or database.

In the typical scenario, the information of the intruder is about some of the attributes published in the protected data set. As always, data are represented by standard files X and X' with the usual structure (r rows (*records*) and k columns (*attributes*)). So, each row contains the values of the attributes for an individual.

Then, the attributes in X can be classified [111,419,486] in the following non-disjoint categories.

- **Identifiers.** These are attributes that *unambiguously* identify the respondent. Examples are passport number, social security number, full name, etc.
- **Quasi-identifiers.** These are attributes that, in combination, can be linked with external information to re-identify some of the respondents. Although a single attribute cannot identify an individual, a subset of them can. For example, the set *(age, zipcode, city)* is a quasi-identifier in some files. Note that although a quasi-identifier is the set of attributes that permits re-identification, we will use also this term to denote any of the attributes in this set. That is, age, zip code, city, birth date, gender, job, etc. will be said to be quasi-identifiers.
- **Confidential.** These are attributes which contain sensitive information on the respondent. For example, salary, religion, political affiliation, health condition, etc. This is usually the information to be studied.
- **Non-confidential.** Attributes not including sensitive information.

Using these categories, an original data set X can be decomposed into $X = id||X_{nc}||X_c$, where id are the identifiers, X_{nc} are the (non-confidential) quasi-identifier attributes, and X_c are the confidential non-quasi-identifier attributes. We do not consider here non-confidential attributes which are not quasi-identifiers as they are not relevant from a disclosure risk perspective. Confidential quasi-identifiers would be treated as non-confidential quasi-identifiers, if it is possible for intruders to access them. We do not mention them explicitly below because the general public will usually not have access to confidential attributes and thus not be able to use them for re-identification.

For re-identification purposes, quasi-identifiers are the relevant attributes as they can uniquely identify a record. Because of that, it is usual to assume that the intruder has information on the quasi-identifiers and these attributes are the ones used for applying record linkage. That is, given a protected database B and an intruder database A, intruders apply record linkage to find the record in the protected file that corresponds to their own records. For this purpose, they compare the values of their quasi-identifiers (represented in file B) with the ones present in the protected file (file A). Figure 3.2 represents this situation. In the figure we represent the quasi-identifiers known by the intruder by $\{a_1, \ldots, a_n\}$. In addition the intruder also knows the identifiers $Id = \{i_1, i_2, \ldots\}$. The identifiers represent e.g. the name of the people, and their identity card numbers to be found in intruders' database. The protected

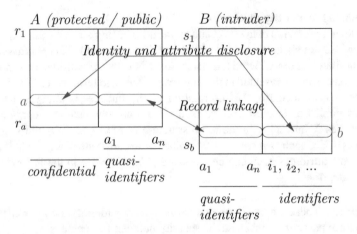

Fig. 3.2 Disclosure risk scenario: attribute and identity disclosure

Table 3.1 Table that permits an adversary to achieve identity disclosure and attribute disclosure. Only attributes city, age, and illness are published

Respondent	City	Age	Illness
ABD	Barcelona	30	Cancer
COL	Barcelona	30	Cancer
GHE	Tarragona	60	AIDS
CIO	Tarragona	60	AIDS
HYU	Tarragona	58	Heart attack

file being attacked has also the same quasi-identifiers $(a_1, \ldots, a_n)$ and, in addition, the file includes some confidential attributes. If the intruder applies record linkage successfully, identity disclosure will usually imply attribute disclosure as some confidential values are then associated to identifiers (through the quasi-identifiers). This is also represented in Fig. 3.2.

When measuring disclosure risk for a file X' that is a protected version of X (i.e., $X' = \rho(X)$), it is usual to consider $A = X'$ and B a subset of X. That is, $B \subset X$.

Note that we are now formalizing the scenario we have discussed in Sect. 1.4.3. See Table 1.3 reproduced here as Table 3.1. We have that when *(city, age, illness)* is published the intruder can find that her friend HYU had a heart attack if she knows that HYU lives in Tarragona and is 58 years old. In this example, *(city, age)* is the quasi-identifier, the illness is the confidential attribute, and the name HYU is the identifier. Following our discussion above on confidential quasi-identifiers, note that we assume intruders do not have this information to attack the database.

In a more general scenario, the database B might have a schema[1] different from the one of database A. That is, the number and type of attributes are different. E.g., while $X_{nc} = \{a_1, \ldots, a_n\}$, the database B might have $X'_{nc} = \{a'_1, \ldots, a'_m\}$.

---

[1] In databases, the schema define the type of attributes, their types and relationships. They roughly correspond to metadata in statistical disclosure control.

Even in the case that there are no common quasi-identifiers in the two files, re-identification may still be possible if there is some structural information common in both files. Algorithms and methods developed in the field of data integration and schema matching are useful for this type of scenarios. These areas are briefly described in the appendix (see Sects. A.1.1 and A.1.2). There are two main types of record linkage algorithms. They are probabilistic and distance-based. They are both described in the appendix (see Sects. A.2 and A.3).

Re-identification

As explained above, we can define a measure of disclosure risk as the proportion of records that an intruder can re-identify. This approximation is empirical (computational) in the sense that re-identification algorithms are implemented and then used to compare and link the masked data set with the data available to the intruder.

Using the notation in Fig. 3.2 (i.e., $A = X' = \rho(X)$: protected set; and $B \subset X$: intruder's set), we define the re-identification risk $Reid(B, A)$ below using a function $true : B \to A$ that for each record b (of the intruder) returns the correct record for re-identification, and a function $r : B \to A$ that models the re-identification algorithm. In order to make the definition general, we consider that r returns a probability distribution on A. That is, given a record b in B, it assigns to each record a in A a probability of matching. Then, we use a function c and with $c(r(b), true(b))$ we evaluate the result for each record in $[0, 1]$.

$$Reid(B, A) = \frac{\sum_{b \in B} c(r(b), true(b))}{|B|}. \tag{3.2}$$

Let us consider two examples.

- When the re-identification algorithm assigns to each record b a single record a_b in A, we model the result of the algorithm by the probability distribution: $r(b)[a_b] = 1$, and $r(b)[a] = 0$ for all $a \neq a_b$. Then, we consider $c(r(b), true(b))$ as one if $a_b = true(b)$. So, the function above corresponds to

$$Reid_d(B, A) = \frac{\sum_{b \in B} |\{b | a_b = true(b)\}|}{|B|}.$$

- When the re-identification algorithm assigns to each record b an anonymity set in A denoted by A_b, we model the re-identification algorithm by the distribution $r(b)[a'] = 1/|A_b|$ for all $a' \in A_b$, and $r(b)[a'] = 0$ for all $a' \notin A_b$. Then, we define $c(r(b), true(b))$ as $r(b)[true(b)]$. Naturally, we will have that $c(r(b), true(b)) = r(b)[true(b)] \leq 1/|A_b|$. Then,

$$Reid_k(B, A) = \frac{\sum_{b \in B} r(b)[true(b)]}{|B|}.$$

- When the re-identification algorithm assigns to each record b a probability distribution $ri(b) : A \to [0, 1]$ then we just define r as ri. That is, $r(b) = ri(b)$. Then, we define $c(r(b), true(b))$ as $r(b)[true(b)]$. So, the function above corresponds to

$$Reid_p(B, A) = \frac{\sum_{b \in B} r(b)[true(b)]}{|B|}.$$

We call these expressions $Reid_d$, $Reid_k$, and $Reid_p$ because distance-based record linkage can be modeled using the first approach, re-identification attacks to k-anonymity can be modeled using the second one, and probabilistic record linkage can be modeled using the third approach.

Can intruders distinguish correct links?

An important issue related to re-identification algorithms is whether intruders can distinguish correct links from incorrect links. Consider a re-identification algorithm that only assigns b to a_b when it is absolutely sure that a_b is the true record for b. In contrast, consider a re-identification algorithm that for any record b it makes a guess a_b which is in some cases correct and in some cases it is not. Then, while $Reid_d(B, A)$ can give the same value for both algorithms, the real risk is not the same.

Whether we are in the first or in the second scenario will depend on the re-identification algorithm itself as well as on some additional information we may have. For example, information on the protection process itself (e.g., if data are published following the transparency principle). Distance-based record linkage assigns to each record b to the nearest record in A. I.e., record a_b using the notation above. The intruder may not be able to know if this assignment is correct. We estimate intruder's performance using $Reid_d$ above. On the other hand, if we know that the protection is achieved by means of generalization (e.g., towns replaced by counties, ages by intervals, and so on), it may be the case that only one pair (b, a_b) is compatible, and the intruder knows that this is a correct link. Even obtaining the same value for $Reid_d$, the risk is different.

So, let K denote the subset of re-identified records for which the intruder is sure that re-identification is correct. Then, we define

$$K.Reid(B, A) = \frac{|K|}{|B|} \tag{3.3}$$

As both measures can be relevant when measuring risk, we define $KR.Reid$ as follows:

$$KR.Reid(B, A) = (K.Reid(B, A), Reid(B, A)). \tag{3.4}$$

Note that $KR.Reid(X, X') = (v_1, v_2)$ with $v_1 = v_2 = 0.001$ can be considered in some contexts more risky than $v_1 = 0$ and $v_2 = 0.25$. The former example means that at least one record over 1000 has been correctly re-identified and the intruder knows which. In contrast, the second example means that 25% of the records can be re-identified but the intruder cannot distinguish the correct matches from the 75% of incorrect ones. We will discuss this issue again in Sect. 6.1.1 when we present a specific attack for rank swapping.

We have already seen that re-identification is an approach that is general enough to be applied in different contexts. It can be applied under different assumptions of intruder's knowledge, and under different assumptions on protection procedures.

Recall Fig. 3.2 and that we can model a range of attacks by means of representing intruder's information in an intruder's file. We have discussed above the case of an intruder having a database with the same schema as the published data set, but also the case of having a different schema.

Record linkage has also been used to measure disclosure risk for synthetic data (i.e., data that is constructed using a particular data model—see Sect. 6.3). More particularly, for partially synthetic data, the approach is the same, as there is at most a single record for each original record. Therefore, the goal is to link intruders' records with the synthetic ones.

From an intruder perspective, the larger the number of re-identifications, the better. It is, therefore, relevant in some situations to have an estimation of how good the best intruder can be. That provides an upper bound of the risk. We discuss this issue below with an analysis of the worst-case scenario.

As re-identification algorithms are the essential component of risk evaluation, we give an overview of data matching and integration, and review different approaches for record linkage in Appendix A. Data integration studies how to establish relationships between different elements of the databases. It includes schema matching (that focuses on establishing relationships between database schema) and data matching (that focuses on the linkage of records).

The worst-case scenario

In any analysis of risk it is important to have an upper bound of the risk. This corresponds to the risk of the worst-case scenario. When using re-identification to assess risk, the data available to the intruder and the re-identification algorithm makes a difference on the number of correct links.

The upper bound of the risk can be computed taking into account the following.

- The best data set for an attack is the complete original file. That is, the one, say X, that has been protected and later released. In general, given two intruders with files B_1 and B_2, the one with more attributes and more records will be the one able to re-identify more. Nevertheless, more records than the ones in the masked file X do not help neither. Similarly, more attributes than the ones in X do not help. Note that records not in X will not help because they can confuse the re-identification algorithm linking records not present. Similarly, attributes other than the ones in X will provide, at most, the same information already present in X. So, the best schema for intruder's database is A.
  Naturally, if a file X has been masked using other information not available in X, this information is also relevant.
- The best information about masking includes both the masking method and its parameters. Recall that the transparency principle states that when data is released we need to inform about all the processes applied to the data (see Sect. 1.4.8). So, this information may be available to intruders. They can use this information to

attack the database and may increase the number of correct links. We call specific record linkage methods the ones that use this information. Deterministic methods are easier to attack with this information. Randomized methods can lead to less re-identifications when the method and its parameters are published. Note the analogy with cryptography where intruders know the algorithms but not the keys. Here, the algorithms are known but not e.g. the random numbers used in the masking.

• The maximum number of re-identifications is obtained with the best re-identification algorithm using the best parameters.

– There are different approaches for re-identification. We have mentioned probabilistic and distance-based record linkage. In the worst-case scenario the intruder will use the one leading to the largest number of re-identifications.

– Most re-identification algorithms are parametric. For example, considering weights for the attributes because some are more relevant than others. In this case, different parameterizations may lead to different number of re-identifications. In the worst-case scenario, intruders will use the parameters that lead to the largest number of re-identifications. We can use machine learning and optimization algorithms to find these successful parameterizations for given datasets. This is discussed in Sect. A.3.3.

As a summary, for $X' = \rho_p(X)$ where ρ is the masking method applied to the data set X and p its parameters, the worst-case scenario results into $KR.Reid(X, X')$ (from Eq. 3.4) where the re-identification algorithm takes advantage of both ρ and p.

Formalization of reidentification algorithms

The definition of k-confusion and (k, t)-confusion (Definitions 3.7 and 3.8) and Example 3.2 poses the question of what is a reidentification algorithm. Recall that they are defined in terms of *all reidentification methods*. Naturally, we do not expect that random methods that by chance achieve 100% reidentifications are taken into account. Note that we also want to discard methods that do not properly take into account available information.

Let us consider here the data of Example 3.2. In the example we create four artificial points

$$X'' = \{(x, 0), (-x, 0), (0, y), (0, -y)\}$$

from four original points

$$X = \{(1, 2), (-2, 4), (4, -2), (-3, -3)\}.$$

For convenience, we set $x = 4$ and $y = 4$. There is no direct correspondence between one particular record in X'' and one in X. Nevertheless, the generation of X'' has (*by chance*) assigned the records in this order. Then, $x''_1 = (4, 0)$, $x''_2 = (-4, 0)$, ...

If we apply distance-based record linkage using an Euclidean distance to these pair of records, we will have the following assignment: $x_1 = (1, 2)$ corresponds to $x''_2 = (-4, 0)$, $x_2 = (-2, 4)$ to $x''_3 = (0, 4)$, $x_3 = (4, -2)$ to $x''_1 = (4, 0)$, and $x_4 = (-3, -3)$ to $x''_4 = (0, -4)$. Therefore, we *reidentify* three records.

We write *reidentify* in italics because it is wrong to state that the worst-case scenario reidentifies three or more records. A proper reidentification algorithm, using information on the masking process, should assign a probability of 1/4 to the link with any record or, equivalently, define an anonymity set of four records. Under a proper definition of reidentification algorithm, it is clear that the method of Example 3.2 satisfies $k = 4$-confusion.

To make this clear, we need a mathematical formulation of what a proper record linkage algorithm is. There is a definition [480, 498] based on true probabilities, and assuming that due to some uncertainty, these probabilities are not fully known by the algorithm. We can model the uncertainty of the algorithm with imprecise probabilities or belief measures. They should be consistent with the true probabilities. Only the algorithms that return probabilities compatible with these belief functions can be called reidentification algorithms. Such definition avoids that the wrong application of the distance-based record linkage above is considered as a re-identification algorithm. Therefore, we can correctly state that the approach in Example 3.2 satisfies $k = 4$-confusion. This mathematical formulation was applied [497] to study different data masking methods.

Disclosure risk and big data

The actual computation of risk using record linkage can be difficult for big data due to its computational cost. We discuss in Appendix A blocking as one of the tools to deal with this problem. Besides of that, in the context of reidentification and k-anonymity it is fundamental to establish the set of quasi-identifiers. With big data the amount of information available to intruders can be very large and thus the set of quasi-identifiers is also large. All attributes may belong to this set.[2] In addition to the information available, effective machine learning and data mining algorithms can infer the values of (sensitive) attributes from other attributes available. E.g. there are results inferring sexual orientation, political and religious affiliation, and even whether parents separated before users of social networks were 21 years old [269]. Such inferences can then be used for reidentification. Linking databases, customary in big data, increases the number of attributes describing an individual. This makes protection more difficult and increases disclosure risk. It is important in this context to recall what we have stated in Sect. 3.3.2: the worst-case scenario for reidentification is when the intruder uses the original data for attacking a data file. This is also the case for big data.

Another important aspect that needs to be clear is the goal of our protection. It is usual to consider that the goal is to protect individuals and not single records. It is usually implicit that records in a database are independent. However, this is not necessarily so. In fact, disclosure risk and also information loss depend [260] on our assumptions on the data. In any case, large databases may contain several data items corresponding to the same individual even if this is not explicit. Observe the case of

---

[2] The discussion of which are the quasi-identifiers for attacking a database is present in e.g. the literature on data protection for graphs and social networks. There are a few competing definitions of k-anonymity for graphs that correspond to different sets of quasi-identifiers. We will discuss them in Sect. 3.4.5 (on k-anonymity and graphs) and in Sect. 6.4.3 (on algorithms for k-anonymity for big data).

anonymizing search logs or shopping carts. Therefore, we need to consider a global perspective for all these records and protect them together. Independent protection of these records may led to disclosure. For example, k-anonymization of k records from the same individual is probably not safe. Detecting and solving these situations in big data may be difficult. E.g. a user can use different devices (and accounts) for accessing a search service and, thus, it may be difficult to detect that different logs belong to the same user if there is no identifier linking them.

Releasing several protected copies of data that change over time (i.e., multiple releases as for dynamic data) also pose disclosure problems. Independent protections of the files do not ensure that individuals are protected when considering all data together. Observe the following example.

Example 3.1 [454] (Example 4) Let us consider a data set X built on data from students from a school class and two independent releases of this data set. The data includes the attribute *month of birth*. There are two students born in each month except for February. Only one student was born in February.

The two releases are k-anonymized versions of X with $k = 2$. One release assigns the student born in February to the group in January, and the other to the group in March. Recordings January-or-February and February-or-March are used for in the protected data sets.

The release of these two sets discloses that there is a student born in February.

Masking cannot be done independent, protection algorithms [344, 350, 380, 454, 501] need to take into account previous releases.

3.4　Privacy Models

Let us begin explicitly defining what a privacy model is.

Definition 3.4 A privacy model is a computational definition of privacy.

As there are different ways to define disclosure and to assess disclosure risk, there are alternative, competing and complementary definitions of privacy. In this section we review some of these definitions. We discuss first privacy models that focus on identity disclosure, and thus related to re-identification. They, therefore, focus on privacy for data releases. Then, we discuss privacy models focusing on attribute disclosure. We include there privacy models for computations.

3.4.1   Privacy from Re-Identification

A basic privacy objective in any data release is to avoid identity disclosure. If re-identification is the process to find a record in the database, a file is safe if this re-identification cannot take place. Then, given a data file X, data protection mechanisms would modify the data in X to produce another file X' in which re-identification is not possible (or difficult).

That is, a database satisfies privacy from re-identification when we avoid completely or up to a certain degree the risk of re-identification. We offer two definitions.

- A protected database A satisfies privacy from re-identification for intruder's knowledge B when (recall Eq. 3.2)

$$Reid(B, A) \leq r_{R1}$$

with a certain privacy level r_{R1} (e.g., $r_{R1} = 0.25$), or, alternatively
- a protected database A satisfies privacy from re-identification when (recall Eq. 3.4)

$$KR.Reid(B, A) \leq (r_K, r_{R1})$$

with certain privacy levels r_K and r_{R1} (e.g., $r_K = 0$ and $r_{R1} = 0.5$).

In this later case with $r_K = 0$ and $r_{R1} = 0.5$ we mean that (i) there is no record that the intruder is absolutely sure about its re-identification (i.e., $r_K = 0$) and (ii) the probability of one record being re-identified (without knowing which) is 0.5.

3.4.2 k-Anonymity

This is a Boolean privacy model, also focusing on identity disclosure, named by Samarati. The definition is closely related to the concept of P-set defined by Dalenius [111] (reviewed in Sect. 1.4.4), and to quasi-identifiers. The concept of k-anonymity is also related to previous works where a minimum and a maximum number of records were required to answer a query or to contribute to the cells in a table. For example, focusing on querying databases, Tendick and Matloff [470] discuss an approach that is called Restricted Query Set Size (RQSS) where a query is denied by a database management system if it is found to involve fewer than k or greater than $|X| - k$ records.

A database A satisfies k-anonymity when for each record in the database there are other $k - 1$ records that are indistinguishable. Indistinguishability is not with respect to all attributes but to the quasi-identifiers that can make a record unique.

Definition 3.5 A database A satisfies k-anonymity with respect to a set of quasi-identifiers QI when the projection of A in this set QI results into a partition of DB in sets of at least k indistinguishable records.

Table 3.2 The data in this table permits an adversary to achieve attribute disclosure without identity disclosure. Attributes city, age, and illness are published and available to intruders

City	Age	Illness
Barcelona	30	Cancer
Barcelona	30	Cancer
Tarragona	60	AIDS
Tarragona	60	AIDS

Note that k-anonymity implies that when we consider any subset of the quasi-identifiers we have an anonymity set of at least k records. In addition, it permits to ensure to any record plausible deniability (see Sect. 1.4.5) at record level, as there will be at least $k - 1$ other possible records. It does not ensure plausible deniability at the database level, as a k-anonymous file may give clues that e.g. a particular outlier record is in the file.

Given a database, a set of quasi-identifiers and a value of k, we can certify whether the database is compliant with k-anonymity or not. For example, the database represented in Table 1.4 (reproduced here as Table 3.2) satisfies k-anonymity for $k = 2$ for the quasi-identifiers *(city, age, illness)*.

This model can be seen as a special case of privacy from re-identification. This is so because any record linkage algorithm cannot distinguish among the at least k records of the anonymity set (they are equally probable to correspond to a given individual). Observe that if a protected database X' built from a database X satisfies k-anonymity then

$$K R.Reid(B, A) \leq (0, 1/k).$$

This is so because for any record $x \in X$ we have k indistinguishable records in X'. So, the intruder cannot know which of the k indistinguishable records corresponds to original one x, and, naturally, the probability of linking the correct link is at most $1/k$.

Variations of this privacy model exist. Some add additional constraints (e.g., l-diversity adds attribute disclosure to k-anonymity) and others generalize these models (n-confusion). If we consider that k-anonymity is about building anonymity sets of cardinality k, n-confusion is a generalization in which the records of such anonymity sets are not required to be all equal.

The standard definition of k-anonymity focus on the available database. That is, we need at least k indistinguishable records in the database for each combination of values (or 0 records). There is a variation called k-map where the focus is on the underlying population. That is, we need a set of k' indistinguishable records corresponding to k individuals in the underlying population. E.g., even when we have only one record in the database with values *(city = Sabadell, Age = 58)*, the database can satisfy $k = 2$-map because there are more than two individuals living in Sabadell with Age equal to 58.

A key aspect of k-anonymity is that the anonymity set provides our anonymity and privacy. For this, we are assuming that the information of the $k-1$ other elements is, of course, not a copy of our own data. In more general terms, k-anonymity is defined under the assumption that the records in the database are independent. This is an important requirement that is not so easy to satisfy in practice. We may have people with correlated information (e.g., all living in the same household). Implementations of k-anonymity need to ensure that this independence assumption holds and proceed appropriately when this does not hold.

3.4.3 k-Anonymity and Anonymity Sets: k-Confusion

From a re-identification point of view what is relevant in k-anonymity is that there are at least k records in the anonymity set that are equally probable, or, equivalently, that the anonymity set of any record has cardinality at least k. It is not so important whether these records have exactly the same values or they are different. This observation has led to several extensions of k-anonymity: k-indistinguishability, (k, t)-confusion [452], k-confusion [450], k-concealment [466], probabilistic k-anonymity [439], and crowd blending [200]. We define k-confusion as follows.

Definition 3.6 If the cardinality of the anonymity set for any record of a database is at least k, then we say that we have k-confusion.

So, if the anonymity set is of size at least k, then the probability of re-identification should be at most $1/k$. Therefore, using the expression above for $KR.Reid$, we have k-confusion when

$$KR.Reid(B, A) \leq (r_K, r_{R1})$$

with $r_K = 0$ and $r_{R1} = 1/k$.

Note that k-confusion does not establish any requirement on the values of the masked data set. The larger the anonymity set, the lower the probability. The definition does not require all probabilities in the anonymity set to be equal. In other words, there is no need that all elements of the anonymity set are equally probable. Because of that, we may have that the probability of one of the elements of the anonymity set is significantly larger than the others. In contrast, (k, t)-confusion forces that the anonymity set for a given probability t is large enough (at least k).

Definition 3.7 [452] Given a space of databases D, a space of auxiliary information A and a method of anonymization of databases ρ, we say that ρ provides (k, t)-confusion if for all re-identification methods r, and all anonymized databases $X \in D$ the confusion (i.e., anonymity set) of r with respect to $\rho(X)$ and A is larger or equal to k for the fixed threshold $0 < t \leq 1/k$.

Definition 3.8 [452] Let notations be as in Definition 3.7. We say that an anonymization method ρ provides n-confusion if there is a $t > 0$ such that ρ provides (n, t)-
confusion.

We introduce now an example [452] to illustrate the difference between
k-anonymity and k-confusion. In particular, we will show that k-confusion permits
us to define methods that lead to solutions with a lower information loss than the
ones that satisfy k-anonymity.

Example 3.2 Let us consider the following data set X consisting of 4 points in $\mathbb{R}^2$:

$$X = \{(1, 2), (-2, 4), (4, -2), (-3, -3)\}.$$

If we want to protect this data set with k-anonymity with $k = 4$ one way is to replace
the four points by their mean. That is,

$$X' = \{(0, 0), (0, 0), (0, 0), (0, 0)\}.$$

In this case, we will have a data set satisfying k-anonymity for $k = 4$ and with the
same mean as the original file. However, the deviation of the attributes of the original
data set is, of course, not equal to the deviation of the attributes of the protected data
set. While the corrected sample standard deviation of the first attribute in X is $\sqrt{10}$
and the one of the second attribute in X is $\sqrt{12.8333}$, the ones in the protected data
set are both zero.

Using k-confusion as our anonymity model we can have four protected records
with different values. Let us consider the following protected records

$$X'' = \{(x, 0), (-x, 0), (0, y), (0, -y)\}.$$

Note that these records satisfy the property that their mean is $(0, 0)$ for any x and y
and, thus, satisfy the same property as the data in X'. In addition, we can compute
x and y so that the deviations of X'' are equal to the deviations of X. To do so, see
that the deviation for the first and the second attribute in X'' are, respectively,

$$s_x = \sqrt{\frac{1}{n-1} \sum (x_i - \bar{x})^2} = \sqrt{\frac{1}{3}(x^2 + x^2 + 0 + 0)} = x\sqrt{2/3},$$

$$s_y = \sqrt{\frac{1}{n-1} \sum (y_i - \bar{x})^2} = \sqrt{\frac{1}{3}(y^2 + y^2 + 0 + 0)} = y\sqrt{2/3}.$$

Therefore, using the equalities $\sqrt{10} = x\sqrt{2/3}$ and $\sqrt{12.83333} = y\sqrt{2/3}$ we
obtain for x and y the following values.

$$x = \sqrt{10}/\sqrt{2/3} = 3.872983$$

$$y = \sqrt{12.8333}/\sqrt{2/3} = 4.387476$$

Figure 3.3 represents the original set X and the protected set X''.

Due to the way we have built the protected data set, the probability of re-identifying
any record of X'' is 1/4. So, this dataset has the same (identity) disclosure risk as the
$k = 4$-anonymous X'.

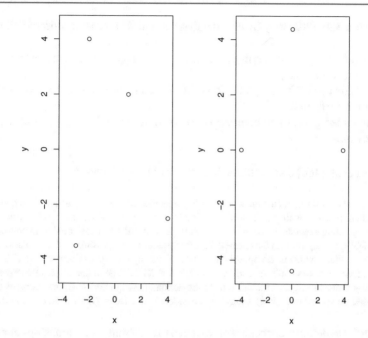

Fig. 3.3 Original data set X (left) and protected data set X'' satisfying k-confusion (right)

If we publish this file following the transparency principle (i.e., informing how the data has been produced), and assess risk applying a record linkage taking advantage of this information, we would get the same risk above. The four masked records in X'' are indistinguishable with respect to each of the records in X.

Observe that applying record linkage without information on the data protection may result into linkages that are not consistent with the protection. That is, all four protected records are associated to the whole set and they are indistinguishable, and it is not true that e.g. record $(0, 4.387476)$ corresponds to $(-2, 4)$.

Exercise 3.2 Consider a data set X and produce a data set X'' compliant with n-confusion. X'' needs to have the same mean and the same correlation as X.

These extensions are related to k-concealment – a privacy model that applies when masking is based on generalization. Generalization is about changing values by more general ones (see Sect. 6.2.1 for details). Let us consider a dataset with records $X = \{x_1, \ldots, x_n\}$, and a masked file $X' = \{x'_1, \ldots, x'_n\}$ where each x'_i has been obtained from x_i through generalization. For example, let attribute A_j provide the place of birth – a city – for each x_i in the database. Then, a possible generalization is to assign $A_j(x'_i)$ the corresponding county for city $A_j(x_i)$. In general, $A_j(x_i) \in A_j(x'_i)$. A record x' is said to be consistent with another record x when x' can be seen as a generalization of x.

Definition 3.9 [202,466] Given a database X and X' a generalization of X; then,

- X' is called a $(1, k)$-anonymization of X if each record in X is consistent with at least k records in X',
- X' is called a $(k, 1)$-anonymization of X if each record in X' is consistent with at least k records in X,
- X' is called a (k, k)-anonymization of X if X' is both a $(1, k)$- and a $(k, 1)$-anonymization of x.

Tassa et al. [466] discuss these three types of anonymization.

A typical adversarial attack aims at revealing sensitive information on a specific target individual. In such an attack, the adversary knows a record $x \in X$ and he tries to locate the corresponding generalized record $x' \in X'$. Alternatively, the adversary could be interested in re-identifying any entity in the released data, for instance to find possible victims to blackmail. Such an attack works in the opposite direction: Focusing on a generalized record $x' \in X'$, the adversary tries to infer its correct preimage $x \in X$. (...) The notion of $(1, k)$-anonymity aims at protecting against the first attack; the notion of $(k, 1)$-anonymity aims at protecting against the second one; (k, k)-anonymity considers both attacks. (Tassa et al. (2012) [466])

In order to define k-concealment, we need to represent the relationships of consistency between pairs of records (x, x') by means of a bipartite graph. The definition follows.

Definition 3.10 Let X be a database, X' be a generalization of X. The bipartite graph $G_{X, X'}$ is defined as the graph with nodes $X \cup X'$ and edges (x, x') when x' is consistent with x.

Recall that in graph theory, we have a perfect matching in a graph bipartite when there is a one-to-one correspondence between the vertexes of the graph. The concept of perfect matching permits to define k-concealment.

Definition 3.11 [466] Let X be a database, X' be a generalization of X and $G_{X, X'}$ be the corresponding bipartite graph. We say that $x' \in X'$ is a match of $x \in X$ if (x, x') is an edge of $G_{X, X'}$ and there exists a perfect matching in $G_{X, X'}$ that includes that edge. If all records $x \in X$ have at least k matches in X', then X' is called a k-concealment of X.

Tassa et al. [466] point out that k-concealment is a generalization of $(1, k)$-anonymity and that similar generalizations can be defined for $(k, 1)$-anonymity and (k, k)-anonymity.

We have underlined before that the definition of n-confusion is based on the idea of anonymity set and on re-identification. Efficient re-identification algorithms would reduce the cardinality of the anonymity set of any record using as much knowledge and making as much inferences as possible. In the case of data protection using generalization, matching and perfect matching would be used to attack a database. In this way, n-confusion and n-concealment can be seen as related, being n-confusion also applicable when masking methods other than generalization are used.

3.4.4 k-Anonymity and Attribute Disclosure: Attacks and Privacy Models

We have discussed in Sect. 3.1.4 that clusters and cells do not necessarily avoid disclosure. This applies to databases that satisfy k-anonymity. They can lead to attribute disclosure. When for a set of records the values of the quasi-identifiers are the same (i.e., they define an anonymity set), the other values can lead to disclosure.

Two types of attacks [121] have been considered in the literature for k-anonymous data sets. There is a correspondence with the attacks discussed in Sect. 3.1.4.

- **Homogeneity attack.** When all indistinguishable records in a cluster are also indistinguishable with respect to a confidential attribute, disclosure can take place. When intruders link a record with this cluster, they can infer the value of the confidential attribute. This is an external attack for attribute disclosure.
- **External knowledge attack.** Information about an individual is used to deduce information of the same or another individual. This corresponds to an internal attack for attribute disclosure. Let us consider k-anonymity with $k = 5$, and a cluster cl_0 with 5 records, four of which with a confidential attribute illness il_1 and one with illness il_2. If an intruder associates two individuals i_1 and i_2 to the cluster cl_0, and knows that i_1 has no illness il_2, then it is clear that i_1 has illness il_1. Similarly, if we know that i_2 has illness il_2 it is also clear that i_1 has illness il_1.

In order to provide solutions that avoid these type of attacks, more strict privacy models have been introduced in the literature. They add constraints on attribute disclosure to the ones on identity disclosure. One of them is p-sensitive k-anonymity, another l-diversity. They all assume that the sensitive attribute is categorical.

Definition 3.12 [504] A data set is said to satisfy p-sensitive k-anonymity for $k > 1$ and $p \leq k$ if it satisfies k-anonymity and, for each group of records with the same combination of values for a set of quasi-identifiers, the number of distinct values for each confidential value is at least p (within the same group).

Therefore, implementations of p-sensitive k-anonymity need to provide anonymity sets in which there are p different values for the sensitive confidential attribute.

Another definition to ensure some level of attribute disclosure is l-diversity. Similar to the case of p-sensitivity, l-diversity forces l different categories in each set. However, in this case, categories should have to be *well-represented*. Different meanings have been given to what *well-represented* means.

Still another privacy model exist. It is t-closeness. In this case it is required that the distribution of the attribute in any k-anonymous subset of the database is similar to the one of the full database. Similarity is defined in terms of the distance between the two distributions and such distance should be below a given threshold t. The Earth Mover distance is used in the definition.

This parameter t permits the data protector to limit the disclosure. Nevertheless, a low threshold forces all the sets to have the same distribution as the full data set. This might cause a large information loss: any correlation between the confidential attributes and the one used for l-diversity might then be lost. For example, if our study is prevalence of cancer in towns, and we want to compare different towns taking into account their main industries (e.g., nuclear power plants), the information conveyed in the original file may be absolutely destroyed by the protection process.

3.4.5 k-Anonymity and Computational Anonymity

In the above definition for k-anonymity, we require that this property holds for all quasi-identifiers. Nevertheless, as the set of quasi-identifiers can be very large some relaxations have been considered. For example, there is a variation [195] based on a set of *virtual identifiers*. Each virtual identifier consists of a set of attributes and an anonymity threshold. Then, for a virtual identifier v_i with anonymity threshold t_i, a database satisfies the anonymity requirement when there are at least t_i records in each of the combinations of values for attributes in v_i (zero records are also allowed).

This approach is related to the computational anonymity, introduced by Stokes [446]. We distinguish between theoretical anonymity and computational anonymity, in a way analogous to theoretical PIR and computational PIR:

> We say that unconditional anonymity is theoretical anonymity. Computational anonymity is conditioned by the assumption that the adversary has some limitation. The limitations can be (...) restricted memory or knowledge. (Stokes (2012) [446]).

Computational anonymity can be seen as the underlying scenario for (k, l)-anonymity. We review first the definition of computational anonymity.

Assumption 1 [446] Let X be a database to protect. Then, we assume that the information the adversary has about any individual is limited to at most l of the attributes in X. The l attributes do not have to be the same for different individuals.

The following definition of (k, l)-anonymity is based on computational anonymity.

Definition 3.13 [446] A data set X satisfies (k, l)-anonymity if it is k-anonymous with respect to every subset of attributes of cardinality at most l.

To illustrate this definition we can consider the following set of records (each one defined on three attributes), which satisfy $(2, 2)$-anonymity. It can be seen that the records are all different, so, the database is 1-anonymous.

$$D = \{(a, b, e), (a, b, f), (c, d, e), (c, d, f), (c, b, e), (c, b, f), (a, d, e), (a, d, f)\}.$$

The case of social networks

There are instantiations of k-anonymity to different types of non-SQL data. This is the case for graphs and social networks. In this case, there is not a single definition but several of them. They differ on the information available to the intruders, and, thus, on how to define quasi-identifiers in the context of social networks. Different background knowledge implies different quasi-identifiers, which means that different types of data protection procedures need to be applied.

We call k-degree anonymity when the information available to an intruder is the degree of a node. Liu and Terzi [304] were among the firsts to consider this problem. An alternative approach is to consider 1-neighborhood anonymity [541]. In this case, intruders have information on the neighbors of a node and the relationship between these nodes (i.e., edges between them). If $\mathcal{N}(n)$ is the graph of neighbors of n and their relationships, we have 1-neighborhood anonymity if for each node n there are $k - 1$ other nodes $n_1, \ldots, n_{k-1}$ such that the graphs $\mathcal{N}(n_i)$ are isomorphic.

An alternative is the one of (k, l)-anonymity. A graph is (k, l)-anonymous if it is k-neighbor anonymous with respect to any subset of cardinality at most l of the neighbor sets of the vertices of the graph. There are two ways to interpret this: one in terms of the neighbors and the other taking also advantage of the non-neighbors. We have the following definition, in case that the non-neighbors are not considered.

Definition 3.14 [453] Let $G = (V, E)$ be a graph. We say that G is (k, l)-anonymous if for any vertex $v_1 \in V$ and for all subset $S \subseteq N(v_1)$ of cardinality $|S| \leq l$ there are at least k distinct vertices $\{v_i\}_{i=1}^{k}$ such that $S \subseteq N(v_1)$ for $i \in [1, k]$.

This definition is related to computational anonymity (see in Sect. 3.4.5), as we restrict intruder's knowledge to l neighbors of v_1.

A more general definition of k-anonymity is to consider structural queries Q. Then, k-candidate anonymity is defined in terms of k-anonymity for such structural query Q. For appropriate queries Q, this definition encompasses the previous ones.

Definition 3.15 [222] Let Q be a structural query. An anonymized graph satisfies k-candidate anonymity given Q if for all x in V and all y in $cand_Q(x)$

$$C_{Q,x}[y] \leq 1/k$$

where $C_{Q,x}[y]$ is the probability, given Q, of taking candidate y for x. The authors define $C_{Q,x}[y] = 1/|cand_Q(x)|$ for each $y \in cand_Q(x)$ and 0 otherwise.

3.4.6 Differential Privacy

This Boolean privacy model, proposed by Dwork in 2006 [161], focuses on disclosure from a computation from a database. So, if q represents a function, a computation, or a query, then $q(X)$ represents the result of this function when applied to the database X.

The privacy model stresses the need to avoid disclosure on whether a particular individual or record was present or not in X. Quoting Dwork [161] "what constitutes a failure to preserve privacy? What is the power of the adversary whose goal it is to compromise privacy?". According to her, the answer comes from the difference of adding or removing an element in the database:

> differential privacy ensures that the removal or addition of a single database item does not (substantially) affect the outcome of any analysis (Dwork (2008) [162], p. 2).

In other words, a function q is differentially private if the presence or absence of a record in the database does not change so much the result. That is, $q(X)$ and $q(X')$ are similar when X and X' only differ in one record. Here, similarity is defined in terms of probability distributions. Differentially private mechanisms are implemented by means of randomization. This can help to understand the definition. For example, if we want to compute the mean of X, we consider q a randomized version of the mean. Then, if we add a record to X, the distribution produced by the randomized mean should not change significantly when we compare with the one obtained on X.

A key concept in differential privacy is the one of neighboring databases. Two neighboring databases D_1 and D_2 are two databases that differ in at most one element. That is, D_1 (or D_2) is a proper subset of D_2 (or, D_1) and the larger database contains just one additional row. The formal definition of differential privacy follows. As we said above, it is defined in terms of probability distributions. Then, given a function or query q, the definition considers a randomized version of q denoted by $K_q(D)$. Then, informally, we state that the output of K_q for two neighboring databases needs to be similar. I.e., the distributions associated to $K_q(D)$ and $K_q(D')$ are similar.

Definition 3.16 A function K_q for a query q gives ε-differential privacy if for all data sets D_1 and D_2 differing in at most one element, and all $S \subseteq Range(K_q)$,

$$Pr[K_q(D_1) \in S] \leq e^{\varepsilon} Pr[K_q(D_2) \in S].$$

Here, ε is the level of privacy required and it should be $\varepsilon \geq 0$. The expression above is often given as

$$\frac{Pr[K_q(D_1) \in S]}{Pr[K_q(D_2) \in S]} \leq e^{\varepsilon},$$

that underlines that e^ε is the bound of the difference between the two probabilities. In this latter expression it is clear that the smaller the ε, the greater the privacy we have. When it is equal to zero, we need that the distributions for two neighboring databases are exactly the same. In other words, if $\varepsilon = 0$, there is no privacy leakage and the function K_q needs to be constant (i.e., the same for all neighboring databases).

Differential privacy permits to implement plausible deniability with respect to the output. Individuals can state that their data have not been used in the computation of the output. The level of credibility of this statement will depend on the value of ε selected.

Several variations of differential privacy have been introduced in the literature. One of them is (ε, δ)-differential privacy (also named δ-approximate ε-indistinguishability in its original definition [164]).

Definition 3.17 A function K_q for a query q gives (ε, δ)-differential privacy if for all data sets D_1 and D_2 differing in at most one element, and all $S \subseteq Range(K_q)$,

$$Pr[K_q(D_1) \in S] \le e^\varepsilon Pr[K_q(D_2) \in S] + \delta.$$

This definition relaxes ε-differential privacy as events with a probability smaller than δ for D_1 are still permitted even if they do not occur in D_2.

Let us reconsider neighboring data sets. The most general definition is the one given above: they are two datasets differing on a single record. Differential privacy with this definition is also known as unbounded differential privacy. In contrast, we may consider the replacement of a record by another one. That is, both data sets have exactly the same number of records. Bounded differential privacy stands for a definition under this type of neighborhood.

When differential privacy is implemented using some randomized process, multiple applications of the privacy mechanism to X will lead to different solutions. Naturally, if we allow users to do multiple queries, they can infer the true value of $q(X)$. To avoid disclosure from multiple queries $q_1, q_2, \ldots$ (same or different), users are usually provided with an initial privacy budget which is reduced by the ε_i parameter associated to query q_i. No queries are allowed to users when their budget is exhausted. We discuss in Sect. 5.1.2 differential privacy guarantees for composition of functions. Multiple queries on the same database correspond to sequential composition.

3.4.7 Local Differential Privacy

Differential privacy focus on privacy for a computation. We have seen that a key element is the query or function q that we want to compute. Then, we define the differential privacy model so that the computation of this function does not lead to disclosure.

Nevertheless, in an extreme case we can consider that q is the identity function that given a database returns this same database. Then, how should we define K_q so that it is differentially private? Alternatively, q can be a function that applies to a single record or datum. Then, how should we define K_q so that differential privacy holds? Local differential privacy is for this latter question.

We can reformulate the problem in another, but equivalent, way. Data is collected from individuals and entities. Then functions are applied to the collection in a centralized manner. That is, we gather information $x_1, x_2, \ldots, x_n$ to build the database $X = (x_1, \ldots, x_n)$ and then apply functions to X. Nevertheless, we can consider a different approach and consider privacy at the collection level. Then, when x_i is transmitted to the central authority, we have a data protection procedure before the transmission. Local differential privacy has this goal: privacy in a distributed setting. Formally, q is the transmission function that is expected to be the identity (i.e., what the user sends is expected to be the same as the central authority receives). Then, K_q is defined so that the respondent has some privacy guarantees.

The formal definition of local differential privacy is the same as above. Given two neighboring databases D_1 and D_2 the query K_q is ε-differentially private if

$$Pr[K_q(D_1) \in S] \leq e^{\varepsilon} Pr[K_q(D_2) \in S].$$

Nevertheless, we have that now D_1 and D_2 are either single records, or just a single value. Then, the neighboring databases are understood as databases where a value is replaced by another one. That is, we are considering bounded differential privacy.

For example, let us consider a set of c categories $C = \{c_1, \ldots, c_c\}$ and that respondents just inform about a value in C. Then, we can understand D_1 and D_2 as two categories in C (i.e., $D_1, D_2 \in C$), and then local differential privacy for individual response $D_1 = c_i$ and $D_2 = c_j$ hold when

$$Pr[K_q(c_i) \in S] \leq e^{\varepsilon} Pr[K_q(c_j) \in S]$$

where $S \subseteq C$, if K_q can deliver any value in C. Note that here, as above, we understand the query q as being the identity, so, $K_q(c_i)$ is a randomized version of just delivering c_i. The same model applies if q returns a number in a range.

As a summary, local differential privacy is a privacy model that protects a single release by means of making the data release (be it a record or a single value) from a user, sensor, or entity *indistinguishable* from the release of another one.

In practice, the use of local differential privacy when users (or sensors) submit data continuously is problematic. As we have discussed above, multiple queries of the same dataset need to be implemented taking into account a privacy budget. Otherwise they can lead to disclosure. When data is decentralized multiple queries usually refer to reporting data at different times. E.g., let x_i^t represent the reading of the ith sensor at time t. Then, the series $x_i^1, \ldots, x_i^T$ for a given T is probably unique and the values x_i^t are probably not independent. Local differential privacy produces $\rho(x_i^1), \ldots, \rho(x_i^T)$ which may not avoid re-identification. If x_i^t are not independent, and we want to provide ε-differential privacy for the whole series (i.e., ε is the privacy budget), we need that ρ provides ε/T differential privacy (see Sect. 5.1.2 on composition of queries in differential privacy).

3.4.8 Integral Privacy

This privacy model also focuses on avoiding inferences from the results of functions f. There are two different definitions, one for a computation from a single database as in differential privacy and another for a computation from two versions of the same database. In short, the result of a computation $y = f(X)$ is integrally private if there are differently enough databases X_i that can provide such result y.

While differential privacy is based on the idea of smooth functions (i.e., adding and removing a record does not modify the result significantly), integral privacy is based on recurrent outputs (i.e., there are different ways to get the same result). Consider a function f that takes a database X and returns 1 if the number of records in X is odd, and 0 if the number of records in X is even. This function is integrally private. Given 1 there is an infinite number of possible databases that can produce 1. The same applies if the outcome is 0. While this function f is already integrally private, it is not differentially private. To define a function K_f differentially private we need to perturbate f significantly.

In integral privacy the concept of generators of a model has a fundamental role. Let f be the function to compute, and let y_0 be a possible output of f. Then, we define the set of generators of y_0 as the set of databases that produce y_0. Informally, this is $f^{-1}(y_0)$. We also consider having some background knowledge, denoted by S^*. It corresponds to a set of records we know to be in the database used to generate y_0. Then,

$$Gen(y_0, S^*) = \{S' | S^* \subseteq S' \subseteq P, f(S') = y_0\}$$

corresponds to the datasets that can produce y_0 and are consistent with this background knowledge. Here, P is the whole population. Then, we have integral privacy when $G(y_0, S^*)$ is large enough and the intersection of the generators (discounting the background knowledge) is empty. I.e., $\cap_{D \in Gen(y_0, S^*)} D \setminus S^* = \emptyset$. Here, large enough can be formally defined as having at least k different databases. I.e., $|Gen(y_0, S^*)| \geq k$. So, the definition is a kind of k-anonymity for computations.

Integral privacy satisfies plausible deniability with respect to the output, as, by default, the output can be computed using other different records. That is, for any record, there is at least one generator that does not include that particular record.

3.4.9 Homomorphic Encryption

The goal is to avoid a non-authorized access to the data X. In fact, not only to the data themselves but also to partial computations of the data. For example, data is stored in a cloud service or, in general, in any other third party storage system. Then, a user is granted to compute $f(X)$ but the third party should learn nothing about X, about partial computations of $f(X)$, nor about $f(X)$ itself.

3.4.10 Secure Multiparty Computation

In this case, there is a set of parties (e.g., individuals or organizations) that want to compute a joint function f of their own databases. Nevertheless, they do not want to share these databases. The only information they want to share is the output of the function. No extra knowledge should be acquired during the process of computing f. We formalize secure multiparty computation below.

Definition 3.18 Let $P_1, \ldots, P_n$ represent a set of parties, and let $X_1, \ldots, X_n$ be their respective databases. The parties want to compute a function f of these databases (i.e., $f(X_1, \ldots, X_n)$) without revealing unnecessary information.

In other words, after computing $f(X_1, \ldots, X_n)$ and delivering this result to each P_i, what P_i knows is nothing more than what can be deduced from X_i and the function f. So, the computation of f has not given P_i any extra knowledge.

A *trivial* approach for solving this problem is to consider a centralized approach. That is, we consider a trusted third party TTP that computes the analysis. In this case, each P_i transfers data X_i using a completely secure channel (e.g., using cryptographic protocols) to the trusted third party TTP. Then, TTP computes the result $y = f(X_1, \ldots, X_n)$, and sends y to each P_i in a secure way. This will satisfy the definition as each P_i knows nothing more than X_i and y.

Secure multiparty computation provides solutions for this problem in a distributed environment in which there is no such trusted third party. Then, the same privacy guarantees are sought.

Privacy-preserving solutions for this privacy model are implemented by means of protocols that describe the information flow among the parties and details their computations. Following the protocol we reach the desired result. We will see some examples in Sect. 5.2. In order to build a protocol that guarantees the privacy model, some assumptions are needed on the behavior of the intruders. In general, the parties themselves can be intruders trying to gain some extra knowledge from their computations. We can even consider parties that try to fool the other parties, break the protocol, and collide with others to learn relevant information from a targeted party. We will discuss the issue of adversaries in Sect. 5.2.1.

3.4.11 Result Privacy

This privacy model focuses on the outcome of data mining algorithms that extract knowledge from a particular database. Some of the knowledge may be sensitive or confidential and, in this case, we want to avoid intruders access to this knowledge. We provide a definition of result privacy. The definition is for a particular database and a particular data mining algorithm.

Definition 3.19 [9] Let X be a database, let A be a parametric data mining algorithm. Then, A run with parameter set Θ is said to have the ability to derive knowledge K

from X if and only if K appears either directly in the output of the algorithm or by reasoning from the output. This is expressed by $(A, X, \Theta) \vdash K$.

Knowledge K is said to be derivable from X, if there exists an algorithm A with parameter Θ such that $(A, X, \Theta) \vdash K$.

Given X the set of derivable knowledge from X is denoted as $K\,Set_X$. Any knowledge K such that $(A, X, \Theta) \vdash K$ is in $K\,Set_X$.

Using these definitions, we formalize result privacy as follows.

Definition 3.20 Let X be a database, let A be a parametric data mining algorithm. Then, A with parameter set Θ is said to satisfy result privacy with respect to a set of sensitive knowledge $\mathcal{K} = \{K_1, \ldots, K_n\}$ when no K_i in $\mathcal{K}$ is derivable from X. That is, no K_i is such that $(A, X, \Theta) \vdash K_i$.

3.4.12   Privacy Models for Clusters and Cells

We have already seen some of the privacy models that apply to clusters and cells. In particular, the variations for k-anonymity that focus on attribute disclosure are privacy models for clusters. Recall l-diversity, t-closeness, and p-sensitive k-anonymity in Sect. 3.4.4. Tools to detect sensitive cells in tabular data are implicitly defining privacy models for cells. These tools are the rule (n, k)-dominance, rule pq, and rule $p\%$. We define them in Sect. 8.2.

3.4.13   Discussion

In this chapter we have seen a large number of alternative privacy models. Some of them can be combined. For example, let us consider the scenario of accessing a cloud service and requiring the output to be privacy compliant. Then, we require homomorphic encryption for computations and differential privacy for the result. If instead of one single user we have multiple ones in a distributed environment, then we may require secure multiparty computation together with differential privacy.

To conclude this section we present in Table 3.3 a list of the most relevant privacy models, and showing whether they address attribute disclosure, identity disclosure, or both. We also show whether they are for a database release or for functions (i.e., outputs of queries). We also indicate if they are usually considered as a Boolean definition of privacy or a quantitative one.

3.5   Classification of Privacy Mechanisms

There are different privacy mechanisms, each developed for a particular scenario and considering certain assumptions on the data. In this section we describe three dimen-

Table 3.3 Data privacy models and disclosure risk measures

Privacy risk model/measure	Attribute disclosure	Identity disclosure	Database release	Query release	Boolean
Re-identification		X	X		Quantitative
Uniqueness		X	X		Quantitative
Result-driven	X		X		Boolean
k-Anonymity		X	X		Boolean
k-confusion		X	X		Boolean
k-concealment		X	X		Boolean
p-sensitive k-Anonymity	X	X	X		Boolean
k-Anonymity, l-diversity	X	X	X		Boolean
k-Anonymity, t-closeness	X	X	X		Boolean
Interval disclosure	X		X		Quantitative
Differential privacy	X			X	Boolean
Local differential privacy		X	X		Boolean
Integral privacy	X			X	Boolean
Homomorphic encryption	X			X	Boolean
Secure multiparty computation	X			X	Boolean

sions that are useful to classify most existing mechanisms. These three dimensions are:

- whose privacy is being sought,
- the computations to be done, and
- the number of data sources.

Individuals and organizations play different roles with respect to information processing. The first dimension focuses on the individual or organization whose data has to be protected. The second on the type of computation a researcher or a data analyzer needs to apply to the data. From the data protection process, it is different if the type of analysis is known or is ill-defined. The third dimension considers whether the data analyser will use one or more data sets. We describe next these three dimensions in more detail, and discuss some of their relationships.

We also discuss the need for knowledge intensive tools in data privacy. We call *knowledge intensive data privacy* the area that encompasses tools and methodologies where knowledge rich tools play a role. Knowledge intensive data privacy is independent of the previous dimensions and can play a role in several different scenarios.

3.5.1   On Whose Privacy Is Being Sought

This dimension can be illustrated considering a scenario that involves three actors. Then, we can observe privacy from the point of view of each of the actors. We consider these three actors: the data respondents, the data holder, and the data user.

The data respondents are the individuals that have generated the data. We consider them as passive subjects that cannot take actions to protect their own privacy. We can consider as typical scenarios the case of data given by people (the respondents) through e.g. research questionaries, interviews and surveys, purchases with fidelity cards, medical treatments in hospitals, and information supplied to insurance companies.

The holder is the organization or individual that has gathered the data and has it in a proprietary database. For example, supermarkets have the listings from fidelity cards that describe all items bought by clients, insurance companies keep all *relevant* data about their clients, and hospitals have the clinical information of their patients, the results of their analyses, and the treatments received. National Statistical Offices have databases with the results of surveys and census.

A user is a person using an information technology service. As in most of the cases, user's access is recorded and stored, we can also consider users as respondents. The main difference between respondents and users is that the latter have an active role in order to protect their own privacy. For example, when Alice is accessing a search engine, all her queries will be typically logged into a database together with some additional information as IP address, time stamps, and so on. Because of that, Alice is a respondent of the database storing all query logs. However, we consider her in the role of a user when she is worried with the privacy of her own queries and she applies herself technological solutions to avoid the disclosure of sensitive information.

Literature also uses the term data owner. Nevertheless, it is understood differently by different authors. Some use it as equivalent to data holder [57,135,509], and others as equivalent to data respondent [194]. We will avoid this term, but consider data owner and data holder as equivalents.

As summary, we have respondent, holder, and user privacy depending on the actor in whose privacy we focus. We define them more formally below, after revisiting the examples.

Example 3.3 A hospital collects data from patients and sets up a server to be used by approved researchers to explore relevant data.

The actors in this scenario are: the hospital as the data holder, and the patients as respondents whose data is in the database.

When the server logs the queries and computations of the approved researchers, we have that these researchers are respondents of the log database.

Example 3.4 An insurance company collects data from customers for their internal use. They are asking a software company to develop new software. For this purpose a fraction of the database will be transferred to the software company for analysis and test of the new system. The insurance company is the data holder, and the customers are the data respondents.

Example 3.5 A car manufacturer collects data from its customers and makes an agreement with a university department so that they will analyze the data, do a segmentation analysis, and make a deep learning prediction model to estimate sales for new customers. The car manufacturer is the data holder, and customers are the respondents.

Example 3.6 A search engine resolves users' queries by sending lists of web pages to these users about the topics queried. Claudia, a user of a search engine, wants to get information about her topics of interest but at the same time she wants these topics out of sight from the search engine company. Because of that, she uses a plugin in her browser that has been developed for this purpose. Claudia is a respondent of the search engine database if, as usual, the engine logs all requests. In addition, Claudia is a user in the sense that she has an active role in order to protect her own privacy.

Example 3.7 Two supermarkets have implemented fidelity cards and use them to record all transactions of their customers. The two directors of the supermarked have decided to mine relevant association rules from their databases. In the extent possible, each director wants to keep their own records private and, thus, inaccessible.

In this scenario, the supermarkets are the data holders, and the customers are the respondents.

Example 3.8 Berta, a journalist of a certain country, is sending reports to a foreign newspaper about some activities of her government. The journalist wants to avoid sniffers to know that she has sent the information to the newspaper.

In this case, the journalist is a user of an emailing system and she has an active role to protect her own privacy.

Let us now review the three main categories of privacy under this dimension.

- **Respondents' privacy**. The goal is to avoid disclosure of sensitive data corresponding to particular respondents. In Example 3.3, regulations force the hospital to avoid the disclosure of e.g. illnesses and medical treatments of patients. For example, Elia, a researcher querying the database, should not be able to find that the reason of her friend Donald visiting the hospital is a vasectomy. Due to this, the hospital has to implement respondents' privacy mechanisms to avoid the disclosure of respondents' sensitive information to researchers. Example 3.4 (the case of software development for the insurance company) is also a problem of respondent's privacy.

- **Holder's privacy**. The goal is to avoid the disclosure of any relevant information of the database as this is against the interest of the holder. The scenario in Example 3.7 where two supermarkets collaborate to mine association rules in a way that none of the supermakets learn anything about the other but the mined association rules corresponds to this type of privacy.
- **User's privacy**. The goal is to ensure the privacy of the user of a particular system, and to achieve this goal, the user acts actively for this purpose. For example, Claudia and Berta in Examples 3.6 and 3.8 apply available technology to avoid as much disclosure of sensitive information as possible. This is also the case of researchers accessing the database in the hospital of Example 3.3 if they try to avoid the hospital to know about their queries.

In this classification, we distinguish between holder's and respondent's privacy. Note that although holders are typically responsible of respondents' privacy according to laws and regulations, holders' interests are not the same as respondents' interests. For example, the director of a hospital may not be really worried that Elia learns about Donald's vasectomy (except for legal liability). The same can apply about Donald's shopping cart in the supermarket. This information is too specific and the holder's focus can be more on generic information and knowledge. For example, the director of the supermarket may be interested in avoiding competitors to know that the pack *(beer, chocolate eggs)* is selling really well, and all people buying them are also buying *chips*. Similarly, the hospital director may be worried that someone learns that most patients of doctor Hyde with appendicitis are back to the hospital after two weeks with a severe illness. In both examples, the information of a particular person may be of no real concern to the data holder.

Methods for user's privacy are discussed in Chap. 4. Methods for respondent and holder privacy are both applied by the data holder. We discuss them in Chaps. 5, 6, and 8.

Exercise 3.3 Discuss the privacy models described in Sect. 3.4 in terms of respondent, holder, and user privacy. Discuss which privacy models apply to each of the actors in the examples presented in this section.

Note that in the EU General Data Protection Regulation (GDPR), there are the terms data subject, data controller, data processor, and recipient with particular definitions related to the actors discussed in this section. These definitions are reproduced in Fig. 3.4.

From EU General Data Protection Regulation, Article 4.

(1) 'personal data' means any information relating to an identified or identifiable natural person ('data subject'); an identifiable natural person is one who can be identified, directly or indirectly, in particular by reference to an identifier such as a name, an identification number, location data, an online identifier or to one or more factors specific to the physical, physiological, genetic, mental, economic, cultural or social identity of that natural person;

(7) 'controller' means the natural or legal person, public authority, agency or other body which, alone or jointly with others, determines the purposes and means of the processing of personal data; where the purposes and means of such processing are determined by Union or Member State law, the controller or the specific criteria for its nomination may be provided for by Union or Member State law;

(8) 'processor' means a natural or legal person, public authority, agency or other body which processes personal data on behalf of the controller;

(9) 'recipient' means a natural or legal person, public authority, agency or another body, to which the personal data are disclosed, whether a third party or not.

Fig. 3.4 Definitions in Article 4 of the EU General Data Protection Regulation (GDPR)

Exercise 3.4 Discuss the relationships between the actors discussed in this section and the data subject, data controller, data processor, and recipient as defined in the EU GDPR (see Fig. 3.4).

3.5.2   On the Computations to Be Done

This dimension focuses on the data use. That is, the prior knowledge the data holder has on the analysis and inferences to be applied to the data. Protection mechanisms can be classified according to their suitability in terms of this available knowledge. For illustration, let us consider the following examples.

Example 3.9 Aitana, the director of hospital A, contacts Beatriu, the director of hospital B. She proposes to compute a linear regression model to estimate the number of days patients stay in hospital using their databases.

Example 3.10 A mobile application helps users to write rhymed verses. The company developing the product claims that the product is privacy-friendly as they do not collect user's verses themselves. They use a federated learning approach based on deep learning for rhyme suggestion, based on ontologies and user's own composition. The app has been extremely trendy and is in use by people of all ages.

Example 3.11 Elia, a researcher on epidemiology, has contacted Aitana the director of a hospital chain. She wants to access the database because she studies flu and she wants to compare how the illness spreads every year in Chicago and in Miami.

In the first example, we find an scenario in which we know the analysis to be computed (a linear regression model) from the data. Then, suitable privacy mechanisms can be optimized with respect to this computation. We can develop and tune privacy approaches so that the two directors can compute the linear model as accurately as possible and the information leakage is minimal. The second example is a similar scenario. The analysis to be computed (a deep learning model) is perfectly known by the software company. The main differences are that we have a massive number of users, and that the system is not fully decentralized because a company is involved and leading the process.

The third example represents a different scenario. The analysis is ill-defined, and, therefore, we need to apply a protection mechanism that permits Elia to have good results (as similar as possible to the ones she would obtain dealing with the original data) for a range of analysis and where the risk of information leakage is minimal.

In general, the knowledge on the intended data use permits us to distinguish three categories. The first two, data-driven and computation-driven procedures, roughly correspond to the two main scenarios above. The third category, result-driven procedures, is loosely related to computation-driven.

Let us consider an additional example to illustrate result-driven procedures.

Example 3.12 A retailer specialized in baby goods publishes a database with the information gathered from customers with their fidelity card. This database is to be used by a data miner to extract some association rules. The retailer is very much concerned about alcohol consumption and wants to avoid the data miner inferring rules about baby diapers and beers.[3]

Let us now review these three categories.

- **Computation-driven and specific purpose protection procedures.** In this case it is known beforehand the analysis to be applied to the data. Because of that we can develop and use a protection procedure that takes advantage of this fact. In other words, protection procedures are tailored for a specific purpose. We call this type of methods computation-driven as the known computation defines the protection mechanism.
  Example 3.9 where Aitana and Beatriu agree on computing a linear regression using the data of the two hospitals corresponds to this case. We are also in this framework when someone, different to the directors, wants to compute the mean of a database. Privacy mechanisms that provide differential privacy are examples of computation-driven procedures.
- **Data-driven and general purpose protection procedures.** In this case, the analysis is ill-defined or simply unknown. This is the case of Example 3.11, and also when data is published in a web server for public use, as some governmental offices or research organizations do. See e.g. information from a National

---

[3] A classic example in the literature of association rule mining is about the discovery of a rule stating that men that buy diapers also buy beers (see the web dssresources [557]).

Statistical Office [555], public repositories and open data (as the UCI repository [32]). The usual way to proceed in data-driven scenarios is sharing a privacy-
preserving version of the data. This privacy-preserving data needs to be similar
enough to the original one to provide good quality results and be different enough
to avoid disclosure. Masking methods are the privacy mechanisms applied in this
case. The quality requirements for the protected data may depend on the type of
scenario. In Example 3.4, the quality of the analysis can be low if our only purpose
is that software engineers can test their software (although in this case data needs
to have enough coverage) as there is no need to do a deep analysis of the output
results of the software. In contrast, when a researcher wants to study the effectiveness of a medical treatment, inferences should be correct. An intermediate case is
when data is generated for educational purposes "to train students in the application of multivariate statistical techniques on 'real' data" (Willenborg (2001) [521],
p. 31). Homomorphic encryption is another type of data-driven or general purpose
approach.
- **Result-driven protection procedures.** In this case, privacy concerns to the result of applying a particular data mining method to some particular data [29,30].
  Example 3.12 illustrates this case.
  Although data protection methods preventing this type of disclosure are specific
  to a given computation procedure, we classify them in a specific class because
  the focus is different. We are interested in the knowledge inferred from the data
  instead of any inference on the data themselves.

   Note that the dimension discussed in this section mainly focuses on respondent's
and holders's privacy, and that methods to ensure their privacy will be applied by the
data holder.

Exercise 3.5 Discuss the correspondence between the privacy models and the classification of protection procedures proposed here.

3.5.3 On the Number of Databases

The last dimension corresponds to the number of databases. We distinguish the
following two cases.

- **Single data sources.** That is, we only consider one database, which is supposed to
  be static. This setting applies for a database release and for building and releasing a
  model built from the database. For example, in Example 3.4 the insurance company
  has a single database to be shared with the software company. Example 3.5 also
  applies here in both user segmentation and sales prediction.
- **Multiple data sources.** There are different scenarios in which multiple data
  sources or multiple databases play a role.
  The first one corresponds to different data holders with a database each, and a join
  analysis of their data. This is the case of Example 3.9, where the databases of the

two hospitals are used to build a join linear regression model. The same applies to Example 3.10, where a massive number of users have relevant information to train the model.

The second scenario is when we need to consider multiple releases from data that change over time. Disclosure risk assessment needs to take into account that adversaries can integrate all released information to improve their attacks. We discuss the problem of multiple releases for e.g. data streams in Sect. 3.3.2.

The most common privacy model for a few multiple parties with a database each is secure multiparty computation. In this case, we need to know the function to compute. When the number of parties is very large, federated learning with differential privacy is an option. For this, we also need to know the model to be computed. Alternative approaches include local anonymization of data and then model building from these data. See e.g. the work by Liu et al. [303].

Multiple data releases are implemented using data-driven approaches, and using e.g. k-anonymity as the privacy model. Integral privacy was defined for multiple-releases of machine learning models taking into account database changes.

3.5.4   Knowledge Intensive Data Privacy

> Uholak eraman du hitzen eta gauzen arteko zubia
>
> K. Uribe, Bitartean heldu eskutik, 2001,
> p. 65 [505]

Initial results in both statistical disclosure control and privacy preserving data mining were on files with numerical and categorical data. Later this evolved in more complex data types (logs, social networks, documents). In the last years there has been a trend to deal not only with the data in a database but also with additional information and knowledge on the data, data schema and even on the semantics attached to the data. Knowledge intensive data privacy focuses on these questions.

We outline here some of the aspects that can be considered as part of knowledge intensive data privacy.

- **Semantics of terms.** In both data protection and disclosure risk the semantics of the terms present in the file can be taken into account. Initial work in this area includes generalization approaches where the generalization schema is known (e.g., recoding cities by counties, and counties by provinces/states). Knowledge rich methods consider ontologies, dictionaries and language technologies (natural language processing and entity recognition) for data protection (e.g., document sanitization) and for risk assesment by means of record linkage.
- **Metadata and constrained data.** Files and tables of databases are not isolated entities, the same applies to attributes in a file or table. It is common to have

relationships (constraints) between the attributes and these relationships have to be taken into account in the data protection process. We discuss this problem in Sect. 6.5.

- **Knowledge rich disclosure risk assessment.** Disclosure risk has to be based on the best technologies for database integration and matching. However, not all information is in a structured way, because there is information in noSQL databases, and in free text form (texts in blogs and online social networks). Disclosure risk assessment may require the analysis of such data.

3.5.5 Other Dimensions and Discussion

The literature considers other ways to classify data protection mechanisms. One of them is on the type of tools used. In such dimension, methods are classified either as following the perturbative or the cryptographic approach. Naturally, perturbative methods are the ones that ensure protection by means of adding some type of noise into the original dataset. On the contrary, cryptographic approaches ensure privacy by means of cryptographic protocols.

Cryptographic approaches are typically developed on the basis that we know which is the analysis to be computed from the data. In most of the cases, a cryptographic protocol is defined to compute a particular function of one or more datasets. As the function to be computed is known, they can be classified as computation-driven protection methods. They are useful to provide homomorphic encryption and secure multiparty computation, as well as to implement user privacy. We will see some of these tools in Chap. 4.

Perturbative approaches are usually understood as tools for database protection. In this case, they are protection mechanisms independent of data use and, therefore, they can be considered as data-driven approaches. We will see these approaches in different chapters of this book. Masking methods for database protection in Chap. 6, for result privacy in Sect. 8.1, and for user privacy in Sect. 4.2.2.1. Perturbative methods are also used to implement differential-privacy, and, in this case, the function is known and, therefore, this correspond to a computation-driven method. We will see perturbative approaches for differential privacy in Sect. 5.1.

We want to underline that in this book we will not use the term *perturbative approach* with this meaning. Instead, we use perturbative methods/approaches in a more restricted way, as it is usual in the statistical disclosure control community. As we show in Chap. 6, we distinguish between perturbative and non-perturbative approaches. Although both reduce the quality of the data, only the first type introduces errors in the data. We will use *masking methods* as the term that encompasses both classes and corresponds to the perturbative approach for databases with the sense above. As a summary, masking methods take the original dataset and construct a protected one reducing the quality of the original one. We will use anonymization methods with a similar meaning. So, in the sense above, all masking methods in Chap. 6 would be relevant for data protection and sharing.

Syntactic and semantic methods

The literature on security distinguishes between perfect secrecy and semantic security. Perfect secrecy ensures that a ciphertext does not provide any information without knowing the key. In semantic security it is possible in theory to get information from the ciphertext, but it is not computationally feasible to get this information.

This distinction has led to distinguish between syntactic and semantic methods in data privacy. k-Anonymity is considered a syntactic [103,291] method while differential privacy is considered an algorithmic and semantic method [291]. From this perspective, computational anonymity as discussed in Sect. 3.4.5 can also be considered as a semantic method (although it is based on k-anonymity).

We will not use this distinction in this book. We will use the term semantic anonymization and e.g. semantic microaggregation when we deal with linguistic terms and take into account their semantics from the point of view of ontologies.

3.6 Summary

In this chapter we have given an overview of disclosure risk measures and privacy models. We have also provided a classification or road-map of privacy mechanisms. There are close connections between the privacy models and the protection mechanisms. We have outlined some of these connections.

Figure 3.5 represents the three dimensions we have studied in a graphical way. The main classification is on the dimension of whose privacy is being sought and on who applies the method. Respondent and holder privacy is considered together because methods will be applied by the data holder. In this case, we include the dimension of the type of computation (data-driven, computation-driven and result-driven), and the third dimension on the number of data sources.

Data-driven approaches are mainly used for respondent privacy. Computation-driven for single database are mainly for respondent privacy, while for multiple databases are for both respondent and holder privacy. Result-driven approaches are mainly applied to ensure holder privacy.

Within the user privacy approaches we shall distinguish two types of scenarios that will be discussed later: the protection of the identity of the user and the protection of the data generated by the user. We will discuss user privacy in Chap. 4, and will explain this distinction and show examples of privacy protection for both communications and information retrieval. Figure 3.5 already shows this distinction.

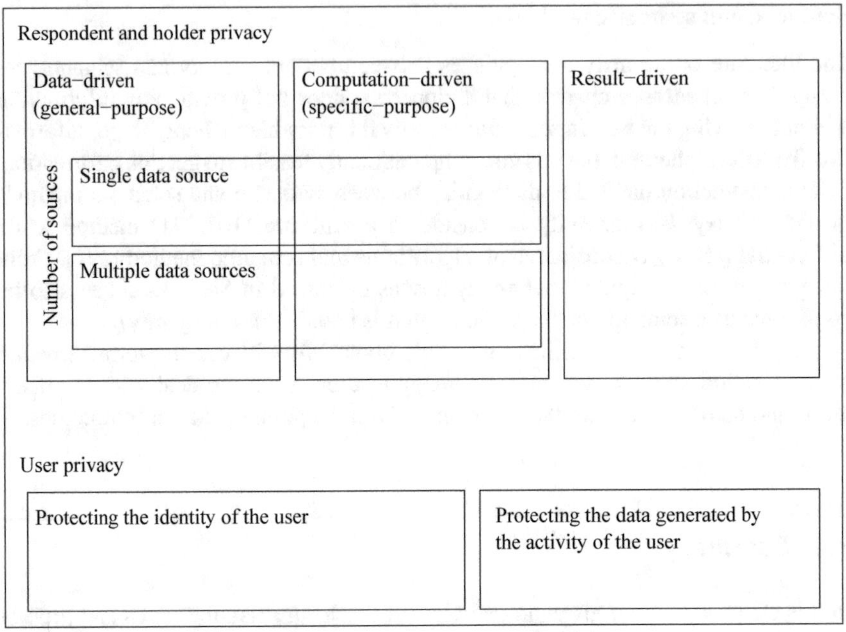

Fig. 3.5 Representation of the three dimensions of data protection methods

3.7 Bibliographical Notes

1. **Attribute disclosure.** Model-based attribute disclosure as described in Sect. 3.2.3 follows the works by Nin [224,358] were risk was evaluated for datasets using classifiers available in WEKA [217] (decision trees, naive Bayes, k-nearest neighbors, and support vector machines). The experiments show that these definitions lead to high values of attribute disclosure for the protection methods selected.
   Our description of membership inference attack follows Shokri et al. [436]. They build a classifier for each single class. They also consider the case of not knowing the structure of the training data of model m. They provide an approach to generate data statistically similar to target's training data. These data is needed to train the shallow models.
2. **Identity disclosure and uniqueness.** Uniqueness as a way to evaluate identity disclosure was studied by Elliot et al. [169,170].
3. **Identity disclosure and re-identification: privacy from re-identification.** The use of re-identification algorithms, and more particularly record linkage for identity disclosure goes back, at least, to Spruill [442] and Paass [371] (using e.g. the algorithm described in Paass and Wauschkuhn [372]) in early 1980s. This scenario with a database to attack a protected file is also mentioned by Sweeney [463]. We have also used this approach extensively [486]. The importance of a correct assessment of re-identification risk is advocated by Cavoukian

and El Emam [86]. They underline the fact that re-identification is not always an easy task.

Re-identification has also been applied to assess risk for partially synthetic data [486,526]. For example, there is a disclosure risk analysis [486] for the family of methods IPSO-A, IPSO-B, and IPSO-C based on record-linkage.

Disclosure risk assessment when files do not share attributes appear in our work at Statistics and Computing [149], and it is based on a previous work [474] used to establish relationships between attributes.

4. **Record-linkage.** The two main record-linkage algorithms are distance-based and probabilistic ones. They are described in Appendix A. The literature presents some other algorithms. For example, Bacher et al. [33] presents a method based on cluster analysis. This is similar to distance-based record linkage, as cluster analysis assigns objects (in this case, records) that are similar (in this case, near) to each other, to the same cluster.

   There are variations of record linkage that take into account the transparency principle (see Sect. 1.4.8), and permit us to implement transparency attacks. These algorithms take advantage of any information available about the data protection procedure. To do so, protection procedures are analyzed in detail to find flaws that can be used for developing more effective, i.e. with larger matching rates, record linkage algorithms. We developed record linkage algorithms to attack microaggregation [356,361,490] (for either univariate and multivariate microaggregation), and rank swapping [354]. This latter algorithm is discussed in Sect. 6.1.1.

5. k-**Anonymity.** This concept was coined by Samarati and is described in seminal papers by Samarati and Sweeney [419,420,462,463]. The concept of k-map appears in Sweeney's PhD Dissertation [461,547]. This concept relates to p-sets, introduced by Dalenius in 1986 [111], which are unique combinations of values (i.e., quasi-identifiers as termed later in the k-anonymity framework).

   Truta et al. [502–504] proposed p-sensitive k-anonymity. They also provided some extensions of this privacy model and algorithms for building compliant datasets. In relation to the other two variations of k-anonymity discussed in this chapter, l-Diversity was introduced by Machanavajjhala et al. [309], and t-closeness by Li et al. [288].

   Our definition of k-confusion follows Stokes and Farràs [450], and the one of k-concealment follows Gionis, Mazza, and Gionis [202,466].

   Computational anonymity was introduced by Stokes [446]. The first definition of (k, l)-anonymity was given [453] in the context of data privacy for graphs.

   The *real anonymity measure* was introduced by Nin et al. [355]. As we have seen in this chapter, it is closely related to k-anonymity.

6. **Differential privacy.** Dwork proposed differential privacy in 2006 [161,162]. Some additional bibliographical notes on differential privacy are given in Chap. 5.

   First definitions of local differential privacy appear in Evfimievski et al. [181] and Kasiviswanathan et al. [256].

7. **Integral privacy.** Integral privacy was introduced [494] with the goal of achieving privacy when database change, and later redefined [495] for a single database and a single computation.

8. **Homomorphic encryption.** There are a few references that describe homomorphic encryption and algorithms to achieve it. See e.g. Yi et al. (2014) [537] where e.g. ElGamal cryptosystem is described.

9. **Secure multiparty computation.** This privacy model was introduced by Yao in 1982 [536]. We provide additional notes on secure multiparty computation in Chap. 5. Secure aggregation is used as an alternative to secure multiparty computation (SMC) in federated learning contexts. The privacy guarantees are lower than SMC but easier to implement in real problems. Pejo et al. [381] discuss the differences of the two approaches in the context of an application on drug discovery.

10. **Result privacy.** Our definition for result privacy is based on Abul [9]. The literature uses different terms to denote result privacy. There are at least the following ones: anonymity preserving pattern discovery [30], result privacy [48], output secrecy [220], and knowledge hiding [9].

11. **Classification of privacy mechanisms.** The dimensions related to whose privacy is being sought was first discussed by Domingo-Ferrer [135].

12. **Knowledge intensive data privacy.** The need to consider knowledge in protection and risk assessment was argued in a work of us [479]. First use of ontologies and dictionaries in data protection, risk assessment, and utility evaluation appears in the works of Batet, Erola and others [43, 175, 316, 410].

    The anonymization and sanitization of documents has been considered for different types of document representation. For example, as full documents [4, 27] and as summaries represented by vectors [3]. In the former case, entity recognition tools are used to identify sensitive information as names and places. Representation of documents in terms of vectors of words permit us to apply the privacy models described in this chapter, and then apply more standard data protection mechanisms (as e.g., k-anonymity) taking advantage of semantics between terms. Lison et al. [298] review data protection methods for documents. Pilan et al. [384] present a benchmark for document anonymization. This area of research is of strong interest for medical texts, so, most applications deal with this type of documents.

13. **Other dimensions.** Semantic privacy is discussed by Clifton and Tassa [103], and Liu et al. [301].

14. **Other disclosure risk measures.** We have presented in this chapter several disclosure risk measures, they are not the only ones in the literature. See e.g. the use of mutual information [35] and statistical dependence [340] (defined as $\theta = 1 - \rho^2$). We can classify these measures as for assessment of attribute disclosure. Note the thin line between risk assessment and information loss when using these type of measures.

Privacy for Users

4

Abstract

User's privacy provides tools to users to help them to protect the information that is sensitive. In this chapter we consider tools for privacy in communications and for privacy in information retrieval. For each scenario, we consider protecting the identity of the user and protecting their data. We describe concepts as anonymity systems (e.g. Tor) and private information retrieval.

> Farfar, får får får?
> Nej, får får inte får,
> får får vattenäpple.
>
> Privacy-preserving Swedish proverb.

In this chapter we review technologies that help people to ensure their own privacy. We have defined in Sect. 3.5.1, user's privacy in terms of people having an active role in protecting their own data. This is the case of Claudia and Berta in Examples 3.6 and 3.8. In this chapter we review a few tools that help users with this purpose.

Methods for user's privacy can be classified in two main classes according to their objective. We have

- methods that protect the identity of the user, and
- methods that protect the data of the user.

This distinction is clear in the case of Claudia (Example 3.6) sending queries to the search engine. The first objective is fulfilled when the search engine receives Claudia's query but is not able to link this query to Claudia. The second objective is fulfilled if Claudia is able to get the information she needs from the search engine without disclosing her interests to the search engine.

In contrast, in Example 3.8, Berta mainly focuses on protecting her identity. The ultimate goal is that the government is unable to link the message to her. Nothing is required about the privacy of the content of the message.

We will consider methods for user's privacy in two scenarios that roughly correspon to the two examples discussed above.

First, we will consider user's privacy in communications. In this case, when a user A sends a message m to B, we may want to hide who is the sender (or the recipient) of the message, or we may want to hide the content of the message. This corresponds to Example 3.8.

Secondly, we will consider user's privacy in information retrieval. In this case, we may want to hide who is sending the query or hide the query itself. This corresponds to Example 3.6.

The chapter finishes with a brief section considering other related types of problems, all providing solutions for user's privacy.

4.1 User's Privacy in Communications

This section is divided in two parts following our discussion above. First, we focus on the tools to avoid the disclosure of the identity of a user. They are tools for user anonymity. Then, we focus on tools to protect the data of the user and, more specifically, to ensure unobservability.

4.1.1 Protecting the Identity of the User

Approaches for anonymous communications can be classified in two main classes as follows.

- **High-latency anonymity systems.** They correspond to applications in which interaction is not needed. This is the case of email. Anonymous systems of this class include mix networks.
- **Low-latency anonymity systems.** In this case interaction is needed, and we need response in real-time. Web browsing is the most typical application. Anonymous systems of this class include onion routing and crowds.

We present these systems below.

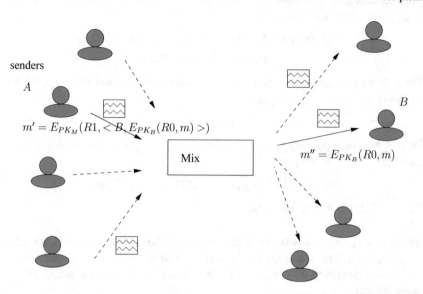

Fig. 4.1 Illustration of A sending a message m to the mix as $m'=E_{PK_M}(R1, <B, E_{PK_B}(R0,m)>)$ and the mix sending the corresponding message to the addressee: $m'' = E_{PK_B}(R0, m)$

4.1.1.1   High-Latency Anonymity Systems

Mix networks were introduced to unlink the sender and the recipient of a message. They are appropriate in scenarios with high-latency. The sender and the recipient of a message are unlinked when a server (a *mix*) receives and sends messages from different senders to different recipients after shuffling them. Messages are encrypted to avoid disclosure on which are their senders and recipients.

The network works using a protocol based on public-key cryptography. We will use $E_K(m)$ to denote the encryption using the key K of the message m, and D_K to denote the decryption mechanism using key K. The whole process of sending a message using a mix is described below. Figure 4.1 illustrates this process. Each user B has a public key PK_B and a private key SK_B, and the mix has a public key PK_M and a private key SK_M.

- **Step 1. Message preparation.** A sender wants to send a message m to recipient B. Using the public key PK_M of the mix and the public key PK_B of B, the sender constructs the following message:

$$m' = E_{PK_M}(R1, < B, E_{PK_B}(R0, m) >)$$

where $R0$ and $R1$ are random strings, B denotes the address of the recipient, (a, b) denotes the message with the string a concatenated with b, and $< a, b >$ denotes a message with the pair a and b.

- **Step 2. Message transmission.** The message m' is sent to the mix. The mix decrypts m' using its private key.

$$m^* = D_{SK_M}(m') = D_{SK_M}(E_{PK_M}(R1, < B, E_{PK_B}(R0, m) >))$$
$$= (R1, < B, E_{PK_B}(R0, m) >)$$

Then, the mix discards the random string $R1$, and sends the message $E_{PK_B}(R0, m)$ to B. Let m'' denote this message.

$$m'' = E_{PK_B}(R0, m)$$

- **Step 3. Message reception.** The recipient B uses his private key to decrypt the message. That is, it computes:

$$D_{SK_B}(m'') = D_{SK_B}(E_{PK_B}(R0, m)) = (R0, m).$$

Then, it discards the random string $R0$ to find m.

In this description we have considered a single mix, but a series of them (a cascade) can also be used. The advantage of a cascade is that all mixes have to collaborate to break the anonymity. In other words, a single non-compromised mix is able to provide secrecy.

We do not give here any explanation on when the messages are sent from the mix to the recipient or, in general, to other mixes. How and when messages are fired by a mix is defined by flushing algorithms. Methods can flush every t_s seconds, or when t_m messages are accumulated in the mix. Note that if the mix applies a first-in first-out approach for sending the messages it may be possible for an intruder to link senders and recipients.

There have been other systems as anon.penet.fi (in Finland, from 1993–1996, a centralized remailer system), and Cypherpunk and Mixminion [550] remailers (distributed remailer systems based on mix networks). Mixminion is the most sophisticated remailer among these ones permitting e.g. recipients to reply the sender without including sender's address in the body of the message.

4.1.1.2 Low-Latency Anonymity Systems

Low-latency anonymity systems have been developed for real-time applications when it is not appropriate to have delays in the reception of the request by the recipient. Recall that flushing algorithms in mixes delay transmissions. In this section we review crowds and onion routing, two of the existing low-latency systems.

Crowds. Crowds were introduced to achieve anonymity of web transactions. A crowd is defined as a collection of users. Then, when a user needs to transmit a transaction, it is either submitted directly or passed to another member of the crowd. Anonymity comes from the fact that users send some of their transactions but also transactions from other members of the crowd.

The process is described below. A graphical representation of the path followed by a request through a crowd is given in Fig. 4.2.

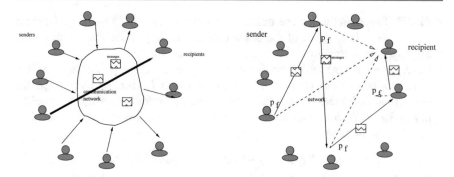

Fig. 4.2 Graphical representation of a crowd system. In the left the standard case of sending the request directly to the recipient. In the right, the request is processed by the crowd. Each process (jondo) forwards the request to another jondo with probability p_f and to the final recipient with probability $1 - p_f$. Solid lines represent actually used communication channels, dotted lines not used communication channels

- **Step 1. Start.** The user starts the local process (this process is known as jondo), that will represent him in the crowd.
- **Step 2. Admission request.** The jondo contacts a server called the blender to request admitance in the crowd.
- **Step 3. Admission.** The blender admits the jondo and sends him the information needed to participate in the crowd.
- **Step 4. Proxy selection.** The user selects this jondo just created as the web proxy for all services.
- **Step 5. Browser's request.** Any request from the browser, is sent to the jondo.
- **Step 6. Processing.** When a jondo receives a request, it submits the request to the end server (the final destination of the request) with probability $1 - p_f$. Otherwise, with probability p_f, it forwards the request to another jondo. In this latter case, the receiver jondo is selected at random among possible ones. Note that this step is applied either for requests sent to the jondo by the browser, or sent to the jondo by other jondos.

Onion routing. This is an approach for real-time and application independent anonymous communication. Both data and communication is made anonymous. Tor [133,563] is a current implementation of onion routing, although its actual mechanism is more sophisticated than the one described here (using e.g. Diffie-Hellman key exchange).

The communication process follows the steps described below.

- **Step 1. Retrieval of known routers.** The user accesses a directory server that provides known routers and their current state.
- **Step 2. Construction of the path.** The list of routers is used to define a path. That is, an ordered list of at least three routers that will be traversed by the message.

- **Step 3. Construction of the onion.** A data structure, called onion, is built for the message. Each layer of the onion defines one hop in the route. Public-key cryptography is used to ensure privacy on the data structure.

  Let $E_{PK}(m)$ denote the encryption of message m using the public key PK. Let $< i, m >$ denote that we send message m to router i. Then, let us consider the message m to be sent through the path traversing nodes 3, 5, and 6 with public keys PK_3, PK_5, and PK_6, respectively. The onion for this message, denoted by o, will be something like:

$$o = E_{PK_3}(< 5, E_{PK_5}(< 6, E_{PK_6}(m) >) >).$$

  This message is to be sent to node 3 first, then node 5, and finally node 6.

- **Step 4. Message passing.** The message is passed to the entry funnel, an onion router with a longstanding connection. The router peels off its layer, identifies the next hop, and sends the embedded onion to this onion router.

  Peeling off the layer consists of applying D_{SK}, the decryption mechanism, to the message. Here SK is the private key of the router.

  In the case above, router 3 is the entry funnel. This router applies D_{SK_3} to the onion o obtaining:

$$D_{SK_3}(o) = D_{SK_3}(E_{PK_3}(< 5, E_{PK_5}(< 6, E_{PK_6}(m) >) >))$$
$$= < 5, E_{PK_5}(< 6, E_{PK_6}(m) >)>.$$

  Then, the onion $o' = E_{PK_5}(< 6, E_{PK_6}(m) >)$ is passed to router 5.

- **Step 5. Message forwarding.** The same approach is applied subsequently by the other routers in the path.

  In this example, router 5 decrypts the message. Then, peels off the onion, identifies the next hop, and sends the embedded onion to 6. That is, node 5 obtains $< 6, E_{PK_6}(m) >$ and forwards $o'' = E_{PK_6}(m)$ to router 6.

- **Step 6. Message delivery.** Once the message arrives to the last router in the path, this router (known as the exit funnel) using the information in m delivers the message to the appropriate address.

- **Step 7. Reply.** The process is reversed for data moving back to the original sender. In this case, each router encrypts the data using the private keys. The recipient (the individual that initiated the communication) will decrypt the message using the original path and the public keys of the routers in the path.

  Following with the example above, the following answer will be received by the original sender:

$$m' = E_{SK_3}(E_{SK_5}(E_{SK_6}(answer))).$$

Applying the decryption mechanism to the message received in the appropriate order, we retrieve the answer:

$$answer = D_{PK_6}(D_{PK_5}(D_{PK_3}(E_{SK_3}(E_{SK_5}(E_{SK_6}(answer)))))).$$

There are some similarities between onion routing and mixes, and more specifically with a cascade of mixes. Reed et al. [397] discuss that one of the differences between onion routing and mixes is that the routers of the former "are more limited in the extent to which they delay traffic at each node". Another difference is that in onion routing, all routers are entry points, and traffic entering or exiting the nodes may not be visible.

4.1.2   Protecting the Data of the User

If the only goal is to provide protection for data in communication, we can use cryptographic tools. A sender can use the public key of the recipient so that only the recipient can decrypt it with the corresponding private key. Recall that public-key cryptography was discussed in Sect. 2.5.2. Similarly, secure multiparty computation protocols can be used to protect the data of users when their data is used to compute a function, and these data are not to be shared. Protocols for secure multiparty computation are discussed in Sect. 5.2.

There are occasions that the data themselves is not the only thing to be protected but also the fact of these data being transmitted. Recall from Sect. 1.4.6 that undetectability is when intruders can not distinguish that the transmission takes place, and unobservability is when there is anonymity on top of undetectability (for those intruders aware of the transmission). An approach to achieve unobservability is dummy traffic. When communication is encrypted, users can send fake data (but indistinguishable from real encrypted data) at appropriate times to confuse intruders and avoid traffic analysis (e.g. to avoid the disclosure of when and to whom data is sent). Some approaches based on secure multiparty computation can also provide unobservability. For example, the problem of the dining cryptographers (see Example 5.1). There, all cryptographers communicate a bit of information, and this communication is independent of whether the bit is one or zero (i.e., whether they have paid the bill or not).

4.2   User's Privacy in Information Retrieval

Information retrieval is about querying a database to get some information. In this setting we can also consider the two cases of protection we have discussed for communications. That is, first, when the user wants to hide her identity and, second, when the user wants to hide her query. We will elaborate on the tools for these two situations.

4.2.1   Protecting the Identity of the User

Anonymous database search, also known as user-private information retrieval [136], is the area that studies how to ensure that the database receives the query without knowing who is the sender of the query.

This problem can be addressed using techniques similar to onion routing and crowds (discussed in Sect. 4.1.1.2). That is, when a user needs to post a query, its software agent posts it in the peer-to-peer (P2P) community, and after a sequence of forwards, another agent (representing another user) forwards the query to the database. When this other agent receives the answer to the query, it forwards it to the interested user.

Queries posted in the P2P community are encrypted so that only members can read them. Different communication spaces can be used. Each communication space is a set of agents/users and the cryptographic key they share. At any point of time, we have in the communication space a set of messages waiting to be processed.

Algorithm 13 describes the procedure that agents need to follow. This is an infinite loop while the agent is active. At each iteration the agent (called ag to make it explicit) selects a communication space and decrypts its content obtaining a queue of messages $M = (M_i)$. Then, each message M_i is processed, and a new set of messages are encrypted and posted to the communication space.

This algorithm should be repeated with frequency f. This frequency does not need to be the same for all users, but it should be higher or equal to the highest query submission frequency among the users. When all communication spaces have the same number of users (k) and all users are in the same number of communication spaces (r), the probability x of self-submission should be fixed to

$$x = 1/(r(k-1) + 1).$$

The use of several communication spaces decrease the risk of compromising keys and at the same time it implies that not all users can see the queries in plain text. Combinatorial configurations [136, 447, 448] can be used to find the optimal way to organize users and communication spaces.

4.2.2   Protecting the Query of the User

The most secure approaches (in terms of the privacy level achieved) to protect the queries of a user are studied in the area of Private Information Retrieval (PIR). In PIR, the database or search engine knows who the user is but learn nothing about the queries of the user. PIR methods, which are based on cryptographic protocols, are explained in Sect. 4.2.3. These methods require the database to collaborate with the users and run appropriate protocols.

There is a family of methods that do not require the collaboration of the database. Their goal is to avoid the re-identification of the user. Some methods are based on applying some perturbation to the data that makes re-identification difficult in line with additive noise in numerical data. Others disassociate queries. These latter ones, exploiting the fact that not all queries are sensitive, increase the size of the anonymity sets.

Algorithm 13: Anonymous database search for each user's agent ag: P2P UPIR 2 protocol.

Data: ag: represents user's agent
1 **begin**
2   **while** *active* **do**
3   l := Select uniformly at random a communication space l of which ag is member
4   M := Decrypt the content on l using the corresponding cryptographic key
5   **foreach** $M_i \in M$ **do**
6   **if** M_i *is a query addressed to* ag **then**
7   M_i is removed from the queue and forwarded to the server. The answer A from the server is encrypted and added at the end of the queue
8   **else**
9   **if** M_i *is an answer to a query belonging to* ag **then**
10   M_i is read and removed from the queue
11   **else**
12   M_i is left on the queue without action
13   **end**
14   **end**
15   **end**
16   **if** ag *has a query* Q **then**
17   With probability x, we define $ag' = ag$; and with probability $1 - x$ the user selects uniformly at random another user $ag' \neq ag$ on l
18   ag addresses Q to ag' and writes Q to the end of the queue
19   **end**
20   **end**
21 **end**

4.2.2.1   Noise Addition for Queries

TrackMeNot [232] and GooPIR [142] are two user's agents implemented as plug-ins in a browser to avoid that a search engine knows with certainty about the interests of a user. The agents send fake queries to the search engine, in addition to the true queries sent by the user. The goal is that the search engine does not distinguish between the real queries and the fake ones. In this way, any profile the search engine builds from the user will be noisy, and, thus, it make re-identification difficult.

TrackMeNot [232] harvests query-like phrases from the web and sends them to the search engine. Queries are constructed using a set of RSS feeds from popular web sites as e.g. the New York Times, CNN, and Slashdot and a list of popular queries gathered from publicly available lists. The reply of the search engine is used for *refining* the query and submitting a new one. The approach implemented causes that each system evolves differently, due to different selections of terms from RSS feeds, terms selected from the search engine response, and the information returned by the search engine (that also evolves with time). In order to mimic user's behavior some links are clicked (selection is done in such a way to avoid revenues to the search engine) and queries are sent in batch similar to what users do.

GooPIR [142] follows a different strategy. While TrackMeNot builds fake queries, GooPIR adds fake terms to the real user queries. It uses a thesaurus to select a number of keywords with frequencies similar to the ones on the query, and then adds the selected keywords with OR to the real query. Then, the query is submitted to the search engine, and, finally, the results given by the search engine are filtered.

Peddinti and Saxena [379] evaluated the effectiveness of TrackMeNot in terms of the privacy level they achieve. To assess privacy, they considered an adversarial search engine that uses users' search histories to determine which queries are generated by TrackMeNot and which are the real queries. Classification is based on machine learning techniques. The experiments, performed using 60 users from the AOL search logs, achieve a 48.88% average accuracy for identifying user queries (predicted as user queries over real user queries), and a 0.02% of incorrectly classified fake queries (incorrectly predicted as belonging to TrackMeNot over the real TrackMeNot queries). The difference of identification between users was large: the range was between 10% and 100%.

4.2.2.2 DisPA: the Dissociating Privacy Agent

DisPA [251,252], which stands for Dissociating Privacy Agent, is an agent implemented as a proxy between the user and the search engine. The goal is to protect the queries of the user, but at the same time permit certain level of profiling by the search engine. In this way, there are privacy guarantees but also personalization on the results delivered by the search engine.

From the point of view of privacy, DisPA is based on the idea that what makes people unique are their set of interests (recall the discussion in Sect. 1.5 that individuals are multifaceted). That is, every person has a set of interests that considered in isolation are usually not enough to identify this person but all together permit the reidentification. In other words, for each interest, the anonymity set is usually large. It is the intersection of these interests what makes the person unique and makes the anonymity set small, if not a singleton.

Similarly, queries considered in isolation do not cause reidentification, but the intersection of them is what can make them linkable to the individual.[1] Based on these principles, DisPA *dissociates* the user identity into different virtual identities, each one with a particular interest. Then, each query is classified into one of these interests, and assigned to the corresponding virtual identity. Then, the query is submitted to the agent by this virtual identity, and the result of the query is received by this virtual identity, and then forwarded to the user. Figure 4.3 represents this process.

For example, if a user is interested in football and piano music. The agent will dissociate these queries and assign one virtual identity to football and another one to piano. Then, each query related to football will be submitted to the database by the corresponding virtual identity. Similarly, the other identity will be used to submit the other queries related to piano. In order to classify queries to the appropriate virtual

---

[1] Note the parallelism with social spheres [51,362] and the privacy problems in online social networks when these spheres are put in contact.

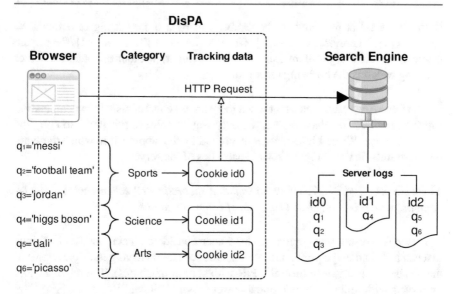

Fig. 4.3 DisPA architecture from [253]

identity, DisPA implements a classifier that uses the taxonomy in the Open Directory Project [561].

It is well known that the use of proper names in queries helps much in any attack. Because of that the DisPA agent implements a filter to detect entities like locations and personal names, unique identifiers and emails. Queries containing these entities are processed by a newly created virtual identity.

As stated above, the dissociation permits the user to have some level of privacy. The more virtual identities, the best privacy level achieved. Personalization is expected to rely on the queries. This means that the more virtual identities, the less personalization. Nevertheless, the search engine will give some personalization to each virtual identity (i.e., personalization for our football queries and for our piano queries). This personalization may be enough for most queries where the different virtual identities do not collide. An example of collision is a query on the Piano scores of F. C. Barcelona.

Virtual identities are processed by DisPA on the assumption that the search engine only uses cookies to identify the users. Additional tools to avoid e.g. device fingerprinting are not currently implemented. Recall that device fingerprinting [12, 166] is an easy path to reidentification.

4.2.3 Private Information Retrieval

Private Information Retrieval (PIR) studies how a user can retrieve an object from a database (or a search engine) in such a way that the database server is not aware of the object being retrieved. This problem can be formalized as follows.

Definition 4.1 Let the database be represented by a binary string of n bits $x = x_0, \ldots, x_{n-1}$. Therefore, $x_i \in \{0, 1\}$. Given a value $i \in \{0, \ldots, n-1\}$, the private information retrieval problem consists of retrieving x_i without the database server knowing which is the bit being retrieved.

The following result states that when there are no constraints on the computation capabilities of the database server, the only way to achieve privacy is to copy the whole database. We call information theoretic PIR this approach in which there are no constraints on the computational capabilities of the server.

Theorem 4.1 *[96,97,272] Any information theoretic PIR scheme with a single-database with n bits requires $\Omega(n)$ bits of communications.*

Due to this result, two approaches have been considered that relax the conditions that can be found in the previous theorem. One focuses on having multiple copies of the database (information theoretic PIR with several databases). The other focuses on servers with limited computational power (computational PIR).

We give examples of privacy mechanisms satisfying information-theoretic PIR in Sect. 4.2.3.1 and of computational PIR in Sect. 4.2.3.4. The literature presents other approaches on both lines.

4.2.3.1 Information-theoretic PIR with k Databases

Let us consider the problem of accessing the bit i in a database with n bits $x_0, \ldots, x_{n-1}$ taking into account that there are k copies of this database. That is, we have k servers $SDB_1, \ldots, SDB_k$ each one with a copy of the database. In addition to the value i, the user will use a random vector of length l_{rnd}.

Then, the user will send k queries, one to each server. Each server will return an answer to the query received. Then, the user will combine the k answers into a value that is the bit x_i.

The next definition formalizes this problem.

Definition 4.2 *[97]* Let us consider the following functions to query k servers, each one with a copy of a database of length n.

- k query functions $Q_1, \ldots, Q_k : \{0, \ldots, n-1\} \times \{0, 1\}^{l_{rnd}} \rightarrow \{0, 1\}^{l_q}$,
- k answer functions $A_1, \ldots, A_k : \{0, 1\}^n \times \{0, 1\}^{l_q} \rightarrow \{0, 1\}^{l_a}$, and
- a reconstruction function $R : \{0, \ldots, n-1\} \times \{0, 1\}^{l_{rnd}} \times (\{0, 1\}^{l_a})^k \rightarrow \{0, 1\}$.

Observe that the query functions build a vector of l_q bits given the ith bit and the random vector of length l_{rnd}. The servers are expected to answer according to $A_1, \ldots, A_k$. That is, they return l_a bits given their database of n bits and a query of l_q bits. Finally, the reconstruction function returns the desired bit using all k vectors of l_a bits, the original random vector of l_{rnd} bits, and the original query bit.

This construction is a theoretic private information retrieval (PIR) scheme for the database of length n if the functions satisfy the following two properties.

- **Correctness.** For every $x \in \{0, 1\}^n$, $i \in \{0, \ldots, n - 1\}$, and $r \in \{0, 1\}^{l_{rnd}}$

$$R(i, r, A_1(x, Q_1(i, r)), \ldots, A_k(x, Q_k(i, r))) = x_i.$$

- **Privacy.** For every $i, j \in \{0, \ldots, n - 1\}$, $s \in \{1, \ldots, k\}$, and $q \in \{0, 1\}^{l_q}$,

$$Pr(Q_s(i, r) = q) = Pr(Q_s(j, r) = q)$$

where the probabilities are taken over uniformly chosen $r \in \{0, 1\}^{l_{rnd}}$.

Correctness means that all works fine and we recover the desired bit, and privacy means that the probability is independent of the bit we query.

We will describe below two schemes that are theoretic private PIR. The first one is for $k = 2$ and the other for $k \geq 2$.

4.2.3.2 Information-theoretic PIR with $k = 2$ Databases

Let $k = 2$ and let SDB_1 and SDB_2 denote the two database servers. Let $i \in \{0, \ldots, n - 1\}$ be the index of the bit the user is interested in. Then, the scheme is as follows.

- **Step 1.** The user selects a random set $S \subset \{0, \ldots, n - 1\}$ where each index $j \in \{0, \ldots, n - 1\}$ is selected with probability $1/2$.
- **Step 2.** The user sends $Q_1 = S$ to server SDB_1 and $Q_2 = S \boxplus i$ to server SDB_2 where $S \boxplus i$ is defined as

$$S \boxplus i = \begin{cases} S \cup \{i\} & \text{if } i \notin S \\ S \setminus \{i\} & \text{if } i \in S \end{cases} \tag{4.1}$$

That is, $Q_1 = b_0^1 \ldots b_{n-1}^1$ where $b_i^1 = 1$ if and only if $i \in S$ and $Q_2 = b_0^2 \ldots b_{n-1}^2$ where $b_i^2 = 1$ if and only if $i \in S \boxplus i$.
- **Step 3.** The server SDB_1 sends an exclusive-or of the bits in S and the server SDB_2 sends an exclusive or of the bits in $S \boxplus i$. That is,

$$A_1 = \bigoplus_{j \in S} x_j \tag{4.2}$$

$$A_2 = \bigoplus_{j \in S \boxplus i} x_j. \tag{4.3}$$

- **Step 4.** The user computes the exclusive or of the bits received. That is,

$$R = A_1 \oplus A_2.$$

We can prove the correctness of the procedure observing that R results into x_i. Note that the following holds. We use the property that the xor of x_j with x_j is always zero (i.e., $x_j \oplus x_j = 0$).

$$R = A_1 \oplus A_2 = \bigoplus_{j \in S} x_j \bigoplus_{j \in S \boxplus i} x_j = \bigoplus_{j \in S \setminus \{i\}} (x_j \oplus x_j) \oplus x_i = x_i.$$

In addition, the servers do not get any information about the index desired by the user. I.e., the privacy condition above is satisfied. This is so because each server receives a uniformly distributed subset of $\{0, \ldots, n-1\}$.

As a final remark note that this solution requires the servers to send a single bit (i.e., $l_a = 1$). Note, however, that the number of bits sent by the user has length n.

4.2.3.3 Information-theoretic PIR with $k \geq 2$ Databases

The second scheme is also for calculating the bit i in $\{0, \ldots, n-1\}$ from a set of k servers. The database is denoted by $x_0, \ldots, x_{n-1}$ as above. The scheme is valid for $k \geq 2$ when k can be expressed as 2^d for a given $d \geq 1$. Here we also assume that $n = l^d$ for a given l.

In order to provide the protocol we need first to embed the database x in a d-dimensional cube. This is done associating each $j \in \{0, \ldots, n-1\}$ a tuple $(j_0, \ldots, j_{d-1}) \in [0, \ldots, l-1]^d$. This transformation is $\phi(j) = (j_0, \ldots, j_{d-1})$.

For example, let us consider $n = 64$, then we need to represent $j \in \{0, \ldots, 63\}$. Let us consider the embedding of this database in the 2-dimensional cube (square) with $d = 2$ and $l = 8$. Then, we can use the representation where $j_0, \ldots, j_{d-1}$ corresponds to j in base l. That is, 0 is represented by $(0, 0)$, 1 is represented by $(1, 0)$, 2 by $(2, 0)$, \ldots, l by $(1, 1)$, $l+1$ is $(2, 1)$ and so on until 63 that is represented by $(7, 7)$. Then the inverse $\phi^{-1}(j_0, \ldots, j_{d-1})$ corresponds to:

$$j = \sum_{i=0}^{d-1} j_i l^i. \tag{4.4}$$

Then, we make a one-to-one correspondence between the $k = 2^d$ servers and the string in $\{0, 1\}^d$.

- **Step 1.** The user calculates $(i_0, \ldots, i_{d-1}) = \phi(i)$ for the given i.
- **Step 2.** The user chooses uniformly and independently d random subsets

$$S_0^0, S_1^0, \ldots, S_{d-1}^0 \subseteq \{0, \ldots, l-1\}.$$

- **Step 3.** The user computes $S_i^1 = S_i^0 \boxplus i_i$ for $i = 0, \ldots, d-1$. Recall that $S \boxplus i$ is defined in Eq. 4.1 and represents either a union or a removal of the element i.
- **Step 4.** There are $k = 2^d$ servers with names $\{0, 1\}^d$. The user sends a query to each server. Let us consider the server named $\alpha = (\alpha_0, \ldots, \alpha_{d-1})$. Note that α_i is either zero or one. The user sends to this server SDB_α the subsets

$$S_0^{\alpha_0}, S_1^{\alpha_1}, \ldots, S_{d-1}^{\alpha_{d-1}}.$$

The number of bits sent to each server are, thus, $d \cdot n^{1/d}$ because each $S_0^{\alpha_0}, \ldots, S_{d-1}^{\alpha_{d-1}}$ has length l and we have defined $n = l^d$. Thus, $l = n^{1/d}$.

- **Step 5.** The product of the sets $S_0^{\alpha_0}, S_1^{\alpha_1}, \ldots, S_{d-1}^{\alpha_{d-1}}$ define a subcube of the d-dimensional cube associated to x.

  Each server SDB_α returns to the user the exclusive-or of the bits in the subcube queried. That is,

$$A_\alpha = \bigoplus_{j_0 \in S_0^{\alpha_0}, \ldots, j_{d-1} \in S_{d-1}^{\alpha_{d-1}}} x_{j_0, \ldots, j_{d-1}},$$

  or, equivalently

$$A_\alpha = \bigoplus_{(j_0, \ldots, j_0) \in S_0^{\alpha_0} \times \cdots \times S_{d-1}^{\alpha_{d-1}}} x_{j_0, \ldots, j_{d-1}}. \tag{4.5}$$

- **Step 6.** The user receives one bit from each server and computes the exclusive-or of these bits. There are $k = 2^d$ bits to combine. That is:

$$R = \oplus_\alpha A_\alpha.$$

The correctness and privacy of this approach was proven by Chor et al. [97]. The number of bits sent in the protocol is

$$k \cdot (d \cdot l + 1) = 2^d (d \cdot n^{1/d} + 1).$$

Note that the user sends $d \cdot n^{1/d}$ bits to each server and receives only one from them. There are 2^d servers. A more balanced scheme was also presented by Chor et al. [97]. Here, a more balanced scheme means that the number of bits sent is reduced increasing the number of bits received.

Example 4.1 Let us consider a database with $n = l^d = 8^2$ bits. Thus, $d = 2$, $l = 8$. Let $k = 2^d = 4$ servers. Let us consider the function $\phi(j) = (j_0, j_1)$ and the computation of j from the pair (j_0, j_1) as given in Eq. 4.4. That is,

$$\phi^{-1}(j_0, j_1) = j_0 l^0 + j_1 l^1 = j_0 + j_1 \cdot 8.$$

Let us consider the case that we look for bit 58 in the database with values $x_0, \ldots, x_{8^2-1=63}$. In Step 1 we need to compute the pair (j_0, j_1) associated to the bit we are searching for. That is, for bit 58 we have that $(j_0, j_1) = (2, 7)$. This is the representation of 58 in base 8.

In Step 2 we choose uniformly and independently $d = 2$ random subsets. Let these subsets be $S_0^0 = \{1, 3\}$ and $S_1^0 = \{0, 1, 2, 3, 6, 7\}$. We will also represent these sets as a vector of binary bits, so,

$$S_0^0 = \{1, 3\} = (01010000) \text{ and } S_1^0 = \{0, 1, 2, 3, 6, 7\} = (1110011).$$

In Step 3 we need to compute $S_0^1 = S_0^0 \boxplus i_0$ and $S_1^1 = S_1^0 \boxplus i_1$. This results into

$$S_0^1 = S_0^0 \boxplus 2 = \{1, 3\} \cup \{2\} = (01110000)$$

and,

$$S_1^1 = S_1^0 \boxplus 7 = \{0, 1, 2, 3, 6, 7\} \setminus \{7\} = (1110010).$$

We represent the four sets S_0^0, S_0^1, S_1^0, and S_1^1 in Fig. 4.4.

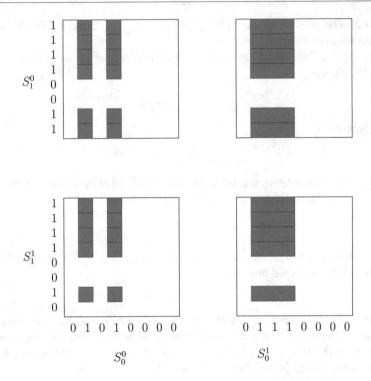

Fig. 4.4 Graphical interpretation of the proof of correctness. The xor of the four figures returns the bit $\phi(58) = (2, 7)$ in the database

Then, Step 4 corresponds to sending the appropriate pairs of sets computed in Step 3 to each server. We have $k = 2^2 = 4$ servers, which are denoted by pairs (α_0, α_1) taking the following values: $(0, 0)$, $(0, 1)$, $(1, 0)$, and $(1, 1)$. Figure 4.4 represents these four servers. Each contains a copy of the database. The databases are represented by the large squares, each with $8 \cdot 8$ cells. Then, each server receives one of the sets S_0^0, S_0^1 and one of the sets S_1^0, S_1^1. With values 0 and 1 in these sets we mark the relevant rows and columns for each server. Here, relevant refers to the bits required on the computation of Step 5.

More precisely, in Step 5 we compute for each server the exclusive-or of the bits in the subcube queried by $S_0^{\alpha_0}$ and $S_1^{\alpha_1}$. This is illustrated in the figure. The marked regions on each database correspond to the bits to be operated according to Eq. 4.5. We obtain a value A_α for each of the four servers.

Finally, the last step combines these four A_α values by means of an exclusive-or. We can see, graphically, in Fig. 4.4, that the only bit highlighted once is the bit $(2, 7)$. It appears highlighted only in the database on the right top corner of the figure. That is, the one of database $\alpha = (1, 0)$. All other bits appear either twice or four times highlighted. So, exclusive-or for all these other bits will just return zero (recall $1 \oplus 1 = 0$ and $0 \oplus 0 = 0$). So, the final combination by means of exclusive-or of all highlighted bits will be just bit $(2, 7)$.

4.2.3.4   Computational PIR

Computational Private Information Retrieval (cPIR) ensures privacy under the assumption that databases have restricted computational capabilities. More specifically, privacy is on the basis that databases are restricted to perform only polynomial-time computations. Initial results in this area were presented in [95,370]. Some methods require several copies of the databases, others can be applied with only one database. That is, replication is not needed.

In this section we present an algorithm for computational PIR without replication of the data. The scheme is based on the intractability of the quadratic residuosity problem. Let us first review this problem. We need the following definition about coprimes.

Definition 4.3 Let N be a natural number, then Z_N^* is the set of numbers defined by:
$$Z_N^* = \{x | 1 \leq x \leq N, gcd(N, x) = 1\}.$$
That is, Z_N^* is the set of numbers coprime with N.

Now, we define the quadratic residue modulo N.

Definition 4.4 An integer y is a quadratic residue modulo N if there is an integer x such that
$$x^2 \equiv y \pmod{N}.$$

We define a predicate for this problem.

Definition 4.5 The quadratic residuosity predicate is defined as follows:
$$Q_N(y) = \begin{cases} 0 \text{ if there exists a number } w \text{ in } Z_N^* \text{ such that } w^2 \equiv y \pmod{N} \\ 1 \text{ otherwise} \end{cases}$$
$$(4.6)$$

That is, $Q_N(y)$ is zero when y is the quadratic residue modulo N of a number w coprime with N. If such number w does not exist, then $Q_N(y) = 1$. In addition, we say that y is QR if it is a quadratic residue ($Q_N(y) = 0$) and that y is QNR if it is a quadratic non-residue ($Q_N(y) = 1$).

Definition 4.6 Given an integer a and an odd primer number p, the Legendre symbol is defined by:
$$\left(\frac{a}{p}\right) = \begin{cases} 0 \text{ if } a \equiv 0 \pmod{p} \\ 1 \text{ if } a \not\equiv 0 \pmod{p} \text{ and } a \text{ is a quadratic residue modulo } p \\ -1 \text{ if } a \not\equiv 0 \pmod{p} \text{ and } a \text{ is a quadratic non-residue modulo } p \end{cases}$$
$$(4.7)$$

The following properties hold for the Legendre symbol.

Proposition 4.1 *Let p be an odd prime number, let a and b be relatively prime integers. Then to p,*

- *the following equality holds*

$$\left(\frac{ab}{p}\right) = \left(\frac{a}{p}\right)\left(\frac{b}{p}\right),$$

- *and also, when $a \equiv b \pmod{p}$, the following holds*

$$\left(\frac{a}{p}\right) = \left(\frac{b}{p}\right).$$

Definition 4.7 Let a be an integer and n be a positive odd integer decomposable in terms of prime numbers $p_1, \ldots, p_k$ as follows $n = p_1^{a_1} \cdot \ldots \cdot p_k^{a_k}$. Then, the Jacobi symbol is defined as follows in terms of the Legendre symbol

$$\left(\frac{a}{n}\right) = \left(\frac{a}{p_1}\right)^{a_1} \cdot \left(\frac{a}{p_2}\right)^{a_2} \cdot \ldots \cdot \left(\frac{a}{p_k}\right)^{a_k}.$$

The Jacobi symbol generalizes the Legendre symbol as n can now be any positive odd integer, and when n is an odd prime both Jacobi and Legendre symbols are equal.

There are a few computational aspects of interest related to the computation of $Q_N(y)$ and the Legendre and Jacobi symbols.

1. Let H_k be the set of integers that are the product of two primes of length $k/2$ bits. That is,

$$H_k = \{N | N = p_1 \cdot p_2 \text{ where } p_1, p_2 \text{ are } k/2 - \text{bit primes}\}. \qquad (4.8)$$

   Then, if $N \in H_k$ and its factorization is known, the computation of $Q_N(y)$ can be done in $O(|N|^3)$. In contrast, when the factorization of N is not known, the computation of $Q_N(y)$ is intractable.
2. For all N (even for $N \in H_k$, and without knowing its factorization), the Jacobi symbol

$$\left(\frac{a}{N}\right)$$

   can be computed in polynomial time of $|N|$.
3. For all $N \in H_k$, given an integer y, the computation of the Jacobi symbol

$$\left(\frac{y}{N}\right)$$

   can either be $+1$ or -1. Let us consider these two cases,

   - if it is -1, we know that y is a quadratic non-residue. In contrast,
   - if it is $+1$, the integer y can be either quadratic residue (QR) or quadratic non-residue (QNR). Not only it can be either QR and QNR, but the sets of QR and QNR for a given N are of the same size.

We will denote the set of integers for which this value is one by Z_N^+. That is,

$$Z_N^+ = \left\{ y \in Z_N^* \mid \left(\frac{y}{N} \right) = 1 \right\}$$

4. For all x, y in Z_N^+ it holds that

$$Q_N(xy) = Q_N(x) \oplus Q_N(y),$$

where $\oplus$ denotes the exclusive or. In other words, the product of two integers is QNR if and only if one of them is QNR.

As a summary we define the quadratic residue problem and review the complexity of solving this problem.

Definition 4.8 Given integers a and N with N the product of two different primes p_1 and p_2 and such that

$$\left(\frac{a}{N} \right) = 1,$$

the quadratic residuosity problem is to determine if a is quadratic residue modulo N or not. That is, compute $Q_N(a)$.

For N in H_k and y in Z_N^+, we have that if we know the factorization of N the computation of $Q_N(y)$ is polynomial but when the factorization is not known the computation of $Q_N(y)$ is intractable.

The algorithm below for computational PIR is based on this fact. The algorithm considers a server SDB with a database. We represent the database as a matrix M (of bits) with s rows and t columns.

The goal of the algorithm is that the user retrieves the bit at the position (a, b) of a matrix M. That is, the content of row a and column b. We denote this value by $M_{a,b}$.

- **Step 1.** The user selects two random primes of $k/2$-bits each and multiplies them. Let N be the result of this multiplication. Therefore, $N \in H_k$ (where H_k as in Eq. 4.8). The user sends N to the server SDB. The factorization is kept secret.
- **Step 2.** The user chooses uniformly at random t numbers $y_1, \ldots, y_t \in Z_N^+$, one for each column. The one of column b, that is y_b, is a QNR and all the others, y_j for $j \neq b$, are QR. The user sends these t numbers to the server. Note that the total number of bits sent corresponds to $t \cdot k$.
- **Step 3.** The database server SDB computes a number z_r for each row $r = 1, \ldots, s$ of the matrix computing first a value for each column, and then multiplying them. The following two steps describe this process for row r.

Fig. 4.5 Computation of values z_a for the scheme in [272] for computational PIR

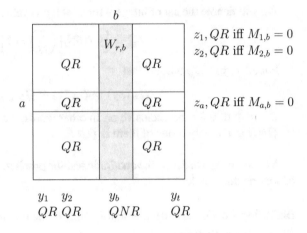

- **Step 1.** Compute $w_{r,j}$ for each column $j = 1, \ldots, t$ as follows

$$w_{r,j} = \begin{cases} y_j^2 & \text{if } M_{r,j} = 0 \\ y_j & \text{if } M_{r,j} = 1. \end{cases}$$

- **Step 2.** Compute z_r using $w_{r,j}$ as follows

$$z_r = \prod_{j=1}^{t} w_{r,j}.$$

Note that this procedure computes a value $w_{r,j}$ for each position (r, j) in the matrix M and then aggregates all the values of the rth row into z_r.

The definition of $w_{r,j}$ is such that $w_{r,j}$ is always a QR when $j \neq b$. This is so because y_j is a QR for $j \neq b$. In contrast, when $j = b$, we have that $w_{r,j}$ is QR if and only if $M_{r,j} = 0$. This is so because when $M_{r,b} = 1$ then $w_{r,b} = y_b$ which is QNR and, in contrast, when $M_{r,b} = 0$ then $w_{r,b} = y_b^2$ which is QR. Because of that, z_r is a QR if and only if $M_{r,b} = 0$ (this follows from the condition above that for x, y in Z_N^+, $Q_N(xy)$ is the exclusive or of $Q_N(x)$ and $Q_N(y)$). This computation is represented in Fig. 4.5.

- **Step 4.** The server SDB sends $z_1, \ldots, z_s$ to the user. The total number of bits sent is $s \cdot k$.
- **Step 5.** The user considers only the number z_a. Recall that a is the row of M which contains the bit the user is interested in. This number is a QR if and only if $M_{a,b} = 0$ (and QNR otherwise).

Since the user knows the factorization of the number N, it can check whether z_a is a QR. If it is QR then the user infers that $M_{a,b} = 0$, otherwise $M_{a,b} = 1$. As the server does not have the factorization of N, determining whether z_a is QR or QNR is intractable.

4.3 Other Contexts

To finish this chapter we want to mention the application of user's privacy into two other contexts: location based services and online social networks.

Gidofalvi [201] developed an approach for location based services where users ensure their privacy by swapping trajectories. It is somehow related to data swapping and because of that we mention this work again in Sect. 6.1.1. Data is expected to be processed in a centralized way, but individuals preprocess the data themselves to ensure their own privacy.

Online social networks are typically centralized. Nevertheless, there are alternative ways of building them from a decentralized perspective. These decentralized online social networks are based on P2P protocols and are constructed to provide user's privacy. See e.g. PeerSoN [64]. Datta et al. [119] give an overview of these systems. These networks need to include mechanisms so that functionalities satisfy appropriate levels of privacy (e.g. event invitations [409]).

4.4 Bibliographical Notes

1. **User's privacy in communications.** For a survey on this topic we refer the reader to the work by Edman and Yener [167]. The main systems for privacy in communications can also be found in the report by Pfitzmann and Hansen [382] (Section 8). Mix networks were introduced by Chaum [89] in 1981 to unlink the sender and the recipient of a message.
   Description of mix systems is given in the report by Serjantov [430]. This report includes a description of threat models. It also includes a discussion on flushing algorithms.
   Crowds were defined by Reiter and Rubin in 1998 [403]. Onion routing was introduced by Reed et al. [397].
2. **User's privacy in information retrieval.** Algorithm 13 is given by Stokes and Farràs [450] following Stokes and Bras [447]. There is a survey on the use of combinatorial configurations for anonymous database search [449].
3. **Information-theoretic PIR.** The solutions we provide here to achieve information-theoretic PIR with k databases were proposed by Chor et al. [97] (both $k = 2$ and $k \geq 2$ solutions).
4. **Computational PIR.** The algorithm for computational PIR was introduced by Kushilevitz and Ostrovsky [272]. The results on number theory used in Sect. 4.2.3.4 can be found in the book by Coppel [106].

Privacy for Computations, Functions, and Queries

5

Abstract

This chapter presents different protection mechanisms that apply when we know which is the function we want to compute, and we want to avoid disclosure from the outcome of this function. Different mechanisms have been developed to provide guarantees for the different privacy models that apply in these scenarios. We structure the chapter in terms of the privacy models including sections on differential privacy and secure multiparty computation.

> Aquesta mar no s'assembla gens a la nostra.
> És una llenca metàl·lica, sense transparències,
> ni colors canviants.
> C. Riera, Te deix, amor, la mar com a penyora,
> 2015, p. 11 [405]

In this chapter we will present privacy mechanisms that provide differential privacy and secure multiparty computation, the main privacy models when we know which is the function we want to compute from a database. Before deepening into the algorithms and their properties, we review some of the alternative mechanisms that exist to provide privacy in this setting.

One of them is query auditing. Following Evfimievski et al. [180], we say that query auditing "is to determine if answering a user's database query could lead to a privacy breach". Fung et al. [194] classify query auditing into the following two classes.

- **Online auditing.** Analysis is made to each query, and queries that compromise information are not served. For example, Deutsch and Papakonstantinou [130] study the case where given a new query, and a set of views from the database already released, the new query is only served when this does only supply information already released. Naturally, when a denial occurs, the denial itself gives information to the user.
- **Offline auditing.** Analysis is done once all queries are already made and served. In this case, if there is a privacy breach, it has already taken place at the time of the analysis.

Privacy with respect to queries has also been studied in relation to multilevel secure databases. They are databases in which different levels of security clearances are granted to different users. A discussion of the problems related to privacy in this type of databases is discussed by Jajodia and Meadows [243]. There are problems related to combining answers from different queries to infer sensitive information, and related to combining the data with metadata.

5.1 Differential Privacy Mechanisms

The definition of differential privacy has been provided in Sect. 3.4.6. We have seen that a mechanism satisfies ε-differential privacy when for two neighboring databases (i.e., two databases that only differ in one record) the results are similar enough. Privacy mechanisms are implemented building randomized versions of the original functions, and then similarity is defined in terms of the probability distributions. We formalized this idea in Definition 3.16, which we reproduce here for convenience as Definition 5.1. We use here q to denote the original function or query and K_q the randomized version of q.

Definition 5.1 A function K_q for a query q gives ε-differential privacy if for all data sets D_1 and D_2 differing in at most one element, and all $S \subseteq Range(K_q)$,

$$\frac{Pr[K_q(D_1) \in S]}{Pr[K_q(D_2) \in S]} \le e^{\varepsilon}.$$

Recall that $\varepsilon \ge 0$, and that with $\varepsilon = 0$, we have maximum privacy. Then, the larger the ε, the smaller our privacy requirements.

5.1.1 Differential Privacy Mechanisms for Numerical Data

For numerical functions, differential privacy is usually implemented modifying the true value with some kind of noise. That is, defining

$$K_q(D) = q(D) + some\ appropriate\ noise.$$

In order that the noise is sufficient to provide the required level of privacy, we need to know the sensitivity of the function with respect to its possible inputs. The definition of sensitivity establishes how the output of the function changes when the input changes. More specifically, it is the maximum difference between the outputs of two arbitrary neighboring databases.

Definition 5.2 [163] Let $\mathcal{D}$ denote the space of all databases; let $q : \mathcal{D} \to \mathbb{R}^d$ be a query; then, the sensitivity of q is defined by

$$\Delta_{\mathcal{D}}(f) = \max_{D,D' \in \mathcal{D}} ||q(D) - q(D')||_1.$$

where $|| \cdot ||_1$ is the L_1 norm, that is, $||(a_1, \ldots, a_d)||_1 = \sum_i |a_i|$.

The most usual approach to provide ε-differential privacy for numerical functions is by means of adding noise following a Laplace distribution on the true value. The Laplace distribution has the following distribution function:

$$f(x|\mu, b) = \frac{1}{2b} exp \left(-\frac{|x - \mu|}{b} \right)$$

where μ is the location parameter, and b is the scale parameter. This scale parameter needs to satisfy $b > 0$. Note we indistinctly use e^a and $exp(a)$, according to convenience.

Some properties of the Laplace distribution are relevant for differential privacy. First, when $b = 1$, the function for $x > 0$ corresponds to the exponential distribution scaled by $1/2$. Second, a Laplace distribution has fatter tails than the normal distribution. This means that the probability for values away from μ is larger in the Laplace distribution than the probability for the same values in the normal distribution.

Given a function q with sensitivity Δ, we can define a mechanism that provides ε-differential privacy using a Laplace distribution with mean equal to zero and parameter $b = \Delta(q)/\varepsilon$. More formally, given a database D and a query q, instead of computing $q(D)$ we compute $K_q(D) = q(D) + r$ with r following $L(0, b)$ with $b = \Delta(q)/\varepsilon$. This is formalized in Algorithm 14. This approach is often known as the Laplace mechanism.

Note that an unbounded Δ does not allow us to set b. So, in practice, the definition of sensitivity is essentially meaningful when data has upper and lower bounds. It is also easy to see that the larger the sensitivity the larger the b, and that the more privacy we require (i.e., a low value for ε), the larger the b. We will illustrate this below. Before giving examples we prove that the Laplace mechanism satisfies differential privacy.

Exercise 5.1 Plot the Laplace and Gaussian distributions for the same scale parameter b, and compare their tails.

Algorithm 14: Differential privacy for a numerical response: $LM(D, q, \epsilon)$.

Data: D: Database; q: query; ϵ: parameter of differential privacy;
Result: Answer to the query q satisfying ϵ-differential privacy
1 **begin**
2      $a := q(D)$ with the original data
3   Compute $\Delta_{\mathscr{q}}(q)$, the sensitivity of the query for a space of databases D
4   Generate a random noise r from a $L(0, b)$ where $b = \Delta(q)/\epsilon$
5   **return** $a + r$
6 **end**

The Laplace mechanism can be defined for (ε, δ)-differential privacy as well. The following proposition provides the expression for b in such case. Note that the Laplace mechanism with any b' larger than b also provides (ε, δ)-privacy.

Proposition 5.1 *Algorithm 14 replacing the expression for b given above by*

$$b = \frac{\Delta(q)}{\varepsilon - \log(1 - \delta)}$$

satisfies (ε, δ)-differential privacy, for $\Delta(q)$ being the sensitivity of function q.

The Laplace mechanism satisfies differential privacy

To prove that the mechanism described in Algorithm 14 satisfies ε-differential privacy, let us begin considering D and D' two neighboring databases. Let S be any subset $S \subseteq Range(K_q)$. Then, we have that for any $r \in S$ and $q(D)$ the Laplace mechanism associates to r the probability

$$P_{q,\Delta(q),\varepsilon}(r; D) = \frac{1}{2\Delta(q)/\varepsilon} exp\left(-\frac{|r - q(D)|}{\Delta(q)/\varepsilon}\right).$$

Similarly, for $q(D')$ it associates to r the probability

$$P_{q,\Delta(q),\varepsilon}(r; D') = \frac{1}{2\Delta(q)/\varepsilon} exp\left(-\frac{|r - q(D')|}{\Delta(q)/\varepsilon}\right).$$

Then, the ratio between these two distributions at r is as follows. We will prove that this is smaller than e^ε.

$$\frac{\frac{1}{2\Delta(q)/\varepsilon} exp\left(-\frac{|r-q(D)|}{\Delta(q)/\varepsilon}\right)}{\frac{1}{2\Delta(q)/\varepsilon} exp\left(-\frac{|r-q(D')|}{\Delta(q)/\varepsilon}\right)} = \frac{exp\left(-\frac{|r-q(D)|}{\Delta(q)/\varepsilon}\right)}{exp\left(-\frac{|r-q(D')|}{\Delta(q)/\varepsilon}\right)} = \frac{exp\left(\frac{|r-q(D')|}{\Delta(q)/\varepsilon}\right)}{exp\left(\frac{|r-q(D)|}{\Delta(q)/\varepsilon}\right)}$$

$$= exp\left(\frac{|r - q(D')| - |r - q(D)|}{\Delta(q)/\varepsilon}\right).$$

Now, we can apply the triangle inequality that establishes that $|a - b| - |b - c| \leq |a - c|$. In this way we obtain

Fig. 5.1 Output of queries $q(D) = 0$ and $q(D') = 1$ with Laplacian noise $L(0, 1)$

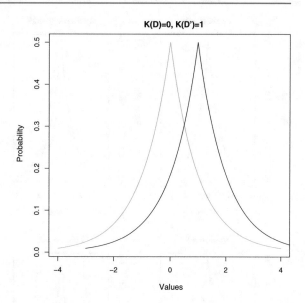

$$exp\left(\frac{|r - q(D')| - |r - q(D)|}{\Delta(q)/\varepsilon}\right) \leq exp\left(\frac{|q(D') - q(D)|}{\Delta(q)/\varepsilon}\right).$$

By definition of sensitivity we have that $|q(D') - q(D)|$ is smaller than the sensitivity. That is, $|q(D') - q(D)| \leq \Delta(q)$. Therefore, we can complete the proof as follows.

$$exp\left(\frac{|q(D') - q(D)|}{\Delta(q)/\varepsilon}\right) \leq exp\left(\frac{\Delta(q)}{\Delta(q)/\varepsilon}\right) = exp(\varepsilon).$$

The Laplace mechanism described above considers that $q(D)$ returns a value in $\mathbb{R}$. If $q(D)$ returns values in $\mathbb{R}^n$, we can define a Laplace mechanism that provides n random values, one for each dimension, and then we can prove that the mechanism satisfies differential privacy in a similar way.

Understanding the Laplacian noise and the ϵ-inequality

Let us first consider a simple query assuming that we have two neighboring databases D and D' for which $q(D) = 0$ and $q(D') = 1$, and let us consider that we use a Laplacian noise with $b = 1$. Figure 5.1 illustrates the probability distributions under these assumptions. That is, for $K_q(D) = 0 + L(0, 1)$ and $K_q(D') = 1 + L(0, 1)$.

Differential privacy for a given ε establishes when two distributions for neighboring databases are similar enough. Let us consider $K_q(D) = 0 + L(0, 1)$ and different values of ε and in what extend a neighboring distribution can be differ from $K_q(D)$. Figure 5.2 illustrates for different values of ε intervals in which the output of a query for a neighboring database (i.e., $K_q(D')$) can lay. Values of $\varepsilon = 0, 0.3829, 0.5, 1, 2, 3$

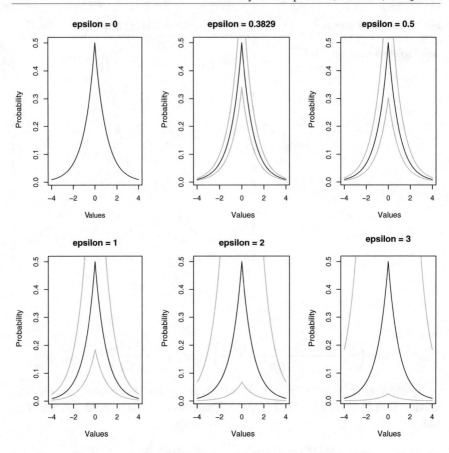

Fig. 5.2 Output of query $K_q(D) = 0 + L(0, 1)$ and boundaries according to different values of ε

are considered. The fringes in the figure describe the region where Eq. 5.1 holds. For $\varepsilon = 0$, the upper and lower fringes overlap with the function. Therefore, we have absolute privacy, and the distribution for $K_q(D')$ needs to be exactly the same as for $K_q(D)$. We can also see that the larger the value of ε, the larger the interval in which a neighboring distribution can lay. The value of 0.3829 is included because this value appears as recommended in a work by Lee and Clifton [282].

We can observe graphically whether a result of a neighboring database $K_q(D') = 1 + L(0, 1)$ would fit to different values of ε. In other words, does the plot of Fig. 5.1 fit into the intervals found in Fig. 5.2? Figure 5.3 combines Figs. 5.1 and 5.2 and we can see clearly that values of $\varepsilon < 1$ make $K_q(D')$ violate differential privacy. Only values larger than $\varepsilon \geq 1$ are consistent with the definition of differential privacy.

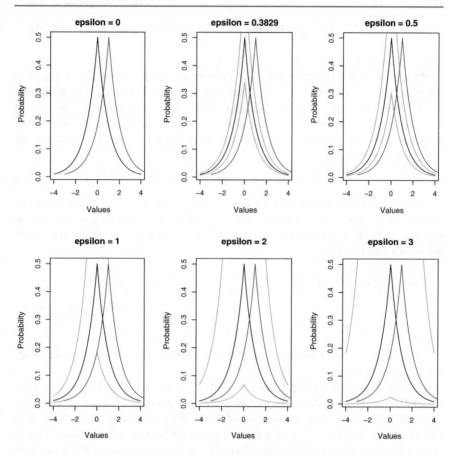

Fig. 5.3 Output of queries $K_q(D) = 0 + L(0, 1)$, $K_q(D') = 1 + L(0, 1)$, and different values of ε

Computing the mean with differential privacy

Let us reconsider the example in Sect. 1.2.2 about computing the mean of incomes. Here, we will work with an *arbitrary* database with an *arbitrary* set of records with *arbitrary* values. We will see what *arbitrary* means. For illustration, we will use the same values (incomes) considered there. Recall that we were considering the incomes of some people from Bunyola (Majorca). These values correspond to our database, say D. That is

$$D = \{1000, 2000, 3000, 2000, 1000, 6000, 2000, 10000, 2000, 4000\}.$$

For this database the mean is $q(D) = 3300\,Euros$. Then, we consider the neighboring database, say D', in which we have added the income of Dona Obdúlia de Montcada, landlord of Bearn. Her income is 100000 Euros. Therefore, D' corresponds to:

D'={1000, 2000, 3000, 2000, 1000, 6000, 2000, 10000, 2000, 4000, 100000}.

Then, the mean becomes $q(D') = 12090.90$.

We have seen that in order to provide a differentially private solution, we need to know the sensitivity of the function. That is, in our case $f = mean$. The sensitivity of the mean depends on the maximum and minimum values that we can find in the database, and, in addition, on the number of values we can assume to be in the database. Let $[min, max]$ denote the range of the attribute, then, the sensitivity of the mean is as follows:

$$\Delta_{\mathscr{G}}(mean) = (max - min)/S. \tag{5.1}$$

This is computed assuming that we have $S - 1$ values in the database all in one extreme of the $[min, max]$ interval (say, with value max) and then we add one in the other extreme of the interval (say, min). Then, naturally, the difference between the means will be

$$\frac{(S-1) \cdot max}{S-1} - \frac{(S-1) \cdot max + min}{S} = max - \frac{(S-1) \cdot max}{S} - \frac{min}{S}$$
$$= \frac{S \cdot min - (S-1) \cdot max - min}{S} = \frac{max - min}{S}$$

Naturally, when no assumption can be made on the number of values in a database, then $\Delta_{\mathscr{G}}(mean) = (max - min)$.

Let us elaborate the example. Assume that we consider that the range of incomes is [1000, 100000]. In addition, let us consider $\varepsilon = 1$ and that we have $S = 5$ records. Then, this means that the sensitivity is $\Delta_{\mathscr{G}}(mean) = (max-min)/S = 19800$. From the sensitivity we can compute the scale parameter b for the Laplace distribution. It will be $b = 19800/1 = 19800$. Therefore, the Laplace mechanism for this problem corresponds to $K_{mean}(D) = q(D) + L(0, 19800)$. Then, applying this mechanism to our database D above, we will compute: $K_{mean}(D) = 3300 + L(0, 19800)$. Figure 5.4 (left) shows the distribution. The distribution is very flat, and although it seems to be zero, it is not. Basically, all numbers (i.e., all incomes) have an almost zero probability to be selected. In other words, this query has a large amount of noise and the output can be anything (so, it is not at all informative). If we compute the mean of D' instead of the one of D (i.e., when we have Dona Obdúlia in the database and her income of 100000 Euro), then, we have a very similar distribution. This corresponds to the computation of $K_{mean}(D') = 12090.90 + L(0, 19800)$.

Let us now consider the same problem but assuming that now the number of incomes in the database is at least one million. So, let us use, $S = 10^6$ values. We will keep the value of $\varepsilon = 1$. In this case the sensitivity will be $\Delta_{\mathscr{G}}(mean) = (max - min)/S = 0.099$, and, therefore, the scale parameter of the Laplace distribution is $b = 0.099/1 = 0.099$. For a database D_1 with mean 3300 we would get the following output: $K_{mean}(D_1) = 3300 + L(0, 0.099)$. Note that we cannot assume that $D_1 = D$ because our example has only 10 values. Figure 5.4 (right) illustrates the distribution of $K_{mean}(D_1)$. We can see that applying Algorithm 14 we will get in this case, with high probability, a value near to 3300.

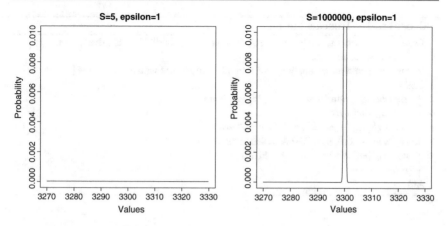

Fig. 5.4 Output of queries $K_q(D) = 3300 + L(0, 19800)$ (left), $K_q(D') = 3300 + L(0, 0.099)$ (right) in the interval [3270, 3330] represented with the same scale. This corresponds to $\varepsilon = 1$ and $S = 5$ (left) and $S = 10^6$ (right)

We cannot illustrate the query of a database including Dona Obdúlia's income. Note that if we have a database with $S = 10^6$ values (i.e., this is roughly speaking the population of all Majorca island according to data from 2019), the influence of Dona Obdúlia will be for sure small and unless all people in Majorca are suddenly rich, the average will be somehow near 3000 euros (some fonts give a mean salary of 2500 euros in Majorca in 2021).

We have seen that when the minimum number of values in the database is small and the range of values is high, the sensitivity is also high. This means that we need to add a lot of noise into the true value of a query to make the solution differentially private. This problem appears frequently in differential privacy. So, how to provide a solution that is reasonable in terms of the amount of noise? To solve this problem, we can try to redefine the function and somehow limit the range of the output or the possible number of different outputs.

In the case of the mean, we force the differentially private query, to give its output within a certain range. So, if we deal with mean income, we will not allow a mean income so large as 12090.90. This will imply that the sensitivity of the query will be smaller and we will need less noise. We will discuss this solution below.

Exercise 5.2 Compute the sensitivity for the variance.

An improvement for the mean: bounded and truncated means

A differential privacy mechanism can introduce a large amount of noise if the sensitivity is large. In the case of the mean, when the number of values is small and their range can be large, the sensitivity is also large. A way to reduce the amount of noise is to reduce the range of the output.

Algorithm 15: Truncated mean.

Data: D: Database; S: minimum size of D; ϵ: parameter of differential privacy; mn, mx: real; max, min: real

Result: *truncated-mean* satisfying ϵ-differential privacy and within the interval $[mn, mx]$

1 **begin**
2 $\quad$ $\Delta_{\mathscr{G}}(mean) = \min((max - min)/S, mx - mn)$
3 $\quad$ $b = \Delta_{\mathscr{G}}(mean)/\epsilon$
4 $\quad$ $m_0 = q'_{mn,mx}(mean(D))$ // A truncated mean
5 $\quad$ $m_1 = m_0 + L(0, b)$ // We add noise to the mean
6 $\quad$ $m_2 = q'(m_1)$ // Our output should also be in $[mn, mx]$
7 $\quad$ **return** (m_2)
8 **end**

We can use the same approach for implementing other differentially private functions for which we expect the value to be in a given range. E.g., non-negative incomes and non-negative ages.

Let us consider again the mean of incomes. Let us consider that we are working in Euros, and that, in this context, we can expect an outcome in the range $[mn, mx]$. Naturally, we assume that $mn \neq mx$. Then, we can reduce the sensitivity forcing that the outcome is really in the interval. This can be done revising our query $q = mean$ defining $\tilde{q}$ in terms of a function q' that checks whether the mean is within $[mn, mx]$ and force it to be in the interval if this is not the case. Let us define q' as follows:

$$q'_{mn,mx}(x) = \begin{cases} mn & \text{if } x < mn \\ x & \text{if } mn \leq x \leq mx \\ mx & \text{if } mx < x \end{cases}$$

Then, $q(D) = mean(D)$, and we define $\tilde{q}(D) = q'_{mn,mx}(mean(D))$. It is clear that $\tilde{q}(D)$ will be always in the interval $[mn, mx]$. Therefore, whatever the size of D, its sensitivity cannot exceed $mx - mn$. Nevertheless, the sensitivity can be smaller than this one. Recall that when we consider the range of the attribute to be $[min, max]$, and S corresponds to the size of the database, the sensitivity of the mean is, according to Eq. 5.1,

$$\Delta_{\mathscr{G}}(mean) = (max - min)/S.$$

So, in general, we will have that the sensitivity of $\tilde{q}$ will be the smaller of the two:

$$\Delta_{\mathscr{G}}(\tilde{q}) = \min((max - min)/S, (mx - mn)).$$

Given a function f that returns a value in $[mn, mx]$, the truncated Laplace mechanism is to apply the Laplace mechanism, and then truncate the results using the function $q'_{mn,mx}$ above. This will satisfy ε-differential privacy by composition, as a function applied to a differential privacy solution will also satisfy differential privacy (see Sect. 5.1.2). This truncated Laplace mechanism is described in Algorithm 15.

Let us consider the application of this algorithm when the interval under consideration is $[mn, mx] = [2000, 4000]$ and with $S = 5$ (as in the example displayed in

Fig. 5.4). Then, the sensitivity is

$$\Delta_{\mathcal{D}}(\tilde{q}) = \min((max - min)/5, (mx - mn))$$
$$= \min((1000000 - 1000)/5, (4000 - 2000)) = 2000.$$

When we apply $\tilde{q}$ to

$$1000, 2000, 3000, 2000, 1000, 6000, 2000, 10000, 2000, 4000$$

we have that the real mean is $mean = 3300$.

For $\varepsilon = 1$ we will have $b = \Delta_{\mathcal{D}}/\varepsilon = 2000/1 = 2000$. Let us consider also $\varepsilon' = 0.4$ and $\varepsilon'' = 2$. Then, we have $b' = \Delta_{\mathcal{D}}/\varepsilon' = 2000/0.4 = 5000$, and $b'' = \Delta_{\mathcal{D}}/\varepsilon'' = 2000/2 = 1000$. Figure 5.5 represents the distributions of the outcomes of the queries under these assumptions for both D and D' (i.e., D' is equal to D adding Dona Obdúlia's income 1000000) and $\varepsilon = 1$ and $\varepsilon'' = 2$. These figures were computed ploting the histogram of applying $\tilde{q}$ 10000 times.

Figure 5.5 (right-top, corresponding to $\varepsilon = 1$ and database D) shows that the distribution is quite uniform in the range $[mn, mx]$, except for the extremes where the probability is accumulated. In contrast to Fig. 5.4 (left), there is an almost imperceptible peak around the right outcome. In the case of database D' Fig. 5.5 (right-bottom), where Dona Obdúlia's income is included, the probability accumulates to the right. When we use $\varepsilon = 2$ (figures on the right) this is more visible.

Exercise 5.3 Represent the distributions corresponding to queries $\tilde{q}(D)$ and $\tilde{q}(D')$ for ε values equal to 0.4, 1, and 2 with $S = 10$ and $S = 20$.

An alternative to truncating the output distribution by means of the function q' (i.e., applying q' on top of the Laplacian mechanism) is to bound the Laplacian mechanism itself into the domain $[mn, mx]$. This bounded Laplace mechanism can be defined in two alternative equivalent ways.

- Use a bounded Laplace distribution with values in $D = [mn, mx]$ as follows:

$$L'(x; \mu, b) = \begin{cases} 0 & \text{if } x \in D \\ \frac{1}{C_q} \frac{1}{2b} exp\left(-\frac{|x-\mu|}{b}\right) \end{cases}$$

- Use the Laplace mechanism and re-draw the mechanism until a value in D is obtained.

This process does not always guarantees differential privacy. When the sensitivity of the query is $(mx - mn)$ then ε-differential privacy is guaranteed when $b = \Delta(q)/\varepsilon$. Otherwise, differential privacy does necessarily holds. A larger scale parameter b than for the Laplace mechanism is needed (i.e., a value $b > \Delta(q)/\varepsilon$).

Exercise 5.4 The Laplacian mechanism with $L(0, b)$ with $b = \Delta(q)/(\varepsilon - \log(1-\delta))$ satisfies (ε, δ)-differential privacy, as introduced in Definition 3.17. Construct figures analogous to the ones in Fig. 5.1, but with $\delta = 0.01$.

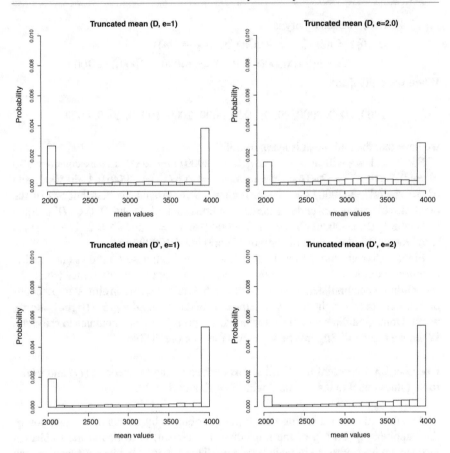

Fig. 5.5 Distribution of the application of the bounded mean for D (without Dona Obdúlia's income) (top) and D' (with Dona Obdúlia's income) (bottom), $S = 5$ and $\varepsilon = 1$ (left) and $\varepsilon = 2$ (right)

Exercise 5.5 The discussion in this section focused on the example of the mean, but most of the discussion is valid for any function f that applies to a database returns a numerical value. Reconsider the definitions under this perspective.

5.1.2 Composition Theorems

Some interesting and useful properties have been proven for differential privacy that establish limits for ε when we are combining two or more functions each one having its own ε value.

Let us consider n functions q_i, each one satisfying differential privacy with ε_i and all applied to the same database D. Then, if $\varepsilon = \sum_{i=1}^{n} \varepsilon_i$, we have that the combination of queries is ε-differential privacy. This is known as the sequential composition theorem.

For example, let us consider a database D. Let us compute the mean and the variance for D. Then $q_1 = mean$ and $q_2 = variance$. Therefore if K_{q_1} is ε_1-differentially private, and K_{q_2} is ε_2-differentially private, publishing both mean and variance will satisfy $\varepsilon_1 + \varepsilon_2$ differential privacy.

This example was for different computations. Nevertheless, it also applies when we apply the same function several times. Note that if we provide a randomized version of the mean, and then we execute this query several times, we will get different randomized versions of the same mean. Then, of course, we can average these means and, the more versions we have, the more similar will be this average to the true mean. It is thus clear that this process will not provide a private mean. The composition theorem gives a bound in this scenario. If we provide a differentially private mean (as in the example above) with $\varepsilon = 1$ and we apply it to obtain 5 randomized versions and then we compute the average, we would have an ε'-differential privacy with $\varepsilon' = 5 * \varepsilon = 5$.

When functions are applied to independent databases, then the publication of all results has a privacy level that is the maximum of the individual privacy levels (i.e., the smallest protection). That is, consider n functions q_i each one satisfying differential privacy with ε_i. Then, if each of them is applied to a disjoint (independent) database D_i, the publication of all outputs is differentially private with ε defined by $\varepsilon = \max \varepsilon_i$. For example, if we have differentially private mean incomes for different towns, each one with its own ε_i, the publication of all incomes will be differentially private with $\varepsilon = \max \varepsilon_i$. This is called parallel composition.

Finally, we can consider the application of a function on top of another one that is ε-differential privacy. Then, the composition is also ε-differential privacy. That is, if q is ε-differential privacy and q' is another function that can be applied on the range of q, then $q'(q(D))$ will be ε-differential privacy. This composition is called post-processing.

For example, let us consider $q = mean$ salary in Euros and its implementation K_{mean} with privacy ε, then, computing $q'(x) = 10x$ to have the salary in SEK will provide $q'(q(D))$ that will be also ε-differentially private. These properties (composition theorems) are summarized in Fig. 5.6.

- **Sequential compisition.** $q_1, \ldots, q_n$ with $\varepsilon_1, \ldots, \varepsilon_n$ all applied to X provide $\varepsilon = \sum_{i=1}^{n} \varepsilon_i$ differential privacy.
- **Parallel composition.** $q_1, \ldots, q_n$ with $\varepsilon_1, \ldots, \varepsilon_n$ each applied to a disjoint X_i provide $\varepsilon = \max_{i=1}^{n} \varepsilon_i$ differential privacy.
- **Post-processing.** q with ε applied to X, and q' applied to the result of q, then $q'(q(X))$ provides ε differential privacy.

Fig. 5.6 Summary of the composition theorems for queries $q, q', q_1, \ldots, q_n$ on databases $X, X_1, \ldots, X_n$

Computing histograms

A histogram represents the frequency of a set of items for a set of buckets (or bins). If we consider the problem from the perspective of differential privacy, it is absolutely relevant to consider whether the set of buckets is predefined or not. That is, the buckets are defined independently of the computation of the histogram, or they are built somehow from the data. It is important to understand that if the set of buckets is not predefined, and, instead, they are actually computed from the database, then we need to compute them in a privacy-preserving way. This naturally adds complexity into the process. So, let us consider that the buckets are predefined.

Let $B = \{b_1, \ldots, b_b\}$ be a set of b buckets, let D be a database, let us see how we can provide the counts $c_D(b_i)$ for each bucket $i = 1, \ldots, b$ in a privacy-preserving way. We can easily observe that given two databases D_1 and D_2 that differ in a single record, the sensitivity of the two corresponding histograms is one (recall Definition 5.2). That is, adding a record means adding a count to any of the buckets.

Let $histogram(B, D)$ denote the histogram of database D using the buckets in B. Then, to provide a histogram that is ε-differential privacy we can apply the Laplace mechanism to each count using $b = \Delta(q)/\varepsilon = 1/\varepsilon$. That is, we add Laplace noise $L(0, b)$ to each bucket. Formally, if $c_{D'}(b_i)$ represents the Laplace mechanism associated to bucket b_i, we define $c_{D'}(b_i) = c_D(b_i) + r_i$ with r_i following $L(0, b)$. In this expression, each r_i for $i = 1, \ldots, b$ is independently drawn from $L(0, b)$, and $c_D(b_i)$ represents the value of the ith bucket for database D.

To illustrate this mechanism, let us consider the following set of values

$$D = \{1234, 1300, 1233, 1250, 1284, 2000, 2300, 2044, 2573, 2745, 2853,$$
$$2483, 3633, 3182, 3274, 3935\}$$

and three buckets $b_1 = [1000, 1999]$, $b_2 = [2000, 2999]$, $b_3 = [3000, 3999]$. Then, the histogram for D for these buckets will be $(5, 7, 4)$. Let us now draw three values r_1, r_2, r_3 (independently) from $L(0, b)$ using $\varepsilon = 1$ (i.e., $b = 1$). Let them be $r = (0.7534844, -0.6143575, -1.5725160)$. Then, the ε-differentially private histogram will be

$$histogram(B, D) = (c_D(b_1), c_D(b_2), c_D(b_3)) = (5, 7, 4) + r$$
$$= (5.753484, 6.385643, 2.427484).$$

Using composition to compute the mean from histograms

We have explained above that given a result already satisfying differential privacy, when we apply another function to it, its result will also satisfy differential privacy. We can take advantage of this fact to compute the average of a set of values from a differentially private histogram. Let us see how this can be computed.

Let D be a database with numerical values. Let $B = \{b_1, \ldots, b_b\}$ be the set of b buckets, each one with its range $b_i = [b_{in}, b_{ix})$ denoting the minimum and the maximum value of the range. Then, the histogram of D using buckets B (i.e., $histogram(B, D)$) will consist of the values $c(b_i)$. They are the counts of the number of elements in D associated to b_i. We also need to consider $m(b_i)$, the mean value of the interval. Using the notation above where $b_i = [b_{in}, b_{ix})$, we have that $m(b_i) = (b_{in} + b_{ix})/2$. Then, for a given set B, a database D and the counts $c(b_i)$, we can compute an approximate average as follows:

$$mean(B, histogram(B, D)) = \sum_{i=1}^{b} c(b_i)m(b_i).$$

Naturally, this average is only an approximation of the actual mean of the values in D because the larger the buckets, the less acurate is the mean. Nevertheless, this lack of accuracy does not imply any privacy guarantee.

Let us consider the values D in the previous section with buckets $b_1 = [1000, 2000)$, $b_2 = [2000, 3000)$, $b_3 = [3000, 4000)$. Then, as the histogram is $(5, 7, 4)$, its mean will be

$$mean(B, histogram(B, D)) = \sum_{i=1}^{b} c(b_i)m(b_i) = \frac{5 \cdot 1500 + 7 \cdot 2500 + 4 \cdot 3500}{5 + 7 + 4}$$
$$= 2437.5.$$

Compare this result with the mean of D which is 2332.688. Observe that the previous result is not differentially private. The difference between both results is just an effect of the discretization of the incomes (i.e., the actual buckets B used). Other discretizations may produce other results which may be more or less accurate than 2437.5.

Let us consider now a differentially private version of this computation. It will consist of the computation of the buckets, then its protection using a differential privacy mechanism, and then the computation of the mean. Instead of the mean, we can compute, in general, any other statistic based on the histogram. The general procedure has, therefore, the following steps, given the buckets B and the database D:

- **Step 1.** Compute $c = histogram(B, D)$
- **Step 2.** Produce a differentially private histogram c'
- **Step 3.** $mean(B, c') = (1/t) \sum_{i=1}^{b} c'(b_i)m(b_i)$ where $t = \sum_{i=1}^{b} c'(b_i)$

If c' is ε-differential privacy, the composition theorems ensure that the mean based on c' also satisfies ε-differential privacy.

For the example above, using the protected version of the histogram (5.753484, 6.385643, 2.427484), we will have

$$mean(B, c') = \sum_{i=1}^{b} c'(b_i)m(b_i)$$
$$= \frac{5.753484 \cdot 1500 + 6.385643 \cdot 2500 + 2.427484 \cdot 3500}{5.753484 + 6.385643 + 2.427484} = 2271.67$$

We can apply this approach to compute the mean for any database. For doing so, it is important to understand that we need buckets to span over the whole range of incomes. So, if we consider the incomes in the range [1000, 100000] as when Dona Obdúlia was in the database, we need either a large bucket (with e.g., all incomes larger than 10000) or a large number of buckets. This will have effects on the output.

5.1.3 Differential Privacy Mechanisms for Categorical Data

Randomized response is the most standard approach to implement differential privacy for categorical data. More particularly, to implement local differential privacy.

Let us consider the most simple definition in which we have a sensitive question with only two possible outcomes: Y and N. Let us consider that Y is the sensitive outcome. For example, let us consider the following questions "Is your car now exceeding the speed limit?" and "Have you consumed drugs this week?". Then, randomized response corresponds to ask the respondent to provide the answer following this procedure:

  (i) toss a coin
 (ii) if heads, return Y
(iii) if tails, return the true answer.

Now, if we have a large enough number of respondents, each one applying this procedure, we can estimate the number of Y and N of the whole set from the actual answers of our respondents. Let us see how this is done. First, let us assume that the true proportion of N is p_N, and, therefore $p_Y = 1 - p_N$ is the true proportion of Y. Second, observe that for a fair coin, we have 50% heads (which lead to Y for all respondents), and 50% tails (which lead to some Ys and some Ns). Let us consider the proportion of N, and let this proportion be r. As this value r just corresponds to half of the respondents (i.e., the 50% that got tails), for the whole set of respondents we estimate the total number as $2r$. That is, $p_N = 2r$ and, therefore, $p_Y = 1 - 2r$. Figure 5.7 represents both randomized response results and estimation of the true values.

As an example, let us consider the following. We ask a group of 100 people if they consumed drugs. Using the procedure above, we get 45 Ns and 55 Ys. Then, we expect that 50 people answered Y just because they got heads. Among the 50 that got tails, 5 answered a true Y, and the remaining 45 answered a true N. So, 45 over 50 are for N, which means $r = 2 \cdot 45 = 90$ over 100 are for N. In other words, $p_N = 0.90$. Then, for Y, we have $p_Y = 1 - 2r = 0.1$.

Although this approach can be used for both local and global differential privacy when data is categorical, it is mainly used for the local one. In this case, a set of respondents or devices need to supply information on a binary attribute. Then, before supplying the value, respondents apply this procedure to their corresponding value $c \in \{Y, N\}$ and obtain $c' \in \{N, Y\}$.

This definition can be modified assuming non-fair coins. That is, we have a probability p of giving the true answer. The outcome in case of heads can also be

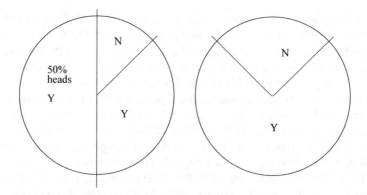

Fig. 5.7 Graphical representation of randomized response and estimation of true results. Randomized response (left): 50% Y due to heads, and then N and Y for tails. Estimation of true results (right): double proportion of N, and remaining are Y

Algorithm 16: Randomized response: $rr(f(X), p, p')$.

Data: $f(X)$: the true outcome of the query; p, p': probability in [0,1]
Result: Randomized response for $f(X)$ with probabilities p, p'
1 **begin**
2     $r :=$ random number in [0,1] according to a uniform distribution
3   **if** $r < p$ **then**
4   **return** $f(X)$
5   **else**
6        $r' :=$ random number in [0,1] according to a uniform distribution
7   **if** $r' < p'$ **then**
8   **return** Y
9   **else**
10   **return** N
11   **end**
12   **end**
13 **end**

---

randomized. That is, when heads, we return Y with probability p' and N with probability $(1 - p')$. This is formally defined in Algorithm 16.

So, if π is the true proportion of Y, for probabilities p and p' we will actually observe the following proportion of Ys

$$o = p * \pi + (1 - p) * p'.$$

Therefore, it is easy to see that given an observed proportion o of Ys, we can estimate π using the following expression:

$$\hat{\pi} = (o - (1 - p) * p')/p.$$

In the example above (that corresponds to $p = 0.5$, $p' = 1$ and where we observe a proportion $o = 0.55$ of Ys), we get using this expression $\pi = (0.55 - 0.5)/0.5 = 0.1$.

Let us consider another example with a true proportion of Ys equal to 0.1 but using this last approach with $p = 0.5$ and $p' = 0.75$. In this case, we will observe a proportion of Ys equal to $o = 1/2 * 0.1 + 1/2 * 3/4 = 0.425$. We can easily see that from this observation, we can infer the true proportion as follows: $\pi = (o - (1 - p) * p')/p = (0.425 - (1 - 0.5) * 3/4)/0.5 = 0.1$.

Although, in theory, the expression above permits to find the true proportion π, in practice, the larger the noise, the more difficult is to recover the correct figure. It is enough to consider that in the extreme case of $p = 0$, we will only observe a proportion of Ys equal to p'. From a statistical perspective, we have that our estimation $\hat{\pi}$ has some variance that depends on the number of respondents (the larger the number, the less the variance) and on the parameters p and p'. Then, when the noise is large (e.g., p near to 0), we need a larger number of respondents to get a small variance. Warner [515] provides some expressions for the variance for the original definition of randomized response.

Randomized response can also be used when the class is not binary. Let us consider the case of c classes $C = \{c_1, \ldots, c_c\}$. Then, we can implement randomized response considering a probability distribution for each c_i. More particularly, for a true response c_i, we consider the probability of delivering a c_j in the set C. We denote this probability by

$$P(c_i, c_j) = P(X' = c_j | X = c_i).$$

Then, for each c_i, we have that $P(X' = c_1 | X = c_i), \ldots, P(X' = c_c | X = c_i)$ define a probability distribution and, thus, we need that for all c_i it holds $\sum_j P(c_i, c_j) = \sum_j P(X' = c_j | X = c_i) = 1$.

The values $P(c_i, c_j)$ define a transition matrix P where the rows add to one (i.e., the ith row jth column is the value $P(c_i, c_j) = P(X' = c_j | X = c_i)$). Algorithm 17 specifies this randomized response for a given transition matrix P. This definition of randomized response corresponds to the masking method PRAM, a masking method we describe in Sect. 6.1.4. That is why we use the name *rrPRAM* in the algorithm.

Given a set of respondents with a true distribution $\pi = (\pi_1, \ldots, \pi_c)$ (i.e., π_k denotes the proportion of respondents of class c_k), randomized response causes us to observe the distribution $o = (o_1, \ldots, o_c)$. Proceeding as we did above for the binary case, we know that the distribution o can be computed from the matrix P and the true distribution π. This corresponds for class c_j to $o_j = \sum_{i=1}^{c} \pi_i P(X' = c_j | X = c_i)$. We can rewrite this expression using matrix form as follows: $o = P\pi$. Then, we can estimate $\hat{\pi} = P^{-1}o$ where P^{-1} is the inverse of the transition matrix P.

Let us now consider the definition of the transition matrix so as it guarantees an appropriate privacy level. That is, given a problem with c classes and a given ε, which matrix P can provide local ε-differential privacy when respondents data is protected using rrPRAM?

We provide a solution that assumes that all categories have the same probability of not being modified. That is, for all c_i, c_j we have $P(X' = c_i | c_i) = P(X' = c_j | c_j)$. In addition, we also assume that $P(X' = c_i | c_i) > P(X' = c_j | c_i)$ for all $i \neq j$. In other words, all values in the diagonal are the same, and are larger than the other values in the matrix. Then, we also assume that all these other values are all equal.

Algorithm 17: Randomized response via PRAM: $rr\,PRAM(c, P)$.

Data: c: the true outcome of the query; P: transition matrix

Result: Randomized response for c according to transition matrix P

1 **begin**

2      $r :=$ random number in $[0,1]$ according to a uniform distribution

3   Select k_0 in $\{1, \ldots, c\}$ such that $\sum_{k=1}^{k_0-1} P(c' = c_i, |C = c) < r \le \sum_{k=1}^{k_0} P(c' = c_i, |C = c)$

4   **return** c_{k_0}

5 **end**

So, we have a matrix of this form

$$\begin{pmatrix} q_d & q & \cdots & q \\ q & q_d & \cdots & q \\ \cdots & & & \cdots \\ q & q & \cdots & q_d \end{pmatrix} \tag{5.2}$$

with $q_d = P(X' = c_i|c_i)$ for all i, and $q = P(X' = c_j|c_i)$ for $j \ne i$.

Given a transition matrix of this form, the algorithm delivers for a class c_i the following probabilities:

$$(P(X' = c_1|c_i), \ldots, P(X' = c_c|c_i)).$$

Similarly, for class c_j, we get the probabilities

$$(P(X' = c_1|c_j), \ldots, P(X' = c_c|c_j)).$$

Then, in order to ensure that we have local ε-differential privacy, we need the following inequalities to hold for all i, j

$$P(X' = c_1|c_i)/P(X' = c_1|c_j) \le e^\varepsilon, \ldots, P(X' = c_c|c_i)/P(X' = c_c|c_j)) \le e^\varepsilon,$$

or, equivalently, that for all i, j the following inequality holds

$$\max_{k=1}^{c} P(X' = c_k|c_i)/P(X' = c_k|c_j) \le e^\varepsilon. \tag{5.3}$$

Now, as we assumed that $P(X' = c_i|c_i)$ is the largest value in a row, and all the non-diagonal values are the same, we have that the maximum will be obtained for $k = i$. In order to get precisely ε privacy (and not $\varepsilon_0 < \varepsilon$ privacy) we require the equality to hold. So, we have

$$P(X' = c_i|c_i)/P(X' = c_i|c_j) = e^\varepsilon. \tag{5.4}$$

In addition, as probability for each row needs to add to one, we have

$$P(X' = c_i|c_i) + (c - 1)P(X' = c_i|c_j) = 1,$$

or, equivalently, $P(X' = c_i|c_j) = (1 - P(X' = c_i|c_i))/(c - 1)$. Using this expression, we have that Eq. 5.4 becomes

$$P(X' = c_i|c_i)/((1 - P(X' = c_i|c_i))/(c - 1)) = e^\varepsilon.$$

This equality implies that $P(X' = c_i | c_i)$ is of the following form:

$$P(X' = c_i | c_i) = e^{\varepsilon}/(c - 1 + e^{\varepsilon}),$$

and, therefore, $P(X' = c_i | c_j)$ for $i \neq j$ is

$$P(X' = c_i | c_j) = 1/(c - 1 + e^{\varepsilon}).$$

These last two expressions determine completely the transition matrix (i.e., Eq. 5.2) so that local ε-differential privacy holds. We can observe that when $c = 2$ and $\varepsilon = 0$, we have the transition matrix contains only 1/2.

Our proof is based on the assumption that the matrix contains only two different values (one for the elements in the diagonal and another for the elements that are not in the diagonal). Wang et al. [513] provide a more general result where other different values in the matrix are allowed. Their solution is to maximize the sum of the elements in the diagonal. That is, their goal is to find a transition matrix so that $\sum_{k=1}^{k} P(X' = c_k | c_k)$ is maximized. Their solution corresponds to the one provided here. It is important to note that there are other matrices that can also provide the same level of privacy ε.

Exercise 5.6 Construct the transition matrix for randomized response *rrPRAM* to satisfy local ε-differential privacy with $\varepsilon = 0$ and $\varepsilon = 1$, for $c = 2$ and $c = 5$.

As we have mentioned above, we present PRAM in Sect. 6.1.4, a masking method for categorical data based on transition matrices. We will discuss there how to determine the level of privacy ε for a given transition matrix. We will also illustrate that when a respondent provides multiple data (e.g., a series or several attributes), the fact that each datum is protected using local differential privacy does not avoid reidentification.

5.1.4 Properties of Differential Privacy

As a summary of this section let us recall some of the properties of differential privacy.

First, we have seen that ε is the privacy level. Then, naturally, the selection of ε has an effect on the outcome. For small ε, we have stronger privacy guarantees which imply that there is more noise into the solution. On the contrary, large ε means that there is less privacy and, thus, less noise.

Second, the sensitivity of the query has also an effect on the amount of noise. We have seen that, e.g., in the Laplacian noise, the scale parameter is proportional to the sensitivity. So, for the same privacy level ε, the larger the sensitivity, the larger the noise. Otherwise, the smaller the sensitivity, the smaller the noise.

Third, implementation of a differentially private mechanism is specific to a given query. For a given query there may be different ways to provide a differentially private solution. These different solutions will provide different types of perturbation. We have seen examples for the mean. We have seen the Laplace mechanism applied to the mean, but also the bounded and truncated means, and an implementation based on histograms. Each of these solutions will provide the user with a different solution, each one with its own probability distribution. For a given function, we need to select the solution that is best in our context. This context includes the privacy level as well as the type of data that we expect to find in the database (e.g., are all incomes in the range of [2000, 4000] or we expect a significant number of incomes larger than 4000?).

Solutions need to take into account not only the privacy level and the quality of the solution, but also the constraints any solution is expected to satisfy. For example, if we are computing the mean of incomes, we really expect this mean to be positive. Note that the Laplace mechanism can produce negative incomes. The same applies to our solution for histograms. We can produce differentially private histograms that have negative counts.

We have focused in this section on a single query. That is, we have a given query q and users have a privacy level ε. When we consider multiple queries, we need to provide users with a privacy budget ε' and then they will reduce this privacy budget for each query. Say, we have queries $q_1, q_2, q_3, \ldots$ for the same database D. Then, if they ask for q_1 with ε_1 then the privacy budget is reduced to $\varepsilon'' = \varepsilon' - \varepsilon_1$ for queries $q_2, q_3, \ldots$.

Note that if differentially private solutions for queries q_1, q_2 are implemented independently, then we will need to consume ε_1 for q_1 and ε_2 for q_2. Nevertheless, in some occasions we can do better than that. For example, assume that we compute a differentially private histogram K_h. Then, if we compute q_1 and q_2 from the histogram K_h, no additional budget is consumed. Recall that any query on K_h will also satisfy the privacy guarantees of K_h. We can apply this approach to compute the mean and the variance of a database.

5.1.5 Machine Learning

In this section we have included examples of applying differential privacy for functions that result into numerical and categorical outcomes. There are mechanisms [289,542] for more complex outputs. In particular there are solutions for machine learning models. This includes decision trees and deep learning models.

There are also applications of differential privacy to other types of objects than just numbers and categories. See e.g, the case of search logs [268], and graphs and social networks [250,465].

5.1.6 Concluding Remarks

We have seen that we can implement differential privacy for numerical data with noise addition. We will discuss in Sect. 6.1.3 additive and multiplicative noise as a masking mechanism. That is, data protection for databases, which relates to local differential privacy. Xiao et al. [529] introduce an alternative approach for achieving differential privacy based on wavelet transforms. Data masking using wavelet transforms is discussed in Sect. 6.1.5.

The selection of an appropriate parameter ε is an open question. To keep a good privacy level, a small parameter is required. A value around 1 is often recommended, but some applications use up to $\varepsilon = 14$. While differential privacy is defined a binary privacy model, the selection of ε is often decided taking into account the utility of the solution. That is, a parameter that achieves a good balance risk-utility.

The following exercise is about the odd function. This function is discussed as one motivating example for the definition of integral privacy.

Exercise 5.7 Consider the implementation of Laplacian noise and randomized response for the odd function (0 if number of records in a database X is even; 1 if number of records is odd).

5.2 Secure Multiparty Computation Protocols

This privacy model, that has been reviewed in Sect. 3.4.10 (see Definition 3.18), applies when several individuals or organizations, called parties, intend to compute together a function of their data. Then, the model has as its goal to protect against disclosure from the data required for the computation as well as from partial results of this calculation.

In short, given parties $P_1, \ldots, P_n$ with databases $X_1, \ldots, X_n$, the goal is to compute

$$y = f(X_1, \ldots, X_n)$$

without revealing unnecessary information to these parties. I.e., the computation of f does not give to party P_i any other knowledge than the one that can be inferred from X_i and y.

We have already discussed in Sect. 3.4.10 that the easiest way to build a solution compliant with secure multiparty computation is to consider a trusted third party TTP. Then, each party sends X_i in a secure way to TTP, then TTP computes $y = f(X_1, \ldots, X_n)$ and sends y to each P_i in a secure way. This corresponds to a centralized solution for computing $f(X)$.

Secure multiparty computation protocols apply when this TTP is not desirable, and, instead, a distributed solution is required. Then, we need to build a protocol to solve the problem. A protocol is a detailed description of how information flows among the parties, as well as the computations each party needs to perform. When we build a distributed solution, the centralized solution using a TTP serves as a reference with respect to the privacy requirements.

It is important to underline that protocols are specific to the function f to be computed. In fact, not only on the function but also on our assumptions on the data as well as on the adversaries. We will explain the most usual assumptions in the next section. Then, we will present some examples of secure multiparty computations.

5.2.1   Assumptions on Data and on Adversaries

For standard data sets described in terms of records and attributes, two typical scenarios are considered in the literature: vertical partitioning of the data and horizontal partitioning. They are as follows.

- **Vertically partitioned data.** All parties share the same records, but different parties have information about different attributes (i.e., different parties have different views of the same records or individuals).
- **Horizontally partitioned data.** All parties have information about the same attributes, nevertheless the records or individuals included in their databases are different.

We have already highlighted that parties should learn nothing else than the output of the function. To achieve this goal, we need to build a protocol that specifies for each party the tasks to do. Information is transmitted during the execution of the protocol and some calculations are done. To warrant that the protocol satisfies our privacy requirements, some assumptions needs to be done on the adversaries (e.g., the parties). Two main types of adversaries are considered. They are the following.

- **Semi-honest adversaries.** Parties follow the cryptographic protocol but they analyse all the information they get during its execution to discover as much information as they can.
- **Malicious adversaries.** Parties try to fool the protocol (e.g. aborting it or sending incorrect messages on purpose) in order to infer confidential information.

We will now provide examples of protocols for computing some specific functions. The first one is about the computation of a sum of numbers. We will discuss how different assumptions on the adversaries would affect the protocol.

5.2.2   Computing a Distributed Sum

Let us consider how to compute the sum of a set of distributed numerical values. More formally, we consider several people (i.e., parties) and each has a database with a single value (e.g., a salary). Our goal is to have as output the sum of these values (e.g., the total salary) but no other information should be disclosed about the participants. Observe that protocols for computing the sum can be used to compute the mean if the number of parties is common knowledge among the participants.

We make the example more concrete considering four people with names Aine, Brianna, Caoimhe, and Deirdre. Then, denote their salaries, respectively by, s_1, s_2, s_3, and s_4. The salaries are confidential and they do not want to share the figures.

The solution is built using public-key cryptography (see Sect. 2.5.2). This means in our context that each party requires two separate keys: a private and a public one. The solution assumes that the sum lies in the range $[0, n]$.

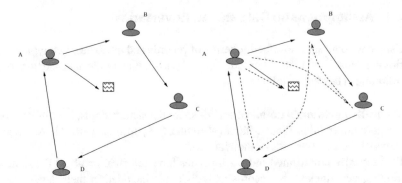

Fig. 5.8 Distributed sum (left) and distributed sum with two shares (right), considering four parties A, B, C, and D that represent Aine, Brianna, Caoimhe, and Deirdre

Under these assumptions, we can define the following protocol to compute the sum of the four salaries. Figure 5.8 (left) represents this protocol.

- Aine starts choosing a secret random number, say r, that is uniformly chosen from the interval $[0, n]$. This number r is added to her salary and sends the computation to Brianna encrypted with Brianna public key. Addition is modulo n. In this way, the outcome of $(r + s_1) \bmod n$ will be a number uniformly distributed in $[0, n]$ and so Brianna will learn nothing about the actual value of s_1.
- Brianna decrypts Aine's message with Brianna's private key, adds her salary (modulo n) and sends the result (i.e., $(r + s_1 + s_2) \bmod n$) to Caoimhe encrypted with Caoimhe's public key.
- Caoimhe decrypts Brianna's message with Caoimhe's private key, adds her salary (modulo n) and sends the result (i.e., $(r + s_1 + s_2 + s_3) \bmod n$) to Deirdre encrypted with Deirdre's public key.
- Deirdre decrypts Caoimhe's message with Deirdre's private key, adds her salary (modulo n) and sends the result (i.e., $(r + s_1 + s_2 + s_3 + s_4) \bmod n$) to Aine encrypted with Aine's public key.
- Aine decrypts Deirdre's message with Aine's private key. She substracts (modulo n) the random number r added in the first step, obtaining in this way $s_1 + s_2 + s_3 + s_4$ (this will be in $[0, n]$).
- Aine announces the result to the participants.

This implementation works fine if the participants follow the protocol and provide the right information. That is, they use their own salary in the computation, Aine announces the correct answer, and participants only take advantage of the output of the system but nothing else. In other words, they are all semi-honest adversaries.

Nevertheless, the protocol is not safe under other assumptions on the adversaries. For example, a participant can lie about her salary. Then, the participant can learn about the salaries of the other participants and the others learn nothing about the salary of this participant. Also, Aine can announce a wrong addition. In this case,

Aine is the only one that gets the correct information and the others learn nothing from the computation. Also, two (or more) parties can collaborate to determine the salaries of other participants. For example, Brianna and Deirdre can collude. Then, they can use their own information to learn about Caoimhe's salary. Note that Brianna is sending to Caoimhe the value $(r + s_1 + s_2) \bmod n$ and Caoimhe is sending to Deirdre the value $(r + s_1 + s_2 + s_3) \bmod n$. Naturally, the subtraction of these two values modulo n is s_3. In other words, there are scenarios than can lead to different types of disclosure. They correspond to the existence of malicious adversaries.

There are alternative protocols that can deal with some malicious adversaries. Let us consider a solution to solve the collusion problem. As we have seen, this problem appears when the two neighbors of a party share information and this is the cause of disclosure. One way to solve this problem is to avoid that only two parties are enough for the disclosure. This can be implemented dividing each salary into t shares. So, for s_1 we have $s_{11}, s_{12}, \ldots, s_{1t}$ so that $s_{11} + s_{12} + \cdots + s_{1t} = s_1$. Then, the sum of each share is computed individually using the protocol above. This will produce t values that will be added. The addition of each share will use a different path (i.e., a different sequence of participants).

In the case above, if we consider two shares, we will need two paths. For the first share we can use the path above: Aine, Brianna, Caoimhe, and Deirdre. Then, for the second share we use the path Aine, Caoimhe, Brianna, and Deirdre. Figure 5.8 (right) represents this case with two shares. If we proceed in this way, the collusion of Brianna and Deirdre is not enough to infer the salary of Caoimhe because the second share goes through Aine and Brianna. Only the three of them can infer Caoimhe salary. Something that they could do anyway from the output.

Using the protocol above, to disclose salary s_i, we need all the neighbors of party P_i. This implies that we need larger coalitions if we have different number of shares and different paths.

5.2.3 Secure Multiparty Computation and Inferences

An important point of this privacy model is that parties should only learn what can be inferred from their own data and the output of the function f that all parties compute together. This naturally means that users can have estimations of the values of other parties. In particular, if we consider the case of two parties and two salaries (e.g., only Aine and Brianna) and $f = sum$, then it is clear that Aine can infer the salary of Brianna from $(s_1 + s_2)$ and vice-versa. Therefore, from a secure multiparty computation perspective, a protocol in which they just share their salaries is privacy-preserving.

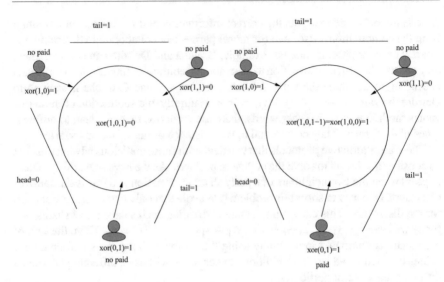

Fig. 5.9 Dining cryptographers: computation of the output when a cryptographer pays (left) and when none of them pay (right)

5.2.4 Computing the Exclusive OR Function

navia aut caput

Let us consider the case that databases consist of a single bit, and we want to compute the exclusive or function of these bits in a secure multiparty computational manner. This problem is usually known in the literature as the problem of dining cryptographers. Let us review the original formulation of this problem.

Problem 5.1 [90] Three cryptographers are sitting down to dinner at their favorite three-star restaurant. Their waiter informs them that arrangements have been made with the maître d'hôtel for the bill to be paid anonymously. One of the cryptographers might be paying the dinner, or it might have been NSA (U.S. National Security Agency). The three cryptographers respect each other's right to make an anonymous payment, but they wonder if NSA is paying.

So, the problem is to know whether one of the cryptographers pay. If we represent by 1 a cryptographer that pays and 0 one that does not, to find whether one paid is equivalent to the (exclusive) or function of these bits. We describe below the steps of a protocol to solve this problem. Let P_i represent the ith cryptographer. Then, we have $P_{(i+1) \bmod 3}$ to represent the cryptographer sitting on the right and $P_{(i-1) \bmod 3}$ to represent the cryptographer sitting on the left. Figure 5.9 illustrates the protocol when one cryptographer is paying (left) and when none pays (right).

- **Step 1.** Each cryptographer flips a coin and shares its outcome with the cryptographer on the right. Let us represent tails and heads by 1 and 0, respectively. Let $coin_i$ be the outcome of the coin of the ith cryptographer.
- **Step 2.** All cryptographers find whether the two coins they know about (the ones they flipped and the one their left-hand neighbor flipped) fell on the same side or not. Let us consider the ith cryptographer, then we can use the *xor* on the results of the two coins to represent cryptographer's computation:

$$c_i = xor(coin_i, coin_{(i-1) \bmod 3}).$$

- **Step 3.** If a cryptographer is the payer, then the answer is the opposite of what is observed. Otherwise, the answer is what is observed. Formally, let us represent the answer of the ith cryptographer by c_i', then

$$c_i' = \begin{cases} c_i & \text{if the } i\text{th cryptographer did not pay the meal} \\ 1 - c_i & \text{if the } i\text{th cryptographer paid the meal.} \end{cases} \tag{5.5}$$

- **Step 4.** Then, let s be the sum of the values c_i'. If the sum is even, no one paid. If odd, one cryptographer paid. The *xor* function can be used for this purpose. That is, the output is:

$$xor(c_1', c_2', c_3').$$

This protocol can be generalized to an arbitrary number of cryptographers. In that case, each cryptographer needs a secret bit with each of the other participants. Each cryptographer computes the sum modulo two (or the *xor* function of all the bits). Then, the ith cryptographer applies the function above to determine c_i' from c_i (i.e., according to Expression 5.5). Finally, as in Step 4 above, let s be the sum of the values c_i'. If the sum is even, no one paid. If odd, one cryptographer paid.

This solution is valid for semi-honest adversaries. Nevertheless, it is not valid when there are malicious parties. If one cryptographer informs incorrectly, the output will be naturally wrong.

The protocol has some limitations. From a computational perspective, for n participants it needs n^2 communications (one communication for each pair of participants). Then, only one bit equal to one can be detected (or an odd number of them equal to one). The protocol computes an exclusive or, and, thus, if two philosophers inform that they have payed, the result is zero. The computation of an exclusive or has two consequences. First, any party can infer the output of all the others. This is fine from a secure multiparty computation perspective. This privacy model allows party P_i all inferences from X_i and from the output of the function $f(X_1, \ldots, X_n)$. Second, a malicious party can inform incorrectly, and then the output will be naturally wrong, but this party will still be able to get the information about the other parties.

This protocol can be seen as providing sender anonymity. That is, we know that a bit is being transmitted but we do not know who is the sender of this bit. From this perspective, it can be seen as an approach for user privacy (see Sect. 4.1.1).

Exercise 5.8 Define a secure multiparty computation protocol to compute exclusive or for only two parties. That is, given parties P_1 and P_2 and bits b_1 and b_2, consider the protocol to compute $xor(b_1, b_2)$.

5.2.5 Secure Multiparty Computation for Other Functions

In secure multiparty computation, we need to know the function to be computed. Protocols are specific for this function, and also about our assumptions on the adversaries. Because of that, the literature offers a plethora of protocols taking into account alternative functions, attacks, as well as computational and communication requirements. Some of these approaches are specific for machine learning and statistics. Some examples are given in the bibliographical notes.

5.3 Bibliographical Notes

1. **Query auditing.** Evfimievski et al. [180] have studied the offline scenario of query auditing. They use the term epistemic privacy, and define it in terms of reasoning about knowledge (in a logical sense) and using the semantics of sets of possible worlds.
2. **Differential privacy: precedents.** Prior to differential privacy, a related approach was proposed by Dwork, Nissim, and others [54,165] for particular types of queries. More particularly, researchers considered a query consisting of a pair (S, f) where S is a set of rows in a database X, and f is a function. The function was restricted first [165] to be from a row to $\{0, 1\}$ and later [54] to $\mathbb{R}$. Then, while the correct response for the pair (S, f) on the database X is $nr = \sum_{x \in S \subseteq X} f(x)$, a noisy version of nr was given to the user to ensure privacy.
3. **Differential privacy: Definitions and Laplace mechanisms.** Differential privacy was introduced by Dwork [161]. First results and research questions were published before 2010 [162,163]. The Laplace mechanism, including the case of functions returning values in $\mathbb{R}^n$, are already described in seminal works by Dwork [161,162]. The sensitivity of queries and the need that data has upper and lower bounds to make sensitivity meaningful was discussed also in early papers [423,517]. A proof that $L(0, b)$ with $b = \Delta(q)/(\varepsilon - \log(1 - \delta))$ satisfies (ε, δ)-differential privacy is given by Holohan et al. [230].
4. **Differential privacy: Bounded and truncated Laplace mechanisms.** The study of the bounded Laplace mechanism and of the truncated Laplace mechanism appears in the works of Holohan et al. [229]. The authors discuss that the truncated mechanism satisfies differential privacy and also give the conditions for when the bounded mechanism is differentially private when $b = \Delta(q)/\varepsilon$. Holohan et al. also give the algorithm to find the appropriate b so that the solution is differentially private when the sensitivity of $\Delta(q)$ is smaller than $(mx - mn)$. Liu [300] has also considered these problems in a multivariate setting calling them truncated and boundary-inflated-truncated (BIT) Laplace mechanisms. The former corresponding to our (and Holohan et al. [229]) bounded and the latter corresponding to our (and Holohan's) truncated.

5. **Differential privacy: categorical data and randomized response.** Warner introduced randomized response in 1965 [515], including estimation of variance. It was defined to help obtaining correct answers in sensitive issues from respondents. Chaudhuri and Mukerjee wrote a book on Randomized response where most relevant results are found [88]. An example of using randomized response for differential privacy is RAPPOR by Google [174]. RAPPOR also tries to avoid longitudinal attacks to the data. Discussion and results on local differential privacy using randomized response, including discussion on RAPPOR is given by Pastore and Gastpar [378].

6. **Differential privacy: on the selection of ε.** Lee and Clifton [282] study the parameter ε in terms of identifying a record, and discuss the case of mean and variance. For their particular problem related to the computation of the mean they recommend $\varepsilon = 0.3829$.

7. **Differential privacy: application.** There are several running applications of differential privacy (for both standard differential privacy and local differential privacy). Abowd, Garfinkel and others explain the adoption of differential privacy by the U. S. Census Bureau in a series of articles [1,2,197].

8. **Differential privacy: others.** Definition of the differentially private mechanism in Algorithm 14 is only based on the $\Delta_{\mathscr{D}}(q)$ and on the Laplace distribution selected. An approach for differential privacy considering previous knowledge was studied by Soria and Domingo-Ferrer [440].

   Differentially private algorithms for machine learning are described by Li et al. [289] and Zhu et al. [542].

   Discussion on the shortcomings of differential privacy for some type of queries are discussed by Bambauer, Muralidhar, and Sarathy [37,423].

9. **Differential privacy: other types of data.** Differential privacy has been applied to graphs. There are definitions for node-differential privacy and edge-differential privacy. The latter provides function outputs that do not change much when an edge is added or removed from a graph. The former is a stronger definition as the output does not change much when a node (with all its edges) is added or removed from a graph.

10. **Secure multiparty computation.** It was introduced by A. C. Yao in 1982 [536]. The problem of the dining cryptographers was first solved by Chaum [90].

    Examples of secure multiparty protocols include the work by Lindell and Pinkas [296,297] on computing a decision tree from two data parties, algorithms for clustering [65]. The book by Vaidya, Clifton and Zhu [506] describes several algorithms for data mining. Bogdanov et al. [55] propose an efficient framework for secure multiparty computation.

Privacy for Data: Masking Methods

6

Abstract

This chapter describes major methods for protecting databases. This includes per-turbative and non-perturbative methods, as well as synthetic data generators. This review includes rank swapping, microaggregation, additive and multiplicative noise, PRAM, and generalization. We also describe the use of GANs to generate synthetic data. The chapter also includes a discussion on methods for achieving k-anonymity and methods appropriate for big data.

> but when you have to turn into a chrysalis –
> you will some day, you know – and then after that
> into a butterfly
>
> L. Carrol, Alice's adventures in wonderland,
> 1865, Chapter V [73].

In this chapter we review data protection methods for sharing or publishing data. They are applicable to data files where each record corresponds to an individual or entity. In the SDC community these data are known as microdata. Masking methods is the usual term for methods to protect a database.

We consider a file or database X and, applying a masking method, we produce a new one X'. We distinguish, according to what we have described in Chap. 3, between identifiers, quasi-identifiers, and confidential attributes. Observe that we may have confidential quasi-identifiers. We process these attributes as follows.

- **Identifiers** id. To avoid disclosure, identifiers are usually removed or encrypted in a preprocessing step. In this way, information cannot be linked to specific respondents.
- **Quasi-identifiers** X_{nc}. They cannot be removed as almost all attributes can be quasi-identifiers. The usual approach to preserve the privacy of the individuals is to apply protection procedures to these attributes. We will use ρ to denote the protection procedure. Therefore, we have $X'_{nc} = \rho(X_{nc})$.
- **Confidential non quasi-identifiers** X_c. These attributes X_c are usually not modified. So, we have $X'_c = X_c$. Confidential quasi-identifiers will be protected as any other quasi-identifier.

Therefore, we have $X' = \rho(X_{nc})||X_c$. Proceeding in this way, we allow third parties to have precise information on confidential data without revealing to whom the confidential data belongs to.

For the sake of simplicity, we will use the simpler notation $X' = \rho(X)$. Then, we use $x_{i,V}$ to represent the value of the attribute V in the ith record.

In this scenario we have identity disclosure when intruders, having some information described in terms of a set of records and some quasi-identifiers, can establish a relationship between their information with the published data set. That is, they are able to link their records with the ones in X'. Then, if the links between records are correct, intruders have achieved reidentification. In addition to reidentification, they may be able to obtain the right values for the confidential attributes. That is, we will have attribute disclosure.

Methods can be classified into three different categories depending on how they manipulate the original data in order to build the protected data set.

- **Perturbative.** The original data set is distorted in some way, and the new data set might contain some erroneous information. E.g. noise is added to an attribute following a normal distribution $N(0, a)$ for a given a. In this way, some combinations of values disappear, and, new combinations appear in the protected data set. As combinations in the masked data set no longer correspond to the ones in the original data set. This obfuscation makes disclosure difficult for intruders.
- **Non-perturbative.** Protection is achieved through replacing an original value by another one that is not incorrect but less specific. For example, we replace a real number by an interval. In general, non-perturbative methods reduce the level of detail of the data set. This detail reduction causes different records to have the same combinations of values, which reduces disclosure.
- **Synthetic Data Generators.** In this case, instead of distorting the original data, new artificial data is generated and used to substitute the original values. Formally, synthetic data generators build a data model from the original data set and, subsequently, a new (protected) data set is randomly generated using the model. As the published data is artificially created, disclosure risk decreases.

An alternative dimension to classify protection methods is based on the type of data. We can distinguish between numerical and categorical data, but other types of data as e.g. time series, sequences of locations and events, search and access logs, graphs and data from online social networks have also been considered in the literature. Some of the methods we review can be applied to different types of databases.

- **Numerical.** As usual, an attribute is numerical when it is represented by numbers and arithmetic operations. I.e., when addition and substraction can be used in a meaningful way and they lead to sound results. Income and age are typical examples of such attributes. With respect to disclosure risk, numerical values are likely to be unique in a database and, therefore, leading to disclosure if no action is taken.
- **Categorical.** In this case, the attribute takes values over a finite set. Even in the case that a numerical representation is used, standard numerical operations do not make sense. Ordinal and nominal scales are typically distinguished among categorical attributes. In ordinal scales the order between values is relevant (e.g. academic degree), whereas in nominal scales it is not (e.g. hair color). Therefore, max and min operations are meaningful in ordinal scales but not on nominal scales.
  Structured attributes are a subclass of categorical attributes. In this case, different categories are related in terms of subclasses or *member of* relationships. In some cases, a hierarchy between categories can be inferred from these relationships. Cities, counties, and provinces are typical examples of these hierarchical attributes. For some attributes, the hierarchy is given but for others it is constructed by the protection procedures.
- **Logs.** For example, search and access logs. Internet services keep track of all actions from users. Access logs include additional information as e.g. IP addresses and time. It is usual to have multiple logs from the same person. Data protection needs to take into account that such logs are not independent.
- **Longitudinal data and time series.** They correspond to sequences of data collected at different times. In longitudinal data, data are obtained from the same sample in all the period of study. This is not usually so usual in time series. Another difference is that time series usually have more repeated observations than studied cases. In contrast, longitudinal studies have more cases than observations. In addition, in time series, uniform time intervals are frequently used. This is not so often the case for longitudinal studies. The stock market index and the unemployment rate are examples of time series. Clinical trials are examples of longitudinal studies.
- **Smart grid.** Smart grids produce a large amount of information. For example, household energy consumption data. Nevertheless, this data is sensitive because they show consumption patterns of individuals and companies, but also because they allow to make other inferences on e.g. religious celebrations. This data has temporal components, as time series, but, in general, protection can be more complex. There may be some dependencies in the data. For example, business with similar internal procedures, and households with similar patterns. In addition, when grids have a hierarchical structure, data aggregates need to be protected in consonance with low level data.

- **Mobility and location data.** This corresponds to sequences of positions and times-tamps. It typically corresponds to data gathered from mobile devices. From the perspective of data privacy, it is important to underline that only a few points of a trajectory can lead to disclosure (e.g., home and workplace).
- **Graphs and social networks.** Graphs are known to represent a large number of structures. Social networks correspond to the most typical example. Shopping carts (or data for recommender systems) can also be represented using graphs, more concretely, using bipartite graphs. Labeled graphs, in addition to vertices and edges include additional information attached to nodes and edges.
- **Documents.** Textual medical documents about patients, their medical history and treatment are of very much research (and commercial!) interest. Nevertheless, the information is clearly sensitive. Other types of documents are of similar character-istics. Depending on the expected data usage, protection is needed for the whole document or just for particular summaries of the document. If we expect public indexing and document ID retrieval, but access to the actual document is restricted, the problem can be reduced to the anonymization of bags of words.
- **Image and video.** This include photograph and video, but also other types of images, as Magnetic Resonance Imaging (RMI).

We will describe in this book some of the existing protection methods follow-ing the classification above: Perturbative methods are described in Sect. 6.1, non-perturbative methods in Sect. 6.2, and synthetic data generators in Sect. 6.3.

In addition, we have devoted a section to k-anonymity (Sect. 6.4). We have already seen (Sect. 3.4.2) that k-anonymity is not a protection method but a privacy model. We will discuss in Sect. 6.4 methods for obtaining data compliant with this definition. We will also discuss how to protect data when there are constraints among attributes. This discussion is in Sect. 6.5, and we use the terms edit constraints and schema constraints to denote them.

6.1   Perturbative Methods

In this section we review the most relevant perturbative methods. Most of the methods described in this section, with some of their variants are implemented in the sdcMicro package in R [467] and in the μ-Argus software [238].

6.1.1   Data and Rank Swapping

Dalenius and Reiss [112, 113] introduced data swapping in 1978 as a way to pro-tect categorical data. The goal of the anonymization process is to preserve t-order frequency tables (contingency tables up to dimension t). The justification is that "for categorical databases, frequency counts embody most of the relevant statistical information".[1] The definition and justification of the method focuses on ordinal data (i.e., there is a pre-established order on the categories) but it can also be applied to numerical data.

Let F_t^X denote the t-order frequency table of data set X. That is, F_0^X is the number of records in the data set X, F_1^X is the frequency of a given value of an attribute, and F_2^X is the frequency given two values of two given attributes. E.g., $F_1^X[V_i = a]$ is the number of records in which the attribute V_i is a in the file X, and $F_2^X[V_i = a, V_j = b]$ is the number of records in which the attribute V_i is a and attribute V_j is b.

Then, data swapping is defined in terms of swaps between values of one or more attributes "subject to the invariance condition that there be" e.g. two-order equivalence. That is, F_2^X equals to $F_2^{X'}$ where X is the original file and X' the masked one.

Reiss [399,400] proposes an algorithm for Boolean data that gives an approximate solution for 2-order frequency tables. We reproduce here in Algorithm 19 how to construct the masked data set from the frequency tables of the original data up to dimension two.

The algorithm uses a function called *Choose*, which assigns a Boolean value given a certain probability. See Algorithm 18.

It can be seen that the algorithm generates as much records as in the original file. Nevertheless, it is easy to generalize this algorithm to any number of records and, thus, this method can be seen as a synthetic data generator based on frequency tables. This scenario was represented in Fig. 3.2.

Each record is constructed iteratively with the value of the jth attribute assigned taking into account the values already assigned to attribute $1, \ldots, j-1$. In particular, the value for the jth value is zero with a probability defined as the average of the probability of having zero in the original file when the attributes $1, \ldots, j-1$ have the same values as the ones of this new record. That is,

$$p_j = \frac{1}{j-1} \cdot \sum_{k=1}^{j-1} \frac{F_2[V_k = X'_{ij}, V_j = 0]}{F_1[V_k = X'_{ik}]}$$

Note that $F_2[V_k = X'_{ij}, V_j = 0]/F_1[V_k = X'_{ik}]$ is the estimated probability in the original file that V_j is zero when $V_k = X'_{ij}$. When $F_1[V_k = X'_{ik}] = 0$ we define the fraction to be $1/2$.

Reiss proves some properties of their method. In particular, that first-order frequency tables tend to be preserved by any method based on the preservation of second- or third-order frequency tables; and that in the rare case of mutually independent attributes, a method that preserves third-order frequency tables will tend to preserve second-order ones. Nevertheless, the author also proves that an algorithm that preserves the first-order frequency tables can lead to data with 50% of error in the second-order ones, and an algorithm preserving the second-order frequency tables can have 25% of error for the third-order ones.

---

[1] We review some information loss measures for categorical data based on contingency tables in Sect. 7.1.3.

Algorithm 18: Random assignment: $Choose(p)$.

Data: p: probability in $[0,1]$
Result: Boolean value in $\{0,1\}$

```
1 begin
2  |   r:= a random value
3  |   if r < p then
4  |   |   return 0
5  |   else
6  |   |   return 1
7  |   end
8 end
```

Algorithm 19: Data swapping approximating second order frequency tables.

Data: F_t: the set of all frequency tables for $0 \leq t \leq 2$, N: number of records in the original file, $|V|$ number of attributes in the original file
Result: X': masked data set consistent with F_t

```
1 begin
2  |   for i = 1 to N do
```
$$3 \qquad p_1 = F_1[V_1 = 0]/F_0$$
$$4 \qquad X'[i, 1] := Choose(p_1)$$
```
5  |   |   for j = 2 to |V| do
```
$$6 \qquad p_j = \frac{1}{j-1} \cdot \sum_{k=1}^{j-1} \frac{F_2[V_k=X'_{ij}, V_j=0]}{F_1[V_k=X'_{ik}]}$$
$$7 \qquad X'[i, j] := Choose(p_j)$$
```
8  |   |   end
9  |   end
10 |   return (X')
11 end
```

Rank swapping

Rank swapping was introduced to improve the quality of data protected by arbitrary swapping. In particular, its goal is to keep multivariate relationships between attributes, and means in subsets.

Definition of rank swapping is given in Algorithm 20. It is defined for a single attribute. When the data file contains several attributes, the method is applied to each of them independently. The algorithm depends on a parameter p that permits the user to control the amount of disclosure risk. It defines the range of possible values with which to swap. Normally, p corresponds to a percent of the total number of records in X.

With this algorithm, the smaller the p, the larger the risk. Note that when p increases the difference between x_i and x_ℓ may increase accordingly. Therefore, the risk decreases. Nevertheless, in this case the differences between the original and the masked data set are higher, so information loss increases.

One of the main advantages of rank swapping is that the marginal distributions of the original file and the masked file are equal because the values are not modified.

Algorithm 20: Rank swapping: $rs(X, p)$.

Data: X: original data file; p: percentage of records for swapping; V attribute

Result: X'_V: attribute V for the masked file

1 **begin**

2      $(a_1, \ldots, a_n) :=$ values of attribute V in X in increasing order (i.e., $a_i \leq a_\ell$ for all $1 \leq i < \ell \leq n$)

3   Mark a_i as unswapped for all i

4   **for** $i = 1$ **to** n **do**

5   **if** a_i *is unswapped* **then**

6   Select ℓ randomly and uniformly chosen from the limited range $[i + 1, \min(n, i + p * |X|/100)]$

7   Swap a_i with a_ℓ

8   **end**

9   **end**

10   Undo the sorting step

11 **end**

Also, the method gives a good trade-off between information loss and disclosure risk when the transparency principle is not taken into account. It was classified [144,473] among the best microdata protection methods for numerical and ordinal attributes. Nevertheless, as we discuss in the next section, it is possible to develop effective transparency attacks.

One of the disadvantages of these methods is that correlations between the attributes are modified by the masking method. This is due to the fact that attributes are masked independently. The effect is more or less intense depending on the data and the number of records.

Rank swapping and transparency: a specific attack

Recall that when we apply the transparency principle, we do not only publish the masked file but also give the information that the data has been masked with rank swapping and report the parameter p used. In this case, any attacker can use this information to attack the database.

In this section we describe a specific record linkage algorithm (rank swapping record linkage, RS-RL) that uses this particular information to link the records of the intruder with the ones in the released masked file. The procedure takes advantage that for any given value, swapping is constrained to a subset of records. Using the notation in Algorithm 20, the value a_i can only be swapped with values ℓ in the limited range $[i + 1, \min(n, i + p * |X|/100)]$.

Therefore, when an intruder knows the value of an attribute V_j about an individual x_i a set $B_j(x_i)$ that contains all masked records which may be the masked version of x_i can be computed. Intruders can apply the same process to all attributes they know, and then the original record should correspond to one in the intersection of all the sets $B_j(x_i)$ for all known attributes j. That is, let $1 \leq j \leq c$ denote the indices

---

Algorithm 21: Rank swapping record linkage (RS-RL).

Data: $Y \subseteq X$: data file of the intruder; X': masked file; p: percentage of records for swapping
Result: linkage between Y and X'

1 **begin**
2     $LP = \emptyset$
3   **for** *each* $x_i \in Y$ **do**
4        $B(x_i) = \cap_{1 \leq j \leq c} B_j(x_i)$
5        $x' = \arg\min_{x' \in B(x_i)} d(x', x_i)$
6        $LP = LP \cup (x', x_i)$
7   **end**
8   **return** (LP)
9 **end**

---

of the attributes known by an intruder. Then, the anonymized record x'_ℓ of x_i should satisfy

$$x'_\ell \in \cap_{1 \leq j \leq c} B_j(x_i). \tag{6.1}$$

This type of attack is an intersection attack. Moreover, $B(x_i) = \cap_{1 \leq j \leq c} B_j(x_i)$ is the anonymity set of x_i.

When this set consists of a single record, this is a true match. Note that in this case, we know for sure that the link is correct because there is no uncertainty in the process and we are absolutely sure that the record is in the intersection of the $B_j(x_i)$. I.e., it is a match. This match will be included in the reidentification measure $K.Reid(B, A)$ (see Eq. 3.3). When the intersection includes several records, we have uncertainty but only within the intersection set. In this case, we can apply e.g. distance-based record linkage to select one of the records of the intersection set. If the method is known but the parameter is not, we can set up an upper bound of the parameter. In case that the set is empty for any of the records, it means that the estimation of the parameter is too low and it should be enlarged. Note that for the correct parameter p, the intersection will never be empty.

Algorithm 21 describes the transparency attack for rank swapping. The following example illustrates this algorithm.

Example 6.1 [354] Let us consider the original and masked files of Table 6.1. Attributes $V_1, \ldots, V_4$ represent quasi-identifiers and attribute V_5 represents a confidential attribute that is not a quasi-identifier. Then, only attributes $V_1, \ldots, V_4$ are masked using rank swapping. For convenience the original and masked files are aligned. I.e., the ith record in the original file corresponds to the ith record in the masked file. In the masking process we used $p = 2/10$. Thus, each value could have been swapped with 4 other values (2 smaller and 2 larger values).

Let us consider that the intruder has information corresponding to attributes V_1, V_2, V_3, V_4 for an individual and that this information is $x_2 = (6, 7, 10, 2)$.

Let us consider the standard distance-based record linkage method (with the Euclidean distance) applied to this record $x_2 = (6, 7, 10, 2)$. That is, we compute the distance between this record and all the masked records. The closest masked record

Table 6.1 Example for rank swapping record linkage: original and masked files (Nin et al. [354])

Original file X					Masked file X'				
V_1	V_2	V_3	V_4	V_5	V_1'	V_2'	V_3'	V_4'	V_5
8	9	1	3	il_1	10	10	3	5	il_1
6	7	10	2	il_2	5	5	8	1	il_2
10	3	4	1	il_3	8	4	2	2	il_3
7	1	2	6	il_4	9	2	4	4	il_4
9	4	6	4	il_5	7	3	5	6	il_5
2	2	8	8	il_6	4	1	10	10	il_6
1	10	3	9	il_7	3	9	1	7	il_7
4	8	7	10	il_8	2	6	9	8	il_8
5	5	5	5	il_9	6	7	6	3	il_9
3	6	9	7	il_{10}	1	8	7	9	il_{10}

corresponds to $x_9' = (6, 7, 6, 3)$. As, this is not the original record for x_2, we have that distance-based record linkage produces an incorrect link between $x_2 = (6, 7, 10, 2)$ and $x_9' = (6, 7, 6, 3)$.

Let us now consider the record linkage described in Algorithm 21 for the same record $x_2 = (6, 7, 10, 2)$. The set of possible masked records consistent with the 6 in the first attribute V_1 corresponds to $B_1(x_2) = B_1(V_1 = 6) = \{(4, 1, 10, 10), (5, 5, 8, 1), (6, 7, 6, 3), (7, 3, 5, 6), (8, 4, 2, 2)\}$. Let us compute also the sets for the other attributes. We obtain $B_2(x_2) = B_2(V_2 = 7) = \{(5, 5, 8, 1), (2, 6, 9, 8), (6, 7, 6, 3), (1, 8, 7, 9), (3, 9, 1, 7)\}$, $B_3(x_2) = B_3(V_3 = 10) = \{(5, 5, 8, 1), (2, 6, 9, 8), (4, 1, 10, 10)\}$ and $B_4(x_2) = B_4(V_4 = 2) = \{(5, 5, 8, 1), (8, 4, 2, 2), (6, 7, 6, 3), (9, 2, 4, 4)\}$. Then, the intersection of these sets (Eq. 6.1) is a single record $(5, 5, 8, 1)$, which is the correct linkage.

Naturally, the more the attributes known by the intruder, the easier that the intersection is a single record. The main characteristics of this approach are summarized below.

- Given a record, when the intersection set is a single record, this is a match. That is, we know for sure that this is the record we are looking for. Recall our discussion in Sect. 3.3.2 (Eq. 3.3 for $K.Reid$).
- Given a masked file, this attack can be done even in the case that the intruder only knows data from a single individual in the masked file. There is no need to have a set of data from several individuals to apply the attack.
- The more attributes the intruder has, the better is the reidentification. The intersection set never increases when the number of attributes increases.
- When the intruder does not know the parameter p, a lower bound of this parameter can be found. Given records in $Y \subseteq X$ known by the intruder, the lower bound of

---

Algorithm 22: Rank swapping p-distribution: $rs(X, p)$.

Data: X: original data file; p: percentage of records for swapping; V: attribute
Result: X'_V: attribute V for the masked file
1 **begin**
2    $(a_1, \ldots, a_n) :=$ values of attribute V in X in increasing order (i.e., $a_i \leq a_\ell$ for all $1 \leq i < \ell \leq n$)
3   Mark a_i as unswapped for all i
4   **for** $i = 1$ **to** n **do**
5   **if** a_i *is unswapped* **then**
6   Select r according to the normal distribution $N(0.5p, 0.5p)$
7          $\ell = i + round(r)$
8   Swap a_i with a_ℓ
9   **end**
10   **end**
11   Undo the sorting step
12 **end**

---

p corresponds to the minimum value that makes all anonymity sets B not empty. To formalize this lower bound of p (denoted p_{lw}), we denote the anonymity set of any record y computed using a particular p_0 by $B^{p_0}(y)$. That is, $B^{p_0}(y)$ is the set of records compatible with y when we are using rank swapping with parameter p_0. Then,

$$p_{lw}(Y) = \min\{p_0| \ |B^{p_0}(y)| \geq 1, \text{ for all } y \in Y\}$$

Note that the larger the set Y, the larger the lower bound and, thus, the better the estimation of p.

Rank swapping p-distribution and p-buckets

Two variants of rank swapping exist to overcome this type of attack with rank swapping-record linkage. They are p-distribution and p-buckets rank swapping. Both variations have in common that the set $B_j(x_i)$, using the terminology of Algorithm 20, is the whole data set. That is, swapping can be done with a value belonging to any record of the file. Probabilities are larger for records with similar values, and lower for records that are dissimilar, but they are never zero. The difference between p-distribution and p-bucket rank swapping is the definition of these probabilities.

In p-distribution rank swapping, the value of the ith record is swapped with the value of record $\ell = i + r$ where r is a random value computed using the $N(0.5p, 0.5p)$ normal distribution. Algorithm 22 describes the process. Here p is the parameter of the method and plays the same role as p in standard rank swapping.

In p-bucket rank swapping, ordered values are clustered into p buckets of similar size and with consecutive values. Let $B_1, \ldots, B_p$ denote these buckets. Then, for each value a_i of a bucket B_r we select a value a_l of a bucket B_s in a two step process. First, we select the bucket B_s with $s \geq r$. Selection is done according to the probability distribution

$$Pr[B_s \text{ is choosen } |B_r] = \frac{1}{K} \frac{1}{2^{s-r+1}}.$$

In this expression K is a normalization constant so that the probabilities add up to one.

Once B_s is known, we select a value a_l from the bucket B_s. In this second step, the selection of a_l is done using a uniform distribution on the elements of the bucket. When $B_s = B_r$, $\ell > i$ is imposed.

Transparency attacks and specific record linkage algorithms can also be designed for these masking methods. For example, rank-based record linkage was applied [335] to p-distribution rank swapping. The results show that p-distribution rank swapping is still more resistant to transparency attacks than standard rank swapping. Alternatively, we can consider a distance-based record linkage based on a linear combination of order statistics (or OWA [533]). Note that these two rank swapping variants discussed above ensure privacy granting that, with a high probability, at least one of the attributes will be swapped with a value in a distant position. Then, we can define an Euclidean-like distance that discards e.g. the largest distance.

Rank swapping: variants and big data

Given an attribute, order is the only property needed to apply rank swapping. Therefore, it can be applied to both numerical and categorical (ordinal) data.

Lasko and Vinterbo [278,279] introduced swapping for high-dimensional data. The approach is based on a spectral transformation of the data using singular value decomposition. I.e., data X is first expressed as UDV^T (where V^T is the transpose of V) and then a new file X' is computed considering a permutation $\tilde{U}$ of U and defining $X' = \tilde{U}DV^T$.

Swapping has been applied to location privacy in [201] in a distributed way. There are also methods for social networks based on swapping edges. As these methods can be seen as noise addition on the adjacency matrix of the graph, we include some references in the corresponding section of this chapter.

In the context of big data, for streaming data, we can apply rank swapping on a sliding window. See e.g. [346].

6.1.2 Microaggregation

Microaggregation consists of building small microclusters and then replacing the original data in each cluster by the cluster representatives. Privacy is achieved because each cluster is required to contain a predefined number of records and, thus, the published data, the cluster representative, is not the data of a single record but a representation of the whole cluster.

This method is currently used by statistical agencies [185]. Comparisons of microaggregation with other methods show that it gives a good trade-off between information loss and disclosure risk (in terms of identity disclosure and reidentification).

Microaggregation is formulated mathematically as an optimization problem. The goal is to find the clusters, i.e. a partition of the data, that minimize a global error. This formalization follows the one of the k-means (see Sect. 2.4.1). Each cluster is represented with a characteristic function χ_i where $\chi_i(x) = 1$ if the record x is assigned

---

Algorithm 23: Optimal Univariate Microaggregation.

Data: $X = (a_1 \ldots a_n)$: original data set (single attribute), k: integer
Result: X': protected data set

1 **begin**
2 | $A :=$ Sort the values of X in ascending order so that if $i < j$ then $a_i \leq a_j$.
3 | Given A and k, a graph $G_{k,n}$ is defined as follows.
4 | **begin**
5 | Define the nodes of G as the elements a_i in A plus one additional node g_0 (this node is later needed to apply the Dijkstra algorithm).
6 | For each node g_i, add to the graph the directed edges (g_i, g_j) for all j such that $i + k \leq j < i + 2k$. The edge (g_i, g_j) means that the values $(a_{i+1}, \ldots, a_j)$ might define one of the possible clusters.
7 | The cost of the edge (g_i, g_j) is defined as the within-group sum of squared error for such cluster. That is, $SSE = \Sigma_{l=i+1}^{j}(a_l - \bar{a})^2$, where $\bar{a}$ is the average record of the cluster.
8 | **end**
9 | Compute the shortest path between the nodes g_0 and g_n. This shortest path can be computed using the Dijkstra algorithm. Each edge represents a cluster
10 | $X' :=$ replace each value in X by the average record of its corresponding cluster
11 | **return** X'
12 **end**

---

to the ith cluster and $\chi_i(x) = 0$ if not. The clusters need to have a minimum number of records to satisfy the privacy requirements. Therefore, this number, denoted by k in the optimization problem, is a parameter of microaggregation. The function to be minimized requires that the partition is made so that the distance between records and their cluster centers is minimal. This is formalized by means of cluster centers p_i and a distance d between records and cluster centers.

The optimization problem includes a parameter c which is the number of clusters and two additional sets of constraints. One that requires that all records are assigned to one cluster, and another that states that the characteristic functions are either zero or one.

The definition of the problem is as follows.

$$\text{Minimize} \quad SSE(\chi, p; X, c, d) = \sum_{i=1}^{c} \sum_{x \in X} \chi_i(x)(d(x, p_i))^2 \qquad (6.2)$$

$$\text{Subject to} \quad \sum_{i=1}^{c} \chi_i(x) = 1 \text{ for all } x \in X$$

$$2k > \sum_{x \in X} \chi_i(x) \geq k \text{ for all } i = 1, \ldots, c$$

$$\chi_i(x) \in \{0, 1\} \text{ for all } x \in X, \text{ for all } i = 1, \ldots, c$$

For numerical data it is usual to require that $d(x, p)$ is the Euclidean distance. Then, given attributes $V = (V_1, \ldots, V_s)$, x and p are vectors, and $(d(x, p))^2 = \sum_{V_i \in V}(x_{v_i} - p_{v_i})^2$. In addition, it is also common to require for numerical data

---

Algorithm 24: General Multivariate Microaggregation.

Data: X: original data set, k: integer
Result: X': protected data set

1 **begin**
2   Let $\Pi = \{\pi_1, \ldots, \pi_p\}$ be a partition of the set of attributes $V = \{V_1, \ldots, V_s\}$
3   **foreach** $\pi \in \Pi$ **do**
4   Microaggregate X considering only the attributes in π
5   **end**
6 **end**

---

that p_i is defined as the arithmetic mean of the records in the cluster. I.e., $p_i = \sum_{j=1}^{n} \chi_i(x_j)x_j / \sum_{j=1}^{n} \chi_i(x_j)$.

In the case of univariate microaggregation, i.e. a single attribute, using the Euclidean distance and the arithmetic mean, algorithms that find an optimal solution in polynomial time can be implemented. Algorithm 23 corresponds to one of such implementation introduced by Hansen and Mukherjee [219]. In contrast, in the case of multivariate data sets the problem becomes NP-Hard [367]. For this reason, heuristic methods have been proposed in the literature.

Heuristic methods for microaggregation

Heuristic methods are usually based on an operational definition of microaggregation. They are defined in terms of the following three steps.

- **Partition.** Records are partitioned into several clusters, each of them consisting of at least k records.
- **Aggregation.** For each of the clusters a representative (the centroid) is computed.
- **Replacement.** Each record is replaced by the cluster representative.

This operational definition has been used to extend microaggregation to a large number of data types. Note that given data in a certain domain, if we define a distance and an aggregation function we can then define a partition method to complete the three steps of the operational definition.

Multidimensional data

Both the general formulation and the multidimensional heuristic operational definition permits us to apply microaggregation to multidimensional data. Nevertheless, when the number of attributes is large, it is usual to apply microaggregation to subsets of attributes; otherwise, the information loss is very high. Algorithm 24 defines this procedure. It considers a partition $\Pi = \{\pi_1, \ldots, \pi_p\}$ of the attributes in the data set X, and applies microaggregation to each subset $\pi \in \Pi$. We discuss how to build this partition in a section below.

Strategies for selecting subsets of attributes

Individual ranking is about an attribute-wise application of microaggregation. In other words, we apply microaggregation to each attribute in an independent way. That is, applying Algorithm 24 with $\pi_i = \{V_i\}$ and $p = s$.

Using a partition Π of the attributes permits us to reduce the information loss at the cost of increasing the disclosure risk. Different partitions can lead to different measures of risk and information loss. It has been shown [355] that when correlated attributes are grouped together, information loss is not as high as when uncorrelated attributes are put together. However, the selection of uncorrelated attributes decreases disclosure risk. Therefore, this is a multi-objective problem and what partition leads to a best trade-off between disclosure risk and information loss will depend on the data available.

A different approach is to microaggregate the given set of records using only a subset of available attributes. Then, the key aspect is to select the attributes. For example, Sun et al. [457] select attributes based on the mutual information measure. The selected set accounts for half the *independence* between the attributes. This roughly corresponds to pick up attributes that are not correlated, and use only these ones to build the clusters. Aggregation and replacement is applied to all the attributes in the set. Note the difference between using the Pearson correlation and the mutual information measure. This approach is justified [457] on the dependency trees introduced by Chow and Liu [98]. Oommen and Fayyoumi [368] proceed similarly, although using an alternative approach to select these few attributes, and reached to the same conclusion: information loss is decreased when independent attributes are selected.

Strategies for building the partition: partitioning

For a given grouping of the set of attributes $\Pi = \{\pi_1, \ldots, \pi_p\}$ we need to apply a multivariate microaggregation method to each subset of data with attributes in π_i to partition, aggregate, and replace the value in the original data set. As stated above, a heuristic approach is usually applied.

Heuristic approaches for sets of attributes can be classified into two categories. One approach consists of projecting the records on a one dimensional space (using e.g. Principal Components or Zscores) and then applying optimal microaggregation on the projected dimension (Algorithm 26 describes this approach). The other is to develop adhoc algorithms. The MDAV [138] (Maximum Distance to Average Vector) algorithm follows this second approach. It is explained in detail in Algorithm 28, when applied to a data set X with n records and A attributes. An alternative heuristic approach is to build the cluster using minimum spanning trees. In this way, it is easy to ensure that all clusters have at least k records but they can contain more than $2k$ records, unless an additional partitioning step is applied to this larger sets. The procedure is as follows:

- **Step 1.** F = minimum spanning tree(X)
- **Step 2.** F' = delete removable edges(F)
- **Step 3.** C = assign data to clusters(F')

Algorithm 25: Minimum spanning tree heuristic microaggregation: $isRemovable((o, d), F)$.

Data: (o, d): edge, F: minimum spanning tree
Result: Boolean
1 **begin**
2   **if** $descendents(o) < k$ **then**
3 | return(false)
4   **end**
5   **else** root = obtain root (o, F)
6   **return** $(descendents(root) - descendents(o) \geq k)$
7 **end**

The construction of the minimum spanning tree is done using the Prim's method. The nodes are the set of records in X, and the costs of the edges correspond to the (Euclidean) distance between records.

Once the minimum spanning tree of the whole data set X is built, some edges are removed in order to obtain smaller components (smaller trees) each with at least k elements. To do so, edges in the tree are considered from larger to lower length and if their removal is permitted (the two new smaller components have at least k records) the edge is cut.

The implementation [280] uses a priority queue of the edges based on their length, and also uses a node structure that links each node with its parent and that contains information on the number of descendents of the node. This latter information is useful when determining if an edge can be cut. Note that an edge linking a node o to a node d (i.e., o is the origin of the edge and d the destination as directed edges are used) can be removed when the number of descendents of o is at least k and the component of node d has also at least k nodes. That a component has at least k nodes can be checked traversing the nodes to the root and then comparing the number of descendents with k. This is detailed in Algorithm 25.

The minimum spanning tree heuristics can lead to clusters with more than $2k$ records when the removal of any edge of the clusters lead to less than k nodes. Such clusters have a star-shape, which are nodes with a central node connecting with several components all of them with less than k nodes. In order to reduce information loss (when measured using SSE) we should split such large clusters. Other microaggregation algorithms can be used for this purpose. This algorithm produce the best results [280] when clusters are well separated.

Another heuristic approach [295] consists of selecting clusters around points with high density. The density is computed taking into account the $k - 1$ nearest records of the record under consideration. This approach can be seen as a microaggregation version of the subtractive method [94] using a potential function as follows

$$d^k(x, T) = \frac{1}{\sum_{x \in N^k(x,T)} ||x - p||^2}$$

where $N^k(x, T)$ are the $k - 1$ nearest records to x in T and p is the average of these records.

Algorithm 26: Heuristic Multivariate Microaggregation: Projected Microaggregation.

Data: X: original data set, k: integer
Result: X': protected data set

1 **begin**
2   Apply a projection algorithm to X, and obtain an univariate vector $z = (z_1, \ldots, z_n)$ where n is the number of records and z_i the projection of the ith record
3   Sort the components of z in increasing order
4   Apply optimal univariate microaggregation to the vector z, using as cost between nodes the within-group sum of square error of the records associated to these nodes (i.e., the SSE of the full records and not only of the projections)
5   For each cluster resulting from the previous step, compute the s-dimensional centroid and replace all the records in the cluster by the centroid
6 **end**

This process can be defined as follows. First, we use $T_0 = X$. In general, for a given T_i, we select the record $x = \arg\max_{x \in T_i} d^k(x, T_i)$. This produces the cluster $N^k(x, T_i)$ and records are replaced by their cluster center. Then we define T_{i+1} as T_i after removing all records in $N^k(x, T_i)$. In other words, $T_{i+1} = T_i \setminus N^k(x, T_i)$. The process stops when T_i has less than $2k$ records.

Heuristic methods lead to partitions that may be suboptimal with respect to the objective function SSE. To improve the result, we can apply a post-processing step after clustering. For example, we can reassign the elements of a cluster with a large variance [87]. The rationale is based on the fact that given a cluster C_i with a large contribution to the error (that is, $\sum_{x \in C_i}(d(x, p_i))^2$ is large), we may be able to reassign all the elements $x \in C_i$ to other clusters in such a way that

(i) the clusters still have between k and $2k - 1$ records, and
(ii) the total distance to the newly assigned cluster centers is smaller than the total distance to C_i. That is,

$$\sum_{x \in C_i}(d(x, p_{n(x)}))^2 < \sum_{x \in C_i}(d(x, p_i))^2$$

where $n(x)$ is the function that assigns the new cluster center to records in C_i.

This post-processing step that reassigns some records is described in Algorithm 27.

Strategies for aggregation

Given a partition, in principle, any aggregation function [491] can be used to build a representative of a cluster. For numerical data, the arithmetic mean is the most used aggregation function. The median and the mode (the plurality rule) have also been used. The median is a good option for ordinal data and the mode for nominal data. As the median and the mode are values in the original data set, they may lead to disclosure.

Algorithm 27: Reassignment of records to reduce SSE.

Data: X: original data set, C: partition of X
Result: C': a new partition
1 **begin**
2   Compute $GSE_i = \sum_{x \in C_i} (d(x, p_i))^2$ for each cluster $C_i \in C$
3   Define $GSE_{\sigma(i)}$ so that $GSE_{\sigma(i)} \geq GSE_{\sigma(i+1)}$
4      $C' = C$
5      $SSE_{C'} = SSE_C$
6   **for** $i = 1$ *to* $|C|$ **do**
7   **for** $x \in C_{\sigma(i)}$ **do**
8   Assign temporarily x in C' to $\arg\min_{i \neq \sigma(i)} d(x, p_i)$
9   Update C' and $SSE_{C'}$ accordingly
10   **end**
11   **if** $SSE_C > SSE_{C'}$ **then**
12              $C = C'$
13   **end**
14   **end**
15 **end**

Strategies for replacement

Almost all approaches replace records by their cluster center. This corresponds to a deterministic replacement. Fuzzy microaggregation (discussed below) is one of the exceptions. It uses a random replacement approach that takes into account several cluster centers. This approach is used to avoid transparency attacks.

Properties: statistics and anonymity

Optimal univariate microaggregation generates a masked file with the same mean as the original file. Note that this is so because a cluster with values $v_1, \ldots, v_k$ replaces these values by their mean. So, the cluster has k copies of the mean $m = (\sum v_i)/k$ and their sum is the sum of the original values (i.e., $km = \sum v_i$). The same applies for heuristic microaggregation when the centroid is computed with the mean. Totals for attributes will be also maintained for the same reason.

In contrast, variance is usually not kept. Not only that, the variance of each attribute is reduced after microaggregation. Observe that, in general, microaggregation replaces different values (e.g., the values $v_1, \ldots, v_k$) by multiple copies of the same value. This, naturally, reduces the variance. The larger the clusters, the smaller the variance.

Exercise 6.1 Given a file, microaggregate it with different values of k and compute the mean and the variance. Observe how variance is reduced when k increases.

Other statistics will also be affected by microaggregation. E.g., correlation coefficients and covariance between attributes. Different partitioning of attributes will produce different effects on the correlation coefficients. We have discussed this problem above.

Microaggregation can be used to obtain a masked file that is compliant with k-anonymity. This is achieved when the partition of the set of attributes contains a set with all attributes $\Pi = \{\pi = \{V_1, \ldots, V_s\}\}$. Section 6.4 discusses the relation between both microaggregation and k-anonymity. As other partitions of the attributes do not ensure k-anonymity, we can define the *real anonymity measure* as the ratio between the total number of records in the original file and the number of protected records which are different. We have already presented this expression in Eq. 3.1.

$$k' = \frac{|X|}{|\{x'|x' \in X'\}|}. \tag{6.3}$$

Post-masking for microaggregation

There have been several attempts to improve the quality of microaggregated files decreasing the information loss of the protected data set. We have seen in Example 3.2 post-masking consisting of replacing different records of a cluster by different values so that the variance of the original and protected files are the same. Let C_i be the ith cluster, $|C_i|$ the cardinality of this set, and c_i the cluster center. Then, for each cluster C_i we define a sphere B_i with center c_i and radius r_i. Instead of replacing the records by the cluster center, we select $|C_i|$ points from the surface of B_i such that their average is the cluster center c_i. In order that the variance is maintained we select $r_i = \sqrt{Var(P_i)}$. Under these conditions, both mean and variance of the original set is preserved.

Blow-up microaggregation [451] is another way to keep both mean and variance of the original file. This is achieved moving all cluster representatives far away from the center of the data in such a way that the original and the protected data have the same variance.

Proposition 6.1 *Let X be the original database and X' be the protected database using standard microaggregation. Then, the database defined by*

$$\tilde{X} = X' + \beta \cdot (X' - \bar{X})$$

with

$$\beta = \sqrt{\frac{\sum (x_i - \bar{X})^2}{\sum_{k \in K} \alpha_k (\bar{x}'_k - \bar{X})^2} - 1}$$

has the same mean and variance as X.

An alternative is to combine microaggregation with synthetic data generators to preserve e.g. the covariances of the original data set. This is called hybrid microdata using microaggregation [137].

Algorithm 27 presented above that modifies the partition to improve SSE can be seen as post-masking. Note however, that in this section we focused on the modification of the whole masked data and not only on reassigning records of the partition.

Microaggregation and transparency

When data is protected using microaggregation visual inspection is enough to know that the file has been microaggregated, which is the parameter k and which is the partition of the attributes used. This permits any intruder to build specific attacks to data masked using microaggregation.

Very effective attacks can be done for optimal univariate microaggregation. This is due to the fact that in optimal microaggregation, clusters are defined with contiguous values. Recall from Algorithm 23 that data is first ordered, and only sets with values $(a_{i+1}, \ldots, a_j)$ are considered. Therefore, if $p_1, \ldots, p_c$ are the cluster centers and z the value in the hands of the intruder, if there is $p_i < z < p_{i+1}$, we know for sure that the record associated to z can only be either in the ith cluster or in the $(i + 1)$th cluster. Then, we define $B(z)$ as the set of records in the ith cluster union the set of records in the $(i + 1)$th cluster. In this way, we can attack the masked data set applying an intersection attack similar to the one we described for rank swapping (see Eq. 6.1). In this case using $B_j(x_i)$ to denote the set of masked records that correspond to a record x_i when we know the value of its V_j attribute, we have that its masked version x'_ℓ should satisfy

$$x'_\ell \in \cap_{1 \leq j \leq c} B_j(x_i).$$

As in the case of rank swapping, this attack can be applied by an intruder even in the case of having information of a single record. Some non-optimal univariate algorithms also result into clusters with contiguous values. In this case, the same attack can be applied.

The following example illustrates a transparency attack.

Example 6.2 Let us consider the following one dimensional set of eight records $X = \{x_0 = 0, x_1 = 1.0, x_2 = 2.1, x_3 = 3.3, x_4 = 4.6, x_5 = 4.7, x_6 = 4.8, x_7 = 4.9\}$. If we apply a microaggregation with $k = 4$ we would obtain the clusters $\{0, 1.0, 2.1, 3.3\}$ and $\{4.6, 4.7, 4.8, 4.9\}$ with cluster centers $p_1 = 1.6$ and $p_2 = 4.75$. It is easy to see that if we look for the record $x_3 = 3.3$ the nearest cluster center is p_2 although it has been assigned to p_1.

- $d(x_3, p_1) = d(3.3, 1.6) = 1.7$
- $d(x_3, p_2) = d(3.3, 4.75) = 1.45$

When an intruder only considers distance-based record linkage for attacking the masked data set, x_3 is assigned to the wrong cluster. The transparency principle would permit the intruder to know that x_3 can be either assigned to p_1 or p_2. Further information on the data (e.g., other records and/or other attributes) permits the intruder to further reduce the set of alternatives.

The partition obtained in this example would also be obtained by some heuristic microaggregation methods when $k = 3$. This is the case, for example, of the method based on minimum spanning trees. MDAV does not return this partition for $k = 3$.

Algorithm 28: MDAV algorithm.

Data: X: original data set, k: integer
Result: X': protected data set
1 **begin**
2 | $C = \emptyset$
3 | **while** $|X| \geq 3k$ **do**
4 | | $\bar{X} :=$ the average record of all records in X
5 | | $x_r :=$ the most distant record from $\bar{X}$
6 | | $x_s :=$ the most distant record from x_r
7 | | $C_r :=$ cluster around x_r (with x_r and the $k - 1$ closest records to x_r)
8 | | $C_s :=$ cluster around x_s (with x_s and the $k - 1$ closest records to x_s)
9 | | Remove records in C_r and C_s from data set X
10 | | $C := C \cup \{C_r, C_s\}$
11 | **end**
12 | **if** $|X| \geq 2k$ **then**
13 | | $\bar{X} :=$ the average record of all records in X
14 | | $x_r :=$ the most distant record from $\bar{X}$
15 | | $C_r :=$ cluster around x_r (with x_r and the $k - 1$ closest records to x_r)
16 | | $C_s := X \setminus C_r$ (form another cluster with the rest of records)
17 | | $C := C \cup \{C_r, C_s\}$
18 | **end**
19 | **else**
20 | | $C := C \cup \{X\}$
21 | **end**
22 | $X' =$ replace in X each record by the cluster center of its cluster
23 | **return** (X')
24 **end**

Attacks for multivariate microaggregation are not so easy. The reason is that a record can turn out to be in different clusters. The constraint of having at least k records in a cluster can cause a record to be in a cluster that is not the nearest one, but far away. Nin et al. [356] attacked microaggregation in different ways. Different multivariate algorithms were attacked using a projected record linkage. For some projected microaggregation, using specific attacks showed a significant improvement (e.g., multiplying by three or even more the number of reidentifications of distance-based and probabilistic record linkage). For MDAV algorithm, the increment was moderate but also significant.

Fuzzy Microaggregation

Fuzzy microaggregation has been proposed as a way to overcome transparency attacks. It is based on fuzzy clustering that permits records to be simultaneously assigned to different clusters with different membership degrees. Cluster centers are then computed using all records assigned to them, each one weighted by their membership. So, the output of the partition step is an assignment of records to all clusters, each assignment has its membership degree. The aggregation step computes the cluster centers. The replacement step uses a probability distribution based on the membership functions to substitute the original values by one of the cluster centers.

Algorithm 29: Decoupled fuzzy c-means based microaggregation with parameters c, m_1, and m_2.

Data: X: original data set, k: integer, m_1, m_2: degrees of fuzziness
Result: X': protected data set

1 **begin**
2   Apply fuzzy c-means with a given c and a given $m := m_1$
3   For each x_j in X, compute memberships u to all clusters in $i = 1, \ldots, c$ for a given m_2. Use:
4

$$u_{ij} = \Big(\sum_{r=1}^{c} \Big(\frac{||x_j - v_i||^2}{||x_j - v_r||^2} \Big)^{\frac{1}{m_2 - 1}} \Big)^{-1}$$

5   For each x_j determine a random value χ in $[0, 1]$ using a uniform distribution in $[0,1]$, and assign x_j to the ith cluster (with cluster center c_i) using the probability distribution $u_{1j}, \ldots, u_{cj}$. Formally, given χ select the ith cluster satisfying $\sum_{k<i} u_{kj} < \chi < \sum_{k \le i} u_{kj}$. Define x'_j as the c_i
6 **end**
7 **return** (X');

We describe an algorithm based on fuzzy c-means. No constraint is used on the number of records in each cluster, and only the usual parameters of fuzzy c-means are used: m_1 (the degree of fuzziness) and c the number of clusters. The parameter c is selected in the range

$$c \in \left[\frac{|X|}{2k}, \frac{|X|}{k} \right]$$

so that clusters have in average between k and $2k$ records.

Once the fuzzy partition is built, we compute the membership of each record to each cluster. For this purpose, we need to select a degree of fuzziness m_2 (which is not necessarily the same m_1 used for clustering). Then, records are assigned to clusters using a probability distribution built from the membership degrees. Algorithm 29 details these steps. We call this algorithm Decoupled fuzzy c-means based microaggregation. This is so because we apply fuzzy c-means using two different fuzziness degrees instead of one as usual.

With appropriate selection of c, m_1, and m_2 we obtain masked files that range from the original file to files with large information loss and high privacy guarantees. In particular, the following can be proven.

Proposition 6.2 *Decoupled fuzzy c-means based microaggregation satisfies the following properties.*

- *For large values of m_2 and $c = |X|/k$, the expected size of all clusters is k (probabilistically expected k-anonymity).*
- *For large m_2, all memberships tend to be $1/c$ and thus any replacement is equally probable.*
- *For large m_1, all cluster centers tend to collide $c_i = c_j = \bar{X}$ for $i, j = 1, \ldots, c$. $\bar{X}$ represents the mean of the whole database.*

- *For $c = 1$, all records are replaced by $\bar{X}$.*
- *For $c = |X|$ and $m_1 = m_2 = 1$, optimal cluster results into $X' = X$.*

Note that implementation of c-means is not always leading to global optimal. So, for the last item we may not achieve in practice $X' = X$ when $c = |X|$.

Here, recall that m_1, m_2 are values larger than 1. With a value near one, fuzzy c-means is equivalent to crisp k-means. In applications, it is usual to consider values between 1 and 2. With respect to this proposition, values larger than 2 are already considered large.

The first property means that we can have probabilistically expected k-anonymity. As we have that assignment is probabilistic, we cannot ensure that all clusters have the same number of records, but the expected number of records is the same for all clusters. The second result implies that we cannot always assume that records are replaced by the nearest cluster center. In fact, they can be replaced by any cluster center when m_2 increases. The last two results give conditions for the largest information loss possible (i.e., either $c = 1$ or a large m_1).

Isolated records can cause disclosure risk problems when m_1 and m_2 are small. Small values of m_1 may imply clusters with only one record with significant membership, and cluster centers may correspond to this very record (or a slight modified version of it).

Microaggregation: variants and big data

In our discussion on k-anonymity as a privacy model (Sect. 3.4.2), we have underlined that independence of the k objects in the anonymity set is a key constraint to ensure privacy. This is naturally also relevant when implementing microaggregation. For example, grouping records based on their similarity may result into clusters containing only members from the same household, which may share some information. In a more extreme case, if we are microaggregating search logs, we may be grouping search logs from the same individual.

Measures need to be taken to ensure that the clusters are diverse enough. From a point of view of anonymity sets, this means that the anonymity sets are defined on the appropriate items of interest. For example, that we have k different people, and not only k different records.

Several algorithms [87,330,334,416,438] for microaggregation have been introduced with the specific goal of being fast and, thus, usable for large volumes of data. Here large is about the number of records. There are also a few methods for a large number of attributes. For example, using the cosine distance [7] or using a spectral basis [278,279]. The latter means transforming data into another space using singular value decomposition.

There are extensions for other types of databases. Observe that the heuristic definition of microaggregation only requires an implementation of a partitioning algorithm (clustering), an aggregation method, and a way to do the replacement. Clustering algorithms exist for almost all types of data, so, we can use similar approaches to properly define microaggregation for any type of data.

For example, microaggregation algorithms exist for the following types of data.

- Time series [360]. Clustering for time series requires a distance, then we can use distances that promote similarity focusing on the shape of the series (short time series distance) or focusing on the values themselves (Euclidean distance).
- Mobility data and location privacy. Trajectories expressed in different forms (e.g., GPS-positions plus time stamps) can be processed as a kind of time series. Nevertheless, this type of information is usually very sensitive as any point can be used for re-identification attacks. Microaggregation algorithms have been proposed [10,11,151,186] with the usual goal to provide k-anonymity.
- Smart metering data. This can also be seen as a type of time series protection problem. Microaggregation algorithms [15] exist that provide protected data at household level. Nevertheless, microaggregation alone may not be enough as the aggregation of the series in a cluster may still lead to disclosure of a household with a significantly different consumption pattern. Some post-processing [15] is needed for an increased protection.
- Graphs and social networks. Variations exist on whether we consider k-degree anonymity or a more strict privacy model. In the former case, microaggregation is about building k-anonymous degree sequences [75,417] and then modify the original graph to be compliant with this sequence. More strict privacy models [223, 388] may imply building clusters of nodes, each cluster with at least k nodes, and then using these clusters as the new nodes—supernodes (including, when needed, k copies of each of them) and adding appropriate edges.
- Access and search logs. Logs contain information of different types (time stamps, terms, numbers, URLs, etc). In addition, they are usually non independent. For example, search logs corresponding to the same person, or access logs from different devices of the same person. Microaggregation, or any other protection mechanism, needs to take this into account. Microaggregation algorithms [43,175,302,345] have been defined for both types of logs. Ontologies may be required to take into account meaning of terms in e.g. search queries.
- Documents. Microaggregation has been applied to documents represented as vectors. Clustering has been defined in terms of distances on the vector space, or taking into account the semantics associated to the terms.

6.1.3   Additive and Multiplicative Noise

As the name indicates, additive noise protects data adding noise into the original file. That is,

$$X' = X + \varepsilon,$$

where ε is noise following a certain distribution. The simplest approach is to require ε to be such that $E(\varepsilon) = 0$ and $Var(\varepsilon) = kVar(X)$ for a given constant k. The two main approaches are correlated and uncorrelated noise.

Uncorrelated noise addition corresponds to the case that for attributes V_i and V_j, noise is such that besides of $E(\varepsilon) = 0$ and $Var(\varepsilon) = kVar(X)$ we have $Cov(\varepsilon_i, \varepsilon_j) = 0$ for attributes $i \neq j$. In this case, additive noise preserves means and covariances, but neither variances nor correlation coefficients. Note that,

$$E(X') = E(X) + E(\varepsilon) = E(X)$$

$$Cov(X'_i, X'_j) = Cov(X_i, X_j) \text{ for } i \neq j$$

$$Var(X') = Var(X) + kVar(X) = (1+k)Var(X)$$

$$\rho_{X'_i, X'_j} = \frac{Cov(X'_i, X'_j)}{\sqrt{Var(X'_i)Var(X'_j)}} = \frac{Cov(X_i, X_j)}{(1+k)\sqrt{Var(X_i)Var(X_j)}} = \frac{1}{1+k}\rho_{X_i, X_j}$$

We can use $\varepsilon \sim N(0, kVar(X))$ and $\varepsilon \sim L(0, \beta)$ with $\beta = \sqrt{k/2Var(X)}$, and other distributions as well, for this purpose. Here, $N(\mu, \sigma^2)$ represents the normal distribution with mean (location) μ and variance (squared scale) σ^2, and $L(\mu, b)$ represents the Laplace distribution with mean (location) μ and scale b. Note that for a Laplace distribution $L(\mu, b)$, the variance is $2b^2$. Recall also that one of the differences between Laplace and normal distribution is that the former has heavier tails (for same variance).

We can implement correlated noise addition that preserves correlation coefficients and means. In this case, however, neither variance nor covariance is preserved: they are proportional to the variance and covariance of the original data set.

In correlated noise addition using a multivariate normal distribution, ε follows a normal distribution $N(0, k\Sigma)$ where Σ is the covariance matrix of X.

$$E(X') = E(X) + E(\varepsilon) = E(X)$$

$$\begin{aligned} Cov(X'_i, X'_j) &= Cov(X_i, Y_j) + Cov(\varepsilon_i, Y_j) + Cov(X_i, \varepsilon_j) + Cov(\varepsilon_i, \varepsilon_j) \\ &= Cov(X_i, Y_j) + 0 + 0 + kCov(X_i, Y_j) \\ &= (1+k)Cov(X_i, X_j) \text{ for } i \neq j \end{aligned}$$

$$Var(X') = Var(X) + kVar(X) = (1+k)Var(X)$$

$$\rho_{X'_i, X'_j} = \frac{Cov(X'_i, X'_j)}{\sqrt{Var(X'_i)Var(X'_j)}} = \frac{(1+k)Cov(X_i, X_j)}{(1+k)\sqrt{Var(X_i)Var(X_j)}} = \rho_{X_i, X_j}$$

These two types of additive noise illustrate a common problem in data privacy. It is difficult that the masked data satisfy all the properties we are interested in. When a new property is required to be satisfied in the masked data (e.g., correlation coefficients preserved) another property is lost (e.g., covariances). Additive noise also illustrates that the transparency principle can help the user to analyse the data. In both types of noise addition, our knowledge on the method and the parameter k permits us to compute correct and exact values for the four statistics listed above. Two of the statistics are directly inferred from the data and two using the computations from the data and our knowledge of k.

Multiplicative noise

Multiplicative noise consists of defining X' as the product of the error by the original data. That is, $X' = X \cdot \varepsilon$. Different strategies can be used for the error. For example, we can consider [335] ε drawn from a uniform distribution on $[1 - b, 1 + b]$ where b is the parameter of the perturbation level.

An advantage of multiplicative noise with respect to additive noise is that the magnitude of the perturbation (the error) applied to a value is proportional to this value. That is, small values have in general small perturbation and large values have large perturbation.

Multiplicative noise has been used to provide privacy from reidentification and differential privacy.

Additive and multiplicative noise: variants and big data

These methods can be easily implemented for numerical data. Definition for other types of data (categorical or structured data) is not so simple. In general, for noise addition, we need to define X' in terms of adding some noise ε from a given distribution on the domain associated to X.

For categorical data, the PRAM method (see Sect. 6.1.4) can be seen as the most natural alternative. There is a related procedure [410] when data consists of terms of text, it consists of introducing semantic noise. That is, noise that takes into account the semantics of the terms, and where semantics is based on an ontology.

Standard additive and multiplicative noise are record-based and, thus, are well suited for files of large dimensions. Masking can be applied in linear time with respect to the number of records, and also in real-time for streaming data. It is also suited for records of high dimensions.

Correlated noise addition needs the covariance matrix which makes its application problematic for high dimensional data. For streaming data, correlation and other properties of the data can change over time, adding complexity to the problem. Otherwise, we can select an initial large subset of records, estimate the covariance matrix, and use it to protect the whole file. In this case, the approach is also cost-efficient once the correlation matrix has been built.

Graph protection can be implemented as a kind of noise addition. In this case, we have a graph G to protect and given a random graph g (i.e., a graph from a distribution of graphs) we define the protected graph $G' = G \oplus g$. We can consider, for example, random graphs following Erdös-Rényi and Gilbert models to generate g. Here $\oplus$ represents the addition or combination of two graphs, defined in terms of the symmetric difference of edges in G and g.

6.1.4 PRAM: Post-Randomization Method

This is a method for categorical data where categories are replaced according to given probabilities defined in terms of a transition matrix.

The most common formulation is considering masking each attribute independently. Then, PRAM uses a transition matrix or Markov matrix on the set of categories. Let $C = \{c_1, \ldots, c_c\}$ denote this set of categories, then P is a transition matrix on C when $P : C \times C \to [0, 1]$ such that $\sum_{c_j \in C} P(c_i, c_j) = 1$. That is, the values are positive and rows add to one.

Then, PRAM constructs X' from X replacing, with probability $P(c_i, c_j)$, each c_i in X by a c_j. Formally, the matrix of probabilities can be seen as a matrix of conditional probabilities. That is,

$$P(c_i, c_j) = P(X' = c_j | X = c_i).$$

The application of PRAM requires an adequate definition of the probabilities $P(c_i, c_j)$. Different matrices lead to different information loss and different disclosure risk. Naturally, maximum risk corresponds to the case of using the identity matrix because in this case $X' = X$. The literature presents different studies on how the Markov matrix can be selected.

Gouweleeuw et al. [204] propose invariant PRAM. Given $T_X = (T_X(c_1) \ldots T_X(c_c))$, the vector of frequencies of categories in C in the original file X, invariant PRAM consists of defining P in such a way that frequencies do not change. That is, $\sum_{i=1}^{c} T_X(c_i) p_{ik} = T_X(c_k)$ for all k. Then, assuming without loss of generality that c_k is the category with smaller frequency (i.e., that $T_X(c_k) \le T_X(c_i)$ for all i), and given a parameter θ such that $0 < \theta < 1$, $p_{ij} = P(c_i, c_j)$ is defined as follows:

$$p_{ij} = \begin{cases} 1 - \frac{\theta T_X(c_k)}{T_X(c_i)} & \text{if } i = j \\ \frac{\theta T_X(c_k)}{(c-1)T_X(c_i)} & \text{if } i \ne j \end{cases}$$

We can observe that for $i \ne j$ we have that

$$p_{ij} = \frac{\theta T_X(c_k)}{((c-1)T_X(c_i))} = \frac{1 - p_{ii}}{c-1}.$$

So, given a category, the probability of changing it is equally divided among all other categories. I.e., for all i we have $p_{ij} = p_{ik}$ for all $j, k \ne i$.

Note that a θ equal to zero implies no perturbation, and θ equal to 1 implies total perturbation. So, θ permits the user to control the degree of distortion suffered by the data set.

An alternative definition of the matrix is to assign the higher exchange probabilities to the categories with less frequency. They are the ones that have a larger probability of being unique and to make unique the records in which they are found. Therefore, this approach is to increase confusion and reduce the risk of reidentification for the records with these categories.

Probabilities p_{ij} for $i \ne j$ are defined by the following expression:

$$p_{ij} = \frac{(1 - p_{ii})(n - T_X(i) - T_X(j))}{(n-2)(n - T_X(i))} \tag{6.4}$$

where $T_x(i)$ is the frequency of category c_i and n is the number of records or the dimension of the file (i.e., $n = \sum_{k=1}^{c} T_X(k)$) and p_{ii} are predefined constant values for all i. It is not required all p_{ii} be the same.

Let us prove that $p_{ii} + \sum_{j=1, j \neq i}^{c} p_{ij} = 1$ for all i.

$$p_{ii} + \sum_{\substack{j=1 \\ j \neq i}}^{c} p_{ij} = p_{ii} + \sum_{\substack{j=1 \\ j \neq i}}^{c} \frac{(1 - p_{ii})(n - T_X(i) - T_X(j))}{(n-2)(n - T_X(i))}$$

$$= p_{ii} + \frac{(1 - p_{ii})}{(n-2)(n - T_X(i))} \sum_{\substack{j=1 \\ j \neq i}}^{c} (n - T_X(i) - T_X(j))$$

$$= p_{ii} + \frac{(1 - p_{ii})}{(n-2)(n - T_X(i))} \left((c-1)(n - T_X(i)) + \sum_{\substack{j=1 \\ j \neq i}}^{c} T_X(j)\right)$$

$$= p_{ii} + \frac{(1 - p_{ii})}{(n-2)(n - T_X(i))} ((c-1)(n - T_X(i)) + (n - T_X(i)))$$

$$= p_{ii} + \frac{(1 - p_{ii})}{(n-2)(n - T_X(i))} (c-2)(n - T_X(i))(n - T_X(i)) = 1$$

An alternative approach is to compute P from a preference matrix $W = \{w_{ij}\}$ where w_{ij} is our degree of preference about replacing category c_i by category c_j. In addition to the weights, we can add the constraints about invariant PRAM, so that the frequencies of the protected file are the same as the ones in the original file. Formally, given W the probabilities P are determined from the following optimization problem.

$$\text{Minimize} \quad \sum_{i,j} w_{ij} p_{ij} \qquad (6.5)$$

$$\text{Subject to} \quad p_{ij} \geq 0$$

$$\sum_{j} p_{ij} = 1$$

$$\sum_{i=1}^{c} T_X(c_i) p_{ij} = T_X(c_j) \text{ for all } j$$

Gross et al. [208] use integers to express preferences, and $w_{ij} = 1$ is the most preferred change, $w_{ij} = 2$ is the second most preferred changes, and so on.

PRAM and transparency

Transparency attacks can also be defined for PRAM. As we have explained above, PRAM is usually applied attribute-wise. This can be exploited as done for microaggregation and rank swapping. Attacks will be effective when the possible values of a given original value is a small subset of the domain. Using the same notation we used previously (i.e., $B_j(x)$ denotes the anonymity set for the jth attribute for x), we have that when $B_j(x) \subset X'$ we may have that $\cap B_j(x)$ can be reduced to a single record and reidentification takes place. When $P(c_i, c_j) \neq 0$ for all i, j we have that $B_j(x) = X'$ and the intersection attack is not so effective. Note, however, that PRAM permits to compute accurate probabilities of transforming a record $x \in X$ (with several attributes) into a record $x' \in X'$.

PRAM and differential privacy

We discuss in Sect. 5.1.3 that local differential privacy can be implemented for categorical data by means of randomized response. When a randomized response mechanism is modeled by a transition matrix, this, of course, is equivalent to PRAM.

In the other way round, when we are masking a categorical attribute by means of a PRAM mechanism and a certain transition matrix P, this process satisfies local differential privacy for a certain ε. Here, local, corresponds to the protection of the value of a particular attribute. We have discussed in Sect. 5.1.3 the construction of a matrix that ensures local differential privacy for a given ε. Naturally, we can use these matrices for PRAM. This will naturally provide differential privacy guarantees.

The same procedure we have considered to build the matrix from ε can be reconsidered here to calculate the ε from a given transition matrix. Recall Eq. 5.3. It establishes that we have local differential privacy when for all i, j we have that

$$\max_{k=1}^{c} P(X' = c_k|c_i)/P(X' = c_k|c_j) \leq e^{\varepsilon}.$$

Or, equivalently,

$$\max_{i=1}^{c} \max_{j=1}^{c} \max_{k=1}^{c} P(X' = c_k|c_i)/P(X' = c_k|c_j) \leq e^{\varepsilon}.$$

Then, we have that given a transition matrix P we have that the PRAM mechanism satisfies local differential privacy for all ε such that $\varepsilon \geq \varepsilon_0$ with ε_0 defined by:

$$\varepsilon_0 = log \left(\max_{i=1}^{c} \max_{j=1}^{c} \max_{k=1}^{c} P(X' = c_k|c_i)/P(X' = c_k|c_j) \right).$$

It is easy to see that we need that all probabilities in the matrix are not zero. Otherwise ε_0 is infinite and there is no privacy guarantee from a differential point of view. This can be seen as related to the intersection attack discussed in the previous section.

PRAM and identity disclosure risk

Naturally, when we are protecting a database and we are considering an individual record, the protection of a value by means of local differential privacy does not mean that the record is fully protected for other privacy models. In particular, it does not ensure privacy against reidentification. We will show an example below.

Consider a database with only two records and 5 categorical attributes $V_1, \ldots, V_5$ each one with categories $C = \{c_1, c_2\}$. Let one record be $x_1 = (c_1, c_1, c_1, c_1, c_1)$ and the other be $x_2 = (c_2, c_2, c_2, c_2, c_2)$. Then, let us consider the following transition matrix for all attributes.

$$P = \begin{pmatrix} 0.8 \; 0.2 \\ 0.2 \; 0.8 \end{pmatrix}.$$

This transition matrix means that about 2 values over 10 (or 1 value over 5) will be updated producing $c' \neq c$. So, for the two records above we may produce a database X' with records $x'_1 = (c_1, c_1, c_2, c_1, c_2)$, $x'_2 = (c_2, c_2, c_2, c_2, c_2)$. Naturally, a reidentification attack based on the majority of coincidences between intruder's record and protected ones will be successful on this data set. For both records (and any other possible record in X'), the majority of the attributes are not modified.

When the transition matrix is such that the elements of the diagonal (i.e., p_{ii}) are larger than the other ones, there will be always databases that even masked can be reidentified. So PRAM does not always avoid reidentification. Similarly, local differential privacy using randomized response will not necessarily protect against reidentification. The examples above are artificial, but when we have records with a large number of attributes, reidentification of local differential privacy is possible and, thus, needs to be analyzed if it is an attack that we want to avoid. We can use the transition matrix to compute the probabilities of e.g. reidentifying a record.

PRAM: variants and big data

Our discussion on PRAM has been for a single categorical attribute described with a set of c classes C. It is naturally possible to define PRAM for a pair of attributes V_1, V_2 with, respectively, classes C^1 and C^2. Then, we need to define appropriate transition matrices $P(X' = (c^1_{i_1}, c^2_{i_2}) | (c^1_{j_1}, c^2_{j_2}))$. Naturally, the same applies to larger sets of attributes. Transition matrices in this way can provide masked files with less risk or better utility. In particular, a multi-attribute transition matrix can be useful if we have correlated attributes as the ones described in the previous section.

Note that it is not necessary that the Markov matrix is explicitly defined. That is, given a value c_i in a domain D, and a random value $r \in [0, 1]$ it is enough to have a function f such that $f(c_i, r)$ returns c_j (the masked value of c_i in D). Typically, for a Markov matrix $P(c_i, c_j)$ this function is defined as follows: if $r \in [0, P(c_i, c_1)]$ we have c_1, if $r \in [P(c_i, c_1), P(c_i, c_2)]$ we have c_2 and so on.

In a more general setting, we can consider $P(c_i, c_j)$ as $P(c_j | c_i)$ which is a valid expression for a probability distribution for any domain D. That is, not solely for categorical data. This formulation links PRAM with other masking methods as additive and multiplicative noise (noise addition as a PRAM for continuous attributes), and shows a way to apply PRAM to types of data different to categorical data. For example, we can apply PRAM to linguistic terms (e.g., words) where the domain of terms D is an ontology or a dictionary as wordnet in which relationships between terms are explicitly given. Then, we define the probability of replacement as uniform between all words in a given distance. Then, we select a word at distance 1 with probability $1/2^2$, at a distance 2 with probability $1/2^3$, and at a distance i with probability $1/2^{i+1}$. Not making any replacement should be $1 - \sum_i 1/2^{i+1}$.

PRAM is well suited for files of large volumes. Once Markov matrices are settled for all attributes, masking is done record-wise. Therefore the cost of the approach is linear with respect to the number of records. The method also applies well to streaming data.

6.1.5 Lossy Compression and Other Transform-Based Methods: De-Noising Data

The idea of reducing the quality of data by means of transforms that permits to remove "noise" or "details" has been used as a data protection mechanism.

The first approach was to use lossy compression [143]. It consists of viewing a numerical data file as a grey-level image. Then, a lossy compression method is applied to the *image*, obtaining a *compressed image*. This *image* is then decompressed and the *decompressed image* corresponds to the masked file.

Different compression rates lead to files with different degrees of distortion. I.e., the more compression, the more distortion. JPEG and JPEG 2000 have been used with this goal. JPEG is based on the Discrete Cosine Transform (DCT) and the latter on wavelets. The transform of the original data file into an *image* requires, in general, a quantization. As JPEG 2000 allows a higher dynamic range (65536 levels of gray because it uses 16 bits of depth) than JPEG (only 256 because it uses 8 bits), this quantization step is more accurate in JPEG 2000.

The use of a wavelet decomposition of a matrix permits to reduce high frequency "noise". Then the inverse discrete wavelet transform is applied to obtain the "de-noised" data in the original space. Other transforms have also been used with the same purpose, as the Haar wavelet transforms and the Fourier transform.

The same idea of transforming the original dataset into another space in order to reduce noise or detail appears in procedures based on singular value decomposition, principal components, and nonnegative matrix factorization. This mechanism can also be seen as a dimensionality reduction process. From a privacy perspective, the number of components used to reconstruct the data in principal components is a parameter of the masking process. The less components, the larger the distortion and the larger the privacy. In contrast, the more components, the less distortion. The same applies to methods based on singular value decomposition and nonnegative matrix factorization.

Autoencoders are an alternative tool that can be used for the same purpose. Autoencoders are neural networks that typically have r neurons as input and output, and s with $s < r$ in a hidden layer. The network is trained to reproduce the input in the output. Then, we can use the autoencoder to trained to learn the records in an original file X. Then, once the network is trained, we apply records $x \in X$ in the input and obtain a slightly modified version x' in the output. These records x' will define the protected file X'. The smaller the s the more difficult is that $x' = x$. In other words, the smaller the s, the larger the distortion.

In general, methods based on lossy compression perform poorly with respect to the trade-off between information loss and disclosure risk (in terms of reidentification). Nevertheless, a good tuning of all the parameters [249] have shown results comparable to those obtained with more effective methods (as rank swapping and microaggregation).

Exercise 6.2 Given a file, use autoencoders to protect it using different values for the parameter s. Study the effect on the mean and the variance of the attributes when modifying s. Compare these results with the ones in Exercise 6.1 (about microaggregation).

Exercise 6.3 Consider how post-masking can be used in data protected using autoencoders.

Lossy compression and transparency

From the point of view of transparency, lossy compression seems difficult to attack unless all the original file is already known by the intruder and, thus, all masking process is reproduced. This difficulty is due to the fact that the modification suffered by any record depends strongly on all the other records in the original file.

The attack of reconstructing the original file has been considered by some authors [40,305]. They use the term breaching algorithm for this type of attack. In other words, the goal is to find the records X that can generate the protected file X'. It has been shown that finding the original records can be easy when data is binary, and researchers discuss the effectiveness of the approach in the more general case of real data.

Lossy compression: variants and big data

These methods have been applied [40] to numerical and categorical data. There are also applications [93] to time series (adding noise to the transform of the series). It is easy to extend these methods for other types of data as e.g. graphs represented as an image (e.g., using the adjacency matrix).

6.2 Non-perturbative Methods

In this section we review some non-perturbative algorithms. They are generalization (also known as recoding), top and bottom coding, and suppression. Sampling [521], which is not discussed here, can also be seen as a non-perturbative method. Recall that sampling [104,307] consists of selecting some records from the whole population.

6.2.1 Generalization and Recoding

This method, mainly applied to categorical attributes, consists of combining a few categories into a more general one. Local and global recoding can be distinguished.

Global recoding [284,521] corresponds to the case that the same recoding is applied to all the categories in the original data file. Formally, if Π is a partition of the categories in C, then each c in the original data file is replaced by the partition element in Π that contains c.

In contrast, in local recoding [464] the same category might be replaced by different generalizations when found in different records. Constrained local recoding is when the data space is partitioned and within the region the same recoding is used, but different regions use different recodings.

In general, global recoding implies a larger perturbation than local recoding. Changes are applied to all records even if the change is not needed to ensure privacy. Nevertheless, local recoding generates a data set that has a larger diversity on the terms used to describe the records. This situation might cause difficulties when using the protected data set in analysis.

While most of the literature considers the recoding as functions of a single attribute (i.e., single-dimension recoding), it is also possible to consider recoding of several attributes at once. This is multidimensional recoding [283]. Formally, when n attributes are considered, recoding is understood as a function of n values. We review a method for multidimensional recoding (Mondrian [283]) in Sect. 6.4.1.

One of the main difficulties for applying recoding is the need for a hierarchy of the categories. In some applications such hierarchy is assumed to be known (e.g. we use an existing ontology or we build it easily from the semantics of terms), while in others it is constructed by the protection procedure. In this later case, the goal of the masking process includes finding the optimal generalization structure. Selection of such optimal generalization can be seen as equivalent to the selection of an optimal partition or an optimal dendrogram, depending on whether we need one or more levels of generalization. The number of partitions of a given set of n categories is the Bell number (see Sect. 2.4.1) and the number of dendrograms is $n!/2$. Because of that, in general, to find an optimal generalization for data protection is a hard problem. Besides of this computational complexity, it is usually preferable that the constructed hierarchy has semantic interpretation. E.g. generalizing Zip codes 08192, 08235, 09398, and 09247 into 0**9* and 0*2** may be inappropriate as these *codes* may correspond to sets of non-adjacent towns. Instead, it would be preferable to generalize them in 08*** and 09***.

Generalization has been extensively used to achieve k-anonymity. We will discuss these algorithms in Sect. 6.4.

Top and bottom coding

Top and bottom coding are two methods that consist of replacing the lowest and largest values (given a threshold) by a generalized category. These two methods can be considered as particular cases of global recoding, and as such are classified here.

These methods are applied when there are only a few records that have extreme values. This kind of generalization permits us to reduce the disclosure risk of outliers as the corresponding records are all generalized to the same category and are indistinguishable.

6.2.2 Suppression

Suppression consists of replacing some values by a special label denoting that the value has been suppressed. Suppression is often applied [420,463] in combination with recoding, and mainly for categorical data.

We can have local and global supression. Global suppression is when suppressing a value c in record r implies that all other appearances of c in the file are also suppressed. Local suppression is when the suppression of c in one record is independent of the suppression of other appearances of c.

Suppression is often combined with generalization to achieve k-anonymity. This is the case of the Datafly algorithm [460]. We discuss algorithms for achieving k-anonymity in Sect. 6.4.

6.3 Synthetic Data Generators

Perturbative and non perturbative approaches are masking methods that try to ensure confidentiality modifying the original data. Synthetic data generators try to ensure confidentiality replacing the original data by artificial ones generated from models of the original data.

There are different approaches to generate synthetic data. Figure 6.1 outlines the requirements for synthetic data generators. Templ and Meindl [469] review some of these methods. They distinguish three major classes.

- **Synthetic reconstruction.** Methods use (i) a data set with some marginal distribution for the whole population, and (ii) conditional probabilities on selected attributes from another data set (a sample) or derived from published contingency tables. Data is generated using several steps. First, some individuals are selected from a population or created. Then, iteratively, values for the required attributes are produced. One attribute is added at a time, creating synthetic values that are consistent with the conditional probabilities. For example, a record is produced, then, the attribute *economically active* is produced (either true or false), and in the next step the individual is assigned an *occupation* if economically active. The iterative proportional fitting (IPF) procedure is an old method (developed at the late 1930s) for building such set. There are more recent procedures for synthetic reconstruction [39,234].
- **Combinatorial optimization.** Methods use a data set which includes the attributes to be simulated, and contingency tables about the characteristics of the synthetic data. The method selects first a random sample from the file of the appropriate size. An iterative process is applied replacing a record in the selection by another in the file and evaluating the suitability of the replacement using a goodness-of-fit statistics (a fitness function using machine learning jargon). With this iterative process we obtain a selection of records that has the same characteristics as the ones in the contingency tables.

Conditions for simulated data.

- Reflect actual sizes of regions and strata.
- Keep marginal distributions and interactions between attributes.
- Keep heterogeneities between subgroups, especially regional aspects.
- Avoid pure replication of units from the underlying sample.
- Ensure data confidentiality.

Fig. 6.1 Conditions required for simulated data from Templ and Meindl [469] (based on Munnich et al. [332,333])

Algorithm 30: Partially synthetic data.

Data: $X|Y$: set of records of a given sample
Result: $X|Y'$: set of records with Y' a masked version of Y
1 **begin**
2      $M_{X,Y} :=$ Build a model of Y in terms of X
3      $Y' := M_{X,Y}(X)$
4   **return** $(X|Y')$
5 **end**

- **Model-based simulation.** The process is based on the construction of models and the use of these models to generate the data. This approach is the one most studied for data protection in both fully and partially synthetic data sets, and it is the one we discuss below. We also use this approach in Algorithm 30.

In the literature we distinguish between partially and fully synthetic data. Fully synthetic data sets are defined in terms of independent samples of records. In contrast, partially synthetic ones comprises the original records. In both cases, approaches differ on the methods used to find the model.

Algorithm 30 outlines how to generate partially synthetic data. The approach considers two types of attributes X and Y. The algorithm builds synthetic versions of Y using models of Y with respect to X. Once the model is built, we replace Y by synthetic data generated using the model.

Following Rubin [411], in fully synthetic data, we consider three sets of attributes (X, Z, Y). We consider a microdata file of n records drawn from a larger population of N individuals. X represents background attributes observed for all N individuals, Z represents non confidential attributes observed for the n samples, and Y represents the confidential attributes observed also for the n samples. First, a model of (Z, Y) is built in terms of the n records in X that are in the sample. Then, the model is used to impute values for the population in X. In order to avoid reidentification problems, Rubin [411] suggests imputation from the $N - n$ records (i.e., the records that are not in the sample). The same process can be used several times to create M different copies of the synthetic data set.

The type of synthetic data generator has implications for disclosure risk, which is larger for partially synthetic data. The more accurate is the model, the more similar are the synthetic records to the original ones. We have results [486] showing effective reidentification of partially synthetic data sets generated using the IPSO method. For fully synthetic data no reidentification experiment has been reported in the literature, nevertheless discussion of disclosure risk for fully synthetic data is discussed by Reiter and Drechsler [402] (p. 408):

> When the imputation models are highly detailed, the imputations could reproduce combinations of quasi-identifiers for real records. Intruders might interpret this to mean that real-data records with those characteristics were in the original sample, which could result in identification disclosures if some of those records are unique in the population. This risk could be magnified when releasing multiple synthetic data sets, because (i) there are several opportunities to impute such records, and (ii) there could be repetitions of realistic synthetic records that might strengthen the intruder's confidence that a similar record was in the original data.

In addition, Reiter [401] discusses predictive disclosure for synthetic data, that can be seen as a type of attribute disclosure.

Synthetic data generators permits us to release multiple protected data sets [401]. This permits users to increase the accuracy of their analysis (e.g., increasing the number of replicates reduces the variability in estimators of variance).

Some of the approaches used for synthetic data generation are the Information Preserving Statistical Obfuscation (IPSO) [66], enhanced GADP [336], methods based on the Latin Hypercube Sampling (LHS)—see e.g. Dandekar et al. [115]. The Enhanced GADP method is described in Algorithm 31. The algorithm includes the computation of Y_A, Y_B and Y_C. The algorithm returns Y_C that is the model that satisfies more properties (the matrices of regression coefficients $\hat{B}$ and covariances $\hat{\Sigma}$ are preserved). Y_A does not preserve them, and Y_B preserves only the regression coefficients. We can see them as three types of synthetic data with more or less precision, similar to IPSO-A, IPSO-B, and IPSO-C.

While most methods for synthetic data generation are based on *statistical* models, there are some based on nonparametric methods from the machine learning literature. Drechsler and Reiter [154] compare classification and regression trees, bagging, random forests, and support vector machines for this purpose and include an empirical evaluation. The authors conclude

> that synthesizers based on regression trees are a particularly attractive option for statistical agencies seeking to release datasets with intense synthesis without intense labor.

Deep learning is currently used to generate synthetic data. More precisely, generative adversarial networks. We review them in the next section.

Algorithm 31: Enhanced GADP.

Data: Y: confidential; S: Non-confidential
Result: $Y'|S$: set of records with Y' a masked version of Y
1 **begin**
2 $\quad$ $\bar{Y} :=$ mean vector of Y
3 $\quad$ $\bar{S} :=$ mean vector of S
4 $\quad$ $\hat{\Sigma}_{YY}, \hat{\Sigma}_{SS}, \hat{\Sigma}_{YS} :=$ covariance matrices of Y,S and between Y and S
5 $\quad$ Regress Y on S as follows
6 $\quad$ **begin**
7 $\quad\quad$ $\hat{\beta}_1 := \hat{\Sigma}_{YS}\hat{\Sigma}_{YS}^{-1}$
8 $\quad\quad$ $\hat{\beta}_0 := \bar{X} - \hat{\Sigma}_{YS}\hat{\Sigma}_{SS}^{-1}\bar{S}$
9 $\quad\quad$ $\hat{\Sigma}_{\epsilon\epsilon} :=$ covariance of the residuals
10 $\quad$ **end**
11 $\quad$ $Y_A := \beta_0 + \beta_1 S$
12 $\quad$ $K :=$ a $(n \times M)$ matrix of random numbers from a standard multivariate normal distribution
13 $\quad$ Regress K on (S and X). $B :=$ the residuals from this regression. ;; The new noise term B is orthogonal to both X and S and $\hat{B} = 0$)
14 $\quad$ $Y_B := Y_A + B$
15 $\quad$ $\hat{\Sigma} :=$ covariance matrix of B
16 $\quad$ Define C and Y computing for $i = 1, 2, \dots, n$
17 $\quad$ **begin**
18 $\quad\quad$ $c_i := \hat{\Sigma}_{\epsilon\epsilon}^{0.5}\hat{\Sigma}_{BB}^{-0.5}b_i$
19 $\quad\quad$ $y_i := \hat{\beta}_0\hat{\beta}_1 s_i + c_i$
20 $\quad$ **end**
21 $\quad$ $Y_C := Y$
22 $\quad$ **return** $(X|Y)$
23 **end**

6.3.1 Synthetic Data Generators and Generative Adversarial Networks

Generative adversarial networks (GAN) have been proposed as a tool for synthetic data generation. They have been extensively used for image synthesis, but also for generation of regular SQL databases.

We describe here one of the GAN model, which is often known as Vanilla GAN. It is based on two neural networks, one called generator and another discriminator. We will use G and D to denote these models. The idea is simple:

- the generator G produces synthetic data and
- the discriminator D tries to distinguish these synthetic data from the real data.

Both generator and discriminator are trained at the same time, using the real data. The generator is trained to produce data as similar as possible to the original, and the discriminator to distinguish between the real and the fake.

When the GAN is trained, the generator is good enough to fool the discriminator, while the discriminator tries as hard as possible to succeed in its task. We now describe these functions. We will use X to denote the real data, and $\mathscr{D}$ to denote the space of data. In particular, for any $x \in X$ we have $x \in \mathscr{D}$. We will use objects to refer to the elements in $\mathscr{D}$ instead of records because, as we have said above, GANs are often used for non-SQL databases (as e.g., images).

Formally, the discriminator can be seen as a function $D(x)$ that takes an object from the space of data, and returns a value in [0,1]. Then, $D : \mathscr{D} \to [0, 1]$. When $D(x) = 1$ the model informs us of x being real data, when $D(x) = 0$ the model states that x is not real but artificially generated. We use s to denote the dimension of $\mathscr{D}$.

Then, the generator is a function G that generates objects in the data space $\mathscr{D}$. It uses as input a noise space $\mathscr{Z}$, which is smaller in dimension than the one of the data. So, we have $G : \mathscr{Z} \to \mathscr{D}$. We use p to denote the dimension of $\mathscr{Z}$. Then, $p < s$. Note that given a random sample z from $\mathscr{Z}$, $G(z)$ is a fake object in the data space.

As we explained above, both G and D are neural networks, and they are defined so that $G(z)$ for z in $\mathscr{Z}$ cannot be distinguished from x in X. The problem is formulated in Vanilla GAN as the following optimization problem:

$$\min_{G} \max_{D} V(G, D) = \mathbb{E}_{x \sim p_{data}(x)} \left[\log D(x) \right] + \mathbb{E}_{z \sim p_z(z)} \left[\log(1 - D(G(z))) \right].$$

or, if we just consider samples of X and of Z, as when we are implementing the system, the problem is formulated in the following terms:

$$\min_{G} \max_{D} V_{S_x, S_Z}(G, D) = \Sigma_{x \in S_X} \left[\log D(x) \right] + \Sigma_{z \in S_Z} \left[\log(1 - D(G(z))) \right], \quad (6.6)$$

where S_X and S_Z are such sets of samples.

Naturally, these expressions are minimized or maximized with respect to the possible generators G and discriminators D. For given neural network models for G and D, this correspond to find the parameters of the models to optimize the expression.

It is easy to see that in this expression,

- the discriminator D that maximizes the equation above, i.e., the one that leads to the largest values, is the one that returns $D(x) = 1$ for real data $x \in X$, and $D(x) = 0$ for generated data from z. These assignments will maximize, respectively, the left and the right part of the expression $V(G, D)$. On the contrary,
- the generator G that minimizes the expression, i.e., the one that leads to the minimal value, is the one that produces objects $G(z)$ that are later incorrectly detected as real. That is, from some noise z the network generates fake data $G(z)$ such that $D(G(z)) = 1$. In this case, the expression on the right will be minimal because it will be zero. Note that the expression on the left has no D, so, it does not play any role in the optimization.

It is usual to use Algorithm 32 for finding the generator G. The algorithm starts initializing the two neural networks G and D. Then, until convergence the process

---

Algorithm 32: Training algorithm for producing a good generator G using generative adversarial networks (GANs). Each iteration uses a mini-batch of m real and m synthetic samples.

Data: X: data set; m: size of mini-batches; k: iterations for generator training
Result: Generator and discriminator

1 **begin**
2   G: initial generator
3   D: initial discriminator
4   **while** *training* **do**
5   **for** k *times* **do**
6           $S_X :=$ create mini-batch of m real samples from X
7           $S_Z :=$ create mini-batch of m samples from the p-dimensional space $\mathscr{Z}$
8           $D :=$ train D using S_x and S_Z maximizing $V_{S_x, S_Z}(G, D)$ (Eq. 6.6)
9   **end**
10       $S_Z :=$ create mini-batch of m samples from the p-dimensional space $\mathscr{Z}$
11       $G :=$ train G using S_Z and minimizing $V_{S_Z}(G, D)$ (Eq. 6.6)
12   **end**
13   **return** (G, D)
14 **end**

---

follows the following structure: (i) train D, (ii) train G. The training of D consists of repeating a predefined number of times (parameter k) the following: (a) selecting m real samples from X and (b) create m artificial objects. The latter are built from the p-dimensional space $\mathscr{Z}$ (e.g., randomly generating p-vectors and then applying G to these vectors to obtain $G(z)$). At this point we have both S_X and S_Z and we can train D. Stochastic gradient descent is used for this training. The objective is to maximize $V_{S_x, S_Z}(G, D)$ (Eq. 6.6). The training of G consists of creating another set of m artificial objects and using them to minimize $V_{S_Z}(G, D)$. Here it is also usual to use stochastic gradient descent. The objective function is to minimize $V_{S_Z}(G, D)$ (Eq. 6.6). Only the right part of this equation is of relevance in the minimization problem, as G only appears in the right part of the equation. The left part is just constant.

GANs were introduced, tested, and used for synthetic images. That is, the space of data $\mathscr{D}$ corresponds to a high-dimensional space representing an image. They have also been used for text generation.

Some variations exist for generating synthetic data for standard databases. Table-GAN and CTAB-GAN are two examples of such approaches.

6.3.2 Table-GANs

The most significant variation of Table-GAN with respect to GAN is that an extra network is added to the discriminator D and the generator D. This network is called classifier and we denote it by C. Both discriminator D and generator G have the same role as in our description of GAN above, although the loss function (the function being optimized) for G is revised here.

The classifier

The role of the classifier C is to help the generator to produce records that are plausible. That is to avoid that values of different attributes of the same record make the record nonsensical. The authors use the term *semantically correct*, which can be understood as records satisfying schema constraints (or edit constraints) using the terminology of this book. Nevertheless, these constraints are not expected to be hard-coded in the method. They are going to be learned from the data. In addition, these constraints are only related to a given attribute, the class, in the data. The classifier is used to help producing such semantically correct records.

The classifier is a function that receives a record of the space of data $\mathscr{D}$ and helps the generator to produce valid records. More precisely, the classifier is built for a given attribute V, the class, which is assumed to be binary, and its output is in the interval $[0, 1]$. Then, C is a function of this form $C : \mathscr{D} \rightarrow [0, 1]$. The function to optimize or loss function for C is defined as follows:

$$\mathbb{E}_{x \sim p_{data}(x)} [V(x) - C(remove_V(x))]. \tag{6.7}$$

Here, $V(x)$ returns the class for x, $remove_V(x)$ removes the attribute V from x, and $C(remove_V(x))$ is the prediction of this class for x using the classifier.

The generator

As we have discussed above, the network G uses a loss function different to the one of standard GANs. More precisely, the loss function extends the one of GAN (i.e., $V(G, D)$) adding some additional components which correspond to (i) the classifier (denoted by $\mathscr{L}_V^C$) and to (ii) the quality of hidden attributes on the generated data (denoted by $L_{m,\sigma}^Q$). The component corresponding to the classifier is similar to Eq. 6.7 but computed for generated data. So, it is

$$\mathscr{L}_V^C = \mathbb{E}_{z \sim p_z(z)} [V(G(z)) - C(remove_V(G(z)))]. \tag{6.8}$$

Then, the component on the quality of hidden attributes on the generated data consists of comparing the last layer of the discriminator for both synthetic and real data. This comparison is not record by record, which would make no sense, but based on statistics for a set of them. More precisely, means and standard deviations are compared. Formally, let $ly(x)$ denote the last layer for input x on the discriminator, and, similarly, let $ly(G(z))$ denote the last layer for the synthetic data generated from z. Then, the means of this last layer for original data and synthetic data are, respectively, $m_X = \mathbb{E}_{x \sim p_{data}(x)} [ly(x)]$ and $m_Z = \mathbb{E}_{z \sim p_z(z)} [ly(G(z))]$. Similarly, the standard deviation for original and synthetic data are denoted by $\sigma_X = \sigma_{x \sim p_{data}(x)} [ly(x)]$ and $\sigma_Z = \sigma_{z \sim p_z(z)} [ly(G(z))]$.

Then, means are expected to be similar and below a given threshold δ_m and standard deviations are also expected to be similar and below a given threshold δ_σ. Similarity between the vectors of means (and standard deviations) is computed using the norm. We denote this term by $\mathscr{L}_{m,\sigma}^Q$, with Q for quality. Then,

$$\mathscr{L}_{m,\sigma}^Q = \max(0, \mathscr{L}_m^Q) + \max(0, \mathscr{L}_\sigma^Q),$$

Algorithm 33: Training algorithm for producing a good generator G using table-generative adversarial networks (table-GANs). Each iteration uses a mini-batch of m real and m synthetic samples.

Data: X: data set; m: size of mini-batches; k: iterations for generator training; w: weight
Result: Generator

1 **begin**
2   G: initial generator
3   D: initial discriminator
4   C: initial classifier
5     $m_X = 0; m_Z = 0; \sigma_X = 0; \sigma_Z = 0;$ **while** *training* **do**
6   **for** *k times* **do**
7           $S_X :=$ create mini-batch of m real samples from X
8           $S_Z :=$ create mini-batch of m samples from the p-dimensional space $\mathscr{Z}$
9           $D :=$ train D using S_x and S_Z maximizing $V_{S_x, S_Z}(G, D)$ (Eq. 6.6)
10          $C :=$ train C using S_x and S_Z minimizing $\mathscr{L}_V^C$ (Eq. 6.8)
11          $m_X := w m_X + (1 - w) m_{S_X}$
12          $m_Z := w m_Z + (1 - w) m_{S_Z}$
13          $\sigma_X := w \sigma_X + (1 - w) \sigma_{S_X}$
14          $\sigma_Z := w \sigma_Z + (1 - w) \sigma_{S_Z}$
15          $G :=$ train G using S_x and S_Z minimizing $\mathscr{L}^G$ (Eq. 6.9)
16   **end**
17   **end**
18   **return** (G, D)
19 **end**

---

where

$$\mathscr{L}_m^Q = ||\mathbb{E}_{x \sim p_{data}(x)}[ly(x)] - \mathbb{E}_{z \sim p_z(z)}[ly(G(z))]||_2 - \delta_m,$$

$$\mathscr{L}_\sigma^Q = ||\sigma_{x \sim p_{data}(x)}[ly(x)] - \sigma_{z \sim p_z(z)}[ly(G(z))]||_2 - \delta_\sigma.$$

All together, the following expression is used for the loss of the generator:

$$\mathscr{L}^G = V(G, D) + \mathscr{L}_V^C + \mathscr{L}_{m,\sigma}^Q. \tag{6.9}$$

The algorithm

To find a solution, this method is implemented using a mini-batch on the original data and a mini-batch on the synthetic data. In each iteration, the values for means and standard deviations are computed for the batch, but using previous values as well. That is, the mean and standard deviation have some inertia on previously computed values. A weight w is used to control this inertia. Algorithm 33 details the computations. Loss functions $V_{S_X, S_Z}(G, D)$, $\mathscr{L}_V^C$, and $\mathscr{L}^G$ are used to improve the discriminator D, the classifier C, and the generator D.

6.4   Masking Methods and k-Anonymity

There are two main approaches for achieving k-anonymity. One is based on generalization and suppression. We present below the algorithm Mondrian as an example
of such algorithm. It has been proven [20,319,456] that optimal k-anonymity with
generalization and suppression is an NP-Hard problem. Because of that, heuristic
algorithms have been defined. The other approach is based on clustering and corresponds to microaggregation when all attributes are implemented at the same time. We
have seen microaggregation algorithms in Sect. 6.1.2, and discussed their connection
with k-anonymity.

6.4.1   Mondrian

Mondrian [283] provides k-anonymity by means of building a multidimensional
partition and applying local recoding to each part. The partition is constructed using
a recursive greedy algorithm.

The algorithm starts with a set of records. Then, it selects an attribute to partition,
and a value in the domain of that attribute to partition the set of records in two sets
of the same size. Then, the same algorithm is applied recursively to each subset.
Recursion is stopped when no further partition is needed (or possible). That is, when
there are between k and $2k - 1$ records in the set. Algorithm 34 formalizes this
process.

More concretely, given the set of records X, we choose an attribute V and then
a value in the domain of V. This value (denoted by i_0 in the algorithm) is selected
so that half of the records in the set are in one of the subsets, and half in the other.
That is, i_0 is the median of the values in X for attribute V_i. As the domain may have
records with the same value, it is possible that there are several records with the value
i_0. These records are distributed in the two subsets to make them of the same size
(or sizes differing in only one record).

Mondrian [283] uses, inspired in previous work to build kd-trees [192], the largest
spread in values for selecting the attribute to split. When a set is not partitionable
because it contains between k and $2k$ records, or because all records are identical, we
return a recoding function γ^X for X that assigns to a record in X a summary of this
set. For example, an interval for each attribute. That is, $\gamma^X(x) = (\gamma_1^X(x), \ldots, \gamma_s^X(x))$
where $\gamma_i^X(x) = [\min_{x' \in X} V_i(x'), \max_{x' \in X} V_i(x')]$.

6.4.2   Microaggregation and Generalization

Naturally, methods based on clustering and those based on generalization are not
worlds apart. We can reconsider the heuristic approach to microaggregation with the
steps (i) partition, (ii) aggregation, and (iii) replacement, and define the representative
of step (ii) as a generalization of records associated to the cluster.

Algorithm 34: Mondrian for achieving k-anonymity: *Mondrian(X, k)*.

Data: X: original data set; k: integer
Result: X': protected data set

1 **begin**
2   **if** *not(partitionable(X))* **then**
3   **return** $\{\gamma^X(x) = \{x \to summary(\mathrm{X})\}|x \in X\}$
4   **else**
5        $V_i :=$ select attribute from X
6        $i_0 :=$ select a value from domain of V_i in X
7        $lhs := \{x \in X | V_i(x) < i_0\}$
8        $rhs := \{x \in X | V_i(x) > i_0\}$
9   Distribute records in $\{x \in X | V_i(x) = i_0\}$ between lhs and rhs
10   **return** Mondrian(lhs, k) $\cup$ Mondrian(rhs, k)
11   **end**
12 **end**

That is, we can observe Mondrian from this microaggregation perspective. This also implies that we can apply Mondrian and define $\gamma^X(x)$ as the centroid of the elements in X. That is a microaggregation algorithm where step (i) is a greedy algorithm based on the selection of attribute V_i and value i_0.

Exercise 6.4 Implement variants of Mondrian where $\gamma^X(x) = (\gamma_1^X(x), \ldots, \gamma_s^X(x))$ is defined with γ_i^X to be the mean, the median, or the most frequent value in X depending on whether the attribute V_i is numerical, ordinal or nominal.

6.4.3 Algorithms for k-Anonymity: Variants and Big Data

We have to distinguish here the variants based on clustering and microaggregation from the ones based on generalization. We refer the reader to Sect. 6.1.2 for the former. About the latter, methods have been proposed to outperform the first algorithms for k-anonymity. For example, algorithms to improve Samarati's method [419], Datafly [460], Incognito [284], and Mondrian [283]. For example, Sun et al. [455] propose an approach to improve Samarati's method, and Russom [413] introduces a parallelization of Mondrian using the map-reduce paradigm. As we have explained, methods based on clustering and on generalization can be combined. Byun et al. [67] propose an efficient algorithm for k-anonymity based on clustering and generalization.

Note that results about efficient implementations of clustering algorithm and of k-nearest neighbors [129] are useful for efficient implementations of k-anonymity.

The k-anonymity model has been applied to all types of data, including time series, location privacy, graphs and social networks, access and search logs, and documents. We have already discussed the application of microaggregation to these types of data in Sect. 6.1.2. There are also examples of using generalization for achieving k-anonymity for location privacy [201,327,349,435], and for social networks [68, 76,77].

6.5   Data Protection Procedures for Constrained Data

Values of different attributes in a dataset are often related, and dependent. When a database is defined, some of these dependences are expressed by means of constraints between attributes. For example, ages are positive, and the number of harvested acres is less than the number of planted acres. These constraints can be stated in the metadata or the schema of the database. When we protect data, these constraints should be taken into account.

In statistical offices it is usual that data is edited before its publication. Data editing [206,383] (see also Fig. 6.2) studies and develops methods to analyze and correct raw data so that it is compliant with the set of constraints that we have assigned to a database. This is needed for the sake of correctness and so data does satisfy expectations (e.g. no negative ages). That is why these constraints are known as edit constraints. They can be also be seen as schema constraints.

Data privacy usually presumes that data is already compliant with the constraints. In statistical disclosure control, it is usual to apply data editing to the original raw data and, in any case, before any perturbation takes place.

Most masking methods ignore the constraints the data are forced to satisfy. This can cause that e.g. a random perturbation of the data invalidates some constraints. For example, adding noise to a data set can cause some ages to be negative or greater than 150 years!, or it can cause some nonsensical combination as e.g. replace the record $(18, woman, pregnant)$ representing a 18 years old pregnant woman by $(2, man, pregnant)$.

The posteriori edition of the masked dataset is always possible but it can cause some additional problems. Consider, for example, a masked data set with information concerning ages and salaries of a set of people. Then, if we add noise in a way that mean is not modified we may have negative ages and salaries. To solve this problem one may consider replacing all negative salaries and ages by zero. But, this process causes the mean age and the mean salary of the people in the sample to increase.

A few masking methods have been developed that take into account edit constraints. When such constraints are explicitly stated, we can set as a goal to produce a masked data set compliant with them. Let us review the constraints considered in the literature.

6.5.1   Types of Constraints

We classify the constraints according to the following types [475]. These types are not exclusive, and some constraints can be seen from different perspectives.

- **Constraints on the possible values.** The values of a given attribute are restricted to a predefined set. For example, salary and age have positive values and, possibly, bounded in an interval. For example,

$$\text{EC-PV: } age \in [0, 125]$$

Data editing is defined as the process of manipulating raw data to reduce the errors present and improve their quality. Other definitions exist strengthening different aspects of the process. Pierzchala [382] distinguishes data editing as either a validating procedure or a statistical process. In the first case, understanding it as a validating procedure, edition is a "within-record action with the emphasis on detecting inconsistencies, impossibilities, and suspicious situations and correcting them. Examples of validation include: checking to see if the sum of parts adds up to the total, checking that the number of harvested acres is less than or equal to that of planted acres". In the second case, editing as a statistical process, we have that "checks are based on a statistical analysis of respondent data". So, while in the first case we have single record checking, in this second case we may have between-record checking. The detection of outliers belong to this second case.

Given a record that does not satisfy a constraint, it is not easy to know which attributes are the wrong ones. A common approach [183] is to look for the minimum number of attributes to be changed so all edit rules are satisfied.

Besides of edit constraints, there is also macro-editing, which consists of checking aggregations of data. This is used when data is aggregated before its publication (e.g. to construct tabular data – following statistical disclosure control jargon – or data summaries).

Fig. 6.2 Definitions of data editing

This type of constraint also applies to sets of attributes. For example, we can restrict values [261] (v_1, v_2) to be such that $v_1/v_2 \in [l, u]$. The set of possible values may also be expressed in terms of an equation. For example, if v_1 and v_2 represent the proportion of nosocomial infections in hospitals, then the values should add up to one (i.e., $v_1 + v_2 = 1$). Linear constraints are discussed below.

- **Values are restricted to exist in the domain.** We require that the values of an attribute appears in a given data set. For example, an attribute *age* is required to be in the range [0, 120] but also that the values exist in the population. When masking data, this constraint forces us that the protected data contains values in the original data. This constraint is useful when linked files are edited [53,431]. For example, the edition of a file with data from a school should be in agreement with the population data from the same town or neighborhood.
- **One attribute governs the possible values of another one.** Given an attribute v_1, we have that the values of an attribute v_2 are constrained by the values of v_1. For example, we can consider [434] the attribute *age* governing the attribute *married*. It is clear that not all values are acceptable for the attribute *married* when *age=2*. Formally,

$$\text{EC-GV1: If } age=2 \text{ THEN } married = FALSE$$

Or, in general, we would define a domain for age where married should be false according to e.g. legal constraints. Another example [434] is represented in the following rule, which links three attributes: *age*, *gross income* and *mean income*.

$$\text{EC-GV2: IF } age < 17 \text{ THEN } gross\ income < mean\ income$$

Finally, we formalize the example [383] given above in form of a rule: the number of harvested acres should be less than or equal to that of planted acres. Formally,

EC-GV3: *harvested acres* $\leq$ *planted acres*

- **Linear constraints.** In this case we have a numerical (and linear) relationship between some numerical attributes. For example, in a data set about economical data the following equation involving attributes *net*, *tax* and *gross* should hold:

EC-LC1: *net* + *tax* = *gross*

- **Non-linear constraints.** This case is similar to the previous one but with a non-linear relationship. The following rule illustrates a non-linear relationship between the attributes *applicable VAT Rate*, *price exc. VAT* and *retail price*.

EC-NLC1: *price exc. VAT* $\cdot$ *(1.00 + applicable VAT Rate)* = *retail price*

Another example [198] of a non-linear relationship based on the attributes *wage sum*, *hours paid for*, and *wage rate* is this one:

EC-NLC2: *wage sum* = *hours paid for* $\cdot$ *wage rate*

- **Other types of constraints.** We include here constraints on non-numerical attributes (ordinal or categorical attributes), and relationships between several attributes that can not be easily represented by an equation.

The following example [475] illustrates edit constraints.

Example 6.3 [475] Table 6.2 represents a file with data from 12 individuals described in terms of the following 7 attributes: *Expenditure at 16%, Expenditure at 7%, Total Expenditure, Hours paid for, Wage rate, Wage sum, Total hours*. We also use $V_1, \ldots, V_7$ to denote these attributes.

The following three constraints are considered.

- A linear one that involves attributes V_1, V_2, and V_3. They satisfy $V_3 = 1.16V_1 + 1.07V_2$.
- A multiplicative constraint. Attributes V_4, V_5, and V_6 satisfy $V_6 = V_4 * V_5$.
- An inequality. Attributes V_4 and V_7 satisfy $V_4 \leq V_7$.

First approaches for masking data taking into account edit constraints were proposed by Shlomo and De Waal [433,434]. They focus on the use of PRAM [433], and propose to use imputation for correcting records that do not satisfy the constraints. Their work also discuss that some of the strategies to decrease disclosure risk can

Table 6.2 A data file satisfying three edit constraint. An additive one involving V_1, V_2, V_3, a multiplicative one involving V_4, V_5, V_6 and an inequality involving V_4, V_7. Example from [475]

Exp 16%	Exp 7%	Total	Hours paid for	Wage rate	Wage sum	Total hours
V_1	V_2	V_3	V_4	V_5	V_6	V_7
15	23	42.01	23	50	1150	37
12	43	59.93	28	70	1960	37
64	229	319.27	12	84	1008	25
12	45	62.07	29	73	2117	30
28	39	74.21	9	30	270	40
71	102	191.5	10	63	630	20
23	64	95.16	9	74	666	10
25	102	138.14	72	30	2160	80
48	230	301.78	26	30	780	35
32	50	90.62	6	45	270	15
90	200	318.4	8	45	360	15
16	100	125.56	34	55	1870	45

reduce the number of records not satisfying the constraints. In particular, the authors mention compounding different attributes into a single one (and apply PRAM to this new attribute). The idea of using imputation and replace records that are not compliant with the constraints can be applied to any data protection method [261]. The imputation procedure needs to be defined so that generated records satisfy the constraints [263]. In the case of noise addition, some constraints can be resolved [69] by means of swapping masked values. Shlomo and De Waal [434] also considered correcting by means of a linear programming problem those records that violated the constraints. They apply this approach to additive noise and microaggregation. All these methods have a common structure. They consist of applying a post-masking approach to correct the records that violate the constraints.

A different approach is to mask data in a way that the constraints are already satisfied once masking is completed, and, thus, there is no need for a post-masking process. It is possible to implement a variation of microaggregation [475] in these terms. For example, attributes need to be partitioned so that all those that belong to the same constraint are in the same set and microaggregated together. Then, the way we compute cluster centers need to take into account the constraints. For example, for linear constraints, cluster representatives need to be computed using the arithmetic mean. Nevertheless, the arithmetic mean is not appropriate to compute the cluster center when constraints are non-linear. For attributes satisfying non-linear constraints of the form $V = \prod_i V_i^{\alpha_i}$, cluster centers have to be computed using the geometric mean. Results are proven using functional equations [13]. This process can be fully automated, and a system [70] where the database schema and the different types of constraints are formally expressed (using Schematron [424]) was built. The system selects the appropriate microaggregation masking method for each subset of attributes.

6.6 Masking Methods and Big Data

This section summarizes some of the results we have already seen in this chapter, but from the big data perspective.

There is no standard definition of big data. Nevertheless, most definitions seem to agree on some basic characteristics (the well-known 3, 4, and 5 V's of big data): volume (large size of data sets), variety (different types of data including text and images), velocity (new data is produced very quickly), variability (data is typically inconsistent), and veracity (the quality of the data can be low). If we combine volume and velocity, we can classify masking methods according to the following three categories.

- **Large volumes.** This corresponds to data of high dimension, but with low velocity. Then, masking methods are for *static* (not changing) databases but of huge dimension.
- **Streaming data.** Data arrives continuously, and needs to be processed in real-time. Data protection methods are usually applied to a sliding window, as it is unfeasible to process all data at once.
- **Dynamic data.** We have this type of data when a database changes with respect to time and we want to publish different copies of this database. Each release needs to take into account previous releases, and how they have been created, otherwise disclosure can take place.

Let us now consider masking methods for these three categories.

- **Large volumes.** In this chapter we have discussed for each masking method variants for data of large volumes: both a large number of records and a high dimension. In particular, we have discussed the case of swapping(Sect. 6.1.1), microaggregation(Sect. 6.1.2), additive noise, PRAM (Sect. 6.1.3), transform-based method (Sect. 6.1.5), and implementations of k-anonymity (Sect. 6.4.3).
We have discussed masking methods for a few types of databases that are usually very large. In particular, we have described and mentioned results concerning time series, mobility and location privacy, graphs and social networks, and logs. There are also anonymization approaches for unstructured data [520].
Additive noise is naturally the best option with respect to time, however, it is not usually so good with respect to the trade-off between information loss and disclosure risk. Other methods as microaggregation are a second option for large databases.

- **Streaming data.** Data protection methods can be adapted to use a sliding window. This is the most usual approach for streaming data as it is unfeasible to process all data at once. Optimal solutions do not exist, and heuristic methods are applied. As records are delayed by the masking method, an additional requirement when developing a solution is to have small delays for processing records.

  There are a few algorithms for masking data streams. For example, methods to achieve microaggregation [539], k-anonymity via generalization [71,290,512, 540], rank swapping [346], and noise for multivariate numerical data streams [293]. An important aspect when we are masking data to achieve k-anonymity is that the k objects we cluster together, are independent. For example, that the k records correspond to k different people and that these people do not belong to the same household. Otherwise, k-anonymity will be usually flawed. This problem, which is discussed by several authors [121,260], is of particular relevance for data streams [540].

- **Dynamic data.** In Sect. 3.3.2 we have summarized an example [454] that illustrates the difficulty of ensuring privacy in this context. Two releases of data from a school class are done independently. Only one child was born in February while there are two childs in the other months. Independent releases of $k = 2$ anonymity can lead to disclosure if we anonymize once the February child with the ones in January and once with the ones in March.

  Algorithms have been designed for dynamic data [344,350,380,454,501]. They deal with standard SQL databases [350] but also for other types [344] as textual documents.

6.7 Bibliographical Notes

1. **Attributes and protection.** The way we process attributes in this book (quasi-identifiers vs. confidentials) is proposed and used in several works in the literature. For example Little [299] (1993, p. 408) states: "Methods that mask the key variables impede identification of the respondent in the file, and methods that mask the target variables limit what is learned if a match is made. Both approaches may be useful, and in practice a precise classification of variables as keys or targets may be difficult. However, masking of targets is more vulnerable to the trade-off between protection gain and information loss than masking of keys; hence masking of keys seems potentially more fruitful".

2. **Masking methods.** There are a few books and reviews on protection procedures for databases [14,143,156,239,521]. Felso et al. [185] reported that the most used ones by statistical agencies were rank swapping and microaggregation. These methods also provide a good balance [144] between risk and utility, with appropriate parameters. In recent years there has been a shift in some statistical offices towards differential privacy [1,2,197].

3. **Data and rank swapping.** The origins of using swapping as a masking method is in Dalenius and Reiss [112,113]. They provided some variants of the algorithm presented in this chapter. A discussion on the contribution of Dalenius and Reiss was given by Fienberg and McIntyre [188].

First definition for rank swapping seems to be by Greenberg for ordinal data [207], and later applied by Moore [328] to numerical data. Moore also proposes an enhanced version with the goal that the masked data set preserves (i) the multivariate dependence or independence (e.g., correlations) in the original file, and (ii) the means of subsets. Rank swapping was introduced as an alternative to arbitrary swapping as the latter "can severely distort the statistics of sub-domains of the universe" [328].

The transparency attack to rank swapping was introduced by Nin et al. [354]. Their experiments show that this attack is quite effective in reidentifying the masked data set. The authors also proposed the two variants p-distribution and p-buckets rank swapping to avoid the transparency attacks [354].

There are other variants of rank swapping [72,464,476]. The last one considers sets of attributes, which requires considering a partial ordering of the values instead of a total order. See also data shuffling [337], a related approach.

4. **Microaggregation.** First definition was given by Defays and Nanopoulos [126]. Then, it was popularized by Domingo-Ferrer and Mateo-Sanz [138] for numerical data. They also introduced MDAV. Microaggregation was defined independently in the data mining community [19,91].

Microaggregation of categorical data has been considered by several authors [127, 473]. While for numerical data heuristic approaches are usually based on Euclidean distance and mean for computing cluster representatives, different strategies can be considered for categorical data. The implementation of MDAV for categorical data [150] uses the median. Comparison of microaggregation and other methods for numerical data [144] and categorical data [473] showed that it leads to a good trade-off risk versus utility.

The problem of the curse of dimensionality in microaggregation, and how this affects information loss and data quality was studied by Aggarwal [16], among others.

The problem of selecting the best partition of attributes for microaggregation is not an easy task when the number of attributes is large. One option [34] is to use genetic algorithms where the fitness function is based on risk and utility. The use of genetic algorithms for grouping problems as this one was studied by Falkenauer [182]. Nevertheless, due to the high cost of genetic algorithms, it may be just more effective to consider a few partitions, evaluate their performance, and select the best one than trying to find the best partition.

Microaggregation based on minimum spanning trees was proposed by Sande [422] (only for bivariate data) and Laszlo and Mukherjee [280] (in multivariate data). The *real anonymity measure* was introduced by Nin et al. [355].

We have mentioned in this chapter the work by Nin et al. [356] about a specific attack for multivariate microaggregation. There was previous work for univariate microaggregation [361]. Winkler [524] was probably the first to describe specific distances that are effective for record linkage for univariate microaggregation. Microaggregation based on fuzzy clustering [147,148,490] was introduced as a way to produce transparency-aware microaggregation. The first approach, called Adaptive *at least k* fuzzy c-means, is to ensure that each cluster has at least k records. In this chapter we have described a simpler algorithm [483,485], decoupled fuzzy c-means based microaggregation, where there are no constraints on the number of elements assigned to the cluster.

5. **Additive and multiplicative noise.** Noise addition and multiplication have been studied in both statistical disclosure control (SDC) and privacy preserving data mining (PPDM) communities. First extensive testing of noise addition was due to Spruill [442] in the SDC community. Fuller [193] further studies this approach. Brand [60] gives an overview of these approaches for noise addition as well as more sophisticated techniques. Domingo et al. [141] describe some of the existing methods as well as the difficulties for its application to privacy.

The first mention of noise addition in the PPDM community is probably Agrawal and Srikant [24]. They discuss the reconstruction of the original distribution. Huang et al. [233] also studied the reconstruction of the original data from the protected data, considering two methods for this reconstruction. One of them based on principal components analysis (PCA).

Noise addition using Laplace distribution has been extensively used to implement differential privacy as we have already discussed in this chapter. Correlated noise using multivariate Laplace distribution can also be implemented. For differential privacy, other distributions have been considered [398] even the more general multivariate elliptical distributions [266].

Multiplicative noise has also been studied in both the SDC [264] and PPDM [303] communities. Kim and Winkler [264] studied reidentification rates for this masking approach.

Noise-graph addition [418,496] permits to represent usual protection procedures [74,222] consisting on adding and removing edges and vertices in graphs, and it permits also to satisfy differential privacy [418] for selected random graphs.

6. **PRAM.** The Post-RAndomization Method was introduced by Gouweleeuw et al. [204] in 1998. They also introduced Invariant PRAM. The approach of defining the transition matrix so that categories with low frequency have larger probabilities of changing was introduced by de Wolf and van Gelder [131]. Invariant PRAM determined from preferences was proposed by Gross et al. [208]. The problem of finding an optimal PRAM matrix for a given data set has been considered in the literature. Given a data file, the goal is to obtain a transition matrix that leads to a file with minimum disclosure risk and minimum information loss. Appropriate definitions of disclosure risk and information loss need to be used. For example, we can define disclosure risk in terms of reidentification. Solutions for arbitrary PRAM matrices [315] and for invariant PRAM [313] have been proposed using genetic algorithms. An alternative of building the transition matrix is to build an analytical expression using genetic programming [314]. From the analytical expression, the transition matrix is built.

7. **Lossy compression and other transform-based methods.** Protection based on lossy compression using both JPEG [143] and JPEG 2000 [248,249] have been used in the literature. Different quantization approaches have been considered and compared [248,249]. Linear quantization transforms linearly the range of the original attributes into the image range [0,255] or [0,65536]. Non uniform quantization can assign more values in the image space to those regions in the original domain that are more dense. A non-uniform quantifier based on histogram equalization [377] has also been used [249].

Independently, Bapna and Gangopadhyay introduced [40] the use of wavelets in similar terms. The approach is based on the decomposition of a matrix using wavelets, and applying a reduction of the number of rows (the number of individuals). Other researchers as Liu et al. [305,306] have used a similar approach also based on wavelet decomposition. Liu et al. [306] also consider applying a normalization step so that the mean and standard deviation is preserved in the protected file. Hajian and Azgomi [212,213] considered the Haar wavelet transforms, focusing on data for clustering, and Mukherjee et al. [331] considered Fourier-related transforms.

The use of singular value decomposition (SVD) appears in works by Xu et al. [530,531], and nonnegative matrix factorization appears in works by Wang et al. [514]. We can also mention here the work by Lasko and Vinterbo [278,279] on microaggregation and rank swapping working on the spectral basis. We have already mentioned this approach in Sects. 6.1.1 and 6.1.2.

Wavelet transforms have been also considered for differential privacy, in particular, differential privacy of range-count queries [529].

8. **Synthetic data generators.** The seminal work of synthetic data generators for its use in data privacy are the works by Little [299] and Rubin [411]. Little's approach corresponds to partially synthetic data sets as only sensitive values (target attributes [299]) or identifiers (key attributes [299]) are synthetic. The second approach corresponds to fully synthetic data sets as all the values in the release are synthetic.

Discussion of the three types of categories for synthetic data generators is provided by Templ and Meindl [468,469]. Synthetic reconstruction is described by several authors [39,234,468,469]. Combinatorial optimization is also described by Huang and Williamson [234]. Huang and Williamson [234] in addition to describe synthetic reconstruction and combinatorial optimization, they also compare them. Model-based approaches are described in detail by Templ and Meindl [468,469]. Drechsler [152] is a reference book on synthetic data generators. A comparison of both fully synthetic and partially synthetic approaches was given by Drechsler et al. [153].

Selection of a Data Protection Mechanism: Information Loss and Risk

Abstract

Masking methods produce a distorted version of the data. This distortion depends on the method as well as of its parameterization. Data utility or the information loss caused by the method can help on method and parameter selection. Disclosure risk may be another element to take also into account. In this chapter we give an overview of information loss measures, and on method selection. Some of the ideas that appear here are useful for protection mechanisms other than masking methods. We complete the chapter with a discussion of data protection in machine learning and federated learning. Federated learning is a very good example to illustrate the difficulties related to data protection mechanism selection.

> No hauria sabut explicar la felicitat que sentia abocada al balcó d'aquella casa, menjant Borregos i una presa de xocolata darrera de l'altra (...)
>
> M. Rodoreda, Mirall trencat, 1974 [408].

In this chapter we discuss the problem of selecting a masking method, or, in general, a protection mechanism. For masking methods, one of the main aspects to take into account is in what extent the resulting database is useful for data analysis or for building machine learning models. This is measured using information loss measures. We devote one section to these measures. Then, we devote another section to the problem of selecting a method itself. We conclude the chapter with a discussion of data protection in relation to machine learning, and more particularly to federated learning. Federated learning provides an excellent example of the difficulties of selecting a good set of privacy technologies.

© The Author(s), under exclusive license to Springer Nature Switzerland AG 2022
V. Torra, *Guide to Data Privacy*, Undergraduate Topics in Computer Science,
https://doi.org/10.1007/978-3-031-12837-0_7

7.1 Information Loss: Evaluation and Measures

Data protection methods introduce distortion to the data. This causes that analyses on the masked data are different to the same analyses performed on the original data. Protection methods for computations (machine learning models, statistics, and aggregates) also modify these computations. We say that some information is lost in this distortion process, or, equivalently, discuss the utility of the result.

The literature presents different ways to evaluate this loss. Some just display in a single framework (a plot or a table) the results of the two analyses (original vs. protected), while others compute an aggregated measure (an information loss measure comparing the two analyses).

In this section we begin discussing (Sect. 7.1.1) the difference between generic and specific information loss and (Sect. 7.1.2) formalizing measures to quantify information loss. Then (Sects. 7.1.3–7.1.5) we give an overview of information loss measures. Most measures are to evaluate data protection mechanisms (i.e., masking methods) but some are also valid for comparing outcomes of computations. First, generic measures, then specific, and finally measures for big data.

7.1.1 Generic Versus Specific Information Loss

When we know which type of analysis the data scientist will perform on the data, the analysis of the distortion of a particular protection procedure can be done in detail. That is, measures can be developed, and protection procedures can be compared and ranked using such measures. *Specific information loss measures* are the metrics that permits us to quantify such distortion.

Nevertheless, when the type of analysis to be performed is not known, only generic metrics can be computed. *Generic information loss measures* are the metrics to be applied in this case. They have been defined to evaluate the utility of the protected data but not for a specific application but for *any* of them. They are usually defined in terms of an aggregation of a few measures, and are based on statistical properties of the data. As these metrics aggregate components, it might be the case that a protection procedure with a good *average* performance behaves badly in a specific analysis.

Generic information loss has been evaluated considering the values of the records [143,144,154,395,396], ranks of values [306], summary statistics [264,336] (means, variance, covariances), regression coefficients [72,153,336,390,402], n-order statistics [399], subgroup analysis (as e.g. means for some combinations [336]), coverage rates for 95% confidence intervals [153,154,402]. We discuss some generic information loss measures in Sect. 7.1.3.

Specific information loss have been defined for e.g. clustering (k-means [212, 303]), classification [24,40,303,331] (including e.g. k-nearest neighbor, Naïve Bayes, (linear) support vector machines, decision trees), and regression [390] (comparison of estimates). We discuss some specific information loss measures in Sect. 7.1.4.

7.1.2   Information Loss Measures

Information loss measures have been defined to quantify information loss. From a general perspective, and for a given data analysis, information loss corresponds to the divergence between the results of the analysis on the original data and the results of the same analysis on the perturbed data. Naturally, the larger the divergence, the larger the information loss.

Definition 7.1 Let X be the original data set on the domain D, and let X' be a protected version of the same data set. Then, for a given data analysis that returns results in a certain domain D' (i.e., $f : D \to D'$), the information loss of f for data sets X and X' is defined by

$$IL_f(X, X') = divergence(f(X), f(X')), \tag{7.1}$$

where $divergence$ is a way to compare two elements of D'.

An analysis of this function seems to point out that it should satisfy for all $X, Y \in D'$ the following axioms:

- $divergence(X, X) = 0$
- $divergence(X, Y) \geq 0$
- $divergence(X, Y) = divergence(Y, X)$

So, $divergence$ is a semimetric on D' instead of a metric or distance (because we do not require to satisfy the triangle inequality). Naturally, any metric or distance[1] function on D' will also be acceptable for computing a $divergence$.

In some circumstances, the condition of symmetry can be removed. Let us consider the case of a function f that distinguishes some objects from X. For example, $f(X)$ selects the sensors in X that malfunction. Consider that having a sensor not working properly can cause major damage, while informing that a valid sensor is malfunctioning is not so relevant (because double testing a sensor is easy and replacing it by a new one has a negligible cost). Then, our goal is to avoid missing any malfunctioning sensors in X. In this context we can use the following divergence measure that is not symmetric:

$$divergence(X, Y) = |malfunctioning(X) \setminus malfunctioning(Y)|$$

Note that this type of measure focuses on false positives, but ignores false negatives.

In addition to the previous axioms, for the sake of commensurability, we usually require the function $divergence$ to be bounded. E.g., $0 \leq divergence(X, Y) \leq 1$. This is to be able to compare different protection mechanisms.

---

[1] Distances and metrics, as well as their properties, are discussed in the Appendix, Sects. A.1.6 and A.3.1.

This definition presumes a particular data use f. Then, different data uses f imply different information loss measures.

Different types of data, usually imply different functions f, so, we may have different information loss measures. Nevertheless, this is not always the case. Observe that, for example, clustering algorithms can be applied to different domains D leading in all cases to a partition of the elements in D. In this case, similar information loss measures can be developed for different data types.

For illustration, we consider now two examples. One for numerical databases and another for search logs.

Example 7.1 Let X be a one-column matrix of numerical data, and X' a protected version of X. Let $f(X) = \bar{X}$ be the average of the matrix X. Then, we can define information loss by

$$IL_{\bar{X}}(X, X') = ||\bar{X} - \bar{X}'||.$$

Let X be a matrix with s columns, with values in $[0, 1]$ and X' a protected version of X. Let $f(X)$ be an d-dimensional vector with the mean of each column in X. Then, we can define information loss by

$$IL_f(X, X') = ||f(X) - f(X)||.$$

Example 7.2 Let X be a search log database, and X' be the protected version of X. Let $f(X)$ be the list of ten more frequent queries in X. Then, we can define information loss by

$$IL_{10+}(X, X') = 1 - \frac{|f(X) \cap f(X')|}{|f(X) \cup f(X')|}$$

In the first example, first case, $f(X) = \bar{X}$ and $divergence(x, y) = ||x - y||$, and in the second case, $f(X)$ is the vector of means and again $divergence(x, y) = ||x - y||$. In the second example, f selects the ten most frequent logs in the set and

$$divergence(x, y) = 1 - \frac{|x \cap y|}{|x \cup y|},$$

for sets x and y. In the first example D' is the set of real numbers or a vector in $[0, 1]^s$, and in the second example D' is a set of logs.

As the two examples above illustrate, different data imply different analyses, and these analyses lead to quite different information loss measures. In addition, for any set, a large number of different data uses can also be conceived.

In the next sections, we discuss some of the existing measures. We start with some generic measures and then we focus on specific measures for classification and clustering.

7.1.3   Generic Information Loss Measures

We review in this section measures for numerical and categorical data.

Numerical data

Information loss measures for numerical data are based on some statistics computed from the data. Some works compute them for the whole domain [139,144] and others [137,336] compute them for the whole domain but also for some subdomains (e.g., for subsets defined in terms of a few attributes).

There are a few works that use means, variance, kth central moments, and covariance to compare masked and original data. In terms of Definition 7.1, they [139, 144] can be seen as: (i) computation of some matrices from the data sets (as e.g. covariance matrices), which stands for the computation of $f(X)$ and $f(X')$, and (ii) computation of the divergence between these matrices. They used three alternative definitions for divergence: mean square error, mean absolute error, and mean variation. Mean square error is defined as the sum of squared componentwise differences between pairs of matrices, divided by the number of cells in either matrix. Mean absolute error is defined as the sum of absolute componentwise difference between pairs of matrices, divided by the number of cells in either matrix. Mean variation corresponds to the sum of absolute percentage variation of components in the matrix computed on the protected data with respect to components in the matrix computed on the original data, divided by the number of cells in either matrix. In the first two definitions, the distinction was on the type of distance used in the measure (square error vs. absolute error). In contrast, in the last definition, we have a relative error. Because of that, a change of the measure scale of the attributes does not change the outcome of the measure.

We provide definitions for some of these measures below.

Definition 7.2 Let X be a numerical microdata file and $X' = \rho(X)$ the protected version of the same file, let V and V' denote the covariance matrices of X and X', and R and R' the correlation matrices of X and X', respectively.

Let us now define three divergence functions to compare two matrices.

- $divergence_{MSE}(M, M') = \frac{\sum_{ij}(M_{ij}-M'_{ij})^2}{c(M)}$ (mean square error)
- $divergence_{MAE}(M, M') = \frac{\sum_{ij}|M_{ij}-M'_{ij}|}{c(M)}$ (mean absolute error)
- $divergence_{MRE}(M, M') = \frac{\sum_{ij}\frac{|M_{ij}-M'_{ij}|}{|M_{ij}|}}{c(M)}$ (mean relative error)

where $c(M)$ is the number of elements in the matrix. For example, for X we have $c(X) = n \cdot p$ where n is the number of records and p the number of attributes, while for R we have $c(R) = p \cdot p$ as M is a square matrix with as many rows as attributes we have in X.

Then, the following information loss measures are defined.

- $IL_{Id}(X, X') = divergence_{MSE}(X, X')$
- $IL_{Cov}(V(X), V(X')) = divergence_{MSE}(V, V')$
- $IL_{Corr}(R(X), R(X')) = divergence_{MSE}(R, R')$

Similar expressions can be defined with the other two divergence functions introduced before $divergence_{MAE}$ and $divergence_{MRE}$.

The expressions for divergence in the previous definition lead to unbounded information loss measures. Yancey et al. [534] considered this problem for the mean relative error of X and X' and proposed to use the following expression that is more stable when the original values are close to zero:

$$IL'_{Id}(X, X') = divergence'_{MRE}(X, X') = \frac{\sum_{ij} \frac{|x_{ij} - x'_{ij}|}{\sqrt{2}S_j}}{n \cdot p}$$

where S_j is the standard deviation of the jth attribute.

Trottini [500] also discussed the unbounded measures and proposed to settle a predefined maximum value of error.

An alternative approach was proposed by Mateo-Sanz et al. [318]. They introduced probabilistic information loss measures to avoid predefined values. This is based on the assumption that X' is a sample from the population, and, the measure is about the discrepancy between a population parameter θ on X and a sample statistic Θ on X'. Let $\hat{\Theta}$ be the value of this statistic for a specific sample. Then, the standardized sample discrepancy corresponds to

$$Z = \frac{\hat{\Theta} - \theta}{\sqrt{Var(\hat{\Theta})}}$$

This discrepancy is assumed [318] to follow a $N(0, 1)$. Accordingly, the probabilistic information loss measure for $\hat{\Theta}$ was defined by:

$$pil(\hat{\Theta}) := 2 \cdot P\left(0 \leq Z \leq \frac{\hat{\theta} - \theta}{\sqrt{Var(\hat{\Theta})}}\right) \tag{7.2}$$

So, from our perspective, we have that information loss corresponds to the following expression for the divergence.

$$divergence(\theta, \hat{\Theta}) = 2 \cdot P\left(0 \leq Z \leq \frac{\hat{\theta} - \theta}{\sqrt{Var(\hat{\Theta})}}\right).$$

When the masking method is microaggregation, it is usual to use SSE/SST [87, 92, 138, 280, 281, 376] as a measure of information loss. Recall from Eq. 6.2 that SSE is defined as

$$SSE(X, \chi, p) = \sum_{i=1}^{c} \sum_{x \in X} \chi_i(x)(d(x, p_i))^2$$

for a set of records X, a partition on X represented by χ, and cluster centers p. Note that the partition χ divides the set X into c clusters, and it is represented with the characteristic function χ_i where $\chi_i(x) = 1$ if the record x is assigned to the ith cluster and $\chi_i(x) = 0$ if not. Each part of the partition has a cluster center: p_i is the cluster center of the ith cluster. While SSE is the overall distance of elements x to the corresponding cluster centers, SST is the distance of elements to the mean of X, or, in other words, to a partition that contains a single cluster with all the elements. Formally,

$$SST(X) = \sum_{x \in X}(d(x, \bar{X}))^2$$

Note that as SST is constant for a given set X, optimization of SSE/SST is only about the optimization of SSE. Then, if we microaggregate X and obtain X' through χ and cluster centers p_i, the information loss is defined as follows. Observe that X' is usually determined from χ as the cluster centers are built from clusters, and then X' is defined replacing records by the cluster centers. We use the following expression.

$$divergence(X, \chi) = SSE(X, \chi, P(\chi, X))/SST(X)$$

where $P(\chi, X)$ represent the cluster centers associated to partition χ and data X. Note that this expression of divergence is equivalent to

$$divergence(X, X') = \frac{\sum(d(x, x'))^2}{SST(X)}$$

and, thus, proportional to $divergence_{MSE}(X, X')$.

Probability distributions

In some applications it is convenient to compare probability distributions. This can also be seen as an alternative to the measures discussed above, when, instead of e.g. the mean of a column in X, we consider the distribution of the values of a column in X.

Therefore, in this case, $f(X)$ is a probability distribution, and divergence is a distance between distributions. Different distances are being used. For example, Agrawal and Aggarwal [21] use the mean absolute difference between distributions (i.e., $\int |f(x) - f(x')|dx$), but it is probably more common to consider the Hellinger distance [432,482].

Given a data set X, a probability distribution can be derived assuming a parametric model. Alternatively, a probability distribution is derived by means of a discretization of the domain of X and counting the number of records in each region. In this latter case, the more intervals are generated in the discretization, the more sensitive is the information loss to noise.

Exercise 7.1 Discuss the effects of microaggregation and rank swapping on the information loss when we compare probability distributions. Consider the following two cases:

- the distributions are univariate, and built independently for each attribute;
- the distributions are multivariate, and built jointly with the different attributes.

Categorical data

In the case of categorical data, we can consider a direct comparison [143] of the categorical data. For this, we can use the distances described in the appendix (Sect. A.1.6, Definition A.2). When there is an underlying hierarchical ontology for the categorical terms, we can use distances [416] taking into account this knowledge (Definition A.3).

An alternative to the comparison of records is the comparison of contingency tables [143,203]. This consists of comparing tables built up to a given dimension. Formally, the divergence is defined in terms of a distance between contingency tables and using f as the function to build the contingency table. For the distance, we can use the absolute distance [143], the Hellinger distance [432], and a difference between entropies [203]. Note that these definitions are a categorical counterpart of comparing probability distributions for numerical data (discussed above).

Two other definitions based on entropy use the probability of replacing a category by another. We define them below.

Definition 7.3 [521] Let X and X' be the original and protected files, let V be a categorical attribute with values $1, \ldots, n$. Let us use $V = i$ and $V' = j$ to represent that X takes value i in attribute i and that X' takes value j for the same attribute. Let $P_{V,V'} = \{p(V' = j | V = i)\}$ be the probability that value i has been replaced by value j. Then, the condicional uncertainty of V given $V' = j$ is defined in terms of the entropy of the distribution given j as follows

$$H(V|V' = j) = -\sum_{i=1}^{n} p(V = i | V' = j) \log p(V = i | V' = j).$$

Note that $p(V = i | V' = j)$ is computed from $P_{V,V'}$ using the Bayes' expression.

This definition was introduced by for the PRAM method. In this case $P_{V,V'}$ is the transition matrix that PRAM requires. For other methods, we can estimate $P_{V,V'}$ from both X and X'.

Using the definition above, the entropy-based information loss measure can be defined as follows.

Definition 7.4 [521] Let X, X', V, V', and $P_{V,V'}$ as above. Then, the entropy-based information loss (EBIL) is defined by

$$EBIL(P_{V,V'}, X') = \sum_{x' \in X'} H(V | V' = V(x')).$$

It is possible to give an expression ([481], Proposition 5) for the expected EBIL for PRAM with matrix $P_{V,V'}$. It is the following one

$$- \sum_i n_i \sum_j p(V' = j|V = i) \sum_k p(V = k|V' = j) \log P(V = k|V' = j) \quad (7.3)$$

where n_i is the number of records in the file X that has value i. I.e,

$$n_i = |\{x \in X|V(x) = i\}|.$$

In EBIL, we have that for a record x the computation of $H(V|V' = j)$ only takes into account the protected value but not the original one. Nevertheless, when we have a recoding of two values into a new one, we can consider that the information loss depends on the proportion of these values in the file (or in the population). This is illustrated in the following example.

Example 7.3 [143,471] Let X, X', V and V' as above. Let V correspond to the attribute town. The masking process for V is to replace location by states. Therefore, locations like New York City and Albany will be recoded into NY (New York State).

Then, all locations in NY will have the same entropy measure according to Definition 7.3.

According to the U.S. Census Bureau's American FactFinder (U.S. Census Bureau 2010) the population of New York State in 2010 was 19,378,102, the population of New York City was 8,175,133, and the population of Albany was 97,856. Thus, the conditional probabilities for NY are:

$$P(V =' Albany'|V = NY) = \qquad 97,856/19,378,102 = 0.005$$
$$P(V =' New York City'|V = NY) = \quad 8,175,133/19,378,102 = 0.421$$

The entropy for recoding all records in the file which belong to NY requires the computation of the following summatory, which goes over the 932 towns and 62 cities in which NY is divided.

$$H(V|V' = NY) = - \sum_{i=1}^{n} p(V = i|V' = NY) \log p(V = i|V' = NY) = 1.69.$$

This measure is used for all records assigned as NY, independently of the size of the town. E.g., to records with an original value equal to New York City (8,175,133 inhabitants), Albany (97,856 inhabitants), and Red House (38 inhabitants).

In order to have a measure that depends on the relative size of the original town, the following per-record measure was introduced.

Definition 7.5 [143,471] Let X, X', V, and V' as above. Let us use also $V = i$ and $V' = j$ as above. Then, we define the per-record information loss measure as:

$$PRIL(P_{V,V'}, i, j) = - \log p(V = i|V' = j).$$

Note that in this case,

$$PRIL(P_{V,V'}, NewYorkCity, NY) = -\log 0.421 = 0.8651$$
$$PRIL(P_{V,V'}, Albany, NY) = -\log 0.005 = 5.298$$

and, thus, the information loss of recoding someone in New York City is smaller than recoding someone in Albany. The following properties about PRIL are of relevance.

Proposition 7.1 *[481] Let X, and V as above. Let $P_{V,V'}$ represent the Markov matrix for PRAM to be used to build X'. Then, the following holds.*

- *For a record in X with value i, its expected PRIL is:*

$$-\sum_j p(V' = j | V = i) \log p(V = i | V' = j).$$

- *For the whole data set X, the expected PRIL is*

$$\sum_i n_i e_i^T \hat{p} \, p(V' | V = i). \tag{7.4}$$

where e_i is the unit vector with one for the ith position and 0 otherwise, e_i^T its transpose, n_i is the number of records in the file X that have value i, and $\hat{p}$ is the matrix defined by $\{-\log p(V = i | V' = j)\}_{ij}$.
- *Let I_j be the values i such that $P(V' = j | V = i) \neq 0$. Then, expected EBIL equals expected PRIL when for all j, $P(V = i_1 | V' = j) = P(V = i_2 | V' = j)$ for all $i_1, i_2 \in I_j$.*

The last condition describes when the two measures EBIL and PRIL lead to the same results for a pair of files X and X'. In short, we need the same probabilities of having i_1 and i_2 in the original files when observing j in the masked file.

7.1.4 Specific Information Loss

We describe in this section information loss for classification, regression, and clustering.

Classification-based information loss

Classification is one of the most common data uses in machine learning. This is to extract a model for a categorical attribute from the data (see Sect. 2.3.1). The (standard) goal of applying machine learning to build classifiers is that the model obtained is as accurate as possible. This is also the case when data is masked.

In this type of data use, research usually compares the results of different machine learning models using tables and figures. Authors compare the performance of models built using the original data and the ones using the masked data. Most of the literature uses accuracy [17,24,40,224], and others have used the area under the curve (AUC) [224]. The comparison of other performance measures can also be useful for assessing information loss.

Some experiments on building classifiers with masked data show that the performance of these classifiers is not always worse than the performance of the classifiers built using the original data. There are cases in which the performance is even improved. Aggarwal and Yu [17] report that "in many cases, the classification accuracy improves because of the noise reduction effects of the condensation process". The same was concluded by Sakuma and Osame [415] for recommender systems: "we observe that the prediction accuracy of recommendations based on anonymized ratings can be better than those based on non-anonymized ratings in some settings". Other similar results [40,224] are also relevant for this discussion. The reason seems to be that methods as microaggregation can be considered as methods for noise/dimensionality reduction. When the number of records is large and they are noisy, reducing the number of these records by means of averaging some of them has positive effects. In addition, when machine learning methods are resistant to errors, some data perturbation does not reduce dramatically the accuracy of the model. In fact, data perturbation may result into models that are better from the point of view of generalization. Some related research [348] on adding noise when training machine learning models, as e.g. deep networks, seem to support this idea. This is an issue not fully understood.

An alternative to accuracy is to consider the similarities between the models themselves. I.e., if we obtain decision trees from X and X', we may want that the two trees are the same (or as similar as possible). Not only that they classify new data in the same way. This approach has not been much considered in the literature. There is some research [494] in the context of integral privacy. Note however, that for some classification models this approach is rather unfeasible as small variations of the data change the model significantly. Observe the case of k-nearest neighbor. Model comparison has been used in regression problems as we discuss below.

Regression-based information loss

Literature on statistical disclosure control considers regression and logistic regression as a usual data use. Evaluation of regression can follow the pattern of classification. We can evaluate the models themselves or the performance of the model.

For example, Raghunathan et al. [390] compare estimates of the regression models, while Muralidhar and Sarathy [336] compare the predictions of different models (sum of squares error). Gomatam et al. [203] consider a measure based on the optimal log-linear model. Some of these comparisons are given graphically, plotting a 2D graph with one prediction in one dimension and the other prediction in the other axis.

Given X and X' and regression models m_X and $m_{X'}$ obtained, respectively, from data sets X and X' using algorithm ML, we can define

$$IL_{regr}(X, X') = ||m_X(X) - m_{X'}(X')||.$$

Here, $m_X(X)$ and $m_{X'}(X')$ are the estimations of appropriate test sets using the models m_X and $m_{X'}$. Different machine and statistical learning algorithms will result into different models and different information loss measures. We have already stated when discussing generic information loss measures, that it is quite common to consider correlation coefficients [72,153,336,390,402]. Such measures are, of course, related to regression.

Exercise 7.2 Consider a data set with a dependent variable. Microaggregate it with increasing values of k. For each protected data set compute the regression of the dependent variable. Observe the effects of k on the regression and the divergence with respect to the original regression.

Apply the same process using rank swapping for different parameterizations, and compare the results with the ones obtained by means of microaggregation.

Clustering-based information loss

Clustering is a typical data analysis in both the statistical and machine learning communities. Because of that, masking methods have been evaluated and compared against its performance with respect to clustering algorithms. In order to do so, we define the two components (i.e., the exact analysis f and the divergence in Eq. 7.1).

The function is one clustering algorithm with its parameters (e.g., the number of clusters). The divergence is to select a function to compare the results of the clustering.

Although there are several types of cluster structures (i.e., clusters, fuzzy clusters, dendrograms), analysis of data masking algorithms has been focused on crisp (mainly k-means) and fuzzy clusters.

In order to compare crisp clusters we can use distances and indices to compare partitions. The Rand, Jaccard, and Wallace indices, the adjusted Rand index, and the Mántaras distance (see Sect. 2.4.1) can be used [43,273] for this purpose. Hajian and Azgomi [212] used the F-measure to compare partitions. Comparison [477] of fuzzy clusters can be done using α-cuts (see Sect. 2.4.1).

Clustering is used extensively within the machine learning community for all types of data (including standard databases, time series, access and search logs, documents, social networks, etc.). In all these cases we can follow the same approach. That is, we can compare partitions (of records, time series, etc.). For example, Batet et al. [43] compare clusters of query logs.

7.1.5   Information Loss and Big Data

Evaluation of information loss for big data follows the same approach formalized in Definition 7.1. That is, we need to evaluate the divergence between analysis for the original data set and the ones for the protected data set. The difficulties we found are due to the nature of the analysis we apply to big data. We can discuss them in relation to the three categories we have considered in Sect. 6.6 for big data: (i) large volumes, (ii) streaming data, and (iii) dynamic data.

(i) **Large volumes.** The analysis of standard databases of huge dimensions and the analysis of typically large datasets (e.g., social networks, location data) has been developed in the last years within the field of data mining. There are effective algorithms for clustering and classification, and also for computing specific indices for some particular types of data.

Research challenges focus on how to compare efficiently the summarizations of the data when these summaries are also of large dimension. In addition, some of the algorithms are not deterministic. This means that even with the same data, different outcomes can be obtained. Because of that effective computation of information loss is difficult. In short, it is difficult to know in what extent divergence in the analysis is due to divergences on the data or to variability on the results.

(ii) **Streaming data.** The research problems of large volumes also apply here. In addition, we have that comparison of results need to be done at run time. This implies that we do not have the full picture of $f(X)$ and $f(X')$ at any instant but only part of this function.

(iii) **Dynamic data.** Information loss needs to consider that at a given point we have a set of databases $X_1, X_2, \ldots, X_n$ together with their masked counterparts $X'_1, X'_2, \ldots, X'_n$. Aggregation of individual divergences

$$d_i = divergence(f(X_i), f(X'_i))$$

using an aggregation function $\mathbb{C}$ as e.g. the arithmetic mean or a weighted mean is the most straightforward way to deal with this problem. An alternative is to consider analysis of several releases. That is

$$IL = divergence(f(X_1, X_2, \ldots, X_n), f(X'_1, X'_2, \ldots, X'_n)).$$

Up to our knowledge, no much research has been done in this area.

We have discussed extensively that data perturbation causes that analysis on the original data and on the protected data differ. This implies some information loss. Nevertheless, it is important to underline that for some data uses, the noise introduced with a data masking procedure still permits us to obtain acceptable results. Naturally this depends on the data and the data use. We have reported in Sect. 7.1.3 the case of building classifiers. Two notes can be made in this respect.

On the one hand, machine learning algorithms are being designed so that they are resistant to errors, and machine learning design strategies are developed to avoid overfitting. In this way, algorithms can deal with some noise added to the data either accidentally or on purpose.

On the other hand, some masking mechanisms can be seen (or can be developed) as privacy-preserving noise reduction methods. It is usual in machine learning to preprocess the data to improve their quality. Attribute selection and dimensionality reduction algorithms are used for this purpose. Microaggregation and other methods to achieve k-anonymity are examples of masking methods that can be seen from this perspective. The process of replacing a set of a few similar data elements by their mean can be seen as a way of consolidating the data and reducing the error.

7.2 Selection of Masking Methods

We have discussed in Chap. 3 (Sect. 3.1.1) that selection of a masking algorithm (and its parameters) can be seen as an optimization problem. When we consider a Boolean privacy model, we need to select the method that minimizes information loss. In contrast, when we consider a measurable privacy model, we need to select the method that is the best in a multicriteria optimization problem. This is so because we need the method to be the best with respect both the information loss and the disclosure risk. In this latter case, if we want to compare different alternatives (i.e., different masking methods and parameters), we can either aggregate the two measures or visualize the outcome.

Note that, in principle, when a masking method has a parameter that relates to the privacy level, increasing the parameter means to increase its information loss. We need to advise that it is usual that this relationship is not strictly monotonic. There is usually some noise in the relationship between protection level and information loss.

7.2.1 Aggregation: A Score

The simplest way to give a trade-off between information loss and disclosure risk for a given masking method m with parameters p and given a data set X is to compute their average.

$$Score(m, p, X) = \frac{IL(X, m_p(X)) + DR(X, m_p(X); m, p)}{2}.$$

where IL corresponds to the information loss and DR to the disclosure risk. Different measures for IL and DR lead to different scores. We have used the expression $DR(X, m_p(X); m, p)$ to denote that disclosure risk may use information on the masking method m and its parameters p.

This definition presumes that both IL and DR are in the same scale, say [0,100], and implies that an increment of 1 in IL can be compensated with a decrement of 1 in DR. Because of that, the following three cases (i.e., three straightforward *masking* methods) are considered as equivalent:

- **The identity method.** A method that publishes the original data without perturbation leads to the minimal information loss ($IL = 0$), the maximum risk ($DR = 100$) and, thus, a score of 50.
- **The random method.** A method that generates a completely random file, that has no resemblance with the original file and thus it is useless for data analysis, has

the maximal loss ($IL = 100$), the minimum risk ($DR = 0$) and, thus, a score of 50.

- **The 50-points method.** Any method that manipulates the data so that $IL = DR = 50$ will also lead to a score of 50.

These considerations also imply that any approach leading to a file with a score larger than 50 is not worth to consider because this trade-off is worse than just generating completely random data, or publishing the original file without perturbation.

Other types of aggregation functions can be used to change the level curves of the score. That is, to give larger importance to one of the components or not allowing compensation between DR and IL. For example, we can use the maximum [314] defining

$$Score(m, p, X) = \max(IL(X, m_p(X)), DR(X, m_p(X); m, p))$$

that will favor methods that are good for both IL and DR. I.e., a method with $IL = DR = 30$ is better rated that one with $IL = 20$ and $DR = 40$, and thus, no so much compensation is allowed. There are alternative aggregation functions [44,205,491] with different properties ranging from maximum to means, and, thus, providing more or less compensation among risk and information loss.

7.2.2 Visualization: R-U Maps

When we have the two dimensions of risk and information loss, we can visualize the performance of a method with a two dimensional graph. The risk-utility maps (R-U maps), first proposed by Duncan et al. [157,158], are such graphical representation. Similarly, we can represent IL-DR maps for information loss and disclosure risk. In an IL-DR map the best methods are the ones that are nearer to (0,0). Following the discussion in the previous section all methods above the line (0,100)–(100,0) are not worth to consider. They are the ones with a score larger than 50.

Figure 7.1 is an example of a IL-DR map from [478] that compares the measures for a few masking methods and parameterizations.

7.2.3 Optimization and Post-Masking

When we consider data protection in terms of an optimization problem, we can consider the combination of one masking method and a post-masking method to further improve the quality of the data. In short, the post-masking is to improve the value of the measures further modifying the data. We have discussed this issue in relation to microaggregation in Sect. 6.1.2. Let us consider a more general case.

We can consider some transformations of the data that we know that can reduce information loss. For example [429], we can consider data normalization (to achieve appropriate means and variances), or a full modification of the outcome (using adhoc methods as e.g. genetic algorithms) to increase the overall measure.

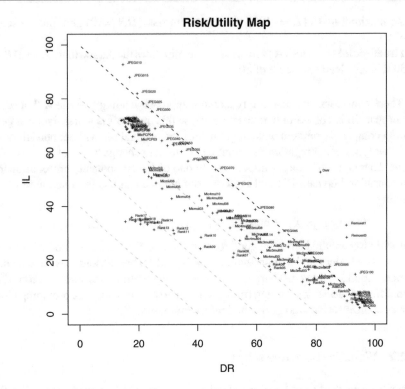

Fig. 7.1 R-U Maps for some protection methods (from [478]). Information loss computed with PIL

Methods described in Sect. 6.5 that are designed to solve the violation of constraints can also be seen from this perspective.

Exercise 7.3 Consider the Iris data set from the UCI repository, and protect the 4 numerical attributes using microaggregation with increasing values of k. Compute information loss for this file using a machine learning model for classification (using the class of the data). Compute disclosure risk for these files using distance-based record linkage. Plot the R-U map to observe the trade-off information loss versus risk.

7.3 Machine Learning

Selection of a data protection mechanism for machine learning needs to take into consideration the desired privacy model. For this, we refer the reader to Chap. 3. Then, we will need to implement the system according to the model.

The most usual approaches are, either to

- apply a differentially private machine learning algorithm to the data and obtain a differentially private model, or
- anonymize the data using a data-driven protection procedure (and data satisfies e.g. privacy from reidentification or k-anonymity) and then apply machine learning algorithms to protected data. We classify in this second category local differential privacy.

As we have seen the first approach has stronger privacy guarantees but the machine learning algorithm needs to be known. In contrast, the second approach has not so strong privacy guarantees and provides more flexibility.

In machine learning, it is usual that the we need to consider a set of steps before the application of a particular machine learning algorithm with a particular parameter. For example, we need data exploration. In most cases, we also apply dimensionality reduction and feature selection. Finally, the machine learning algorithm. Most of these steps consist not in just an application of a single method but consider the application of different alternative methods, analyze their results, until we are convinced that a certain combination of methods and parameters is the good one. For applying this process, the second approach has clear advantages.

In some cases, we can consider both. For example, exploration and analysis of anonymized data, and a model construction using a differentially private algorithm.

For selection of a particular protection procedures, either a masking method or a differentially private machine learning algorithm, we would use information loss measures. That is, we would use e.g. accuracy for classification or error for regression (as described in Sect. 7.1.4).

7.4   Privacy in Federated Learning

Federated learning is a machine learning framework in which a massive number of devices, each one with its own data, are considered. These data are used to train a centralized model (hosted at a central server). Nevertheless, data is not expected to be shared. Therefore, it has some connections with secure multiparty computation but also some major differences. Among the differences, we have the following ones. First, on the number of parties, which are expected to be few in secure multiparty computation models. In contrast, in federated learning we have a large number of them. Second, in secure multiparty computation the computation is fully distributed. In contrast, in federated learning it is usually assumed the existence of a third party. This third party, who is interested in the model, is not fully trusted. Because of that, data is not transmitted and the model is built in an iterative way using information from the devices, but not the data themselves. The typical scenario is about a massive number of mobile or IoT devices from which data we build a machine learning model. Some kind of deep learning model is usually assumed but any model is, in principle, possible.

The general framework of federated learning consists of a set of agents, say n, each with its local database X_i and a local objective function F_i for $i = 1, \ldots, n$. Functions F_i are parametric in terms of a certain parameter w. It is relevant to note that w can be a simple value, a vector, a matrix, or even a set of matrices depending on the problem. Then, $F_i(w)$ can be understood as the value of the objective function for a given parameter w. For example, when each agent is training a deep learning model, w represents the matrices of weights for such models. The importance or relevance of each agent in the system is denoted by p_i for $i = 1, \ldots, n$. These importances are positive and such that $\sum_{i=1}^{n} p_i = 1$. Finally, the goal of the whole federated learning system is to find the parameters w that minimize a global objective function F that is a weighted sum of the F_i. More formally

$$\min_{w} F(w) = \min_{w} \sum_{i=1}^{n} p_i F_i(w). \tag{7.5}$$

Some examples of federated learning include defining $p_i = 1/n$ (i.e., all agents have the same relevance) and $p_i = |X_i|$ where the importance is proportional to the size of the database (e.g., the number of records in X_i). Then, if X_i consists of records $\{(x_k, y_k)\}$ we can consider F_i in terms of a loss function $f_i(w; x_k, y_k)$ (e.g., that evaluates the prediction/classification of x_k for a model based on parameter w).

Solutions for federated learning are usually implemented using an iterative process that helps to build the model cooperatively. The iterative step follows the following structure, which is built assuming that the central server has a model.

- The server sends the model to a selection of devices.
- Selected devices train the model with their own data.
- Devices compute the differences between the server model and their own model after training. We use the gradient to denote this difference.
- Devices send their gradient to the server.
- The server averages these gradients, the result is the average gradient.
- The server updates its own model using the average gradient

This process is repeated until convergence, or until the desired number of iterations is achieved. To bootstrap the process the central server needs to initialize the model.

From a privacy point of view, federated learning has the advantage that data is not sent to the central server. Only the gradients are shared between an agent and the central server. Nevertheless, this is not enough to provide complete privacy to the agents. The gradients may convey enough information about the database X_i associated to an agent, and this can be exploited by the server. For example, there are attacks to deep learning based on gradients to estimate the data used in the training. In addition, the model itself can lead to disclosure.

A combination of privacy models may be required to ensure that the whole system provides enough privacy guarantees. Some requirements will be implemented at the local level, and others at the global level.

- Global level. To avoid disclosing agents' gradients to the central server, we may require secure multiparty computation for computing the average gradient. In this way, the server cannot extract information from individual agents using data reconstruction attacks from gradients. Note that this will protect agents against data reconstruction by the server, but this does not avoid inferences from the model itself. A differentially private machine learning model may be needed for this. A more stronger guarantee is to require secure multiparty computation for this latter computation, so, e.g. not only individual gradients are not disclosed but neither the average gradient is disclosed.
- Local level. Agents may consider their own privacy policies, as well as the implementation of a suitable privacy model to avoid any undesired leakage of their own data (e.g. accidental leakages from the server). Two alternatives are (i) to compute a differentially private gradient, and (ii) to first anonymize its own data and then compute gradients using anonymized data. k-Anonymity or privacy from reidentification can be used for the latter.

7.5 Bibliographical Notes

1. **Generic information loss measures.** Some statistical measures, including EBIL, appear in the book by Willenborg and de Waal (2001) [521]. They were used in two papers [139, 144] that compared masking methods for both numerical and categorical data. In this analysis, numerical measures include the ones given in this chapter based on differences in the values of the files, as well as the ones based on some statistics, and categorical measures include the ones based on contingency tables, EBIL, and PRIL. PRIL was introduced in these latter works.

2. **Comparison and selection of masking methods.** The score was first used [144] to compare a plethora of methods with different parameters. Both IL and DR were defined in terms of an aggregation of a few other information loss and disclosure risk measures.

3. **Machine learning.** We have provided extensive references on the effects of masking to machine learning in the chapter, mainly concerning accuracy and error. It is useful to underline the references that express that data protection does not necessarily imply a high information loss as the works by Aggarwal, Yu, Sakuma and others [17, 40, 224, 415].
   In relation to machine learning and local differential privacy it is also relevant the worky by Kasiviswanathan et al. [256].

4. **Federated learning.** A discussion of federated learning together with its challenges is given by Li et al. [292, 535]. Use of secure multiparty computation in federated learning is studied by e.g. Bonawitz et al. [56]. An attack to deep learning through gradients to reconstruct the data is given by Zhu et al. [543].

Other Data-Driven Mechanisms

8

Abstract

In this chapter we describe privacy mechanisms for two additional types of protections. We describe result-driven approaches with examples on rule mining. We describe how we can modify a database so that some rules cannot be extracted once the protected database is published. We introduce tabular data protection. We understand tabular data as aggregates of data in table form. We describe rules to detect when a cell in the table is sensitive and two approaches for tabular data protection.

> La natura
> diligent ens procura
> una bèstia
> per a cada molèstia.
>
> Pere Quart, Bestiari, 1986 [389].

This chapter presents additional data protection mechanisms for data publishing. We focus on two types of data. First, we consider databases of transactions, as for market basket analysis. Our privacy model is result privacy, as we want to avoid intruders to learn particular patterns from the database. We describe a perturbative method for this purpose. Second, we consider tabular data. Tabular data are tables built from a data file summarizing frequencies as well as other attributes. We will discuss ways to detect that cells in the table are sensitive, and two approaches for protecting these tables. One based on cell suppression and the other based on a perturbation of the table.

8.1 Result-driven Approaches

The goal of result-driven protection procedures is to ensure that the results of a data mining process do not lead to disclosure of sensitive information. So, if we publish a protected data set, we want to avoid that researchers applying a certain data mining method to this dataset obtain some undesired outcome.

One application of this type of approaches is for holder privacy, when the holder wants to hide a certain knowledge that can be used by competitors. This is not the only application. The approach can also be used [214] to avoid the mining of discriminatory knowledge.

The case of holder privacy was illustrated in Example 3.12 where a supermarket wants to avoid the disclosure of rules relating the consumption of *baby diapers* and *beers*. We also discussed the case of a holder avoiding competitors to know that people buying the pack *(beer, chocolate eggs)* are also buying *chips*.

With respect to discrimination, as Hajian et al. [215] state, one may tend to think that the application of data mining algorithms to raw data, and the posterior use of the inferred knowledge in decisions is free from discrimination bias. The automatic application of both data mining algorithms and decision support systems gives this impression. Nevertheless, subtle (and not so subtle) bias in the data can cause the inference of discriminatory rules. Let us consider the following example.

Example 8.1 [214,215] We have a dataset containing the attribute race in which most of the people of a certain race had delay in returning previous credits (or failed with them). However, although the ultimate cause can be low salary, data mining algorithms may use race in classification rules and, therefore, defining discriminatory knowledge.

The case of race is of direct discrimination because a sensitive attribute is used in the rule. We will have indirect discrimination if the database contains the attribute Zip code and this is correlated with race. Indirect discriminatory knowledge can be inferred by a data mining algorithm and lead to a rule denying credits for people living in a particular ZIP code. Some result-driven algorithms can be used to avoid data mining algorithms to infer such discriminatory rules. See [214] for details.

We have introduced in Definitions 3.19 and 3.20 result privacy. Then, from an operational point of view and with the aim of defining a protection procedure, our goal is to produce a file X' from a database X so that sensitive knowledge $\mathcal{K} = \{K_1, \ldots, K_n\}$ cannot be inferred. We have denoted by $KSet_X$ the knowledge inferred from X (using a particular algorithm A). In general, our objective is to find X' so that

1. $\mathcal{K} \cap KSet_{X'} = \emptyset$, and
2. X is similar to X', or, in other words, the information loss from X to X' is minimal.

To make this definition concrete we need to formalize what means minimal information loss in our context. Following Abul [9], we express information loss in terms of misses (false negative) and fakes (false positive). In our context a false negative is when a certain knowledge that should appear in the result (because it is derivable from X) does not appear in the result from X'. On the contrary, a false positive is when a certain result that is not derivable from X can be derived from X'. Therefore, we replace condition 2 above by [9]:

- The number of false negative is minimized. That is, minimize $|K\,Set_X \setminus K\,Set_{X'}|$. Note that here $A \setminus B$ is the set of elements in A not in B,
- The number of false positive is minimized. That is, minimize $|K\,Set_{X'} \setminus K\,Set_X|$.

Let us now consider the case in which the knowledge inferred from the database are itemsets, and our goal is to prevent the user to infer itemsets. Recall from Sect. 2.4.2 that rule mining finds rules (see Eqs. 2.8 and 2.9) such that

$$Support(R) \geq thr - s$$

and

$$Confidence(R) \geq thr - c$$

for certain thresholds $thr - s$ and $thr - c$.

Due to these two conditions, there are two main approaches [118,510] for avoiding the disclosure of rules. We can

- **Case 1.** Reduce the support of the rule, or
- **Case 2.** Reduce the confidence of the rule. This can be achieved either

  - **Case 2a.** increasing the support of the antecendent, or
  - **Case 2b.** decreasing the support of the consequent (to decrease the support of the rule without decreasing the one of the antecedent).

In order to increase the support of an antecedent, some transactions partially supporting the antecedent (i.e., supporting some subsets of the antecedent but not the antecedent) will be modified to support the antecedent completely. This implies the addition of some items to a transaction. For example, if we have the rule $\{a, b, c, d\} \Rightarrow \{e\}$, and we have the transaction (a, b, c, e, f) which partially supports the rule because d is not present in the transaction, we can increase the support of this rule adding d into the transaction. In order to decrease the support of a consequent, or of a rule, some items will be removed from a transaction. For example, if we have the same rule as before $\{a, b, c, d\} \Rightarrow \{e\}$ and the transaction (a, b, c, d, e, f) we can reduce the support of this rule removing any of the items (a, b, c, d, e) from the transaction.

Note that decreasing the support of the consequent reduces at the same time the support of the rule and the confidence of the rule. As we will see later, Algorithm 35 proceeds in this way, and, because of that, it checks both the confidence and the support of the rule.

Algorithm 35: Modification of a database of transactions by Atallah et al. [29] to avoid the disclosure of an association rule.

Data: HI: itemset to be hidden; X: database
Result: A database from which HI is not inferred
1 $X' := X$
2 **while** $Support_{X'}(HI) \geq thr - s$ **do**
3 | $HI' := HI$
4 | **while** $|HI'| > 2$ **do**
5 | | $P :=$ subsets of HI' with cardinality $|HI'| - 1$
6 | | $HI' := \arg\max_{hi \in P} Support_{X'}(hi)$
7 | **end**
8 | $T_{HI} :=$ set of transactions in X' that support
9 | $T_s :=$ transaction in T_{HI} that affects the minimum number of itemsets of cardinality 2
10 | $X' :=$ remove from X' one item from transaction HI' that is in Ts
11 **end**
12 **return** X'

Case 1. Reduce the support of the rule. We follow here the approach proposed by Atallah et al. [29]. The only modifications allowed on X are removing items in transactions. Then, we consider that information loss relates to the number of itemsets that were supported in X and that after the modification are not.

Definition 8.1 [9] Let X be a database with transactions on the itemset I. Let $thr - s$ be a disclosure threshold. Let $\mathcal{K} = \{K_1, \ldots, K_n\}$ be the set of sensitive itemsets and $\mathcal{A}$ the set of non-sensitive itemsets.

Naturally, for all $K \in \mathcal{K} \cup \mathcal{A}$, it holds $K \in 2^I \setminus \emptyset$. In addition, $Support(K) \geq thr - s$ for $K \in \mathcal{K} \cup \mathcal{A}$.

Then, the problem of hiding itemsets $\mathcal{K}$ from X consists of transforming X into a database X' such that

1. $Support_{X'}(K) < thr - s$ for all $K \in \mathcal{K}$
2. The number of itemsets K in $\mathcal{A}$ such that $Support_{X'}(K) < thr - s$ is minimized.

This problem is NP-hard [29], and a generalized version of it is also NP-hard [216] (Section 3.4). Because of that, association rule hiding is solved by means of heuristic algorithms [29,508,510].

We present the algorithm proposed by Atallah et al. [29], one of the first approaches to this problem, which focuses on hiding a single itemset. The algorithm, reproduced in Algorithm 36, begins with the itemset to be hidden, we use HI, and traverses the itemsets that are subsets of HI until one with only two items is reached. Each step of this traversal consists of going from one itemset to another one with one item less and

Table 8.1 Database with three transactions X and protected version of this database X'. Example by Atallah et al. [29]

Transaction Number	Original X (Items)	Protected X' (Items)
T1	a, b, c, d	a, b, c, d
T2	a, b, c	b, c
T3	a, c, d	a, c, d

that has maximum support (selection of new HI' in the algorithm). Once the set with two items is determined, one of the items in this set is removed from a transaction in the database. This process is repeated while the itemset HI is not hidden in X'. This algorithm focus on the support, so, hidden means $Support_{X'}(HI) < thr - s$ for the threshold $thr - s$.

It is easy to see that this algorithm only decreases the support of itemsets. Therefore, it does not cause false positives in the set of inferred rules. Because of that, information loss focuses on false negatives, and the goal of the algorithm is to avoid that valid association rules are no longer inferred from the database.

We give now an example of the application of this algorithm. We use the database of transactions in Table 8.1 (left).

Example 8.2 [29] Let X be the database of transactions in Table 8.1 (left) and let $HI = \{a, b, c\}$ be the itemset to be hidden. We use $thr - s = 2$.

First, we need to consider all subsets of HI with cardinality $|HI| - 1 = 2$. This defines P in the algorithm. In our case, P consists of $\{a, b\}$, $\{b, c\}$, and $\{a, c\}$. Table 8.2 provides the supports of these itemsets. We have $Support_{X'}(\{a, b\}) = Support_{X'}(\{b, c\}) = 2$, and $Support_{X'}(\{a, c\}) = 3$. Therefore, in the next step we select the itemset with largest support as HI'. That is, $HI' = \{a, c\}$.

The next step is to find the set of transactions in the database that support HI. We see that HI is a subset of $T1$ and of $T2$, but it is not a subset of $T3$. Therefore, T_{HI} is $\{T1, T2\}$. Naturally, all transactions that support HI support also HI' (recall Lemma 2.1).

Table 8.2 Support for itemsets in the database of transactions X and in the database of transactions x' (in Table 8.1)

Itemsets	Counts on X	Counts on X'
a, b	2	1
b, c	2	2
a, c	3	2
a, b, c	2	1

Let us compute Ts. This is a transaction in T_{HI} that affects the minimum number of itemsets of cardinality 2. We consider $T1 = \{a, b, c, d\}$ and $T2 = \{a, b, c\}$ in T_{HI}. $T2$ affects less itemsets than $T1$. So, we take $Ts = T2$.

Finally, we remove one of the items in $HI' = \{a, c\}$ that is in $T2$. Both items have the same support, we select one of them at random. Say, a. So, $T2'$ will be $T2' = \{b, c\}$. This produces a new version of the database X' (this is given in Table 8.1 (right)).

To iterate, we need to recompute the support of $HI = \{a, b, c\}$ in X'. Table 8.2 (right) gives the support of the itemsets in X'. We see that $Support_{X'}(HI) = 1$. So the itemset is hidden, and we return X'.

Case 2. Reduce the confidence of the rule by means of decreasing the support of the consequent (case 2b). We provide in Algorithm 35 a method to protect a database following this idea. This algorithm was introduced by Verykios et al. [510] (Algorithm 1.b), and the support of the consequent of a rule is reduced until the confidence or the support of the rule are below the corresponding thresholds.

The algorithm starts with a rule HI to be hidden in a database X, the algorithm determines the set of transactions in X that support HI and their size. This is the table of sizes ts. Then, we need to order the transactions in T_{HI} in ascending order according to size ts. Smallest transaction first. We define use a priority queue for this. We call it Q.

Algorithm 36: Modification of a database of transactions. Algorithm 1.b from [510] to avoid the disclosure of an association rule.

Data: HI: rule to be hidden, X: database
Result: A database where HI is not inferred
1 $X' := X$
2 $T_{HI} :=$ set of transactions in X' that support HI
3 **forall** $t \in T_{HI}$ **do**
4 $\quad$ $ts[t] := |t|$
5 **end**
6 $Q = Q(T_{HI}, ts)$ – priority queue with transactions sorted according to size (lowest first)
7 $NumIterConf := \left\lceil |D| \cdot \left(\frac{Support_{X'}(HI)}{thr-c} - Support_X(antecedent(HI)) \right) \right\rceil$
8 $NumIterSupp := \left\lceil |D| \cdot \frac{Support_{X'}(HI)}{thr-s} \right\rceil$
9 $NumIter := \min (NumIterConf, NumIterSupp)$
10 **for** $i := 1$ *to* $NumIter$ **do**
11 $\quad$ $< t, Q > :=$ firstAndDequeue(Q)
12 $\quad$ $j :=$ chooseItem(t, consequent(HI))
13 $\quad$ $X' :=$ remove from X' item j from transaction t
14 $\quad$ $Support_{X'}(HI) := Support_{X'}(HI) - 1$
15 $\quad$ $Conf(HI) := Support_{X'}(HI)/Support_{X'}(antecedent(HI))$
16 **end**
17 **return** X'

Then, we have a loop in which at each step the smallest transaction is selected. Note that the smallest is the first in the priority queue Q. We call this
transaction t. Verykios et al. [511] explain this selection in the following terms:
generate all subsets of $consequent(HI)$ with cardinality $|consequent(HI)| - 1$,
and choose the item with the highest support, thus minimizing the impact on the
$(|consequent(HI)| - 1)$-itemsets. In the algorithm this process corresponds to the
call: chooseItem(t, consequent(HI)), and the selected item is j.

Then, the item j is removed from t. In this way, we are updating the database
X'. Removing j from t, t does not longer support HI. So, it should also be deleted
from T_{HI}. This is already done, as we have dequeued Q and removed t producing
a new version of Q. Accordingly, $Support(HI)$ and $Conf(HI)$ of the rule are also
recomputed.

The process is repeated an appropriate number of times, and then X' is returned.
The number of iterations corresponds to $NumIter$ in the algorithm. This number
is computed as the minimum between the number of iterations required to decrease
the confidence below the confidence threshold $thr - c$, and the number of iterations
required to decrease the support below the threshold. These number of iterations are,
respectively, $NumIterConf$ and $NumIterSupp$ in the algorithm. Expressions for these
values are given below. A proof of these values being correct is given by Verykios
et al. [510] (Lemma 4.1 and 4.2).

8.2 Tabular Data

In statistics, tabular data correspond to aggregates of data with respect to a few
attributes. We illustrate tabular data with an example by Castro [81,84].

Example 8.3 [81,84] Let us consider a file X with records described in terms of at
least the following attributes: profession, town and salaries.

From the information in the file we build a table with aggregate values. One dimension is defined by professions and the other by towns. Cells in the table correspond to
the frequency of each pair *(profession, town)*. Table 8.3 represents this information.
So, the cell (M_2, P_3) corresponds to the number of people with profession P_3 living
in municipality M_2.

Table 8.4 is built using the same dimensions: professions and towns. Cells contain
the total salary received by people with a certain job and living in a certain place.

In both tables we have totals for rows and columns, and a grand total for the full
table.

We have discussed in Sect. 3.1.4 privacy models and disclosure risk in what
concerns computations and aggregates. We have seen that in cells we may have
internal and external attacks. The first is when the intruder is one of the contributors
to the cell and can estimate information about the other contributors. In contrast, an
external attack is when the intruder is only aware of the information published and
nothing else.

Table 8.3 Two-dimensional table of frequencies (adapted from Castro [81])

	P_1	P_2	P_3	P_4	P_5	Total
M_1	2	15	30	20	10	77
M_2	72	20	1	30	10	133
M_3	38	38	15	40	5	136
TOTAL	112	73	46	90	25	346

Table 8.4 Two-dimensional table of magnitudes (adapted from Castro [81])

	P_1	P_2	P_3	P_4	P_5	Total
M_1	360	450	720	400	360	2290
M_2	1440	540	22	570	320	2892
M_3	722	1178	375	800	363	3438
TOTAL	2522	2168	1117	1770	1043	8620

8.2.1   Sensitivity Rules

Protection in tabular data typically consists of removing or modifying some of the elements in the table so that the intruder cannot make good estimations. In order to apply protection, we need first to determine which cells can lead to disclosure. I.e., which cells are sensitive. Sensitive rules are those rules used to assess when a cell is sensitive. The most common rules are described below. These rules are applied to each cell independently. We will give formulations of these rules using $c_1, \ldots, c_t$ to denote the t contributions to the cell. We assume that all contributions are positive ($c_i > 0$).

- **Rule (n, k)-dominance.** A cell is sensitive when n contributions represent more than the k fraction of the total. That is, the cell is sentitive when

$$\frac{\sum_{i=1}^{n} c_{\sigma(i)}}{\sum_{i=1}^{t} c_i} > k$$

  where $\{\sigma(1), \ldots, \sigma(t)\}$ is a permutation of $\{1, \ldots, t\}$ such that $c_{\sigma(i-1)} \geq c_{\sigma(i)}$ for all $i = \{2, \ldots, t\}$ (i.e., $c_{\sigma(i)}$ is the ith largest element in the collection $c_1, \ldots, c_t$). Hundepool et al. [239] recommend to use this rule with $n = 1$ and $k = 0.6$, or $n = 2$ and $k > 0.6$.
- **Rule pq.** This rule is also known as the prior/posterior rule. It is based on two positive parameters p and q with $p < q$. Prior to the publication of the table, any intruder can estimate the contribution of contributors within the q percent. Then, a cell is considered sensitive if an intruder on the light of the released table can estimate the contribution of a contributor within p percent.

  Among all contributors, the best estimation can be done by the second largest contributor on the first largest contributor. Let us consider estimations of values for contributor r by the contributor s. Although derivation is general for any r and s ($r \neq s$), we will apply this to $s = \sigma(2)$ (to denote the second largest contributor) and $r = \sigma(1)$ (to denote the first largest contributor).

Note that in general, assuming that the q percent holds, the estimation of the lower bound of any contributor i is lower than $c_i - (q/100)c_i$. I.e.,

$$lower\text{-}estimation(c_i) < c_i - \frac{q}{100}c_i.$$

Then, the upper bound estimation of c_r computed by c_s is

$$upper\text{-}estimation(c_r) = \sum_{i=1}^{t} c_i - \sum_{i \neq s,r} lower\text{-}estimation(c_i) - c_s$$

$$= \sum_{i=1}^{t} c_i - \sum_{i \neq s,r} \left(c_i - \frac{q}{100}c_i\right) - c_s$$

$$= \sum_{i=1}^{t} c_i - \sum_{i \neq r} c_i + \frac{q}{100} \sum_{i \neq s,r} c_i$$

$$= c_r + \frac{q}{100} \sum_{i \neq s,r} c_i$$

A cell will be sensitive if the estimations are inside the p percent interval. That is,

$$estimation(c_i) \in \left[c_i - \frac{p}{100}c_i, c_i + \frac{p}{100}c_i\right].$$

So, the upper estimation of c_r is sensitive if smaller than $c_r + \frac{p}{100}c_r$. Using the expression of the upper estimation of c_r we have that the cell is sensitive if

$$upper\text{-}estimation(c_r) = c_r + \frac{q}{100} \sum_{i \neq s,r} c_i < c_r + \frac{p}{100}c_r$$

So, equivalently, the cell is sensitive if

$$q \sum_{i \neq s,r} c_i < p \cdot c_r.$$

Taking into account what we have stated above that the better estimation is the one of the second largest contributor on the first largest contributor, we need to apply this expression with $s = \sigma(2)$ and $r = \sigma(1)$. This results into the following expression for the pq rule

$$q \sum_{i=3}^{t} c_{\sigma(i)} < p c_{\sigma(1)}. \tag{8.1}$$

That is, we check this condition for all cells and the cells that satisfy the inequality are sensitive.

We have developed this rule starting with an estimation of the lower bound and then applying the p percent on the upper bound. We can proceed starting with the upper bound and then apply the p percent on the lower bound. We would obtain the same Eq. 8.1.

- **Rule p%.** This rule can be seen as a special case of the previous rule when no prior knowledge is assumed on any cell. Because of that, it can be seen as equivalent to the previous rule with $q = 100$. Using Eq. 8.1 and using $q = 100$ we would say that a cell is sensitive when the contributions satisfy:

$$\sum_{i=3}^{t} c_{\sigma(i)} < \frac{p}{100} c_{\sigma(1)}. \tag{8.2}$$

A value larger than 60% is recommended. Hundepool et al. [239] recommend the use of $p' = (1 - k)/k$ (and $p\% = 100p'$) as providing a risk assessment similar to the $(2, k)$-dominance rule. E.g., for $n = 2$ and $k = 0.6$, we would have $p = 66\%$.

According to Daalmans and de Waal [122], the pq rule and the p rule are preferred. Robertson and Ethier [407] discuss in details the drawbacks of the (n, k)-dominance rule.

8.2.2   Tabular Data Protection

Once sensitive cells are determined, we can apply a data protection method for tabular data. We classify the methods for tabular data protection into two categories following Castro [84]. They are perturbative and non-perturbative ones. Observe that these categories are also used to classify masking methods in Chap. 6 with similar interpretations.

- **Perturbative.** The values of the cells are modified and an alternative table where some cells contain inaccurate values is published. The two main methods are controlled rounding and controlled tabular adjustment. Rounding consists of replacing all values by multiples of a given base number. The controlled tabular adjustment consists of finding the nearest table (given an appropriate distance) of the table to be protected. We explain this approach below (Sect. 8.2.4).
  These approaches are known as post-tabular methods to distinguish them with pre-tabular perturbation. In such methods [179], noise is added to the original file before the table is prepared. Note the connection of pre-tabular perturbation and masking methods.
- **Non-perturbative.** The table does not include any inaccurate value. Privacy is achieved by means of suppressions and modifications on the structure of the table. We explain below cell suppression for tables (Sect. 8.2.3).

8.2.3   Cell Suppression

Methods for cell suppression consist of removing the values in the sensitive cells. Nevertheless, this is not enough. Sensitive values should not be inferred from the

Table 8.5 Two-dimensional table of magnitudes with suppressed cells (primary and secondary suppressions) (adapted from Castro [81,84])

	P_1	P_2	P_3	P_4	P_5	Total
M_1	360	450		400		2290
M_2	1440	540		570		2892
M_3	722	1178	375	800	363	3438
TOTAL	2522	2168	1117	1770	1043	8620

published data and due to the fact that tables include marginals, it is not enough to remove the values that lead to disclosure.

Note that removing the value of the cell (M_2, P_3) in Table 8.4 does not avoid disclosure. The adversary can use the subtotals to find the value of the cell. A way to ensure anonymity for cell (M_2, P_3) is to suppress the value of this cell and also the ones of some other cells. In this case we have primary and complementary (or secondary) suppression. The suppression of the value in (M_2, P_3) is a primary suppression and the one of other cells secondary suppression. With secondary suppression, we can obtain something like Table 8.5. In this case cells (M_1, P_3), (M_1, P_5), and (M_2, P_5) correspond to a secondary suppression. Observe that when these cells are suppressed, the value in (M_2, P_3) cannot be inferred.

This problem can be formulated in terms of an optimization problem which consists of minimizing the deletions (secondary cell suppression) in a way that the constraints are satisfied. We formalize this optimization problem. To do so, we need the following elements.

- **Positive table with n cells.** This is expressed by means of values $a_i \geq 0$ for $i = 1, \ldots, n$. In addition we have some linear relationships expressed in a matrix form $Aa = b$. Note that these relationships permit us to express marginals of the table (as well as other conditions, if required).
- **Weights of each cell.** They correspond to the cost of modifying or removing each cell. These weights are denoted by w_i for $i = 1, \ldots, n$ and are such that $w_i \geq 0$. When all cells have equal weight $w_i = 1$ for all i.
- **Upper and lower bounds of a_i.** They are the bounds known by the intruders on the values of the cells (i.e., the background knowledge). We denote them by kup_i and klo_i for $i = 1, \ldots, n$. Naturally, $klo \leq a \leq kup$. For positive tables $klo = 0$. We use M and $-M$ as the default values (for M a large value). Therefore, default values are $(0, M)$ for positive tables, and $(-M, M)$ for arbitrary tables.
- **Set of sensitive cells $\mathscr{P}$.** It is a subset of all cells. That is, $\mathscr{P} \subseteq \{1, \ldots, n\}$.
- **Upper and lower protection levels.** For each cell p in $\mathscr{P}$ we denote its upper and lower protection level by up_p and lo_p. Then, we expect the estimated value of cell p, say x_p, to be outside the interval $[a_p - lo_p, a_p + up_p]$ (either above the upper limit or below the lower limit).

In order to formulate the problem, we need additional variables.

- **Variables for suppression.** Variables y_i for all cells $i = 1, \ldots, n$ represent whether a cell is suppressed or not. Formally, y_i takes values in $\{0, 1\}$, and when $y_i = 1$ we understand that the ith cell has to be suppressed, and when $y_i = 0$ that the cell is not modified. The goal of the problem is to determine the set of cells to be deleted, or in other words, to find the secondary suppressions $\mathscr{S}$ to be added to the primary suppressions $\mathscr{P}$. As all these cells will have $y_i = 1$, we have that

$$\mathscr{P} \cup \mathscr{S} = \{i \,|\, y_i = 1\}.$$

- **Variables for estimations.** Variables $x^{l,p}$ and $x^{u,p}$ for each primary cell p denote the lower and upper estimation of the intruders for primary cells $p \in \mathscr{P}$. So, $x^{l,p}$ will be the minimum of possible values x_p and $x^{u,p}$ will be the maximum of possible values x_p.

  The formulation of the problem is based on the fact that for each set of primary and secondary suppressions intruders can establish these lower and upper bounds for primary cells. These bounds $x^{l,p}$ and $x^{u,p}$ can be computed as follows:

  - **Lower estimation.** For all $p \in \mathscr{P}$, the lower estimation is the solution of the following optimization problem

$$x^{l,p} = \min x_p$$
$$\text{subject to} \quad Ax = b$$
$$klo_i \leq x_i \leq kup_i \text{ for all } i \in \mathscr{P} \cup \mathscr{S}$$
$$x_i = a_i \text{ for all } i \notin \mathscr{P} \cup \mathscr{S} \tag{8.3}$$

    That is, the lower estimation is the lowest value that can be achieved that satisfies the linear relationships ($Ax = b$), the constraints on the background knowledge of the intruder ($klo_i \leq x_i \leq kup_i$), and the fact that undeleted cells keep their original value ($x_i = a_i$ if $i \notin \mathscr{P} \cup \mathscr{S}$).

  - **Upper estimation.** For all $p \in \mathscr{P}$, the upper estimation is found solving the following problem, which is similar to the one above for the lowest estimation

$$x^{u,p} = \max x_p$$
$$\text{subject to} \quad Ax = b$$
$$klo_i \leq x_i \leq kup_i \text{ for all } i \in \mathscr{P} \cup \mathscr{S}$$
$$x_i = a_i \text{ for all } i \notin \mathscr{P} \cup \mathscr{S} \tag{8.4}$$

Let us formulate the optimization problem for cell suppression. For convenience, this formulation uses $d^{l,p}$ and $d^{u,p}$ instead of $x^{l,p}$ and $x^{u,p}$, respectively. Here, $d^{l,p}$ is the difference between the lower estimation and the real value of the cell $p \in \mathscr{P}$, and $d^{n,p}$ is the difference between the upper estimation and the real value of the cell p (i.e., a_p). Formally,

$$d^{l,p} = x^{l,p} - a_p \quad \text{and} \quad d^{u,p} = x^{u,p} - a_p.$$

Note that in general, $d^{l,p}$ will be negative.

The goal of the protection is that after deletion $x^{l,p}$ and $x^{u,p}$ are out of the interval defined by the lower and upper protection levels. I.e.,

$$x^{l,p} \leq a_p - lo_p \quad \text{and} \quad a_p + up_p \leq x^{u,p}$$

for all $p \in \mathscr{P}$, or, equivalently, using $d^{l,p}$ and $d^{u,p}$

$$d^{l,p} \leq -lo_p \quad \text{and} \quad up_p \leq d^{u,p}.$$

These latter equations are the ones we include in the mathematical formulation below.

The mathematical problem also includes constraints so that the lower and upper constraints are within lower and upper limits of a_i known by intruders. That is, if $y_i = 1$ then for the lower limits we have $klo_i - a_i \leq d^{l,i} \leq kup_i - a_i$ or, equivalently, in terms of $x^{l,i}$, the inequalities $klo_i \leq x^{l,i} \leq kup_i$, and for the upper limits we require $klo_i - a_i \leq d^{u,p} \leq kup_i - a_i$.

In addition, we need that estimates x^l and x^u satisfy the linear constraints. That is, $Ax^l = b$ and $Ax^u = b$. This constraint in terms of d^l and d^u corresponds to $Ad^l = 0$ and $Ad^u = 0$.

The objective function corresponds to the weights of the cells being suppressed. This is, $\sum_{i=1}^{n} w_i y_i$ as y_i is one for suppressed cells.

Therefore, the optimization problem becomes.

$$\min \sum_{i=1}^{n} w_i y_i$$

subject to

$$Ad^l = 0$$
$$(klo_i - a_i)y_i \leq d^{l,i} \leq (kup_i - a_i)y_i \quad \text{for all } i = 1, \dots, n$$
$$d^{l,p} \leq -lo_p \quad \text{for all } p \in \mathscr{P}$$

$$Ad^u = 0$$
$$(klo_i - a_i)y_i \leq d^{u,i} \leq (kup_i - a_i)y_i \quad \text{for all } i = 1, \dots, n$$
$$d^{u,p} \geq up_p \quad \text{for all } p \in \mathscr{P}$$

$$y_i \in \{0, 1\} \quad \text{for } i = 1, \dots, n$$

This is a linear problem with liner constraints. Some variables are integers and others are not. Therefore, it is a mixed-integer linear programming problem.

Exercise 8.1 Consider Tables 8.3 and 8.4. Consider that all cells with less than 3 people are sensitive. Consider primary and secondary suppressions for Table 8.4 according to these assumptions.

8.2.4   Controlled Tabular Adjustment

This approach consists of replacing the original table by another one that is similar, and that satisfies a set of requirements. There will be no suppressed cells, but cells with noisy values. The problem of finding a similar one can be expressed as an optimization problem. The formulation requires a set of variables, which are detailed below. Note that these variables are exactly the ones used in Sect. 8.2.3.

- **Positive table with n cells.** We use $a_i \geq 0$ with $i = 1, \dots, n$ to denote the values of the cells. In addition we have some linear relationships expressed in a matrix form $Aa = b$. Note that these relationships permit us to express marginals of the table as well as other relationships.
- **Weights of each cell.** The cost of modifying or removing each cell is denoted by w_i for $i = 1, \dots, n$ and are such that $w \geq 0$.
- **Upper and lower bounds of a_i.** These bounds correspond to what is known by the intruder. They are denoted, respectively, by kup_i and klo_i for $i = 1, \dots, n$. Naturally, the bounds should be such that $kup \leq a \leq klo$. We use a default value M and $-M$ for the upper and lower bounds. For positive tables, the default values are $(0, M)$, and for arbitrary tables $(-M, M)$.
- **Set of sensitive cells $\mathscr{P}$.** This set is defined by primary cells that need to be suppressed. It is a subset of all cells. That is, $\mathscr{P} \subseteq \{1, \dots, n\}$.
- **Upper and lower protection levels.** For each primary cell p (i.e., p in $\mathscr{P}$) we have the bounds of the protection. These bounds are, respectively, up_p and lo_p for $p \in \mathscr{P}$. Then, we expect the protected value of cell p, that is x_p, to be outside the interval $[a_p - lo_p, a_p + up_p]$ (either above the upper limit or below the lower limit).

The goal is to find a table near to a where near is defined in terms of a distance. The new table is denoted by x which corresponds to the values $x_1, \dots, x_n$ (one value for each cell). The distance between x and a is expressed as $||x - a||_{L_s(w)}$ and corersponds to the following expression

$$||x - a||_{L_s(w)} = \sum_{i=1}^{n} w_i |x_i - a_i|^s$$

for x_i and a_i the components of x and a, respectively.

Note that in this formulation x_p is the value of cell p in the new matrix, and this is different to the role of x_p in Sect. 8.2.3 (x_p were estimations for the cells in the set $\mathscr{P}$ of suppressed values).

Controlled tabular adjustment is formulated in terms of the following optimization problem. We can see that in this problem we minimize the distance between x and a subject to the fact that the linear relationship on A (as e.g. the marginals) are not modified ($Ax = b$) and that the values of the new matrix are whithin the bounds known by the intruder ($klo \leq x \leq kup$) but outside the sensitive intervals (either $x_p \leq ap - lo_p$ or $x_p \geq a_p + up_p$).

$$\min_{x} \quad ||x - a||_{L_s(w)}$$
$$s.t. \quad Ax = b$$
$$klo \le x \le kup$$
$$x_p \le a_p - lo_p \text{ or } x_p \ge a_p + up_p \text{ for } p \in \mathscr{P}$$

This more general definition allows x_p to be either below the limits of the interval or over the limits of the interval. Nevertheless, this formulation results into a difficult optimization problem. An alternative is to allow values only on one side of the interval. In this case the problem is a continuous optimization problem that is easier to solve.

There is [82] an exhaustive empirical analysis of risk for different tables using both L_1 and L_2 distances. Castro [82] summarizes his study stating that "if the attacker does not have good knowledge on the original data, he/she could hardly obtain good estimates of the sensitive cells, in general. However, if the attacker has good information about the protection levels and which are the sensitive cells, or he/she knows the lower and upper bounds of the optimization problem (which is a stronger condition), then the method has a high disclosure risk". An analysis of the risk and data utility for these methods seems to indicate [82,83] that L_2 is more suitable than L_1.

8.3 Bibliographical Notes

- **Result driven approaches.** We have described the algorithm proposed by Atallah et al. [29] as an example of how reducing the support of the rule can avoid its disclosure. Then, we provide an algorithm based on decreasing the support of the consequent. This algorithm was introduced by Verykios et al. [510] (Algorithm 1.b). There are other algorithms with the same objectives. Verykios [508] reviews some of these algorithms for association rule hiding.

- **Tabular data protection.** The example for tabular data protection that illustrates disclosure risk is taken from [81,84]. Several authors [122,145,407] have studied and proposed sensitivity rules. An example of another type of sensitive rule is the one based on entropy [145]. In this chapter, properties and proofs of sensitivity rules follow Daalmans and de Waal [122]. Castro [84] explains the algorithms for cell suppression described in Sect. 8.2.3 as well as methods to solve the mixed-integer linear programming problem.

  Controlled tabular adjustment was independently developed by Dandekar and Cox [114] and Castro [79] (using L_1 or L_2 distance), and defined in its extended form by Castro [80]. It was also called [79] minimum-distance controlled perturbation method. Castro [80,82,84] provides details on how the optimization problem can be solved.

Conclusions

9

Jođi lea buoret go oru
Sami proverb [199]

This book has given an introduction to data privacy. We have presented the main areas and some of the methods and tools to ensure privacy and avoid disclosure. We have tried to show the difficulties of correctly assessing disclosure risk and provided two examples, already in the first chapter, that are paradigmatic of the problems we encounter on building privacy-aware systems. In this chapter we provide some guidelines for implementing privacy. That is, even a few innocent attributes may lead to reidentification, even an aggregate or a summary can lead to disclosure of sensitive information.

We have presented different privacy models and disclosure risk measures. It is important to underline that different privacy models focus on different aspects of privacy. We have seen, for example, attribute and identity disclosure, and then mechanisms to protect these different types of disclosure. The methods that are suitable for one type of model may be ineffective for the other. The selection of our privacy model will depend on the context (e.g., data and privacy threats).

For example, we have seen that methods ensuring k-anonymity may be unsuitable for avoiding attribute disclosure. As an alternative, l-diversity considers both types of disclosure. Often, more privacy is at the expenses of data utility. We need to find a good balance.

We have seen that differential privacy considers privacy from a different perspective. The goal is to avoid that intruders learn whether a record is in the database. With this purpose in mind, it masks the result of a query usually adding some noise. Because of that, when the query is e.g. the mean of one of the variables of the file, it is possible that the result diverges (even largely) from the correct mean. On the contrary, masking methods or methods that are compliant with k-anonymity can produce a masked data set with a mean that is similar or equal to the original mean. The latter methods can ensure that the probability of linking a given record to the masked file

© The Author(s), under exclusive license to Springer Nature Switzerland AG 2022
V. Torra, *Guide to Data Privacy*, Undergraduate Topics in Computer Science,
https://doi.org/10.1007/978-3-031-12837-0_9

is lower than a certain threshold, but they are not compliant with differential privacy definition.

Cryptographic approaches provide 100% privacy for the privacy model selected, and 100% exact output, for the desired computation. Nevertheless, privacy models as homomorphic encryption and secure multiparty computation need usually to be combined with others to provide stronger privacy guarantees. In this case, of course, the quality of the solution will depend on these other models and how they are implemented.

As a summary, each privacy model has its pros and cons. Selection needs to be done taking into account our requirements, and in particular, the data we are dealing with and possible privacy threats. We need to find a solution that represents a good compromise on all requirements.

9.1 Guidelines

We outline below some guidelines that we consider fundamental for ensuring privacy. These guidelines are based and complement the ones provided by several authors [108,177,441,492].

- Privacy by design. We have discussed their principles in Chap. 1. We consider that they are mandatory requirements for any system working with data, and they need to be taken into account when developing and using data-driven models. The tools described in this book are to help developing systems following these principles.
- Transparency. We have advocated in this book the need for transparency. Transparency is also one of the principles of privacy by design. Data protection methods should be resistant to transparency attacks. We have discussed this issue extensively in Chap. 6 and we have seen that there are masking methods that have been designed to be resistant to these transparency attacks. Unfortunately, however, new effective transparency attacks may be further designed for masking methods unless privacy guarantees have been formally proven. The study of attacks to masking methods and, specially, transparency attacks is essential in order to have accurate assessments of disclosure risk.
- Data minimization. We consider that data minimization should be a driving force for privacy-preserving solutions. In machine learning, and computer science in general, there is the tendency to store as much as possible and track all changes and updates. We need to question if this is really needed for developing particular solutions.
- Models and generalizations. Data mining provides algorithms that are resistant to errors, so we can still apply them when data is anonymized. Data utility may be low for those applications in which we focus on the outliers (as e.g. anomaly

detection[1]) or, in general, to individual records. In this discussion it is relevant the comment from Little [299] (p. 408) on masking versus information loss:

> The key distinction is that masking is primarily concerned with identification of *individual* records, whereas statistical analysis is concerned with making inferences about *aggregates*. (...) Methods that exploit this distinction can achieve great gains in confidentiality at little cost. (...) masking becomes inherently difficult when the distinction between aggregate and individual is not clear-cut, as when one large firm dominates a business file, or analysis is required for small subdomains of the population.

- User privacy and decentralized anonymity. They need to be put in place (whenever possible) so that users keep their data as long as possible in their devices, and anonymize their data in origin. In this way there is no need to trust the data collector. This need was also highlighted in COVID-19 times by several authors [341], in relation to contact tracing and mobile apps.
- User privacy and user awareness. Technology for user privacy should increase user awareness of privacy risks. That is, technology should help people to know what others know or can infer about them. User interfaces should help users to declare some attributes as sensitive but also inform what (which other attributes, links to friends in social networks, membership to societies, etc.) can be used to infer such sensitive data.
- Anonymization in origin. Databases should be anonymized in origin, before data use, data integration, and database linkage, to reduce disclosure risk. Data should be stored in anonymized form as much as possible.
- Controlled linkability. Anonymization can provide controlled linkability. So, if data is protected in origin, we can still establish relevant connections between databases. For example, k-Anonymity permits to link groups.
- Composability. Privacy models need to be composable in order to know the privacy guarantees when protected databases are integrated, and functions combined.

Another aspect we think is relevant is the use of knowledge intensive tools. In the era of big data, when data of all kinds are integrated at large, and when ontologies and natural-language processing technologies are used for all type of applications, data privacy needs to take advantage of these technologies to have accurate estimations of risk, and provide effective solutions for ensuring privacy. We have described this issue in Sect. 3.5.4.

Finally, in a real world scenario, a particular data analysis or the actual construction of a model is just one of the steps of a complex process. Researchers need to explore the data, and, usually test several models before deciding which model better

---

[1] There are two main types of methods for anomaly detection: models based on misuses (a database of misuses is used to learn what an anomaly is) and models based on correct activity (the model we learn explains normal activity, and what diverges from the model is classified as an anomaly). The latter approach seems more suitable when data is protected if this process can eliminate outliers, and, thus, the anomalies of a database.

suits the problem. Steps related to data exploration and data analysis previous to the construction of the model include e.g. feature engineering and dimensionality reduction. In this context, one cannot just decide a machine learning model and apply a computation-driven privacy solution to obtain a privacy-preserving model. This simply does not work. Privacy by design is required for the whole process.

A final consideration. Data privacy is a complex area that is influenced by variables in different dimensions (technological, sociological, psychological, legal, economical, political, educational, ethical, etc.). In this book we have focused on the technological aspects. To ensure privacy, the development of the technological dimension is not enough, these other dimensions need to be taken into account.

Abstract

This chapter describes tools for database integration. In particular, tools for matching and record linkage. We review distance-based record linkage and probabilistic
record linkage. These tools for database integration are useful when measuring
identity disclosure risk.

> Elàstics blaus subjectats amb candaus
> porta el meu enamorat i el barret de costat,
> de color verd, que és el que em perd.
>
> I porta un gec, catacric, catacrec,
> un gec d'astracan pelut, ribetat de vellut,
> i a l'armilla hi duu cigrons per botons.
>
> Joan Casas i Vila, El vestir d'en Pasqual, 1920s.

We have claimed that reidentification, and, in general, matching, is a flexible way to
model and assess disclosure risk. Database integration supplies us with a set of tools
that can be used for this purpose. We will describe them in this chapter.

There are other tools that can be also useful in extracting relevant information from
multimodal data, and, thus, useful to attack databases. As an example of the diversity
of sources, recall the Netflix case [342] where the data in the Netflix database was
linked to data from Internet Movie Database (IMDb) users. Tools useful in this context include natural language processing algorithms and ontology matching software.

V. Torra, *Guide to Data Privacy*, Undergraduate Topics in Computer Science,
https://doi.org/10.1007/978-3-031-12837-0_A

Ontologies have also been used [316] in combination with standard reidentification algorithms.

A.1 Heterogeneous Distributed Databases

It is well known that available data are not centralized but highly distributed. It is usually the case that records corresponding to a particular person are spread within several subsidiary companies or departments of the same organization (e.g. sales department, customer department and suppliers department).

In order to take full advantage of available data in distributed databases, software systems have been defined to find and link records that while belonging to different databases they correspond to the same individual. Although it could be possible that the different databases have the same software and the same schema (i.e., we have an homogeneous database) the most common and problematic case is that they have different software and different schema. In this case, the *set of different databases* and the corresponding integration system is known in the literature by *heterogeneous database*. Han et al. [218] define heterogeneous databases as follows:

> A Heterogeneous database consists of a set of interconnected, autonomous component databases. The components communicate in order to exchange information and answer queries. Objects in one component database may differ greatly from objects in other component databases, making it difficult to assimilate their semantics into the overall heterogeneous databases.

Difficulties in the integration in a heterogeneous database are due to the fact that different databases contain partially overlapping data and this overlapping information is usually non-uniformly standardized and subject to all kind of errors and accuracies. Robust integration methods are needed to avoid that the result of a query is incorrect or inconsistent with previously reported results.

Data integration is the field that studies how data from different databases are combined in a single one. This is an active area of research, and there exist nowadays several commercial solutions for this purpose. Some of the existing solutions are for a virtual data integration. In this case, there is a wrapper based on a global schema but there is no real integration of the databases. Some others materialize this integration.

A.1.1 Data Integration

There exist several technologies for data integration. Let us discuss first some of the problems we can encounter in data integration. We follow Rahm and Do [392] and consider four different scenarios, as well as the most typical problems for these scenarios. The scenarios are classified in two dimensions. As some of the problems are specific to data integration (i.e., to multiple databases) and others also appear in scenarios of a single database (e.g., the problem of finding an individual in a database or the problem of database deduplication) one dimension is the number of sources. The other dimension is the problem level.

- **Number of sources.** That is, the number of data suppliers considered in the process. We consider single source and multi-source (multi-database) problems.
- **Problem level.** Inconsistencies and integration difficulties can appear in both instance (or record) level and schema level. Schema level problems are the ones that can be solved with an appropriate schema and the corresponding integrity constraints. Naturally, instance level problems are the ones strictly related to the data represented in the records of the database.

We review below the four scenarios that can be obtained according to these two dimensions.

- **Single source at instance level (SSIL).** In this scenario we have data integration in deduplication (removal of duplicate records in a database). Typical problems are misspellings, missing values but also contradictory records (e.g., different addresses for the same person).
- **Single source at schema level (SSSL).** Here problems typically arise because the database schema is not strict enough and some integrity constraints are not checked. This is the case of illegal values (e.g. a record with Name = John, Sex = Male, Age = 2, Pregnant = true) or inconsistent values (e.g. current date $\neq$ birthday + age).
- **Multi-source at instance level (MSIL).** Problems specific to this scenario include differences on representation formalisms. For example, different databases may use different recodifications, different scales or different granularity. For different recodification, let us consider one database using the 10th revision of the International Classification of Diseases [548] to codify illnesses while the second one uses a full text description of the illness. For different scales consider Celsius versus Fahrenheit scales for temperature. For different granularity consider one database where fever is represented using real numbers (from data recorded in a hospital) and another using linguistic terms (e.g., no-fever, a little) and numbers in a mixed way because data was collected in interviews with the patients.
- **Multi-source at schema level (MSSL).** Problems correspond to naming and structural conflicts. With respect to names we may have the same name for different objects (homonyms) and different names for the same object (synonyms). More complex structural problems arise when one attribute in one database (e.g. address) correspond to several attributes in the other (street, zip code, city).

In Table A.1, we report some of the problems typically found in these four scenarios and provide some example [392].

Table A.1 Single and multi-source (SS/MS) problems at instance and schema level (IL/SL) according to Rahm and Do [392]

	Problem	Example
SSIL	Missing values	Null values
	Misspellings	
	Misfielded values	
	Unknown abbreviations	
	Multiple attributes: non-consistent use	Different order: name/first name
		"Joan John" versus "John, Joan"
	Contradictory records	Same name/different address
		"Joan John, Alpha street"
		"Joan John, Beta street"
	Wrong or outdated data	
SSSL	Illegal values	Data outside rang, negative age
	Violation of attribute dependencies	Price ≠ net price + taxes
		City and zip code not consistent
	Uniqueness violation	Passport not unique
	Referential integrity violation	Reference to an unknown record
MSIL	Different scales	Temperatures: Celsius versus Fahrenheit
	Different codifications	True/false 1/0 t/f t/nil
	SSIL problems	
MSSL	Name conflicts	Synonyms: customer/client, sex/gender
	Structural conflicts	(address) versus (num. str. zip city)
		"203, Alfa street 08201 Sabadell"
		"Alfa st." "2003" "08201" "Sabadell"
	SSSL problems	

The distinction between schema and instance level problems is not always clear. Some problems can be considered from the two perspectives. For example, the problem with the temperature scale and the divergence of illness codification can be seen as a problem at instance level but also as a schema level problem if we consider that the schema should include information about scales and codification.

In the remaining part of this section we further elaborate into the problems related to data integration. Now we focus on the simpler problem of considering two databases and a single attribute in each database. Although we can consider in this case that, again, some of the problems are due to discrepancies on the schema, we

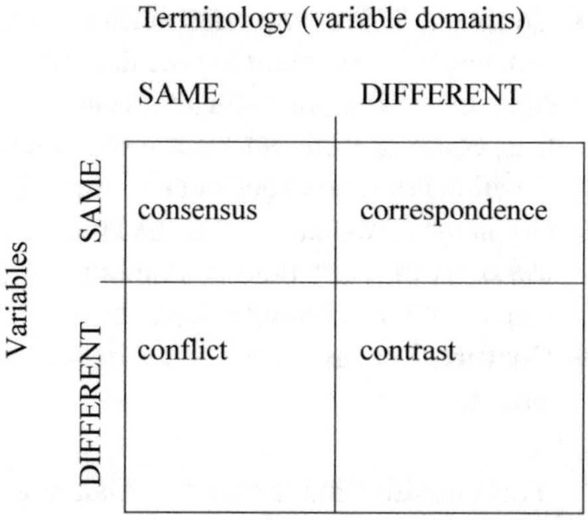

Fig. A.1 Attribute-related dimensions in data integration problems

Terminology (variable domains)

		SAME	DIFFERENT
Variables	SAME	consensus	correspondence
	DIFFERENT	conflict	contrast

consider them as divergences on the attributes. We classify the situations according to two dimensions. One is about the coincidence on attributes and the other one is about the coincidence on terminology. A graphical interpretation of this classification is given in Fig. A.1.

- **Coincidence on attributes.** Attributes describing data can be the same in both databases or can be (partially) different.
- **Coincidence on terminology.** Terminology in this framework corresponds to the domain on the attributes. That is, terminology is the set of terms used to evaluate the individuals. As before, two cases are considered: equal and different terminology. By the way, in some situations it would be appropriate to distinguish a third case corresponding to small differences between attributes domain (*small* from a semantics point of view). This latter case includes the case of terms that although different when considered from its syntactical definition (e.g. the terms "low" and "small" are different) they refer to the same concept or idea. Similarly, we classify in this group the case of two terms that are subject to errors (for example, surnames with misspelling: *Green* vs. *Grene*).

The combination of both dimensions leads to four different cases (see Fig. A.1). Following [196], the following terms are used for describing these cases.

- **Consensus.** The databases use both attributes and terminology in the same way. In this case, records can be moved from one database to the other with no changes.
- **Correspondence.** The database use the same attributes but the terminology for describing these attributes are different. For example both databases contain an attribute named *location* but while in one database it corresponds to *town* in the other refers to *counties*. In this case, mapping between both terminologies are required. The example given above about an attribute *temperature* expressed either in Celsius or in Fahrenheit also belongs to this case.

- **Contrast.** This case corresponds to using the same terminology for different attributes. It is important to note that different attribute names in different databases can either correspond to a unique underlying attribute or to two different attributes (i.e., equal or different from a semantics point of view). An example of the first situation is when we consider an attribute *city* and another *location* both containing city names. An example of the latter situation is when we consider the attributes *work/city* and *city* both containing city names but one referring to a work-place and the other to household place.
- **Conflict.** The last case is when databases differ in both terminology and attribute names.

This classification is based on Gaines and Shaw [196] (for knowledge elicitation methods from groups). They consider the problem of integrating grid data [58] from two experts.

In order to solve the problems described in this section, data integration considers three tasks [100, 101].

- **Schema matching.** This is to find correspondences between schemas of two or more databases.
- **Data matching.** Presuming that different databases use the same schema, this is to find which objects in one database correspond to which objects in another database.
- **Data fusion.** This is to consolidate in a single database the data that is known to correspond to the same object.

From the point of view of disclosure risk assessment only schema and data matching are of interest. Schema and data matching are discussed below in Sects. A.1.2 and A.1.3, respectively.

There are several ways to fuse and consolidate data. For example, we can use the mean of the values or select the most recent one. Aggregation functions and data fusion methods [491] provide a large number of tools, which can be selected on the basis of their mathematical properties or experimental results.

We will see that record linkage is used in one of the steps of data matching. In data privacy, record linkage is mainly used when we have *consensus* between the two databases, and when we have *correspondence* with small variations in the terminology (e.g. due to transcription errors), or with a clear correspondence between the set of terms. Knowledge-based record linkage [316] based on ontologies can be used in this latter case. Ontologies are also used in schema matching. We will review some of the existing approaches in the next section. Contrast and conflict is not considered.

The use of semantics in data privacy to attack a database links data integration, schema and data matching with ontology matching. We will not address this topic further. Euzenat and Shvaiko [178, 437] provide overviews on ontology matching tools.

A.1.2   Schema Matching

As the name indicates, schema matching is about establishing correspondences between the schema of two or more databases. The goal is to match attributes that represent the same information.

One of the difficulties of this task is that databases may be defined in terms of a large number of attributes, and this causes the matching process to work with a combinatorial explosion. Another difficulty is that not only 1 : 1 relationships are possible (one attribute in one database with another one in another database), but also 1 : n or m : n relationships. That is, it may be possible that m attributes in one file correspond to n attributes in another file. Name and address are typical examples of such relationships. We may have one or more fields for title, names and surnames. Similarly, address can be splitted into different components in the databases.

Attribute correspondence identification methods focus on finding correspondences between pairs of attributes.

In the literature we find methods that are solely based on attribute names and data types while others use some kind of structural information [47,134] or characteristics of data instances [173]. Other methods [47,173] combine the information in the database with some other information or, following Artificial Intelligence terminology, background knowledge. This corresponds to knowledge about the attributes or terms that can be represented in ontologies or dictionaries (as e.g. Wordnet [554]). Hybrid approaches have also been considered. They combine several identification methods following the machine learning approach of combining several classifiers. One of such systems is COMA [134] that provides an extensible library off attribute-matching algorithms and supports different ways for combining matching results. Structure-level matching methods [391] match combinations of elements.

Operators for data transformation can help schema matching. For example, Haas et al. [211] use user-defined functions supported in SQL for some data transformations. In general, such operations permit us to define new views from an initial table so that the schema matching procedure can be found more easily. This is the case, for example, of decomposing a *raw* address field in a file, say A, into the following attributes: Address, City, Zip code, State, and Country. In this way, the Zip code in a file B can be easily matched with the corresponding Zip code in file A.

Data analysis tools are also helpful in schema matching. They can be used to increase our knowledge about the data and extend meta-data description. On the one hand we have data profiling tools, which extract basic information about data types (type, length, typical patterns, ...) and basic statistics about the data (frequency or variance, value range). For example, there is a method [474] that permits to characterize the probability distributions of the attributes and then link attributes in the two files with the same distributions. On the other hand we have tools for model building. They will find relationships between the attributes that can be latter used for matching. For example, regression models and decision trees can be used to establish relationships between attributes. Such analysis can help the user to find incorrect records. For example, records not compliant with high frequency models might contain errors.

Machine learning has been used as a data analysis tool for finding typical patterns in complex string attributes. Borkar et al. [59] describe a tool for extracting structured elements like *Street name*, *Company* and *City name* from an address record occurring as a free text string. The method is based on Hidden Markov Models (HMM). Churches et al. [102] present a similar system also based on the hidden Markov model. Methods for automaton and grammar determination can also be used in similar contexts.

In some situations, it is not even known if databases share attributes. SEMINT [287], a tool for identifying relationships between attributes in different database schemas, was developed to deal with this problem. It is based on neural networks and uses both schema information and data contents for building such relationships.

Note that all these tools can be used by an intruder whose database has different schema than the one published.

A.1.3 Data Matching

Data matching focuses on establishing relationships between the records. The goal is to identify the records that belong to the same individual but that are in different databases. This problem is sometimes known [392] as the object identity problem and the merge/purge problem.

Given two databases, the process of matching them can be described in terms of the five steps [100, 101] described below. Note that there is some overlapping between the steps here and the problems considered in schema matching.

- **Data preprocessing.** In this step data files are transformed so that all attributes have the same structure and the data have the same format. In data fusion, this is said to make data commensurate. That is, data should refer to the same point in time and refer to the same position in space. The same should be done here to make data comparable. Major steps in data preprocessing [100] (Sect. 2.2) are: (i) remove unwanted characters and words (stop words), (ii) expand abbreviations and correct misspellings, (iii) segment attributes into well defined and consistent output attributes, (iv) verify correctness of attributes values (e.g., that ages are always positive). Note that (iii) is related to schema matching.
- **Indexing.** In most data matching problems it is unfeasible to compare all pairs of records in order to know which pairs correspond to the same individual. Note that the number of comparisons is the product of the number of records in the two databases. In order to reduce the number of comparisons, only some pairs are compared. Indexing is about the determination of which are the pairs interesting to be compared.
- **Record pair comparison.** This consists in the calculation of a value for each pair of records of interest. The comparison can be either a vector of Boolean values (stating whether each pair of attributes coincide or not) or a vector of *similarities*

(stating in a quantitative way how similar are the values of the corresponding attributes).

- **Classification.** Using the comparison we need to establish whether the two records in the pair correspond to the same object or they correspond to different objects.
- **Evaluation step.** The result of the data matching system is analyzed and evaluated to know its performance.

We discuss the steps related to data privacy in more detail below. Preprocessing in Sect. A.1.4, indexing in Sect. A.1.5, record pair comparison in Sect. A.1.6 and classification in Sect. A.1.7. We do not discuss here the evaluation step of data matching systems. Instead, we describe how to tune the parameters of distance-based record linkage in a supervised perspective (Sect. A.3.3).

A.1.4 Preprocessing

Assuming that there is no discrepancy between attributes, data need to have the same format. Different forms of the same name (e.g., Robert, Bob), company names (e.g., Limited, Ltd., LTD) and addresses (e.g. street, st.) are transformed into a single form. This step can be seen as a final standardization step prior to the comparison. It consists of:

1. Parsing attributes to build a uniform structure.
2. Detecting relevant keywords to help in the process of recognizing the components that form the values of an attribute.
3. Replacing all the (common) forms of a word by a single one (for example, expand abbreviations).

The goal of parsing is to ensure that, when the value of the attribute consists of several elements, these always appear in the same order. For example "Robert Green, Ph.D.", "Dr. Bob Green" and "Green, Robert" are translated into "Ph.D. Robert Green", "Dr. Bob Green" and "Robert Green", respectively, following a *title + name + surname* structure.

The detection of special keywords can help in this process. For example, detection of "Ms.", "Ph.D." or "Dr." is usually an indication of the presence of a personal name and "Ltd." indicates the presence of a company name. Detection would trigger specific parsing routines when appropriate.

The third standardization procedure replaces variants of values by a standard form. Depending on the meaning and the values of the attribute, this procedure can either be applied to the whole attribute value (e.g., to the string used to represent the name) or to components of the attribute value. This latter case occurs when the attribute corresponds to personal names and they include for example title and middle letters, or when the attribute is an address with street names, numbers or a P. O. box.

The substitutions required by standardization can be efficiently implemented by building a database with lists of words and their corresponding standard form so that the forms that appear in the files can be *replaced* by the standard ones. It is important to note that this *standard* form does not need to be a "dictionary" form (the root of a word or any not-shortened version of the name) but only an abstract identifier. This abstract identifier can be useful when a single spelling can have different origins (e.g. Bobbie might refer to Robert but also to Roberta).

Winkler [523] gives details on the standardization processes. Examples of name and address parsing are provided there.

A.1.5 Indexing and Blocking

Let **A** and **B** be the files to be linked. When these files contain a huge number of records, considering all possible pairs is rather costly. Note that we need to consider $|A| \cdot |B|$ pairs. Among these pairs, only $\min(|A|, |B|)$ pairs can be effectively linked when each individual appears at most once in each file. Blocking methods are defined to eliminate most of the unsuccessful comparisons. They define blocks of records and then comparisons between records are restricted to records in the same block. There are different approaches to blocking. We classify them into three categories following Steorts et al. [443].

- **Blocking attributes.** Attributes are sometimes used for this purpose. They are selected by the user among the most error-free ones present in both files (those attributes most likely to maintain their values across files). Only records with equal values for all blocking attributes are compared. To implement this approach, files are ordered according to blocking attributes.

  Typical examples of blocking attributes are the gender, ZIP code and other geographical attributes. When string attributes are used, a good alternative is to use the first letter or a particular coding so that all the symbols with a similar sound are mapped onto the same block (for example, the SOUNDEX codification—see Definition A.4, Sect. A.1.6). This is to reduce the possibility that records that should be compared are in different blocks.

- **Cluster-based blocking.** In this approach, records are clustered and comparisons are only applied within records in the cluster. In this case, blocks are built not on the basis of a single attribute but a set of them, expecting that errors will not make records that should be linked together differ too much.

  The use of clustering methods that require a large number of comparisons (between pairs of record pairs) is discouraged. This will not reduce the cost of record linkage.

- **Locality-sensitive hashing.** Hashing functions are used so that similar records are mapped into the same blocks. Functions are selected to maximize the number of linked records that are mapped into the same block. Christen [99] presents a survey of some indexing techniques, and compares them experimentally. Steorts et al. [443] also used this type of blocking method. An alternative is semantic blocking [359], which also falls in this area.

  Note the difference between standard hash functions [25] and locality-sensitive hashing. In the former, we expect similar values to be associated with different blocks or buckets to avoid collisions, while in locality-sensitive hashing it is precisely the opposite. The goal is to put similar values in the same block or bucket.

As blocking methods are not always correct, some of the linked pairs are not detected. I.e., we will have *missed matches*. An unsuitable selection of the blocking method can result in a large number of missed matches. An approach to reduce the negative effects is to apply several times the record linkage method using in each iteration a different blocking method (e.g., a different blocking attribute). Naturally, this process increases the complexity of the data matching process. Blocking methods correspond to a compromise between a high-cost detailed analysis of all possible pairs with few missed matches and a low-cost analysis of only a few pairs with more missed matches. Machine learning can help [320] in the process of defining the blocking method.

A.1.6   Record Pair Comparison: Distances and Similarities

The comparison between any pair of records is rarely based only on a binary coincidence of the values in the two records. In real-world databases, data includes errors. This is similar in data privacy although in this case masking methods introduce noise in the data on purpose to decrease disclosure risk. Because of that, comparison is usually expressed in terms of a distance between pairs of records. More specifically, the distance between pairs of records is usually expressed in terms of specific distances for each attribute.

Due to this, we can consider distances at record level and distances at attribute level. The former will be defined in terms of the latter. We discuss in this section the basics of distances between records, focusing on the distances between attributes. Other distances at record level will be discussed in Sect. A.3.

One of the most usual definitions is to consider that all attributes have equal weight and define the distance between two records as the addition of the distance between values. This definition follows.

Definition A.1 Let a and b two records defined on attributes $\{V_1, V_2, \ldots, V_n\}$. Assuming equal weight for all attributes, we define $d(a, b)$ as follows.

$$d(a, b) = \sqrt{\sum_{i=1}^{n} d_{V_i}^2 (V_i^A(a), V_i^B(b))}$$

where $d_{V_i}^2 (a_i, b_i)$ is the square of a distance on attribute V_i.

Recall that, formally, given a set X and a real function on $X \times X$, d is a metric [428] on X if and only if for all $a, b, c \in X$, d is positive ($d(a, b) \geq 0$ with $d(a, b) = 0$ only if $a = b$), d is symmetric ($d(a, b) = d(b, a)$), and d satisfies the triangle inequality ($d(a, b) \leq d(a, c) + d(c, b)$). Then, we call the number $d(a, b)$ the distance between a and b with respect to the metric d. Note also that we can define similarities from distances as follows when the distance is bounded by 1: $similarity = f(distance)$ (with $f(0) = 1$ and decreasing) as e.g. $similarity = 1\text{-}distance$. Note that triangle inequality will not hold for a distance defined from a similarity if an equivalent property does not hold for the similarity.

Distances at attribute level depend on the type of attribute. We review here some distances used in the literature of data privacy for numerical, ordinal, and nominal attributes. We will discuss later distances for strings. Alternatively, if V_i are partitions we can use the expressions discussed in Sect. 2.4.1. Note that this review is by no means exhaustive. For any type of data the literature on distances is large.

Definition A.2 The following distances have been used extensively for numerical, ordinal, and nominal attributes.

1. For a numerical attribute V, it is usual to use the expression above with $d_V^2(c, d) = (c - d)^2$. In order to avoid scaling problems, it is convenient to standardize the attributes. This results into the Euclidean distance.
2. For an ordinal attribute V, let $\leq_V$ be the total order operator over the range of V. Then, the distance between categories c and c' can be defined as the number of categories between the minimum and the maximum of c and c' divided by the cardinality of the range:

$$d_V(c, c') = \frac{|c'' : min(c, c') \leq_V c'' \leq_V max(c, c')|}{|D(V)|}$$

3. For a nominal attribute V, the only permitted operation is comparison for equality. This leads to the following definition:

$$d_V(c, c') = \begin{cases} 0 \text{ if } c = c' \\ 1 \text{ if } c \neq c' \end{cases}$$

where c and c' correspond to categories for attribute V.

In the case of nominal attributes for which a hierarchical structure has been defined, Salari et al. [416] used the following distance which is based on the closest common generalization of two given categories. The closest common generalization of two categories c_1 and c_2 corresponds to the nearest category that has both c_1 and c_2 as descendants.

Definition A.3 Let H be a hierarchical structure representing the categories of an attribute V. Let $dpt(c)$ be the depth of the category c in the hierarchical structure, and let $CCG(c_1, c_2)$ the closest common generalization of categories c_1 and c_2. Then, the distance between c_1 and c_2 is defined as

$$distance(c_1, c_2) = dpt(c_1) + dpt(c_2) - 2dpt(CCG(c_1, c_2)).$$

There is large number of distances defined for strings [343,444]. We start reviewing SOUNDEX, which transforms a string into a code that tends to bring together all variants of the same name. Therefore, the application of this method for string comparison leads to a Boolean comparison (strings are either encoded in the same or in a different way). A description of this method, originally developed by Odell and Russell [365,366], can be found in Knuth's book [265]. The SOUNDEX code of any string is a sequence of four characters. For example, both strings "Smith" and "Smythe" are encoded as "S530". Then, comparison between strings is achieved by means of comparison of sequences. This coding has been used to deal with surnames. Jaro [247] recommends its use as a blocking attribute in the indexing step.

> To maximize the chance that similarly spelled surnames reside in the same block, the SOUNDEX system can be used to code the names, and the SOUNDEX code can be used as a blocking attribute. There are better encoding schemes than SOUNDEX, but SOUNDEX with relatively few states and poor discrimination helps ensure that misspelled names receive the same code (Jaro, 1989, p. 418 [247])

Jaro [247] only recommends it for blocking attributes, in other cases it does not recommend its application because nonphonetic errors leads to different codes. Newcombe [353] states that the coding is effective except when the names are of Oriental origin.

Definition A.4 Given a string, the SOUNDEX method encodes it into a sequence of one character and three digits as follows.

1. The first letter of the string is selected and used as the first character of the codification.
2. Vowels A, E, I, O, U and letter Y are not encoded. Letters W and H are also ignored.
3. All the other letters are encoded as follows:

$$
\begin{array}{ll}
B, F, P, V & \text{encoded as 1} \\
C, G, J, K, Q, S, X, Z & \text{encoded as 2} \\
D, T & \text{encoded as 3} \\
L & \text{encoded as 4} \\
M, N & \text{encoded as 5} \\
R & \text{encoded as 6}
\end{array}
$$

4. When the coding results into two or more adjacent codes with the same value only one code is kept. The others are removed. E.g., "S22" is reduced to "S2" and "S221" to "S21".
5. All strings are encoded into a string with the following structure: `Letter`, `digit`, `digit`, `digit`. Additional elements are truncated and in case the string is too short, additional "0" are appended.

Table A.2 displays some examples taken from Knuth [265]. Examples of pairs of surnames that do not lead to the same codification include *(Rogers, Rodgers)* and *(Tchebysheff, Chebyshev)*.

Table A.2 SOUNDEX codification

Surnames		Coding
Euler	Ellery	E460
Gauss	Ghosh	G200
Hilbert	Heilbronn	H416
Knuth	Kant	K530
Lloyd	Ladd	L300
Lukasiewicz	Lissajous	L222

There exist other methods that proceed in a way similar to SOUNDEX by transforming a large number of strings into a single codification. These methods are classified [444] as hashing techniques. For example, Blair [52] builds the so-called r-letter abbreviations. This procedure transforms all strings s to r-letter strings removing $length(s) - r$ irrelevant characters. In this method, relevance of a character is computed in terms of relevance of letters (e.g., "A" has relevance 5 and "B" relevance 1) and relevance of position (e.g., relevance of second position is larger than relevance of first position). Some example codings for 4-letter abbreviations are: *Euler* and *Ellery* are transformed to ELER and *Tchebysheff* and *Chebyshev* are transformed to ESHE. *Rogers* is translated to OERS and *Rodgers* can either be translated to OERS or GERS (letters "O" and "G" in *Rodgers* have the same importance but only one of them can be deleted).

Bigrams have been used to compare strings and compute a similarity measure. A bigram is defined as a pair of consecutive letters in a string. Therefore, the word bigram contains the following bigrams: bi, ig, gr, ra, am. The value of the function $simB$ applied to two strings $s1$ and $s2$ is a value in the [0, 1] interval corresponding to the number of bigrams in common divided by the mean value of bigrams in both strings:

$$simB(s1, s2) = \frac{|bigrams(s1) \cap bigrams(s2)|}{(|bigrams(s1)| + |bigrams(s2)|)/2}$$

where $bigrams(s)$ corresponds to the bigrams in string s.

Naturally, this function defines a similarity function and is equal to 1 when both strings are equal.

As said above, bigrams correspond to two consecutive characters. In fact, the literature also considers the general structure of n-grams (n consecutive characters in a string—a substring of length n). Similarity measures have been considered for n-grams with $n > 2$.

Another approach is the Jaro algorithm [246].

Definition A.5 The similarity between two strings $s1$ and $s2$ according to the Jaro algorithm is defined as follows.

Algorithm 37: Levenshtein distance.

Data: $s1$: string; $s2$: string
Result: Levenshtein distance between $s1$ and $s2$

```
1  for i = 0 to m do
2  |   d[i,0] = i;
3  end
4  for i = 0 to n do
5  |   d[0,i] = 0;
6  end
7  for j = 1 to n do
8  |   for i = 0 to m do
9  |   |   if s1[i] == s2[j] then
10 |   |   |   d[i, j] = d[i − 1, j − 1];
11 |   |   else
12 |   |   |   d[i, j] = 1 + min(d[i − 1, j], d[i, j − 1], d[i − 1, j − 1]);
13 |   |   end
14 |   end
15 end
16 return d[m, n];
```

---

1. Compute the length of the strings $s1$ and $s2$:

   - $strLen1 = length(s1)$
   - $strLen2 = length(s2)$

2. Find the number of common characters. These characters are the ones that appear in both strings at a distance that is at most $minLen/2$ where $minLen = \min(strLen1, strLen2)$:

   $$common = \{c | c \in chars(s1) \cap chars(s2) \text{ and } pos(s1) - pos(s2) \leq minLen/2\}$$

3. Find the number of transpositions among the common characters. A transposition happens whenever a common character from one string does not appear in the same position as the corresponding character from the other string. Let $trans$ be the number of transpositions.

Then, the Jaro similarity is defined as follows:

$$jaro(s1, s2) = \frac{1}{3} \left(\frac{common}{strLen1} + \frac{common}{strLen2} + \frac{1}{2} \frac{trans}{common} \right)$$

McLaughlin, Winkler and Lynch have studied this similarity and defined some enhancements which, when combined with record linkage, improve the performance of the latter. Enhancements and results are given by Porter and Winkler [387] (the code for this distance is available [564]).

Another approach for computing similarities between strings is based on dynamic programming. Algorithm 37 describes how to compute the Levenshtein distance [286] between two strings. This distance is defined on any pair of strings (not necessarily of the same length) and gives the same weight (assumed to be 1 in the algorithm) to insertions, deletions and substitutions.

Improvements of this method exist [444] so that the computation time and the working space requirement are reduced.

A.1.7 Classification of Record Pairs

Record linkage algorithms are used to classify pairs of records. There are two main approaches.

- **Distance-based record linkage methods.** They assign each record in one file to the nearest record in the other file. They are simple to implement and to operate. The main difficulty consists of establishing appropriate distances for the attributes under consideration. The advantage of distance-based record linkage is that it allows inclusion of subjective information (individuals or attributes can be weighted) in the reidentification process.
- **Probabilistic record linkage methods.** They are less simple to implement. Assignment is done according to a probabilistic model. However, they do not assume rescaling or weighting of attributes and require the user to provide only two probabilities as input. Probability of having false positives and false negatives.

Other record linkage methods include cluster-based and rank-based record linkage. The cluster-based approach [33] is based on merging the two files in a single file and then building a large number of clusters (ideally, equal to the number of people) expecting records from the same individuals to be located in the same cluster. Rank-based record linkage [335] consists of computing the distance on ranked data instead on the original values. That is, original values are ordered and each value is replaced by its position in the order. Distance-based and probabilistic record linkage can then be applied to these ranks.

Probabilistic record linkage is described in Sect. A.2 and distance-based record linkage in Sect. A.3. These two methods are applicable when the two files have the same set of attributes. In Sect. A.4 we consider the case of files not sharing attributes. Section A.5 is a summary and analysis of the different approaches.

In order to compare in what extent the number of correct reidentifications an intruder obtains can be due to randomness, we give below the following result.

Proposition A.1 ([472]) *Let A and B be two files corresponding to the same set of n individuals. The probability of finding at random a permutation with exactly r records in the correct position is*

$$\frac{\sum_{v=0}^{k} \frac{(-1)^k}{v!}}{(n-k)!} \tag{A.1}$$

where $k := n - r$.

In most real problems, the probability of finding a few reidentifications by chance is negligible. In the case of 35 objects, finding [472] more than or equal to 3 correct links is less than 0.1.

A.2 Probabilistic Record Linkage

The goal of probabilistic record linkage is to establish whether pairs of records $(a, b) \in \mathbf{A} \times \mathbf{B}$ either belong to the set $\mathbf{M}$ or to the set $\mathbf{U}$, where $\mathbf{M}$ is the set of matches (i.e., correct links between records in $\mathbf{A}$ and $\mathbf{B}$) and $\mathbf{U}$ is the set of unmatches (i.e., incorrect links). That is, whether both records a and b correspond to the same individual or to different individuals. Decision rules classify pairs as linked or non-linked by placing them, respectively in $\mathbf{M}$ and $\mathbf{U}$). Some decision rules in probabilistic record linkage consider an additional classification alternative: clerical pairs. They are the ones that cannot be automatically classified neither in $\mathbf{M}$ nor in $\mathbf{U}$. Classification of clerical pairs is done manually. As a summary, the following classes are considered by decision rules: $\mathbf{DR} = \{\mathbf{LP}, \mathbf{CP}, \mathbf{NP}\}$.

1. **LP**: Set of linked pairs
2. **CP**: Set of clerical pairs
3. **NP**: Set of non-linked pairs

In probabilistic record linkage, a basic assumption is that files share a set of attributes. Taking this into account, decision rules rl are defined as mappings from the comparison space (the space of all comparisons Γ) into probability distributions over $\mathbf{DR}$. If $\gamma \in \Gamma$ then $rl(\gamma) = (\alpha_1, \alpha_2, \alpha_3)$ where $\alpha_1, \alpha_2, \alpha_3$ are, respectively, the membership probabilities for $\{\mathbf{LP}, \mathbf{CP}, \mathbf{NP}\}$. Naturally, $\alpha_1 + \alpha_2 + \alpha_3 = 1$ and $\alpha_i \geq 0$.

Example A.1 ([487]) Let us consider the files $\mathbf{A}$ and $\mathbf{B}$ in Table A.3. Both files contain 8 records and 3 attributes (Name, Surname and Age). For the sake of understandability, the files are defined so that records in the same row correspond to

Table A.3 Files $\mathbf{A}$ and $\mathbf{B}$ used in Example A.1

$Name^A$	$Surname^A$	Age^A	$Name^B$	$Surname^B$	Age^B
Joana	Casanoves	19	Joana	Casanovas	19
Petra	Joan	17	Petra	Joan	17
J.M.	Casanovas	35	J.Manela	Casanovas	35
Johanna	Garcia	53	Johanna	Garcia	53
Ricardo	Garcia	14	Ricard	Garcia	14
Petra	Garcia	18	Petra	Garcia	82
Johanna	Garcia	18	Johanna	Garcia	18
Ricard	Tanaka	14	Ricard	Tanaka	18

matched pairs and records in different rows correspond to unmatched pairs. The goal of record linkage in this example is to classify all possible pairs so that pairs with both records in the same row are classified as linked pairs and all the other pairs are classified as non-linked pairs.

To do so, we consider all pairs $(a, b) \in \mathbf{A} \times \mathbf{B}$. Note that $\gamma(a, b)$ is a coincidence vector in Γ. In this example, $\Gamma = \{\gamma^1 = 000, \gamma^2 = 001, \gamma^3 = 010, \gamma^4 = 011, \gamma^5 = 100, \gamma^6 = 101, \gamma^7 = 110, \gamma^8 = 111\}$. In probabilistic record linkage, the classification of any pair (a, b) is solely based on its corresponding coincidence vector $\gamma(a, b)$. Note that the number of different coincidence vectors (8) is much less than the number of pairs in $\mathbf{A} \times \mathbf{B}$ (64).

Decision rules are defined for $\gamma \in \Gamma$ and they are based on the following expression:

$$\frac{P(\gamma = \gamma(a, b) | (a, b) \in \mathbf{M})}{P(\gamma = \gamma(a, b) | (a, b) \in \mathbf{U})}. \tag{A.2}$$

Definition A.6 Let (a, b) be a pair of records in $\mathbf{A} \times \mathbf{B}$ and let (lt, ut) be two thresholds (lower and upper) in $\mathbb{R}$ such that $lt < ut$. Then the FS (for Fellegi and Sunter [184]) decision rule is:

1. If $R_p(a, b) \geq ut$ then (a, b) is a Linked Pair (**LP**)
2. If $R_p(a, b) \leq lt$ then (a, b) is a Non linked Pair (**NP**)
3. If $lt < R_p(a, b) < ut$ then (a, b) is a Clerical Pair (**CP**)

where the index $R_p(a, b)$ is defined in terms of the vector of coincidences $\gamma(a, b)$ as follows:

$$R_p(a, b) = R(\gamma(a, b)) = \log\left(\frac{P(\gamma(a, b) = \gamma(a', b') | (a', b') \in \mathbf{M})}{P(\gamma(a, b) = \gamma(a', b') | (a', b') \in \mathbf{U})}\right). \tag{A.3}$$

Remark that, in the above example, $R(\gamma)$ does not really use the values in records a and b but only their coincidences. The rationale of Expression A.3 is made clear in the rest of this section. Nevertheless, note that this rule associates large values of R to those pairs whose γ is such that $P(\gamma = \gamma(a', b') | (a', b') \in \mathbf{M})$ is large and $P(\gamma = \gamma(a', b') | (a', b') \in \mathbf{U})$ is small. Therefore, larger values are assigned to $R(\gamma)$ when the probability of finding the coincidence vector γ is larger in $\mathbf{M}$ than in $\mathbf{U}$. Otherwise, small values of R are assigned to coincidence vectors with larger probabilities in $\mathbf{U}$ than in $\mathbf{M}$.

In what follows, we will use m^i and u^i to denote the conditional probabilities of the coincidence vector γ^i:

$$m^i = P(\gamma^i = \gamma(a', b') | (a', b') \in \mathbf{M}) \tag{A.4}$$

$$u^i = P(\gamma^i = \gamma(a', b') | (a', b') \in \mathbf{U}) \tag{A.5}$$

In general, for any decision rule rl, the following two probabilities are of interest:

$$P(\mathbf{LP}|\mathbf{U}) = \mu \tag{A.6}$$

and

$$P(\mathbf{NP}|\mathbf{M}) = \lambda. \tag{A.7}$$

Note that they are the probabilities that the rule causes an error. In particular, the first probability corresponds to the classification as a linked pair of a pair that is not a matched pair. This situation corresponds to a *false linkage*. The second probability corresponds to the classification as a non-linked pair of a matched pair. This situation corresponds to a *false unlinkage*. Note that false linkage and false unlinkage can be seen as false positives and false negatives of the classification rule.

In addition to the two conditional probabilities above, another probability is also relevant in decision rules: the probability of classifying pairs of records into the set **CP**. As this latter set corresponds to pairs that should be further revised, the smaller the probability, the better. Therefore, it is clear that, given the set of all decision rules with the same probabilities $P(\mathbf{LP}|\mathbf{U})$ and $P(\mathbf{NP}|\mathbf{M})$, we are interested in finding the one (or ones) with the smallest probability of classifying a pair as **CP**.

To that end, Fellegi and Sunter [184] considered the following definitions.

Definition A.7 Let rl be a decision rule in the space Γ and let μ and λ be the two values in the interval $(0, 1)$ for its conditional probabilities $P(\mathbf{LP}|\mathbf{U})$ and $P(\mathbf{NP}|\mathbf{M})$ (Expressions A.6 and A.7). Then rl is a *rule with levels μ and λ* and is expressed by $rl(\mu, \lambda, \Gamma)$.

Definition A.8 Let **rl** be the set of all decision rules over Γ with levels μ and λ. Then $rl(\mu, \lambda, \Gamma)$ is the *optimal decision rule* if it satisfies:

$$P(\mathbf{CP}|rl) \leq P(\mathbf{CP}|rl')$$

for all $rl'(\mu, \lambda, \Gamma)$ in **rl**.

In these definitions, it is assumed that μ and λ lead to a non-empty set of decision rules. It is said that μ and λ are admissible when they satisfy simultaneously Expressions A.6 and A.7 and when the set of decision rules is not empty. Fellegi and Sunger [184] give details on the admissibility of μ and λ.

Definition A.9 ([184]) Let μ and λ be an admissible pair of error levels and σ be a permutation of $\{1, \ldots, |\Gamma|\}$ such that $\sigma(j) < \sigma(k)$ if

$$\frac{P(\gamma^{\sigma(j)} = \gamma(a', b')|(a', b') \in \mathbf{M})}{P(\gamma^{\sigma(j)} = \gamma(a', b')|(a', b') \in \mathbf{U})} > \frac{P(\gamma^{\sigma(k)} = \gamma(a', b')|(a', b') \in \mathbf{M})}{P(\gamma^{\sigma(k)} = \gamma(a', b')|(a', b') \in \mathbf{U})} \tag{A.8}$$

and let $limit$ and $limit'$ be the indexes such that

$$\sum_{i=1}^{limit-1} u^{\sigma(i)} < \mu \leq \sum_{i=1}^{limit} u^{\sigma(i)} \tag{A.9}$$

Algorithm 38: Distance-based record linkage.

Data: A: file; B: file
Result: LP: linked pairs; NP: non-linked pairs
1 **for** $a \in A$ **do**
2   b' = arg $\min_{b \in B} d(a, b)$; $LP = LP \cup (a, b')$;
3   **for** $b \in B$ **such that** $b \neq b'$ **do**
4          $NP := NP \cup (a, b)$;
5   **end**
6 **end**
7 **return** (LP, NP);

$$\sum_{i=limit'+1}^{|\Gamma|} m^{\sigma(i)} < \lambda \leq \sum_{i=limit'}^{|\Gamma|} m^{\sigma(i)} \tag{A.10}$$

where u^i and m^i correspond to the conditional probabilities in Expression A.4 and A.5.

Then, the optimal decision rule ODR_p for the pair (a, b) is a probability distribution $(\alpha_1, \alpha_2, \alpha_3)$ on $\{\textbf{LP}, \textbf{CP}, \textbf{NP}\}$ defined by $ODR_p(a, b) = ODR(\gamma(a, b))$ with ODR defined as follows:

$$ODR(\gamma^{\sigma(i)}) = \begin{cases} (1, 0, 0) & \text{if } 1 \leq i \leq limit - 1 \\ (P_\mu, 1 - P_\mu, 0) & \text{if } i = limit \\ (0, 1, 0) & \text{if } limit < i < limit' \\ (0, 1 - P_\lambda, P_\lambda) & \text{if } i = limit' \\ (0, 0, 1) & \text{if } limit' + 1 \leq i \leq |\Gamma| \end{cases} \tag{A.11}$$

and where P_μ and P_λ are the solutions of the equations:

$$u^{\sigma(limit)} P_\mu = \mu - \sum_{i=1}^{limit-1} u^{\sigma(i)} \tag{A.12}$$

$$m^{\sigma(limit')} P_\lambda = \lambda - \sum_{i=limit'+1}^{|\Gamma|} m^{\sigma(i)} \tag{A.13}$$

This decision rule is optimal. This is established in the next theorem.

Theorem A.1 ([184]) *The decision rule in Definition A.9 is a best decision rule on Γ at the levels μ and λ.*

According to the procedure outlined above, the classification of a pair (a, b) requires: (i) computing the coincidence vector γ; (ii) determining the position of this γ vector in Γ once elements in Γ are ordered according to Expression A.8 and (iii) computing the probability distribution over **DR** for this $\gamma^{\sigma(i)}$.

The estimation of the probabilities involved in the computation of R_p is usually based on the EM (Expectation-Minimization) algorithm (Sect. 2.4.3).

A.3   Distance-Based Record Linkage

This approach consists of computing distances between records in the two data files being considered. Then, the pair of records at minimum distance are considered linked pairs.

Let $d(a, b)$ be a distance function between records in file **A** and file **B**. Then, Algorithm 38 describes distance-based record linkage. Naturally, the effectiveness of this record linkage algorithm heavily relies on the effectiveness of the distance function.

We have seen in Sect. A.1.6 the basics for comparing records. We have seen some distances for different types of attributes and Definition A.1 to compute distance between pairs of records.

Definition A.1 assumes that all attributes are equally important and that they are all independent. We present below weighted distances that can be used when these assumptions fail. They are necessary when different attributes have different discriminatory power for record linkage.

A.3.1   Weighted Distances

Let us reconsider Definition A.1. For the sake of simplicity we use the square of the distance.

Note that the square of the distance is not really a distance (as it does not satisfy the triangular inequality) but from a practical point of view there is no difference. In Algorithm 38, replacing d by its square d^2 and/or multiplying d by a constant will result in exactly the same sets (LP, NP). Because of that, we consider the following expression.

Definition A.10 Assuming equal weight for all attributes $\mathbf{V} = \{V_1, V_2, \ldots, V_n\}$, the square distance between records a and b is defined by:

$$d^2(a, b) = \frac{1}{n} \sum_{i=1}^{n} d_{V_i}(V_i^A(a), V_i^B(b)).$$

Weighted generalizations of this expression replace the implicit arithmetic mean in the previous expression by other aggregation functions [44,205,491]. Examples are the weighted mean, a linear combination of order statistics (with total weights equal to one, i.e., ordered weighted aggregation—OWA), and the Choquet integral. Note that if $AM(a_1, \ldots, a_n) = \sum a_i/n$ represents the arithmetic mean, then

$$d^2(a, b) = AM(d_{V_1}(V_1^A(a), V_1^B(b)), \ldots, d_{V_n}(V_n^A(a), V_n^B(b))). \qquad (A.14)$$

The weighted mean and the OWA operators use a weighting vector to represent the importance in the variables/data. A vector $w = (w_1, \ldots, w_n)$ is a weighting vector of dimension n if $w_i \geq 0$ and $\sum w_i = 1$. The Choquet integral uses a non-additive measure (also known as a fuzzy measure) to represent the importance of the variables/data. A non-additive measure μ is a set function on the set of variables $\mathbf{V}$ such that $\mu(\emptyset) = 0$, $\mu(\mathbf{V}) = 1$ and for all $A, B \subseteq \mathbf{V}$ such that $A \subseteq B$ we have that $\mu(A) \leq \mu(B)$.

Definition A.11 Given $a_1, \ldots, a_n \in \mathbb{R}$ the weighted mean (WM), the ordered weighted averaging (OWA) operator (a liner combination of order statistics), and the Choquet integral (CI) are defined as follows.

- Let $\mathbf{p}$ be a weighting vector of dimension n; then, a mapping WM: $\mathbb{R}^n \to \mathbb{R}$ is a *weighted mean* of dimension n if $WM_p(a_1, \ldots, a_n) = \sum_{i=1}^n p_i a_i$.
- Let $\mathbf{w}$ be a weighting vector of dimension n; then, a mapping OWA: $\mathbb{R}^n \to \mathbb{R}$ is an *Ordered Weighting Averaging (OWA) operator* of dimension n if

$$OWA_{\mathbf{w}}(a_1, \ldots, a_n) = \sum_{i=1}^n w_i a_{\sigma(i)},$$

where $\{\sigma(1), \ldots, \sigma(n)\}$ is a permutation of $\{1, \ldots, n\}$ such that $a_{\sigma(i-1)} \geq a_{\sigma(i)}$ for all $i = \{2, \ldots, n\}$ (i.e., $a_{\sigma(i)}$ is the ith largest element in the collection $a_1, \ldots, a_n$).
- Let μ be a non-additive measure on $\mathbf{V}$; then, the *Choquet integral* of a function $f : \mathbf{V} \to \mathbb{R}^+$ with respect to the measure μ is defined by

$$(C) \int f d\mu = \sum_{i=1}^n [f(x_{s(i)}) - f(x_{s(i-1)})] \mu(A_{s(i)}), \qquad (A.15)$$

where $f(x_{s(i)})$ indicates that the indices have been permuted so that $0 \leq f(x_{s(1)}) \leq \cdots \leq f(x_{s(n)}) \leq 1$, and where $f(x_{s(0)}) = 0$ and $A_{s(i)} = \{x_{s(i)}, \ldots, x_{s(n)}\}$.
When no confusion exists over the domain $\mathbf{V}$, we use the notation

$$CI_\mu(a_1, \ldots, a_n) = (C) \int f d\mu,$$

where, $f(x_i) = a_i$, as before.

These definitions permits us to introduce the following distances.

Definition A.12 Given records a and b on variables $\mathbf{V} = \{V_1, V_2, \ldots, V_n\}$, and weighting vectors p, w and a non-additive measure μ on $\mathbf{V}$ we define the following (square) distances:

- $d^2 WM_p(a, b) = WM_p(d_1(a, b), \ldots, d_n(a, b))$,
- $d^2 OWA_w(a, b) = OWA_w(d_1(a, b), \ldots, d_n(a, b))$,
- $d^2 CI_\mu(a, b) = CI_\mu(d_1(a, b), \ldots, d_n(a, b))$,

where $d_i(a, b)$ is defined as $d_{V_i}(V_i^A(a), V_i^B(b))$.

Note that although we are using here the term distance, these expressions are not always, properly speaking, a distance because the triangular inequality is not satisfied.

Due to the properties [491] of aggregation functions, d^2WM and d^2OWA are generalizations of d^2AM. That is, they are more flexible than d^2AM. This means that all results achieved by d^2AM can be achieved by the others with appropriate parameters p and w. Similarly, d^2CI is more general than d^2AM, d^2WM, and d^2OWA. Thus, using the distance d^2CI we can obtain at least as much correct reidentifications as with the other distances but may be more.

The difficulty of using these expressions is that we have to tune the parameters. That is, we have to know how to assess the importance of the different variables, or the importance of the different sets of variables in the reidentification process. In any case, when $w = p = (1/n, \ldots, 1/n)$ and $\mu(A) = |A|/n$ we have that all distances are equivalent. This corresponds to stating that all variables have the same importance, as implicitly stated in the Euclidean distance.

We have stated that these distances permit us to represent different importance of the variables. In addition, the distance based on the Choquet integral permits to represent situations in which there is no independence between the variables. The measure μ permits to express the interactions [491]. Nevertheless, this is not the only possible approach for considering non independent variables. Another one is the Mahalanobis distance and, in general, any symmetric bilinear form.

In symmetric bilinear forms, the importance or weights will be represented by a symmetric matrix. That is, given a set of n variables, we consider a $n \times n$ symmetric matrix. Recall that a symmetric matrix is one where $a_{ij} = a_{ji}$ for all i, j.

Definition A.13 Given records a and b on attributes $\mathbf{V} = \{V_1, V_2, \ldots, V_n\}$, and a $n \times n$ symmetric matrix Q, we define the square of a symmetric bilinear form as

$$d^2SB_Q(a, b) = SB_Q(d_1(a, b), \ldots, d_n(a, b))$$

where

$$SB_Q(c_1, \ldots, c_n) = (c_1, \ldots, c_n)'Q^{-1}(c_1, \ldots, c_n),$$

with c' being the transpose of c, and where $d_i(a, b)$ is defined as $d_{V_i}(V_i^A(a), V_i^B(b))$.

A symmetric matrix M is said to be positive definite if $x'Mx > 0$ for all non zero vectors x, and positive semi-definite if $x'Mx \geq 0$ for all vectors x.

When the matrix is positive definite we have that the root square of the bilinear form is a distance satisfying the triangular inequality, and also the identity of indiscernibles. For positive semi-definite matrices the triangular inequality is satisfied but the identity of indiscernibles is not.

When Q is the covariance matrix (i.e., $Q = \Sigma$ for Σ the covariance matrix of the data), which is semi-definite positive, we have that Definition A.13 leads to the Mahalanobis distance. That is, $\sqrt{d^2SB_\Sigma(a, b)}$ is the Mahalanobis distance between a and b for the covariance matrix Σ.

Recall that the covariance matrix Σ is computed by

$$\Sigma = [Var(V^X) + Var(V^Y) - 2Cov(V^X, V^Y)],$$

where $Var(V^X)$ is the variance of variables V^X, $Var(V^Y)$ is the variance of variables V^Y and $Cov(V^X, V^Y)$ is the covariance between variables V^X and V^Y.

The bilinear form generalizes the Euclidean distance when Q^{-1} is diagonal and such that $a_{ii} = 1/n$ and generalizes the weighted mean when Q^{-1} is diagonal and such that $a_{ii} = w_i$. However, in all other cases $d^2 SB$ and $d^2 CI$ lead to different results. Both distances permit to represent situations in which there is no independence between the variables but the type of relationship between the variables is different.

Kernel distances have also been considered. Their definition is for numerical data. The main idea is that instead of computing the distance between records a and b in the original n dimensional space, records are compared in a higher dimensional space H. The definition follows.

Definition A.14 Let $\Phi(x)$ be the mapping of x into the higher space. Then, the distance between records a and b in H is defined as follows:

$$\begin{aligned} d_K^2(a, b) &= ||\Phi(a) - \Phi(b)||^2 = (\Phi(a) - \Phi(b))^2 \\ &= \Phi(a) \cdot \Phi(a) - 2\Phi(a) \cdot \Phi(b) + \Phi(b) \cdot \Phi(b) \\ &= K(a, a) - 2K(a, b) + K(b, b) \end{aligned}$$

where K is a kernel function (i.e., $K(a, b) = \Phi(a) \cdot \Phi(b)$).

The following family of polynomial kernels have been considered in the literature

$$K(x, y) = (1 + x \cdot y)^d$$

for $d > 1$. With $d = 1$, the kernel record linkage corresponds to the distance-based record linkage with the Euclidean distance.

A.3.2 Distance and Normalization

In the previous definitions we have been using $d_i(a, b)$ defined as $d_{V_i}(V_i^A(a), V_i^B(b))$. However, we have not given much detail on how to compute $d_{V_i}(V_i^A(a), V_i^B(b))$. In part, this refers to the expressions in Sect. A.1.6 where distances at variable level where considered.

At this point we want to underline that record linkage needs to consider standardization of the data. Otherwise variables with large values would weight more than variables that only take values in a small interval. The following two different standardizations can be considered. The first one corresponds to an attribute-standardizing distance (das).

$$das_V^2(V^A(a), V^B(b)) = \left(\frac{V^A(a) - \overline{V^A}}{\sigma(V^A)} - \frac{V^B(b) - \overline{V^B}}{\sigma(V^B)} \right). \tag{A.16}$$

which is the most common in the literature.

The second one corresponds to a distance-standardizing distance (dds).

$$dds_V^2(V^A(a), V^B(b)) = \left(\frac{V^A(a) - V^B(b)}{\sigma(V^A - V^B)} \right). \qquad (A.17)$$

Both definitions are for numerical values, but the second one can be easily modified to be appropriate for non numerical, e.g. categorical, values. The modification consists of using the distance between values instead of the difference, and using the σ of the distance instead of the one of the difference.

$$dds_V'^2(V^A(a), V^B(b)) = \left(\frac{d(V^A(a), V^B(b))}{\sigma(d(V^A(a), V^B(b)))} \right)$$

A.3.3 Parameter Determination for Record Linkage

As we have seen, distance-based record linkage requires a distance. Distances depend implicitly or explicitly on weights for the variables (and on the interactions between the variables). For distance based record linkage on numerical data it is common to use the Euclidean distance between pairs of records. We have already discussed briefly alternative distances in the previous section.

In order to have better estimation of the worst-case disclosure risk (see Sect. 3.3.2), we can try to tune the parameters in an optimal way so that the number of reidentifications is maximum. To do so, we can use machine learning and optimization techniques, assuming that we know which are the correct links (i.e., supervised machine learning).

Although this section focuses on supervised approaches for distance based record linkage, we could proceed in a similar way for probabilistic record linkage.

Let us first recall that in Eq. A.14 we have expressed the distance between pairs of records in terms of the arithmetic mean, and that this expression was later generalized in Definitions A.12 and A.13 so that other parametric distances were taken into account. In particular, we have seen that we can use a weighted distance (using the weighted mean, the OWA or the Choquet integral) or a symmetric bilinear form.

In general, given records a and b on variables $\mathbf{V} = \{V_1, V_2, \ldots, V_n\}$, we can define a distance between a and b in terms of an aggregation (combination) function $\mathbb{C}$ that aggregates the values of the distances between each variable. If we denote the distance for the ith variable as $d_{V_i}(V_i^A(a), V_i^B(b))$, the distance between a and b corresponds to

$$d^2(a, b) = \mathbb{C}_p(d_{V_1}(V_1^A(a), V_1^B(b)), \ldots, d_{V_n}(V_n^A(a), V_n^B(b)))$$

where p is the parameter of the function $\mathbb{C}$. In Definitions A.12 and A.13 we considered different alternatives for $\mathbb{C}$. For the sake of simplicity, we will use $\mathbb{C}_p(a, b)$ to denote the following.

$$\mathbb{C}_p(a, b) = \mathbb{C}_p(d_{V_1}(V_1^A(a), V_1^B(b)), \ldots, d_{V_n}(V_n^A(a), V_n^B(b))).$$

If $\mathbb{C}$ is known, to find the worst-case disclosure risk is to find the parameter p that permits us to achieve the maximum number of reidentifications. When A and B are given and we know which pairs correspond to the same record, this problem can be formulated mathematically. Note that this information is available to those that protect the file. For the sake of simplicity we assume that A and B consist of the same number of records and that records are aligned. That is, a_i and b_i correspond to the same individual.

Using this notation, it is clear that the record a_i is correctly linked to b_i when the following equation holds

$$\mathbb{C}_p(a_i, b_i) < \mathbb{C}_p(a_i, b_j) \tag{A.18}$$

for all $b_j \neq b_i$ in B.

Ideally, we could require all a_i in A to behave in this way, and eventually get the parameter p. This would correspond to have $|A| \times |B|$ equations and find the parameter p that satisfies all of them. Unfortunately, this is usually not possible because there is no p with 100% success. In contrast, we need to permit some incorrect links. In other words, the optimal solution is only able to link correctly some of the pairs. In this case, we can still formalize the problem mathematically. This is done by means of considering blocks of equations.

We consider a block as the set of equations that correspond to a certain record a_i. We then consider a variable K_i associated to this block. When $K = 0$ it means that the constraints are satisfied for a_i, and when $K = 1$ it means that the constraints are not satisfied for a_i. Then, we want to minimize the blocks (i.e., the records a_i) that do not satisfy the constraints. This approach is based on the fact that if there is j_0 such that

$$\mathbb{C}_p(a_i, b_i) > \mathbb{C}_p(a_i, b_{j_0})$$

for $i \neq j_0$ then as the pair (a_i, b_i) is not correctly linked, it does not matter which are the values of $\mathbb{C}_p(a_i, b_i)$ and $\mathbb{C}_p(a_i, b_{j_0})$. I.e., what is relevant is the number of correct and incorrect blocks not the distances themselves.

Using the variables K_i and a constant C that corresponds to the maximum insatisfaction of the inequality, we can rewrite the equation above (Eq. A.18). We have that for a given record a_i the equation

$$\mathbb{C}_p(a_i, b_j) - \mathbb{C}_p(a_i, b_i) + C K_i > 0.$$

has to be satisfied for all $j \neq i$, for a given C, and for $K_i \in \{0, 1\}$.

Then, the optimization problem is to find the p that minimizes the number of K_i equal to one. Naturally, this is equivalent to minimize $\sum K_i$. This sum will be the number of times we are not able to reidentify correctly, $|A| - \sum_{i=1}^{|A|} K_i$ will be the correct number of reidentifications.

Therefore, the optimization problem results as follows:

$$\text{Minimize} \sum_{i=1}^{|A|} K_i$$

Subject to:

$$\mathbb{C}_p(a_i, b_j) - \mathbb{C}_p(a_i, b_i) + CK_i > 0, \qquad \forall i = 1, \ldots, |A|,$$
$$\forall j = 1, \ldots, |B|, i \neq j$$
$$K_i \in \{0, 1\}$$

We need to add to this optimization problem constraints on the parameter p if the function $\mathbb{C}$ requires such constraints for the parameter. For example, if we consider $\mathbb{C}$ to be the weighted mean (so, the distance is a weighted Euclidean distance) we need p to be a weighting vector $p = (p_1, \ldots, p_n)$ with all weights positive $p_i \geq 0$ and adding one $\sum p_i = 1$. This results into the following optimization problem.

$$\text{Minimize} \sum_{i=1}^{A} K_i$$

Subject to:

$$WM_p(a_i, b_j) - WM_p(a_i, b_i) + CK_i > 0, \qquad \forall i = 1, \ldots, |A|,$$
$$\forall j = 1, \ldots, |B|, i \neq j$$
$$K_i \in \{0, 1\}$$

$$\sum_{i=1}^{n} p_i = 1$$

$$p_i \geq 0 \qquad\qquad\qquad \text{for } i = 1, \ldots, n$$
$$(A.19)$$

Other distances in Definition A.12 and A.13 imply other constraints on the parameters p. Constraints for the OWA (linear combination of order statistics) are similar (w is a weighting vector with positive elements that add to one). The constraints for the Choquet integral force μ to be a non-additive (i.e., constraints so that $\mu(\emptyset) = 0$, $\mu(\mathbf{V}) = 1$ and for all $A, B \subseteq \mathbf{V}$ such that $A \subseteq B$ we have that $\mu(A) \leq \mu(B)$), and the constraints for the symmetric bilinear form are to force the matrix Q to be symmetric and semidefinite positive.

The optimization problem described in Eqs. A.19 with the constraints for the weighted mean, the OWA and the Choquet integral, is a linear optimization problem with linear constraints. As some of the variables are integers (i.e., K_i), it is in fact a Mixed Integer Linear mathematical optimization problem (MILP). This type of problems can be solved effectively using standard solvers. When we use a bilinear form, the problem is more complex because the matrix Q needs to be semidefinite positive, and this cannot be expressed in terms of linear constraints. Semi-definite programming can be used to solve this problem.

It can be proven mathematically that the distance based on the Choquet integral always outperforms the weighted mean and the OWA, and that the bilinear form outperforms the weighted mean. However, using such distances is at the cost of an optimization problem with more constraints, and more difficult to solve. E.g., for $t = |A| = |B|$ records and n variables we need

$$t(t-1) + t + n + 1$$

constraints for the weighted mean (and the OWA) and we determine n parameters, but for the Choquet integral we look for $2^n - 1$ parameters with a problem of

$$t(t-1) + t + 2 + \sum_{k=2}^{n} \binom{n}{k} k$$

constraints, and in the case of the bilinear form we look for $n(n-1)/2$ parameters using $t(t-1) + t + t^2$ constraints.

A.4   Record Linkage Without Common Attributes

When two databases do not share the schema, reidentification may still be possible if the information in both databases is similar. The following hypothesis makes explicit when reidentification may take place.

Hypothesis 1 ([472]) *A large set of common individuals is shared by both files.*

Hypothesis 2 ([472]) *Data in both files contain, implicitly, similar structural information. In other words, even though there are no common variables, there is some amount of redundancy between variables in both files.*

In this second hypothesis, structural information corresponds to an explicit representation of the underlying relationship between the individuals in the database. Once this structural information is extracted from the data, reidentification algorithms can be applied to the extracted structure. For example, the structural information can be expressed in terms of partitions [472]. If this information is implicit in both files, then e.g. clustering algorithms can extract it. Partitions has an advantage with respect to other data structures as dendrograms, as they are more robust to changes in the data [351].

A.5   Comparison of Record Linkage Algorithms

The comparison of the different generic record linkage algorithms in experiments show that, in general, probabilistic record linkage and distance-based record linkage with unweighted distances lead to similar results for most of the distances used for both the numerical data [144] and categorical data [146]. The use of Mahalanobis distance [486] is for some very particular experiments significantly better than other distances (Euclidean, kernel-based distances), but in general results are also similar. Although results are similar in percentage of correctly reidentified records, this does not mean that the pairs of records reidentified are always the same. There are differences among these pairs.

Distance-based record linkage, in its basic version, is simpler to implement and operate than probabilistic record linkage. Distance-based record linkage permits us to incorporate easily knowledge on the variables. In contrast, optimal parameters for distance-based record linkage are not easy to find if we do not have a training set.

The use of supervised approaches to determine the parameters of the distances, as explained in Sect. A.3.3 has also been proven successful. It is clear that using record linkage with weighted means and other kind of distances that generalize the Euclidean and the Mahalanobis distance should lead to larger reidentification rates than when simply using the Euclidean and Mahalanobis distance. Nevertheless, the computational cost of these approaches can be very large, and even unfeasible to get the optimal solution in reasonable time.

Abril et al. [8] compared these supervised approaches for 6 different data files and showed that the distance based on the bilinear form was the one that leads to the largest number of reidentifications. This however depends on the files and the type of protection. It seems that when variables are protected independently, the Euclidean distance and weighted Euclidean distance are enough to give a good upper bound of the risk (the improvement achieved is not very much significant). When sets of variables are protected together, other distances as the ones based on the Choquet integral and the bilinear form may be preferable. In any case, results depend on specific original and protected data files.

A.6   Bibliographical Notes

1. **Data matching and record linkage.** Data matching and record linkage is described in Christen's books [100,101]. We describe in detail distance-based and probabilistic record linkage in a book chapter [487], including details on the estimation of probabilities based on the expectation-maximization algorithm.
2. **Probabilistic-record linkage.** Probabilistic record linkage is described in detail in the book by Herzog, Scheuren, and Winkler [227], as well as in few reviews [172,527,560]. Protocols to ensure private probabilistic record linkage [507] have also been developed.
   Most literature on probabilistic record linkage assumes the independence of the variables. Nevertheless, it is usual that some variables are not independent. Consider e.g., postal code and city of residence. Winkler [525] discusses the problem of record linkage in the case of non-independent variables introducing interaction models. In each interaction model, a set of interaction patterns are considered. The paper compares two interaction models, the one in Larsen and Rubin [277] and the one in a previous paper by Winkler [522]. Tromp et al. [499] also discuss

the case of non independent variables. Daggy et al. [109] also introduce a model that includes terms to model dependences between pairs of fields.

3. **Distance-based record linkage.** Distance-based record linkage was first described for disclosure risk assessment by Pagliuca and Seri [373], in a very restricted formulation.

   In our discussion we have not made any assumption on the relationship between the links the record-linkage provides. In short, we permit two different records of an intruder (e.g., b_1 and b_2) to be assigned to the same record a. There are authors [225, 285, 404] that force different records in B to be linked to different records in A. When A and B have the same number of records, such algorithms find a one-to-one correspondence between the records of both files. This is known as perfect matching in graph theory. The RELAIS record linkage software [404] developed by ISTAT permits users to consider one-to-one, one-to-many, and many-to-many re-identification problems. Herranz et al. [225] present a detailed analysis of the performance (with respect to the number of re-identifications) of perfect matching algorithms comparing them with those not requiring this property. Their approach is based on the Hungarian algorithm. An $O(n^3)$ combinatorial optimization algorithm that solves the assignment problem.

4. **Distances.** There are plenty of references for distances, see e.g. the dictionary of distances [132]. The ones reviewed here for numerical and categorical data have been used [144, 486] to evaluate and compare the performance of masking methods. More particularly, the following distances have been considered to evaluate disclosure risk for masked files: the Mahalanobis distance [486], distance based on a bilinear form [8], distances based on kernels [486], distance based on the weighted means [6, 493], distance based on OWA [493], and distance based on the Choquet integral in [5].

   As we have explained in this chapter, the determination of optimal parameters for most of these distances in the context of disclosure risk assessment [5, 6, 493] can be formalized in terms of an optimization problem. Experiments are reported using IBM ILOG CPLEX tool [240] (version 12.1). In the case of the bilinear form, in order to make the optimization problem linear, constraints on Q to make the problem semi-definite, were replaced [8] by a set of equations requiring the distance for the records under consideration to be positive. That is, requiring for all a, b in A and B that $SB_Q(a, b) \geq 0$.

   Cohen et al. [105] present a comparison of several efficient string distances in the particular context of record matching. Herranz et al. [226] propose another distance which satisfies all axioms of a distance and is also efficient.

References

1. J.M. Abowd, The U.S. Census Bureau adopts differential privacy, in *Proceedings of the KDD 2018* (2018)
2. J. Abowd, R. Ashmead, R. Cumings-Menon, S. Garfinkel, D. Kifer, P. Leclerc, W. Sexton, A. Simpson, C. Task, P. Zhuravlev, An uncertainty principle is a price of privacy-preserving microdata, in *NeurIPS 2021* (2021)
3. D. Abril, G. Navarro-Arribas, V. Torra, Towards semantic microaggregation of categorical data for confidential documents. Proceedings of the MDAI **2010**, 266–276 (2010)
4. D. Abril, G. Navarro-Arribas, V. Torra, On the declassification of confidential documents. Proceedings of the MDAI **2011**, 235–246 (2011)
5. D. Abril, G. Navarro-Arribas, V. Torra, Choquet integral for record linkage. Ann. Oper. Res. **195**, 97–110 (2012)
6. D. Abril, G. Navarro-Arribas, V. Torra, Improving record linkage with supervised learning for disclosure risk assessment. Inf. Fusion **13**(4), 274–284 (2012)
7. D. Abril, G. Navarro-Arribas, V. Torra, Spherical microaggregation: anonymizing sparse vector spaces. Comput. Secur. **49**, 28–44 (2015)
8. D. Abril, G. Navarro-Arribas, V. Torra, Supervised learning using a symmetric bilinear form for record linkage. Inf. Fusion **26**, 144–153 (2016)
9. O. Abul, Knowledge hiding in emerging application domains, in *Privacy-Aware Knowledge Discovery*. ed. by F. Bonchi, E. Ferrari (CRC Press, Boca Raton, 2011), pp.59–87
10. O. Abul, F. Bonchi, M. Nanni, Never walk alone: uncertainty for anonymity in moving objects databases, in *Proceedings of the 24th ICDE 2008* (2008), pp. 376–385
11. O. Abul, F. Bonchi, M. Nanni, Anonymization of moving objects databases by clustering and perturbation. Inf. Sci. **35**, 884–910 (2010)
12. G. Acar, M. Juarez, N. Nikiforakis, C. Diaz, S. Gürses, F. Piessens, B. Preneel, FPDetective: dusting the Web for Fingerprinters, in *Proceedings of the ACM Conference on Computer and Communications Security (CCS)* (2013), pp. 1129–1140
13. J. Aczél, *A Short Course on Functional Equations* (D (Reidel Publishing Company (Kluwer Academic Publishers Group), Boston, 1987)
14. N.R. Adam, J.C. Wortmann, Security-control for statistical databases: a comparative study. ACM Comput. Surv. **21**, 515–556 (1989)
15. K.S. Adewole, V. Torra, DFTMicroagg: a dual-level anonymization algorithm for smart grid data (2022) (manuscript)
16. C. Aggarwal, On k-anonymity and the curse of dimensionality, in *Proceedings of the 31st International Conference on Very Large Databases* (2005), pp. 901–909

V. Torra, *Guide to Data Privacy*, Undergraduate Topics in Computer Science,
https://doi.org/10.1007/978-3-031-12837-0

17. C.C. Aggarwal, P.S. Yu, A condensation approach to privacy preserving data mining, in *Proceedings of the EDBT* (2004), pp. 183–199
18. C.C. Aggarwal, P.S. Yu (eds.), *Privacy-Preserving Data Mining: Models and Algorithms* (Springer, Berlin, 2008)
19. G. Aggarwal, T. Feder, K. Kenthapadi, S. Khuller, R. Panigrahy, D. Thomas, A. Zhu, Achieving anonymity via clustering, in *Proceedings of the PODS 2006* (2006)
20. G. Aggarwal, T. Feder, K. Kenthapadi, R. Motwani, R. Panigrahy, D. Thomas, A. Zhu, Anonymizing tables, in *Proceedings of the 10th International Conference on Database Theory (ICDT05)* (2005), pp. 246–258
21. D. Agrawal, C.C. Aggarwal, On the design and quantification of privacy preserving data mining algorithms, in *Proceedings of the PODS'01* (2001), pp. 247–255
22. R. Agrawal, T. Imielinski, A.N. Swami, Mining association rules between sets of items in large databases, in *Proceedings of the 1993 ACM SIGMOD International Conference on Management of Data* (1993), pp. 207–216
23. R. Agrawal, R. Srikant, Fast algorithms for mining association rules, in *Proceedings of the 20th International Conference on VLDB. Also as Research Report RJ 9839, IBM Almaden Research Center, San Jose, California, June 1994* (1994), pp. 478–499
24. R. Agrawal, R. Srikant, Privacy preserving data mining, in *Proceedings of the ACM SIGMOD Conference on Management of Data* (2000), pp. 439–450
25. A.V. Aho, J.D. Ullman, J.E. Hopcroft, *Data Structures and Algorithms* (Addison-Wesley, Boston, 1988)
26. A.N. Albatineh, M. Niewiadomska-Bugaj, D. Mihalko, On similarity indices and correction for chance agreement. J. Classif. **23**, 301–313 (2006)
27. A. Alfalahi, S. Brissman, H. Dalianis, Pseudonymisation of personal names and other PHIs in an annotated clinical Swedish corpus, in *Proceedings of the 3rd LREC Workshop Building and Evaluating Resources for Biomedical Text Mining (BioTxtM 2012)* (2012), pp. 49–54
28. D.T. Anderson, J.C. Bezdek, M. Popescu, J.M. Keller, Comparing fuzzy, probabilistic, and possibilistic partitions. IEEE Trans. Fuzzy Syst. **18**(5), 906–918 (2010)
29. M. Atallah, E. Bertino, A. Elmagarmid, M. Ibrahim, V. Verykios, Disclosure limitation of sensitive rules, in *Proceedings of IEEE Knowledge and Data Engineering Exchange Workshop (KDEX)* (1999)
30. M. Atzori, F. Bonchi, F. Giannotti, D. Pedreschi, Anonymity preserving pattern discovery. VLDB J. **17**, 703–727 (2008)
31. C. Babbage, *Passages from the Life of a Philosopher (Longman, Green, Longman* (Roberts & Green, London, 1864)
32. K. Bache, M. Lichman, *UCI Machine Learning Repository* (University of California, School of Information and Computer Science, Irvine, 2013)
33. J. Bacher, R. Brand, S. Bender, Re-identifying register data by survey data using cluster analysis: an empirical study. Int. J. Uncertain. Fuzziness Knowl. Based Syst. **10**(5), 589–607 (2002)
34. J. Balasch-Masoliver, V. Muntés-Mulero, J. Nin, Using genetic algorithms for attribute grouping in multivariate microaggregation. Intell. Data Anal. **18**, 819–836 (2014)
35. E. Balsa, C. Troncoso, C. Díaz, A metric to evaluate interaction obfuscation in online social networks. Int. J. Uncertain. Fuzziness Knowl.-Based Syst. **20**, 877–892 (2012)
36. J. Bambauer, Tragedy of the deidentified data commons: an appeal for transparency and access, in *Joint UNECE/Eurostat Work Session on Statistical Data Confidentiality, Ottawa, Canada, 28–30 October 2013* (2013)
37. J. Bambauer, K. Muralidhar, R. Sarathy, *Fool's gold: an illustrated critique of differential privacy* (Vanderbilt J. Entertain, Technol, Law, 2014). ((in press))
38. D. Barth-Jones, K. El Emam, J. Bambauer, A. Cavoukioan, B. Malin, Assessing data intrusion threats. Science **348**, 194–195 (2015)

39. J. Barthelemy, P.L. Toint, Synthetic population generation without a sample. Transp. Sci. **47**(2), 266–279 (2013)
40. S. Bapna, A. Gangopadhyay, A wavelet-based approach to preserve privacy for classification mining. Decis. Sci. **37**(4), 623–642 (2006)
41. M. Barbaro, T. Zeller, S. Hansell, A face is exposed for AOL searcher no. 4417749. New York Times, 9 August 2006
42. M. Barni, V. Cappellini, A. Mecocci, Comments on "A possibilistic approach to clustering". IEEE Trans. Fuzzy Syst. **4**(3), 393–396 (1996)
43. M. Batet, A. Erola, D. Sánchez, J. Castellà-Roca, Utility preserving query log anonymization via semantic microaggregation. Inf. Sci. **242**, 49–63 (2013)
44. G. Beliakov, A. Pradera, T. Calvo, *Aggregation Functions: a Guide for Practitioners* (Springer, Berlin, 2007)
45. S.I. Benn, Privacy, freedom, and respect for persons. Reproduced as Chapter 8 in [425] (1971)
46. D. Berend, T. Tassa, Improved bounds on bell numbers and on moments of sums of random variables. Probab. Math. Stat. **30**(2), 185–205 (2010)
47. S. Bergamaschi, S. Castano, M. Vincini, D. Beneventano, Semantic integration of heterogeneous information sources. Data Knowl. Eng. **36**(3), 215–249 (2001)
48. E. Bertino, D. Lin, W. Jiang, A survey of quantification of privacy preserving data mining algorithms, in *Privacy-Preserving Data Mining: Models and Algorithms*. ed. by C.C. Aggarwal, P.S. Yu (Springer, Berlin, 2008), pp.183–205
49. J.C. Bezdek, *Pattern Recognition with Fuzzy Objective Function Algorithms* (Plenum Press, New York, 1981)
50. J.C. Bezdek, The parable of Zoltan, in *On Fuzziness: Volume 1 (STUDFUZZ 298)*. ed. by R. Seising, E. Trillas, C. Moraga, S. Termini (Springer, Berlin, 2013), pp.39–46
51. J. Binder, A. Howes, A. Sutcliffe, The problem of conflicting social spheres: effects of network structure on experienced tension in social network sites, in *Proceedings of the CHI'09* (2009)
52. C.R. Blair, A program for correcting spelling errors, information and control **3**(1), 60–67 (1960)
53. O. Blum, Evaluation of editing and imputations supported by administrative records, in *Conference of European Statisticians, WP7* (2005)
54. A. Blum, C. Dwork, F. McSherry, K. Nissim, Practical privacy: the SuLQ framework. Proceedings of the PODS **2005**, 128–138 (2005)
55. D. Bogdanov, S. Laur, J. Willemson, Sharemind: a framework for fast privacy-preserving computations, in *Proceedings of the ESORICS 2008*. LNCS (2008)
56. K. Bonawitz, V. Ivanov, B. Kreuter, A. Marcedone, H.B. McMahan, S. Patel, D. Ramage, A. Segal, K. Seth, Practical secure aggregation for privacy-preserving machine learning, in *Proceedings of the CCS'17* (2017)
57. F. Bonchi, Y. Saygin, V.S. Verykios, M. Atzori, A. Gkoulalas-Divanis, S.V. Kaya, E. Savaş, Privacy in spatiotemporal data mining, in *Mobility, Data Mining and Privacy: Geographic Knowledge Discovery*. ed. by F. Giannotti, D. Pedreschi (Springer, Berlin, 2008), pp.297–333
58. J.H. Boose, *Expertise Transfer for Expert System Design* (Elsevier, Amsterdam, 1986)
59. V. Borkar, K. Deshmukh, S. Sarawagi, Automatic segmentation of text into structured records, in *Proceedings of the ACM SIGMOD Conference* (2001)
60. R. Brand, Microdata protection through noise addition, in *Inference Control in Statistical Databases*, ed. by J. Domingo-Ferrer. LNCS, vol. 2316 (2002), pp. 97–116
61. M. Bras-Amorós, J. Domingo-Ferrer, On overlappings of digitized straight lines and shared steganographic file systems. Trans. Data Priv. **1**(3), 131–139 (2008)
62. L. Breiman, Statistical modeling: the two cultures. Stat. Sci. **16**(3), 199–231 (2001)
63. R.K. Brouwer, Extending the Rand, adjusted Rand and Jaccard indices to fuzzy partitions. J. Intell. Inf. Syst. **32**, 213–235 (2009)
64. S. Buchegger, D. Schiöberg, L.-H. Vu, A. Datta, PeerSoN: P2P social networking: early experiences and insights, in *Proceedings of the SNS2009* (2009), pp. 46–52

65. P. Bunn, R. Ostrovsky, Secure two-party k-means clustering, in *Proceedings of CCS'07* (ACM Press, 2007), pp. 486–497

66. J. Burridge, Information preserving statistical obfuscation. Stat. Comput. **13**, 321–327 (2003)

67. J.-W. Byun, A. Kamra, E. Bertino, N. Li, Efficient k-anonymization using clustering techniques, in *Proceedings of the DASFAA 2007* (2007)

68. A. Campan, T.M. Truta, Data and structural *k*-anonymity in social networks. Proceedings of the PinkDD. LNCS **5456**, 33–54 (2008)

69. I. Cano, V. Torra, Edit constraints on microaggregation and additive noise. LNCS **6549**, 1–14 (2011)

70. I. Cano, G. Navarro-Arribas, V. Torra, A new framework to automate constrained microaggregation, in *Proceedings of the PAVLAD Workshop in CIKM 2009* (2009)

71. J. Cao, B. Carminati, E. Ferrari, K.-L. Tan, Castle: a delay-constrained scheme for ks-anonymizing data streams, in *Proceedings of the 24th ICDE* (2008), pp. 1376–1378

72. M. Carlson, M. Salabasis, A data swapping technique using ranks: a method for disclosure control. Res. Off. Stat. **5**(2), 35–64 (2002)

73. L. Carrol, Alice's adventures in wonderland, *Project Gutenberg's* (1865)

74. J. Casas-Roma, J. Herrera-Joancomartí, V. Torra, Comparing random-based and k-anonymity-based algorithms for graph anonymization, in *Proceedings of the MDAI 2012*. LNCS, vol. 7647 (2012), pp. 197–209

75. J. Casas-Roma, J. Herrera-Joancomartí, V. Torra, An algorithm for *k*-degree anonymity on large networks, in *Proceedings of 2013 IEEE/ACM ASONAM* (2013)

76. J. Casas-Roma, J. Herrera-Joancomartí, V. Torra, A survey of graph-modification techniques for privacy-preserving on networks. Artif. Intell. Rev. (2017). https://doi.org/10.1007/s10462-016-9484-8, in press

77. J. Casas-Roma, J. Herrera-Joancomartí, V. Torra, k-degree anonymity and edge selection: improving data utility in large networks. Knowl. Inf. Syst. **50**, 447–474 (2017)

78. J. Castro, Internal communication to partners of the European Union IST-2000-25069 CASC project (2002)

79. J. Castro, Computational experiments with minimum-distance controlled perturbation methods, in *Proceedings of the PSD 2004*. LNCS, vol. 3050 (2004), pp. 73–86

80. J. Castro, Minimum-distance controlled perturbation methods for large-scale tabular data protection. Eur. J. Oper. Res. **171**, 39–52 (2006)

81. J. Castro, *Taules estadístiques i privadesa* (Universitat Estiu URV, La lluita contra el big brother, 2007)

82. J. Castro, On assessing the disclosure risk of controlled adjustment methods for statistical tabular data. Int. J. Uncertain. Fuzziness Knowl.-Based Syst. **20**, 921–942 (2012)

83. J. Castro, Comparing L1 and L2 distances for CTA, in *Proceedings of the PSD 2012*. LNCS, vol. 7556 (2012), pp. 35–46

84. J. Castro, Recent advances in optimization techniques for statistical tabular data protection. Eur. J. Oper. Res. **216**, 257–269 (2012)

85. A. Cavoukian, Privacy by design. The 7 foundational principles in privacy by design. Strong privacy protection - now, and well into the future (2011), https://www.ipc.on.ca/wp-content/uploads/Resources/7foundationalprinciples.pdf, https://www.ipc.on.ca/wp-content/uploads/Resources/PbDReport.pdf

86. A. Cavoukian, K. El Emam, Dispelling the myths surrounding de-identification: anonymization remains a strong tool for protecting privacy (2011)

87. C.-C. Chang, Y.-C. Li, W.-H. Huang, TFRP: an efficient microaggregation algorithm for statistical disclosure control. J. Syst. Softw. **80**, 1866–1878 (2007)

88. A. Chaudhuri, R. Mukerjee, *Randomized Response: Theory and Techniques* (Marcel Dekker, New York, 1988)

89. D.L. Chaum, Untraceable electronic mail, return addresses, and digital pseudonyms. Commun. ACM **24**(2), 84–88 (1981)

90. D. Chaum, The dining cryptographers problem: unconditional sender and recipient untraceability. J. Cryptol. **1**, 65–75 (1985)

91. S. Chawla, C. Dwork, F. McSherry, A. Smith, H. Wee, Toward privacy in public databases, in *Proceedings of the Theory of Cryptography Conference* (2005), pp. 363–385

92. L. Cheng, S. Cheng, F. Jiang, ADKAM: a-diversity k-anonymity model via microaggregation, in *Proceedings of the ISPEC 2015*. LNCS, vol. 9065 (2015), pp. 553–547

93. S.K. Chettri, B. Borah, On analysis of time-series data with preserved privacy. Innov. Syst. Softw. Eng. **11**, 155–165 (2015)

94. S.L. Chiu, *A cluster estimation method with extension to fuzzy model identification* (Proc, IEEE Fuzzy Syst, 1994)

95. B. Chor, N. Gilboa, Computationally private information retrieval, in *Proceedings of the 29th STOC* (1997), pp. 304–313

96. B. Chor, O. Goldreich, E. Kushilevitz, M. Sudan, Private information retrieval, in *Proceedings of the IEEE Conference on Foundations of Computer Science* (1995), pp. 41–50

97. B. Chor, O. Goldreich, E. Kushilevitz, M. Sudan, Private information retrieval. J. ACM **45**(6), 965–982 (1999)

98. C. Chow, C. Liu, Approximating discrete probability distributions with dependence trees. IEEE Trans. Inf. Theory **14**(3), 462–467 (1968)

99. P. Christen, A survey of indexing techniques for scalable record linkage and deduplication. IEEE Trans. Knowl. Data Eng. **24** (2012)

100. P. Christen, *Data Matching - Concepts and Techniques for Record Linkage, Entity Resolution, and Duplicate Detection* (Springer, Berlin, 2012)

101. P. Christen, T. Ranbaduge, R. Schnell, *Linking Sensitive Data: Methods and Techniques for Practical Privacy-Preserving Information Sharing* (Springer, Berlin, 2020)

102. T. Churches, P. Christen, K. Lim, J.X. Zhu, Preparation of name and address data for record linkage using hidden Markov models. BMC Med. Inform. Decis. Mak. **2**(9) (2002)

103. C. Clifton, T. Tassa, On syntactic anonymity and differential privacy. Trans. Data Priv. **6**, 161–183 (2013)

104. W.G. Cochran, *Sampling Techniques*, 3rd edn. (Wiley, New York, 1977)

105. W.W. Cohen, P. Ravikumar, S.E. Fienberg, A comparison of string metrics for matching names and records, in *Proceedings of the KDD 2003* (2003)

106. W.A. Coppel, *Number Theory: an Introduction to Mathematics* (Springer, Berlin, 2009)

107. Council of Europe, European Court of Human Rights, European Data Protection Supervisor, European Union Agency for Fundamental Rights, Handbook on European data protection law: 2018 edition, Publications Office (2019), https://data.europa.eu/doi/10.2811/343461. Accessed May 2022

108. G. D'Acquisto, J. Domingo-Ferrer, P. Kikiras, V. Torra, Y.-A. de Montjoye, A. Bourka, Privacy by design in big data: an overview of privacy enhancing technologies in the era of big data analytics, ENISA report (2015)

109. J.K. Daggy, H. Xu, S.L. Hui, R.E. Gamache, S.J. Grannis, A practical approach for incorporating dependence among fields in probabilistic record linkage. BMC Med. Inform. Decis. Mak. **13**(97) (2013)

110. T. Dalenius, Towards a methodology for statistical disclosure control. Stat. Tidskr. **5**, 429–444 (1977)

111. T. Dalenius, Finding a needle in a haystack - or identifying anonymous census records. J. Off. Stat. **2**(3), 329–336 (1986)

112. T. Dalenius, S.P. Reiss, Data-swapping - a technique for disclosure control, in *Proceedings of the ASA Section on Survey Research Methods* (1978), pp. 191–194

113. T. Dalenius, S.P. Reiss, Data-swapping: a technique for disclosure control. J. Stat. Plan. Inference **6**, 73–85 (1982)

114. R.A. Dandekar, L.H. Cox, *Synthetic tabular data: an alternative to complementary cell suppression, manuscript* (Energy Information Administration, US Department of Energy, 2002)

115. R.A. Dandekar, M. Cohen, N. Kirkendall, Applicability of Latin hypercube sampling technique to create multivariate synthetic microdata. Proceedings of the ETK-NTTS **2001**, 839–847 (2001)

116. R. Dandekar, J. Domingo-Ferrer, F. Sebé, LHS-based hybrid microdata vs rank swapping and microaggregation for numeric microdata protection. LNCS **2316**, 153–162 (2002)

117. G. Danezis, J. Domingo-Ferrer, M. Hansen, J.-H. Hoepman, D. Le Métayer, R. Tirtea, S. Schiffner, Privacy and data protection by design - from policy to engineering, ENISA report (2014)

118. E. Dasseni, V.S. Verykios, A.K. Elmagarmid, E. Bertino, Hiding association rules by using confidence and support (2001)

119. A. Datta, S. Buchegger, L.-H. Vu, T. Strufe, K. Rzadca, Decentralized online social networks, *Handbook of Social Network Technologies* (2010), pp. 349–378

120. R.N. Davé, Characterization and detection of noise in clustering. Pattern Recognit. Lett. **12**, 657–664 (1991)

121. S. De Capitani di Vimercati, S. Foresti, G. Livraga, P. Samarati, Data privacy: definitions and techniques. Int. J. Uncertain. Fuzziness Knowl. Based Syst. **20**(6), 793–817

122. J. Daalmans, T. de Waal, An improved formulation of the disclosure auditing problem for secondary cell suppression. Trans. Data Priv. **3**, 217–251 (2010)

123. Y.-A. de Montjoye, L. Radaelli, V.K. Singh, A.S. Pentland, Unique in the shopping mall: on the reidentifiability of credit card metadata. Science (30 January) 536–539 (2015)

124. Y.-A. de Montjoye, A.S. Pentland, Response. Science **348**, 195 (2015)

125. Y.-A. de Montjoye, A.S. Pentland, Response to comment on "Unique in the shopping mall: on the reidentifiability of credit card metadata". Science (18 March 1274-b)

126. D. Defays, P. Nanopoulos, Panels of enterprises and confidentiality: the small aggregates method, in *Proceedings of 92 Symposium on Design and Analysis of Longitudinal Surveys, Statistics Canada* (1993), pp. 195–204

127. D. Defays, M.N. Anwar, Masking microdata using micro-aggregation. J. Off. Stat. **14**, 449–461 (1998)

128. A.P. Dempster, N.M. Laird, D.B. Rubin, Maximum likelihood from incomplete data via the EM algorithm. J. R. Stat. Soc. **39**, 1–38 (1977)

129. Z. Deng, X. Zhu, D. Cheng, M. Zong, S. Zhang, Efficient kNN classification algorithm for big data. Neurocomputing **195**, 143–148 (2016)

130. A. Deutsch, Y. Papakonstantinou, Privacy in database publishing, in *Proceedings of the ICDT 2005*. LNCS, vol. 3363 (2005), pp. 230–245

131. P.P. De Wolf, I. Van Gelder, An empirical evaluation of PRAM. Discussion paper 04012. Statistics Netherlands, Voorburg/Heerlen (2004)

132. E. Deza, M.-M. Deza, *Dictionary of Distances* (Elsevier, Amsterdam, 2006)

133. R. Dingledine, N. Mathewson, P. Syverson, Tor: the second-generation Onion Router, in *13th USENIX Security Symposium* (2004)

134. H.-H. Do, E. Rahm, COMA - A system for flexible combination of schema matching approaches, in *Proceedings of the VLDB* (2002), pp. 610–621

135. J. Domingo-Ferrer, A three-dimensional conceptual framework for database privacy, in *Proceedings of the SDM 2007*. LNCS, vol. 4721 (2007), pp. 193–202

136. J. Domingo-Ferrer, M. Bras-Amorós, Q. Wu, J. Manjón, User-private information retrieval based on a peer-to-peer community. Data Knowl. Eng. **68**(11), 1237–1252 (2009)

137. J. Domingo-Ferrer, U. González-Nicolás, Hybrid microdata using microaggregation. Inf. Sci. **180**, 2834–2844 (2010)

138. J. Domingo-Ferrer, J.M. Mateo-Sanz, Practical data-oriented microaggregation for statistical disclosure control. IEEE Trans. Knowl. Data Eng. **14**(1), 189–201 (2002)

139. J. Domingo-Ferrer, J.M. Mateo-Sanz, V. Torra, Comparing SDC methods for microdata on the basis of information loss and disclosure risk, in Pre-proceedings of ETK-NTTS'2001. Eurostat **2**, 807–826 (2001)

140. J. Domingo-Ferrer, D. Sánchez, J. Soria-Comas, *Database Anonymization: Privacy Models, Data Utility, and Microaggregation* (Morgan and Claypool Publishers, San Rafael, 2016)

141. J. Domingo-Ferrer, F. Sebe, J. Castella-Roca, On the security of noise addition for privacy in statistical databases, in *Proceedings of the PSD 2004*. LNCS, vol. 3050 (2004), pp. 149–161

142. J. Domingo-Ferrer, A. Solanas, J. Castella-Roca, $h(k)$-private information retrieval from privacy-uncooperative queryable databases. Online Inf. Rev. **33**(4), 720–744 (2009)

143. J. Domingo-Ferrer, V. Torra, Disclosure control methods and information loss for microdata, in *Confidentiality, Disclosure, and Data Access: Theory and Practical Applications for Statistical Agencies*, ed. by P. Doyle, J.I. Lane, J.J.M. Theeuwes, L. Zayatz (North-Holland, 2001), pp. 91–110

144. J. Domingo-Ferrer, V. Torra, A quantitative comparison of disclosure control methods for microdata, in *Confidentiality, Disclosure and Data Access: Theory and Practical Applications for Statistical Agencies*, ed. by P. Doyle, J.I. Lane, J.J.M. Theeuwes, L. Zayatz (North-Holland, 2001), pp. 111–134

145. J. Domingo-Ferrer, V. Torra, A critique of the sensitivity rules usually employed for statistical table protection. Int. J. Uncertain. Fuzziness Knowl.-Based Syst. **10**(5), 545–556 (2002)

146. J. Domingo-Ferrer, V. Torra, Validating distance-based record linkage with probabilistic record linkage. LNCS **2504**, 207–215 (2002)

147. J. Domingo-Ferrer, V. Torra, Towards fuzzy c-means based microaggregation, in *Soft Methods in Probability and Statistics*, ed. by P. Grzegorzewski, O. Hryniewicz, M.A. Gil (2002), pp. 289–294

148. J. Domingo-Ferrer, V. Torra, Fuzzy microaggregation for microdata protection. J. Adv. Comput. Intell. Intell. Inform. **7**(2), 153–159 (2003)

149. J. Domingo-Ferrer, V. Torra, Disclosure risk assessment in statistical microdata protection via advanced record linkage. Stat. Comput. **13**, 343–354 (2003)

150. J. Domingo-Ferrer, V. Torra, Ordinal, continuous and heterogeneous k-anonymity through Microaggregation. Data Min. Knowl. Discov. **11**(2), 195–212 (2005)

151. J. Domingo-Ferrer, R. Trujillo-Rasúa, Microaggregation- and permutation-based anonymization of movement data. Inf. Sci. **208**, 55–80 (2012)

152. J. Drechsler, *Synthetic Datasets for Statistical Disclosure Control: Theory and Implementation* (Springer, Berlin, 2011)

153. J. Drechsler, S. Bender, S. Rässler, Comparing fully and partially synthetic datasets for statistical disclosure control in the German IAB establishment panel. Trans. Data Priv. **1**, 105–130 (2008)

154. J. Drechsler, J.P. Reiter, An empirical evaluation of easily implemented, nonparametric methods for generating synthetic datasets. Comput. Stat. Data Anal. **55**, 3232–3243 (2011)

155. R. Dubes, A.K. Jain, Clustering techniques: the user's dilemma. Pattern Recognit. **8**, 247–260 (1976)

156. G.T. Duncan, M. Elliot, J.J. Salazar, *Statistical Confidentiality* (Springer, Berlin, 2011)

157. G.T. Duncan, S.A. Keller-McNulty, S.L. Stokes, Disclosure risk vs. data utility: the R-U confidentiality map, Technical report 121, National Institute of Statistical Sciences (2001)

158. G.T. Duncan, S.A. Keller-McNulty, S.L. Stokes, Database security and confidentiality: examining disclosure risk vs. data utility through the R-U confidentiality map, Technical report 142, National Institute of Statistical Sciences (2001)

159. G.T. Duncan, D. Lambert, Disclosure-limited data dissemination. J. Am. Stat. Assoc. **81**, 10–18 (1986)

160. G.T. Duncan, D. Lambert, The risk disclosure for microdata. J. Bus. Econ. Stat. **7**, 207–217 (1989)

161. C. Dwork, Differential privacy, in *Proceedings of the ICALP 2006*. LNCS, vol. 4052 (2006), pp. 1–12

162. C. Dwork, Differential privacy: a survey of results, in *Proceedings of the TAMC 2008*. LNCS, vol. 4978 (2008), pp. 1–19

163. C. Dwork, The differential privacy frontier, in *Proceedings of the TCC 2009*. LNCS, vol. 5444 (2009), pp. 496–502

164. C. Dwork, K. Kenthapadi, F. McSherry, I. Mironov, M. Naor, Our data, ourselves: privacy via distributed noise generation. Proceedings of the EUROCRYPT **2006**, 486–503 (2006)

165. C. Dwork, N. Nissim, Privacy-preserving datamining on vertically partitioned databases, in *Proceedings of the CRYPTO 2004*. LNCS, vol. 3152 (2004), pp. 528–544

166. P. Eckersley, How unique is your browser? in *Proceedings of the 10th Privacy Enhancing Technologies Symposium (PETS)* (2010), pp. 1–17

167. M. Edman, B. Yener, On anonymity in an electronic society: a survey of anonymous communication systems. ACM Comput. Surv. **42** (2009)

168. E.A.H. Elamir, Analysis of re-identification risk based on log-linear models, in *Proceedings of the PSD 2004*. LNCS, vol. 3050 (2004), pp. 273–281

169. M. Elliot, Integrating file and record level disclosure risk assessment, in *Inference Control in Statistical Databases*, ed. by J. Domingo-Ferrer. LNCS, vol. 2316 (2002), pp. 126–134

170. M.J. Elliot, C.J. Skinner, A. Dale, Special uniqueness, random uniques and sticky populations: some counterintuitive effects of geographical detail on disclosure risk. Res. Off. Stat. **1**(2), 53–67 (1998)

171. M.J. Elliot, A.M. Manning, R.W. Ford, A computational algorithm for handling the special uniques problem. Int. J. Uncertain. Fuzziness Knowl. Based Syst. **10**(5), 493–509 (2002)

172. A.K. Elmagarmid, P.G. Ipeirotis, V.S. Verykios, Duplicate record detection: a survey. IEEE Trans. Knowl. Data Eng. **19**(1), 1–16 (2007)

173. D.W. Embley, D. Jackman, L. Xu, Multifaceted exploitation of metadata for attribute match discovery in information integration (2001)

174. U. Erlingsson, V. Pihur, A. Korolova, RAPPOR: randomized aggregatable privacy-preserving ordinal response, in *Proceedings of the 2014 ACM SIGSAC Conference on Computer and Communications Security (CCS 14)* (2014)

175. A. Erola, J. Castellà-Roca, G. Navarro-Arribas, V. Torra, Semantic microaggregation for the anonymization of query logs, in *Proceedings of the PSD 2010*. LNCS, vol. 6344 (2010), pp. 127–137

176. V. Estivill-Castro, L. Brankovic, Data swapping: balancing privacy against precision in mining for logic rules, in *Proceedings of the DaWaK-99*. LNCS, vol. 1676 (1999), pp. 389–398

177. V. Estivill-Castro, D.F. Nettleton, Privacy tips: would it be ever possible to empower online social-network users to control the confidentiality of their data? Proceedings of the ASONAM **2015**, 1449–1456 (2015)

178. J. Euzenat, P. Shvaiko, *Ontology Matching* (Springer, Berlin, 2013)

179. T. Evans, L. Zayatz, J. Slanta, Using noise for disclosure limitation of establishment tabular data. J. Off. Stat. **14**(4), 537–551 (1998)

180. A. Evfimievski, R. Fagin, D. Woodruff, Epistemic privacy. J. ACM **58**(1) (2010)

181. A. Evfimievski, J. Gehrke, R. Srikant, Limiting privacy breaches in privacy preserving data mining, in *Proceedings of the PODS* (2003)

182. E. Falkenauer, *Genetic Algorithms and Grouping* (Wiley, New York, 1998)

183. I.P. Fellegi, D. Holt, A systematic approach to automatic edit and imputation. J. Am. Stat. Assoc. **71**, 17–35 (1976)

184. I.P. Fellegi, A.B. Sunter, A theory for record linkage. J. Am. Stat. Assoc. **64**(328), 1183–1210 (1969)

185. F. Felsö, J. Theeuwes, G. Wagner, Disclosure limitation in use: results of a survey, in *Confidentiality, Disclosure, and Data Access: Theory and Practical Applications for Statistical Agencies*, ed. by P. Doyle, J.I. Lane, J.J.M. Theeuwes, L. Zayatz (North-Holland, 2001), pp. 17–42

186. C. Ferreira Torres, R. Trujillo-Rasua, The Fréchet/Manhattan distance and the trajectory anonymisation problem, in *Proceedings of the DBSec 2016*. LNCS, vol. 9766 (2016), pp. 19–34

187. C.E. Ferreiro, *Longa noite de pedra* (Xerais, 1990)

188. S.E. Fienberg, J. McIntyre, Data swapping: variations on a theme by Dalenius and Reiss, in *Proceedings of the PSD 2004*. LNCS, vol. 3050 (2004), pp. 14–29

189. S. Foresti, *Preserving Privacy in Data Outsourcing* (Springer, Berlin, 2011)

190. L. Franconi, S. Polettini, Individual risk estimation in μ-Argus: a review, in PSD 2004. LNCS **3050**, 262–272 (2004)

191. J.H. Friedman, Data mining and statistics: what's the connection? (1997), http://www-stat.stanford.edu/~jhf/ftp/dm-stat.pdf

192. J. Friedman, J. Bentley, R. Finkel, An algorithm for finding best matchings in logarithmic expected time. ACM Trans. Math. Softw. **3**(3), 209–226 (1977)

193. W.A. Fuller, Masking procedures for microdata disclosure limitation. J. Off. Stat. **9**, 383–406 (1993)

194. B.C.M. Fung, K. Wang, A.W.-C. Fu, P.S. Yu, *Introduction to Privacy-Preserving Data Publishing: Concepts and Techniques* (CRC Press, Boca Raton, 2011)

195. B.C.M. Fung, K. Wang, P.S. Yu, Top-down specialization for information and privacy preservation, in *Proceedings of the ICDR 2005* (2005)

196. B.R. Gaines, M.L.G. Shaw, Knowledge acquisition tools based on personal construct psychology. Knowl. Eng. Rev. **8**, 49–85 (1993)

197. S.L. Garfinkel, J.M. Abowd, S. Powazek, Issues encountered deploying differential privacy, in *Proceedings of the WPES 2018* (2018)

198. S. Gasemyr, Editing and imputation for the creation of a linked micro file from base registers and other administrative data, in *Conference of European Statisticians, WP8* (2005)

199. H. Gaski, *Time Is a Ship That Never Casts Anchor* (ČálliidLágádus, Karasjok, 2006)

200. J. Gehrke, M. Hay, E. Lui, R. Pass, Crowd-blending privacy, in *32nd International Cryptology Conference (CRYPTO 2012)* (2012)

201. G. Gidófalvi, Spatio-temporal data mining for location-based services, Ph.D. dissertation (2007)

202. A. Gionis, A. Mazza, T. Tassa, k-anonymization revisited, in *Proceedings of the ICDE 2008* (2008)

203. S. Gomatam, A.F. Karr, A.P. Sanil, Data swapping as a decision problem. J. Off. Stat. **21**(4), 635–655 (2005)

204. J.M. Gouweleeuw, P. Kooiman, L.C.R.J. Willenborg, P.-P. De Wolf, Post randomisation for statistical disclosure control: theory and implementation. J. Off. Stat. **14**(4), 463–478 (1998). Also as Research Paper No. 9731 (Statistics Netherlands, Voorburg, 1997)

205. M. Grabisch, J.-L. Marichal, R. Mesiar, E. Pap, *Aggregation Functions*. Encyclopedia of Mathematics and Its Applications, vol. 127 (Cambridge University Press, Cambridge, 2009)

206. L. Granquist, The new view on editing. Int. Stat. Rev. **65**(3), 381–387 (1997)

207. B. Greenberg, Rank swapping for masking ordinal microdata, US Bureau of the Census (1987) (unpublished manuscript)

208. B. Gross, P. Guiblin, K. Merrett, Implementing the post randomisation method to the individual sample of anonymised records (SAR) from the 2001 Census, paper presented at *"The Samples of Anonymised Records, an Open Meeting on the Samples of Anonymised Records from the 2001 Census"* (2004)

209. S. Gürses, C. Troncoso, C. Diaz, Engineering privacy by design. Comput. Priv. Data Prot. **14**(3) (2011)

210. S. Gurses, C. Troncoso, C. Diaz, Engineering privacy by design reloaded, in *Proceedings of the Amsterdam Privacy Conference 2015* (2015)

211. L.M. Haas, R.J. Miller, B. Niswonger, M. Tork Roth, P.M. Schwarz, E.L. Wimmers, Transforming heterogeneous data with database middleware: beyond integration. Bull. IEEE Comput. Soc. Tech. Comm. Data Eng

212. S. Hajian, M.A. Azgomi, A privacy preserving clustering technique using Haar wavelet transform and scaling data perturbation (IEEE, 2008)

213. S. Hajian, M.A. Azgomi, On the use of Haar wavelet transform and scaling data perturbation for privacy preserving clustering of large datasets. Int. J. Wavelets Multiresolution Inf. Process. **9**(6), 867 (2011)

214. S. Hajian, Simultaneous discrimination prevention and privacy protection in data publishing and mining, Ph.D. dissertation, Universitat Rovira i Virgili (2013)

215. S. Hajian, J. Domingo-Ferrer, A. Martínez-Ballesté, Rule protection for indirect discrimination prevention in data mining, in *Proceedings of the MDAI 2011*. LNCS, vol. 6820 (2011), pp. 211–222

216. A. HajYasien, Preserving privacy in association rule hiding, Ph.D. dissertation, Griffith University (2007)

217. M. Hall, E. Frank, G. Holmes, G. Pfahringer, P. Reutemann, I.H. Witten, The WEKA data mining software: an update. SIGKDD Explor. **11**(1) (2009)

218. J. Han, M. Kamber, J. Pei, *Data Mining: Concepts and Techniques*, 3rd edn. (Morgan Kaufmann Publishers, Waltham, 2011)

219. S. Hansen, S. Mukherjee, A polynomial algorithm for optimal univariate microaggregation. IEEE Trans. Knowl. Data Eng. **15**(4), 1043–1044 (2003)

220. J.R. Haritsa, Mining association rules under privacy constraints, in *Privacy-Preserving Data Mining: Models and Algorithms*. ed. by C.C. Aggarwal, P.S. Yu (Springer, Berlin, 2008), pp.239–266

221. T. Hastie, R. Tibshirani, J. Friedman, *The Elements of Statistical Learning* (Springer, Berlin, 2009)

222. M. Hay, G. Miklau, D. Jensen, P. Weis, S. Srivastava, *Anonymizing Social Networks*. Computer Science Department Faculty Publication Series, vol. 180 (2007)

223. M. Hay, G. Miklau, D. Jensen, D.F. Towsley, C. Li, Resisting structural reidentification in anonymized social networks. J. VLDB **19**, 797–823 (2010)

224. J. Herranz, S. Matwin, J. Nin, V. Torra, Classifying data from protected statistical datasets. Comput. Secur. **29**, 875–890 (2010)

225. J. Herranz, J. Nin, P. Rodríguez, T. Tassa, Revisiting distance-based record linkage for privacy-preserving release of statistical datasets. Data Knowl. Eng. **100**, 78–93 (2015)

226. J. Herranz, J. Nin, M. Solé, Optimal symbol alignment distance: a new distance for sequences of symbols. IEEE Trans. Knowl. Data Eng. **23**(10), 1541–1554 (2011)

227. T.N. Herzog, F.J. Scheuren, W.E. Winkler, *Data Quality and Record Linkage Techniques* (Springer, Berlin, 2007)

228. J.-H. Hoepman, Privacy design strategies. Proceedings of the IFIP SEC **2014**, 446–459 (2014)

229. N. Holohan, S. Antonatos, S. Braghin, A.P. Mac Aonghusa, The bounded Laplace mechanism in differential privacy. J. Priv. Confid. **10**(1), TPDP (2018)

230. N. Holohan, D.J. Leith, O. Mason, Differential privacy in metric spaces: numerical, categorical and functional data under the one roof. Inf. Sci. **305**, 256–268 (2015)

231. F. Höppner, F. Klawonn, R. Kruse, T. Runkler, *Fuzzy Cluster Analysis* (Wiley, New York, 1999)

232. D.C. Howe, H. Nissenbaum, TrackMeNot: resisting surveillance in web search, in *Lessons from the Identity Trail: Anonymity, Privacy, and Identity in a Networked Society*. ed. by I. Kerr, V. Steeves, C. Lucock (Oxford University Press, Oxford, 2009), pp.417–436

233. Z. Huang, W. Du, B. Chen, Deriving private information from randomized data, in *Proceedings of the SIGMOD'05* (2005), pp. 37–48

234. Z. Huang, P. Williamson, A comparison of synthetic reconstruction and combinatorial optimization approaches to the creation of small-area microdata, Working Paper, Department of Geography, University of Liverpool, UK (2002)

235. L.J. Hubert, P. Arabie, Comparing partition. J. Classif. **2**, 193–218 (1985)

236. E. Hüllermeier, M. Rifqi, A fuzzy variant of the Rand index for comparing clustering structures, in *Proceedings of the IFSA/EUSFLAT 2009* (2009)

237. E. Hüllermeier, M. Rifqi, S. Henzgen, R. Senge, Comparing fuzzy partitions: a generalization of the Rand index and related measures. IEEE Trans. Fuzzy Syst. **20**(3), 546–556 (2012)
238. A. Hundepool, A. van de Wetering, R. Ramaswamy, L. Franconi, C. Capobianchi, P.-P. de Wolf, J. Domingo-Ferrer, V. Torra, R. Brand, S. Giessing, μ-ARGUS version 3.2 software and user's manual (Statistics Netherlands, Voorburg NL, 2003); version 4.0 published on May 2005 (2003)
239. A. Hundepool, J. Domingo-Ferrer, L. Franconi, S. Giessing, E.S. Nordholt, K. Spicer, P.-P. de Wolf, *Statistical Disclosure Control* (Wiley, New York, 2012)
240. IBM ILOG CPLEX, High-performance mathematical programming engine. International Business Machines Corp. (2010)
241. H. Ichihashi, K. Honda, N. Tani, Gaussian mixture PDF approximation and fuzzy c-means clustering with entropy regularization, in *Proceedings of the 4th Asian Fuzzy System Symposium, May 31–June 3, Tsukuba, Japan* (2000), pp. 217–221
242. A.K. Jain, R.C. Dubes, *Algorithms for Clustering Data* (Prentice Hall, Englewood Cliffs, 1988)
243. S. Jajodia, C. Meadows, Inference problems in multilevel secure database management systems, in *Information Security*, ed. by M.D. Abrams, S. Jajodia, H.J. Podell (IEEE, 1995), pp. 570–584
244. M. Jändel, Decision support for releasing anonymised data. Comput. Secur. **46**, 48–61 (2014)
245. M. Jändel, Anonymization of personal data is impossible in practice, presented in Kistamässan om Samhällssäkerhet 2015 (2015)
246. M.A. Jaro, *UNIMATCH: a Record Linkage System: User's Manual* (U.S. Bureau of the Census, Washington, 1978)
247. M.A. Jaro, Advances in record-linkage methodology as applied to matching the 1985 Census of Tampa. Florida. J. Am. Stat. Assoc. **84**(406), 414–420 (1989)
248. J. Jiménez, V. Torra, Utility and risk of JPEG-based continuous microdata protection methods, in *Proceedings of the International Conference on Availability, Reliability and Security (ARES 2009)* (2009), pp. 929–934
249. J. Jiménez, G. Navarro-Arribas, V. Torra, JPEG-based microdata protection, in *Proceedings of the PSD 2014*. LNCS, vol. 8744 (2014), pp. 117–129
250. F.D. Johansson, O. Frost, C. Retzner, D. Dubhashi, Classifying large graphs with differential privacy, in *Proceedings of the MDAI 2015*. LNCS, vol. 9321 (2015), pp. 3–17
251. M. Juárez, V. Torra, Toward a privacy agent for information retrieval. Int. J. Intell. Syst. **28**(6), 606–622 (2013)
252. M. Juárez, V. Torra, A self-adaptive classification for the dissociating privacy agent. Proceedings of the PST **2013**, 44–50 (2013)
253. M. Juàrez, V. Torra, DisPA: an intelligent agent for private web search, in *Advanced Research on Data Privacy*. ed. by G. Navarro-Arribas, V. Torra (Springer, Berlin, 2015), pp.389–405
254. M. Kantarcioglu, A survey of privacy-preserving methods across horizontally partitioned data, in *Privacy-Preserving Data Mining: Models and Algorithms*. ed. by C.C. Aggarwal, P.S. Yu (Springer, Berlin, 2008), pp.313–335
255. A.F. Karr, The role of transparency in statistical disclosure limitation, Joint UNECE/Eurostat Work Session on Statistical Data Confidentiality (2009)
256. S.P. Kasiviswanathan, H.K. Lee, K. Nissim, S. Raskhodnikova, A. Smith, What can we learn privately? in *Proceedings of the Annual Symposium on Foundations of Computer Science* (2008)
257. J. Katz, Y. Lindell, *Introduction to Modern Cryptography* (Chapman and Hall/CRC, Boca Raton, 2008)
258. L. Kaufman, P.J. Rousseeuw, *Finding Groups in Data: an Introduction to Cluster Analysis* (Wiley, New York, 1990)
259. A. Kerckhoffs, La cryptographie militaire. Journal des sciences militaires IX Janvier 5–38 (1883)

260. D. Kifer, A. Machanavajjhala, No free lunch in data privacy, in *Proceedings of the SIGMOD 2011* (2011)

261. H.J. Kim, A.F. Karr, J.P. Reiter, Statistical disclosure limitation in the presence of edit rules. J. Off. Stat. **31**(1), 121–138 (2015)

262. H.J. Kim, J.P. Reiter, A.F. Karr, Simultaneous edit-imputation and disclosure limitation for business establishment data. J. Appl. Stat. **45**, 63–82 (2018)

263. H.J. Kim, J.P. Reiter, Q. Wang, L.H. Cox, A.F. Karr, Multiple imputation of missing or faulty values under linear constraints. J. Bus. Econ. Stat. **32**(3), 375–386 (2014)

264. J. Kim, W. Winkler, Multiplicative noise for masking continuous data, U.S. Bureau of the Census, RR2003/01 (2003)

265. D.E. Knuth, *The Art of Computer Programming, Vol. 3: Sorting and Searching* (Addison-Wesley, Reading, 1973)

266. T. Kollo, D. von Rosen, *Advanced Multivariate Statistics with Matrices* (Springer, Berlin, 2005)

267. D. Korff, Country report on different approaches to new privacy challenges in particular in the light of technological developments. Country Studies. A.4 - Germany. European Commission. Directorate-General Justice, Freedom and Security (2010), https://op.europa.eu/en/publication-detail/-/publication/9c7a02b9-ecba-405e-8d93-a1a8989f128b. Accessed May 2022

268. A. Korolova, K. Kenthapadi, N. Mishra, A. Ntoulas, Releasing search queries and clicks privately, in *Proceedings of the WWW 2009* (2009)

269. M. Kosinski, D. Stillwell, T. Graepel, Private traits and attributes are predictable from digital records of human behavior. PNAS (2013)

270. D.H. Krantz, R.D. Luce, P. Suppes, A. Tversky, *Foundations of Measurement, Vol. 1: Additive and Polynomial Representations* (Academic, New York, 1971)

271. R. Krishnapuram, J.M. Keller, A possibilistic approach to clustering. IEEE Trans. Fuzzy Syst. **1**, 98–110 (1993)

272. E. Kushilevitz, R. Ostrovsky, Replication is not needed: single database, computationally-private information retrieval, in *Proceedings of the 38th Annual Symposium on Foundations of Computer Science* (1997), pp. 364–373

273. S. Ladra, V. Torra, On the comparison of generic information loss measures and cluster-specific ones. Int. J. Uncertain. Fuzziness Knowl.-Based Syst. **16**(1), 107–120 (2008)

274. D. Lafky, The safe harbor method of de-identification: an empirical test, Department of Health and Human Services. Office of the National Coordinator for Health Information Technology (2009), pp. 15–19, http://www.ehcca.com/presentations/HIPAAWest4/lafky_2.pdf. Accessed May 2022

275. D. Lambert, Measures of disclosure risk and harm. J. Off. Stat. **9**, 313–331 (1993)

276. J. Lane, V. Stodden, S. Bender, H. Nissenbaum, *Privacy, Big Data, and the Public Good* (Cambridge University Press, Cambridge, 2014)

277. M.D. Larsen, D.B. Rubin, Iterative automated record linkage using mixture models. J. Am. Stat. Assoc. **79**, 32–41 (2001)

278. T.A. Lasko, Spectral anonymization of data, Ph.D. dissertation, MIT (2007)

279. T.A. Lasko, S.A. Vinterbo, Spectral anonymization of data. IEEE Trans. Knowl. Data Eng. **22**(3), 437–446 (2010)

280. M. Laszlo, S. Mukherjee, Minimum spanning tree partitioning algorithm for microaggregation. IEEE Trans. Knowl. Data Eng. **17**(7), 902–911 (2005)

281. M. Laszlo, S. Mukherjee, Iterated local search for microaggregation. J. Syst. Softw. **100**, 15–26 (2015)

282. J. Lee, C. Clifton, How much is enough? Choosing ε for differential privacy, in *Proceedings of the ISC 2011*. LNCS, vol. 7001 (2011), pp. 325–340

283. K. LeFevre, D.J. DeWitt, R. Ramakrishnan, Multidimensional k-anonymity, Technical report 1521, University of Wisconsin (2005)

284. K. LeFevre, D.J. DeWitt, R. Ramakrishnan, Incognito: efficient full-domain K-anonymity, in *SIGMOD 2005* (2005)
285. R. Lenz, A graph theoretical approach to record linkage, Joint ECE/Eurostat Work Session on Statistical Data Confidentiality, Working Paper No. 35 (2003)
286. V.I. Levenshtein, Binary codes capable of correcting deletions, insertions, and reversals. Dokl. Acad. nauk SSSR **163**(4), 845–8 (1965) (in Russian) (also in Cybern. Control Theory **10**(8), 707–10 (1966))
287. W.-S. Li, C. Clifton, SEMINT: a tool for identifying attribute correspondences in heterogeneous databases using neural networks. Data Knowl. Eng. **33**, 49–84 (2000)
288. N. Li, T. Li, S. Venkatasubramanian, T-closeness: privacy beyond k-anonymity and l-diversity, in *Proceedings of the IEEE ICDE 2007* (2007)
289. N. Li, M. Lyu, D. Su, W. Yang, *Differential Privacy: from Theory to Practice* (Morgan and Claypool Publishers, San Rafael, 2016)
290. J. Li, B.C. Ooi, W. Wang, Anonymizing streaming data for privacy protection, in *Proceedings of the 24th ICDE 2008* (2008), pp. 1367–1369
291. N. Li, W. Qardaji, D. Su, On sampling, anonymization, and differential privacy: or, k-anonymization meets differential privacy, in *Proceedings of the 7th ASIACCS'12* (2011)
292. T. Li, A.K. Sahu, A. Talwalkar, V. Smith, Federated learning: challenges methods, and future directions (2019)
293. F. Li, J. Sun, S. Papadimitriou, G.A. Mihaila, I. Stanoi, Hiding in the crowd: privacy preservation on evolving streams through correlation tracking, in *Proceedings of the IEEE 23rd ICDE 2007* (2007), pp. 686–695
294. C.K. Liew, U.J. Choi, C.J. Liew, A data distortion by probability distribution. ACM Trans. Database Syst. **10**, 395–411 (1985)
295. J.-L. Lin, T.-H. Wen, J.-C. Hsieh, P.-C. Chang, Density-based microaggregation for statistical disclosure control. Expert Syst. Appl. **37**, 3256–3263 (2010)
296. Y. Lindell, B. Pinkas, Privacy preserving data mining. J. Cryptol. **15**(3) (2002)
297. Y. Lindell, B. Pinkas, Privacy preserving data mining, Crypto'00. LNCS **1880**, 20–24 (2000)
298. P. Lison, P. Ildikó, D. Sánchez, M. Batet, L. Øvrelid, Anonymisation models for text data: state of the art, challenges and future directions, in *Proceedings of the 59th Annual Meeting of the Association for Computational Linguistics and 11th International Joint Conference on Natural Language Processing* (2021)
299. R.J.A. Little, Statistical analysis of masked data. J. Off. Stat. **9**(2), 407–426 (1993)
300. F. Liu, Statistical properties of sanitized results from differentially private Laplace mechanism with univariate bounding constraints. Trans. Data Priv. **12**(3), 169–195 (2019)
301. J. Liu, L. Xiong, J. Luo, Semantic security: privacy definitions revisited. Trans. Data Priv. **6**, 185–198 (2013)
302. J. Liu, K. Wang, Anonymizing bag-valued sparse data by semantic similarity-based clustering. Knowl. Inf. Syst. **35**, 435–461 (2013)
303. K. Liu, H. Kargupta, J. Ryan, Random projection based multiplicative data perturbation for privacy preserving data mining. IEEE Trans. Knowl. Data Eng. **18**(1), 92–106 (2006)
304. K. Liu, E. Terzi, Towards identity anonymization on graphs, in *Proceedings of the SIGMOD 2008* (2008)
305. L. Liu, J. Wang, Z. Lin, J. Zhang, Wavelet-based data distortion for privacy-preserving collaborative analysis, Technical report N. 482-07, Department of Computer Science, University of Kentucky (2007)
306. L. Liu, J. Wang, J. Zhang, Wavelet-based data perturbation for simultaneous privacy-preserving and statistics-preserving, IEEE ICDM Workshops (2008)
307. S. Lohr, *Sampling: Design and Analysis* (Duxbury, 1999)
308. R.D. Luce, D.H. Krantz, P. Suppes, A. Tversky, *Foundations of Measurement, Vol. III: Representation, Axiomatization, and Invariance* (Academic, New York, 1990)

309. A. Machanavajjhala, J. Gehrke, D. Kiefer, M. Venkitasubramanian, L-diversity: privacy beyond k-anonymity, in *Proceedings of the IEEE ICDE* (2006)
310. H. Mannila, H. Toivonen, A.I. Verkamo, Efficient algorithms association for discovering rules, AAAI technical report WS-94-03 (1994), http://www.aaai.org/Papers/Workshops/1994/WS-94-03/WS94-03-016.pdf
311. A.M. Manning, D.J. Haglin, J.A. Keaner, A recursive search algorithm for statistical disclosure assessment. Data Min. Knowl. Discov. **16**, 165–196 (2008)
312. R. López de Mántaras, A distance-based attribute selection measure for decision tree induction. Mach. Learn. **6**, 81–92 (1991)
313. J. Marés, N. Shlomo, Data privacy using an evolutionary algorithm for invariant PRAM matrices. Comput. Stat. Data Anal. **79**, 1–13 (2014)
314. J. Marés, V. Torra, N. Shlomo, Optimisation-based study of data privacy by using PRAM, in *Advanced Research in Data Privacy*. ed. by G. Navarro-Arribas, V. Torra (Springer, Berlin, 2015), pp.83–108
315. J. Marés, V. Torra, An evolutionary algorithm to enhance multivariate post-randomization method (PRAM) protections. Inf. Sci. **278**, 344–356 (2014)
316. S. Martínez, A. Valls, D. Sánchez, An ontology-based record linkage method for textual microdata. Artif. Intell. Res. Dev. **232** (IOS Press) 130–139 (2011)
317. J.M. Mateo-Sanz, F. Sebé, J. Domingo-Ferrer, Outlier protection in continuous microdata masking, in PSD 2004. LNCS **3050**, 201–215 (2004)
318. J.M. Mateo-Sanz, J. Domingo-Ferrer, F. Sebé, Probabilistic information loss measures in confidentiality protection of continuous microdata. Data Min. Knowl. Discov. **11**(2), 181–193 (2005)
319. A. Meyerson, R. Williams, On the complexity of optimal k-anonymity, in *Proceedings of the 23rd ACM-SIGMOD-SIGACT-SIGART Symposium on the Principles of Database Systems* (2004), pp. 223–228
320. M. Michelson, C.A. Knoblock, Learning blocking schemes for record linkage, in *AAAI* (2006)
321. W. Min, B. Liu, *Multimedia Data Hiding* (Springer, Berlin, 2003)
322. S. Miyamoto, *Introduction to Fuzzy Clustering (in Japanese)* (Ed. Morikita, Japan, 1999)
323. S. Miyamoto, H. Ichihashi, K. Honda, *Algorithms for Fuzzy Clustering* (Springer, Berlin, 2008)
324. S. Miyamoto, M. Mukaidono, Fuzzy c-means as a regularization and maximum entropy approach, in *Proceedings of the 7th International Fuzzy Systems Association World Congress (IFSA'97)*, vol. II (1997), pp. 86–92
325. S. Miyamoto, K. Umayahara, Fuzzy c-means with variables for cluster sizes (in Japanese), in *16th Fuzzy System Symposium* (2000), pp. 537–538
326. D. Mokrosinska, Privacy and autonomy: on some misconceptions concerning the political dimensions of privacy. Law Philos. **37**(2), 1–27 (2018)
327. A. Monreale, G. Andrienko, N. Andrienko, F. Giannotti, D. Pedreschi, S. Rinzivillo, S. Wrobel, Movement data anonymity through generalization. Trans. Data Priv. **3**, 91–121 (2010)
328. R. Moore, Controlled data swapping techniques for masking public use microdata sets, U.S. Bureau of the Census (unpublished manuscript) (1996)
329. L. Morey, A. Agresti, The measurement of classification agreement: an adjustment to the Rand statistic for chance agreement. Educ. Psychol. Meas. **44**, 33–37 (1984)
330. R. Mortazavi, S. Jalili, Fast data-oriented microaggregation algorithm for large numerical datasets. Knowl.-Based Syst. **67**, 192–205 (2014)
331. S. Mukherjee, Z. Chen, A. Gangopadhyay, A privacy-preserving technique for Euclidean distance-based mining algorithms using Fourier-related transforms. VLDB J. **15**, 293–315 (2006)
332. R. Münnich, J. Schürle, On the simulation of complex universes in the case of applying the German microcensus. DACSEIS Research Paper Series No. 4, University of Tübingen (2003)

333. R. Münnich, J. Schürle, W. Bihler, H.-J. Boonstra, P. Knotterus, N. Nieuwenbroek, A. Haslinger, S. Laaksoner, D. Eckmair, A. Quatember, H. Wagner, J.-P. Renfer, U. Oetliker, R. Wiegert, Monte Carlo simulation study of European surveys. DACSEIS Deliverables D3.1 and D3.2, University of Tübingen (2003)

334. V. Muntés-Mulero, J. Nin, Privacy and anonymization for very large datasets, in *Proceedings of the 18th ACM IKM* (2009), pp. 2117–2118

335. K. Muralidhar, J. Domingo-Ferrer, Rank-based record linkage for re-identification risk assessment, in *Proceedings of the PSD 2016* (2016)

336. K. Muralidhar, R. Sarathy, An enhanced data perturbation approach for small data sets. Decis. Sci. **36**(3), 513–529 (2005)

337. K. Muralidhar, R. Sarathy, Data shuffling-A new masking approach for numerical data. Manag. Sci. **52**(5), 658–670 (2006)

338. K. Muralidhar, R. Sarathy, Generating sufficiency-based non-synthetic perturbed data. Trans. Data Priv. **1**(1), 17–33 (2008)

339. K. Muralidhar, A Re-examination of the Census Bureau Reconstruction and Reidentification Attack, in *Proceedings of the PSD 2022*, LNCS 13463 pp. 312–323 (2022)

340. M. Muralidhar, R. Sarathy, Statistical dependence as the basis for a privacy measure for microdata release. Int. J. Uncertain. Fuzziness Knowl.-Based Syst. **20**, 893–906 (2012)

341. M. Nanni, G.L. Andrienko, A.-L. Barabási, C. Boldrini, F. Bonchi, C. Cattuto, F. Chiaromonte, G. Comandé, M. Conti, M. Coté, F. Dignum, F. Dignum, J. Domingo-Ferrer, P. Ferragina, F. Giannotti, R. Guidotti, D. Helbing, K. Kaski, J. Kertész, S. Lehmann, B. Lepri, P. Lukowicz, S. Matwin, D. Megías, A. Monreale, K. Morik, N. Oliver, A. Passarella, A. Passerini, D. Pedreschi, A. Pentland, F. Pianesi, F. Pratesi, S. Rinzivillo, S. Ruggieri, A. Siebes, V. Torra, R. Trasarti, J. van den Hoven, A. Vespignani, Give more data, awareness and control to individual citizens, and they will help COVID-19 containment. Trans. Data Priv. **13**, 61–66 (2020)

342. A. Narayanan, V. Shmatikov, Robust de-anonymization of large sparse datasets, in *Proceedings of the 2008 IEEE Symposium on Security and Privacy (SP'08)* (2008), pp. 111–125

343. G. Navarro, A guided tour to approximate string matching. ACM Comput. Surv. **33**(1), 31–88 (2001)

344. G. Navarro-Arribas, D. Abril, V. Torra, Dynamic anonymous index for confidential data, in *Proceedings of the 8th DPM and SETOP* (2013), pp. 362–368

345. G. Navarro-Arribas, V. Torra, Tree-based microaggregation for the anonymization of search logs, in *Proceedings of the 2009 IEEE/WIC/ACM WI'09* (2009), pp. 155–158

346. G. Navarro-Arribas, V. Torra, Rank swapping for stream data, in *Proceedings of the MDAI 2014*. LNCS, vol. 8825 (2014), pp. 217–226

347. G. Navarro-Arribas, V. Torra (eds.), *Advanced Research in Data Privacy* (Springer, Berlin, 2015)

348. A. Neelakantan, L. Vilnis, Q.V. Le, I. Sutskever, L. Kaiser, K. Kurach, J. Martens, Adding gradient noise improves learning for very deep networks (2015), arXiv:1511.06807

349. M.E. Nergiz, M. Atzori, Y. Saygın, Towards trajectory anonymization: a generalization-based approach, in *Proceedings of the SIGSPATIAL ACM GIS International Workshop on Security and Privacy in GIS and LBS* (2008)

350. M.E. Nergiz, C. Clifton, A.E. Nergiz, Multirelational k-anonymity. IEEE Trans. Knowl. Data Eng. **21**(8), 1104–1117 (2009)

351. D.A. Neumann, V.T. Norton Jr., Clustering and isolation in the consensus problem for partitions. J. Classif. **3**, 281–297 (1986)

352. H.B. Newcombe, J.M. Kennedy, S.L. Axford, A.P. James, Automatic linkage of vital records. Science **130**, 954 (1959)

353. H.B. Newcombe, Record linking: the design of efficient systems for linking records into individuals and family histories. Am. J. Hum. Genet. **19**(3), Part I (1967)

354. J. Nin, J. Herranz, V. Torra, Rethinking rank swapping to decrease disclosure risk. Data Knowl. Eng. **64**(1), 346–364 (2007)

355. J. Nin, J. Herranz, V. Torra, How to group attributes in multivariate microaggregation. Int. J. Uncertain. Fuzziness Knowl.-Based Syst. **16**(1), 121–138 (2008)

356. J. Nin, J. Herranz, V. Torra, On the disclosure risk of multivariate microaggregation. Data Knowl. Eng. **67**(3), 399–412 (2008)

357. J. Nin, J. Herranz, V. Torra, Towards a more realistic disclosure risk assessment. LNCS **5262**, 152–165 (2008)

358. J. Nin, J. Herranz, V. Torra, Using classification methods to evaluate attribute disclosure risk, in *Proceedings of the MDAI 2010*. LNCS, vol. 6408 (2010), pp. 277–286

359. J. Nin, V. Muntés-Mulero, N. Martínez-Bazan, J.-L. Larriba-Pey, On the use of semantic blocking techniques for data cleansing and integration. Proceedings of the IDEAS **2007**, 190–198 (2007)

360. J. Nin, V. Torra, Extending microaggregation procedures for time series protection. LNCS **4259**, 899–908 (2006)

361. J. Nin, V. Torra, Analysis of the univariate microaggregation disclosure risk. New Gener. Comput. **27**, 177–194 (2009)

362. H. Nissenbaum, *Privacy as contextual integrity* (Wash, Law Rev, 2004)

363. H. Nissenbaum, *Privacy in Context: Technology, Policy, and the Integrity of Social Life* (Stanford University Press, Stanford, 2010)

364. B. Nowok, G.M. Raab, C. Dibben, Synthpop: bespoke creation of synthetic data in R. J. Stat. Softw. **74**(11), 1–26 (2016). https://doi.org/10.18637/jss.v074.i11

365. M.K. Odell, R.C. Russell, U.S. Patents 1261167 (1918)

366. M.K. Odell, R.C. Russell, U.S. Patents 1435663 (1922)

367. A. Oganian, J. Domingo-Ferrer, On the complexity of optimal microaggregation for statistical disclosure control. Stat. J. U.N. Econ. Commission Eur. **18**(4), 345–354 (2000)

368. B.J. Oommen, E. Fayyoumi, On utilizing dependence-based information to enhance microaggregation for secure statistical databases. Pattern Anal. Appl. **16**, 99–116 (2013)

369. G. Orwell, *Nineteen Eighty-Four, a Novel* (Harcourt, Brace, New York, 1949)

370. R. Ostrovsky, V. Shoup, Private information storage, in *Proceedings of the 29th STOC* (1997), pp. 294–303

371. G. Paass, Disclosure risk and disclosure avoidance for microdata. J. Bus. Econ. Stat. **6**, 487–500 (1985)

372. G. Paass, U. Wauschkuhn, *Datenzugang, Datenschutz und Anonymisierung - Analysepotential und Identifizierbarkeit von Anonymisierten Individualdaten* (Oldenbourg Verlag, Munich, 1985)

373. D. Pagliuca, G. Seri, Some results of individual ranking method on the system of enterprise accounts annual survey, Esprit SDC Project, Deliverable MI-3/D2 (1999)

374. N.R. Pal, K. Pal, J.C. Bezdek, A mixed c-means clustering model, in *Proceedings of the 6th IEEE International Conference on Fuzzy Systems* (1997), pp. 11–21

375. N.R. Pal, K. Pal, J.M. Keller, J.C. Bezdek, A possibilistic c-means clustering algorithm. IEEE Trans. Fuzzy Syst. **13**(4), 517–530 (2005)

376. C. Panagiotakis, G. Tziritas, Successive group selection for microaggregation. IEEE Trans. Knowl. Data Eng. **25**(5), 1191–1195 (2013)

377. J.R. Parker, *Practical Computer Vision Using C* (Wiley, New York, 1994)

378. A. Pastore, M.C. Gastpar, Locally differentially-private randomized response for discrete distribution learning. J. Mach. Learn. Res. **22**, 1–56 (2021)

379. S.T. Peddinti, N. Saxena, On the privacy of web search based on query obfuscation: a case study of TrackMeNot, in *Proceedings of the Privacy Enhancing Technologies*. LNCS, vol. 6205 (2010), pp. 19–37

380. J. Pei, J. Xu, Z. Wang, W. Wang, K. Wang, Maintaining k-anonymity against incremental updates, in *Proceedings of the SSDBM* (2007)

381. B. Pejo, M. Remeli, A. Arany, M. Galtier, G. Acs, Collaborative drug discovery: inference-level data protection perspective. Trans. Data Priv. **15**, 87–107 (2022)

382. A. Pfitzmann, M. Hansen, A terminology for talking about privacy by data minimization: anonymity, unlinkability, undetectability, unobservability, pseudonymity, and identity management (2010)

383. M. Pierzchala, A review of the state of the art in automated data editing and imputation, in *Statistical Data Editing, Vol. 1, Conference of European Statisticians Statistical Standards and Studies N. 44* (United Nations Statistical Commission and Economic Commission for Europe, 1994), pp. 10–40

384. I. Pilán, P. Lison, L. Øvrelid, A. Papadopoulou, D. Sánchez, M. Batet, The text anonymization benchmark: a dedicated corpus and evaluation framework for text anonymization (2022), arXiv:2202.00443

385. B. Pinkas, Cryptographic techniques for privacy-preserving data mining. ACM SIGKDD Explor. **4**(2) (2002)

386. J. Polonetsky, C. Wolf, M.W. Brennan, Comments of the future of privacy forum (2014)

387. E.H. Porter, W.E. Winkler, *Approximate string comparison and its effect on an advanced record linkage system, Report RR97/02, Statistical Research Division* (U.S. Bureau of the Census, USA, 1997)

388. F. Prost, J. Yoon, Parallel clustering of graphs for anonymization and recommender systems (2016)

389. P. Quart, *Bestiari* (Proa, Barcelona, 1986)

390. T.E. Raghunathan, J.P. Reiter, D.B. Rubin, Multiple imputation for statistical disclosure limitation. J. Off. Stat. **19**(1), 1–16 (2003)

391. E. Rahm, P.A. Bernstein, A survey of approaches to automatic schema matching. VLDB J. **10**, 334–350 (2001)

392. E. Rahm, H.-H. Do, Data cleaning: problems and current approaches. Bull. IEEE Comput. Soc. Tech. Comm. Data Eng. **23**(4), 3–13 (2000)

393. W.M. Rand, Objective criteria for the evaluation of clustering methods. J. Am. Stat. Assoc. **66**(336), 846–850 (1971)

394. P. Ravikumar, W.W. Cohen, A hierarchical graphical model for record linkage, in *Proceedings of UAI 2004* (2004)

395. D. Rebollo-Monedero, J. Forné, E. Pallarés, J. Parra-Arnau, A modification of the Lloyd algorithm for k-anonymous quantization. Inf. Sci. **222**, 185–202 (2013)

396. D. Rebollo-Monedero, J. Forné, M. Soriano, An algorithm for k-anonymous microaggregation and clustering inspired by the design of distortion-optimized quantizers. Data Knowl. Eng. **70**(10), 892–921 (2011)

397. M.G. Reed, P.F. Syverson, D.M. Goldschlag, Anonymous connections and onion routing. IEEE J. Sel. Areas Commun. **16**(4), 482–494 (1998)

398. M. Reimherr, J. Awan, Elliptical perturbations for differential privacy, in *Proceedings of the NeurIPS 2019* (2019)

399. S.P. Reiss, Practical data-swapping: the first steps. ACM Trans. Database Syst. **9**(1), 20–37 (1984)

400. S.P. Reiss, Practical data-swapping: the first steps, in *Proceedings of the 1980 Symposium on Security and Privacy* (1980), pp. 38–45

401. J.P. Reiter, Releasing multiply-imputed, synthetic public use microdata: an illustration and empirical study. J. R. Stat. Soc. Ser. A **168**, 185–205 (2005)

402. J.P. Reiter, J. Drechsler, Releasing multiply-imputed synthetic data generated in two stages to protect confidentiality. Stat. Sin. **20**, 405–421 (2010)

403. M. Reiter, A. Rubin, Crowds: anonymity for web transactions. ACM Trans. Inf. Syst. Secur. **1**(1), 66–92 (1998)

404. M. Scannapieco, N. Cibella, L. Tosco, T. Tuoto, L. Valentino, M. Fortini, L. Mancini, RELAIS (REcord Linkage At IStat): user's guide (2015)

405. C. Riera, *Te deix, amor, la mar com a penyora* (Edicions 62, Barcelona, 2015)
406. F.S. Roberts, *Measurement Theory* (Addison-Wesley, Reading, 1979)
407. D.A. Robertson, R. Ethier, Cell suppression: experience and theory. LNCS **2316**, 8–20 (2002)
408. M. Rodoreda, *Mirall trencat* (Club Editor, 1974)
409. G. Rodríguez-Cano, B. Greschbach, S. Buchegger, Event invitations in privacy-preserving DOSNs - Formalization and protocol design. IFIP Adv. Inf. Commun. Technol. **457**, 185–200 (2015)
410. M. Rodriguez-Garcia, M. Batet, D. Sanchez, Semantic noise: privacy-protection of nominal microdata through uncorrelated noise addition, in *Proceedings of the 27th ICTAI* (2015)
411. D.B. Rubin, Discussion: statistical disclosure limitation. J. Off. Stat. **9**(2), 461–468 (1993)
412. E.H. Ruspini, A new approach to clustering. Inf. Control **15**, 22–32 (1969)
413. Y.K. Russom, Privacy preserving for big data analysis, Master's thesis, University of Stavanger (2013)
414. T.P. Ryan, *Modern Regression Methods* (Wiley, New York, 1997)
415. J. Sakuma, T. Osame, Recommendation based on k-anonymized ratings. Trans. Data Priv. **11**, 47–60 (2017)
416. M. Salari, S. Jalili, R. Mortazavi, TBM, a transformation based method for microaggregation of large volume mixed data. Data Min. Knowl. Discov. (2016). https://doi.org/10.1007/s10618-016-0457-y, in press
417. J. Salas, V. Torra, Graphic sequences, distances and k-degree anonymity. Discret. Appl. Math. **188**, 25–31 (2015)
418. J. Salas, V. Torra, Differentially private graph publishing and randomized response for collaborative filtering, in *Proceedings of the SECRYPT 2020* (2020)
419. P. Samarati, Protecting respondents' identities in microdata release. IEEE Trans. Knowl. Data Eng. **13**(6), 1010–1027 (2001)
420. P. Samarati, L. Sweeney, Protecting privacy when disclosing information k-anonymity and its enforcement through generalization and suppression, SRI International, Technical report
421. D. Sánchez, S. Martínez, J. Domingo-Ferrer, Comment on "Unique in the shopping mall: reidentifiability of credit card metadata". Science (18 March 1274-a) (2016)
422. G. Sande, Exact and approximate methods for data directed microaggregation in one or more dimensions. Int. J. Uncertain. Fuzziness Knowl.-Based Syst. **10**(5), 459–476 (2002)
423. R. Sarathy, K. Muralidhar, Some additional insights on applying differential privacy for numeric data, in *Proceedings of the PSD 2010*. LNCS, vol. 6344 (2010), pp. 210–219
424. Schematron, ISO/IEC. Information technology – Document schema definition language (DSDL) – Part 3: rule-based validation – Schematron. ISO/IEC 19757-3:2006 Standard JTC1/SC34 (2006)
425. F.D. Schoeman, Privacy: philosophical dimensions of the literature, Reproduced as Chapter 1 in [425] (adapted from Privacy: philosophical dimensions. Am. Philos. Q. **21** (1984)) (1984)
426. F.D. Schoeman, *Philosophical Dimensions of Privacy: an Anthology* (Cambridge University Press, Cambridge, 1984)
427. F.D. Schoeman, *Privacy and Social Freedom* (Cambridge University Press, Cambridge, 1992)
428. M.O. Searcóid, *Metric Spaces* (Springer, Berlin, 2007)
429. F. Sebe, J. Domingo-Ferrer, J.M. Mateo-Sanz, V. Torra, Post-masking optimization of the tradeoff between information loss and disclosure risk in masked microdata sets. Inference Control in Statistical Databases. LNCS **2316**, 187–196 (2002)
430. A. Serjantov, On the anonymity of anonymity systems, Technical report, University of Cambridge, Computer Laboratory (2004)
431. N. Shlomo, Making use of alternate data sources, in *Statistical Data Editing, Vol. 3: Impact on Data Quality* (United Nations Statistical Commission and Economic Commission for Europe, 2006), p. 301
432. N. Shlomo, L. Antal, M. Elliot, Measuring disclosure risk and data utility for flexible table generators. J. Off. Stat. **31**(2), 305–324 (2015)

433. N. Shlomo, T. De Waal, Preserving edits when perturbing microdata for statistical disclosure control, in *Conference of European Statisticians, WP11* (2005)
434. N. Shlomo, T. De Waal, Protection of micro-data subject to edit constraints against statistical disclosure. J. Off. Stat. **24**(2), 229–253 (2008)
435. R. Shokri, C. Troncoso, C. Diaz, J. Freudiger, J.-P. Hubaux, Unraveling an old cloak: k-anonymity for location privacy, in *Proceedings of the WPES 2010* (2010)
436. R. Shokri, M. Stronati, C. Song, V. Shmatikov, Membership inference attacks against machine learning models (2017), arXiv:1610.05820v2
437. P. Shvaiko, J. Euzenat, Ontology matching: state of the art and future challenges. IEEE Trans. Knowl. Data Eng. **25**(1), 158–176 (2013)
438. M. Solé, V. Muntés-Mulero, J. Nin, Efficient microaggregation techniques for large numerical data volumes. Int. J. Inf. Secur. **11**(4), 253–267 (2012)
439. J. Soria-Comas, J. Domingo-Ferrer, Probabilistic k-anonymity through microaggregation and data swapping. FUZZ-IEEE **2012**, 1–8 (2012)
440. J. Soria-Comas, J. Domingo-Ferrer, Sensitivity-independent differential privacy via prior knowledge refinement. Int. J. Uncertain. Fuzziness Knowl.-Based Syst. **20**(6), 855–876 (2012)
441. J. Soria-Comas, J. Domingo-Ferrer, Big data privacy: challenges to privacy principles and models. Data Sci. Eng. **1**(1), 21–28 (2016)
442. N.L. Spruill, The confidentiality and analytic usefulness of masked business microdata, in *Proceedings of the Section on Survey Research Methods 1983* (American Statistical Association, 1983), pp. 602–610
443. R.C. Steorts, S.L. Ventura, M. Sadinle, S.E. Fienberg, A comparison of blocking methods for record linkage, in PSD 2014. LNCS **8744**, 253–268 (2014)
444. G.A. Stephen, *String Searching Algorithms* (World Scientific Publishing Co, Singapore, 1994)
445. J.F. Stephen, *Liberty, Equality and Fraternity* (Henry Hold and Co, New York, 1873)
446. K. Stokes, On computational anonymity, in *Proceedings of the PSD 2012*. LNCS, vol. 7556 (2012), pp. 336–347
447. K. Stokes, M. Bras-Amorós, On query self-submission in peer-to-peer user-private information retrieval, in *Proceedings of the 4th PAIS 2011* (2011)
448. K. Stokes, M. Bras-Amorós, Optimal configurations for peer-to-peer user-private information retrieval. Comput. Math. Appl. **59**(4), 1568–1577 (2010)
449. K. Stokes, M. Bras-Amorós, A survey on the use of combinatorial configurations for anonymous database search, in *Advanced Research in Data Privacy*, ed. by G. Navarro-Arribas, V. Torra (Springer, 2015)
450. K. Stokes, O. Farràs, Linear spaces and transversal designs: k-anonymous combinatorial configurations for anonymous database search. Des. Codes Cryptogr. **71**, 503–524 (2014)
451. K. Stokes, V. Torra, Blow-up microaggregation: satisfying variance (2011) (manuscript)
452. K. Stokes, V. Torra, n-confusion: a generalization of k-anonymity, in *Proceedings of the Fifth International Workshop on Privacy and Anonymity on Information Society (PAIS 2012)* (2012)
453. K. Stokes, V. Torra, Reidentification and k-anonymity: a model for disclosure risk in graphs. Soft Comput. **16**(10), 1657–1670 (2012)
454. K. Stokes, V. Torra, Multiple releases of k-anonymous data sets and k-anonymous relational databases. Int. J. Uncertain. Fuzziness Knowl.-Based Syst. **20**(6), 839–854 (2012)
455. X. Sun, M. Li, H. Wang, A. Plank, An efficient hash-based algorithm for minimal k-anonymity, in *Proceedings of the ACSC 2008* (2008)
456. X. Sun, H. Wang, J. Li, On the complexity of restricted k-anonymity problem, in *Proceedings of the 10th Asia Pacific Web Conference (APWEB2008)*. LNCS, vol. 4976 (2008), pp. 287–296
457. X. Sun, H. Wang, J. Li, Microdata protection through approximate microaggregation, in *Proceedings of the CRPIT* (2009)
458. P. Suppes, D.H. Krantz, R.D. Luce, A. Tversky, *Foundations of Measurement, Vol. II, Geometrical, Threshold, and Probability Representations* (Academic, New York, 1989)

459. L. Sweeney, Simple demographics often identify people uniquely, Carnegie Mellon University, Data Privacy Working Paper 3. Pittsburgh 2000 (1997)
460. L. Sweeney, Datafly: a system for providing anonymity in medical data, in *Proceedings of the IFIP TC11 WG11.3 11th International Conference on Database Security XI: Status and Prospects* (1998), pp. 356–381
461. L. Sweeney, Computational disclosure control: a primer on data privacy protection, Ph.D. dissertation, Massachusetts Institute of Technology (2001)
462. L. Sweeney, Achieving *k*-anonymity privacy protection using generalization and suppression. Int. J. Uncertain. Fuzziness Knowl. Based Syst. **10**(5), 571–588 (2002)
463. L. Sweeney, *k*-anonymity: a model for protecting privacy. Int. J. Uncertain. Fuzziness Knowl. Based Syst. **10**(5), 557–570 (2002)
464. A. Takemura, Local recoding and record swapping by maximum weight matching for disclosure control of microdata sets. J. Off. Stat. **18**, 275–289 (2002). Preprint (1999) Local recoding by maximum weight matching for disclosure control of microdata sets
465. C. Task, C. Clifton, A guide to differential privacy theory in social network analysis, in *Proceedings of the 2012 IEEE/ACM International Conference on Advances in Social Networks Analysis and Mining* (2012)
466. T. Tassa, A. Mazza, A. Gionis, k-concealment: an alternative model of k-type anonymity. Trans. Data Priv. **5**(1), 189–222 (2012)
467. M. Templ, Statistical disclosure control for microdata using the R-Package sdcMicro. Trans. Data Priv. **1**, 67–85 (2008)
468. M. Templ, *Statistical Disclosure Control Microdata: Methods and Applications in R* (Springer, Berlin, 2017)
469. M. Templ, B. Meindl, Methods and tools for the generation of synthetic populations. A brief review, in *PSD 2014* (2014)
470. P. Tendick, N. Matloff, A modified random perturbation method for database security. ACM Trans. Database Syst. **19**, 47–63 (1994)
471. V. Torra, On information loss measures for categorical data, Report 3, Ottilie Project (2000)
472. V. Torra, Towards the re-identification of individuals in data files with non-common variables. Proceedings of ECAI **2000**, 326–330 (2000)
473. V. Torra, Microaggregation for categorical variables: a median based approach, in *Proceedings of the PSD 2004*. LNCS, vol. 3050 (2004), pp. 162–174
474. V. Torra, OWA operators in data modeling and reidentification. IEEE Trans. Fuzzy Syst. **12**(5), 652–660 (2004)
475. V. Torra, Constrained microaggregation: adding constraints for data editing. Trans. Data Priv. **1**(2), 86–104 (2008)
476. V. Torra, Rank swapping for partial orders and continuous variables. Proceedings of the ARES **2009**, 888–893 (2009)
477. V. Torra, On the definition of cluster-specific information loss measures, in *Advances in Artificial Intelligence for Privacy Protection and Security*. ed. by A. Solanas, A. Martínez-Ballesté (World Scientific, Singapore, 2009), pp.145–163
478. V. Torra, Privacy in data mining, in *Data Mining and Knowledge Discovery Handbook 2010*. ed. by O. Maimon, L. Rokach (Springer, Berlin, 2010), pp.687–716
479. V. Torra, Towards knowledge intensive data privacy, in *Proceedings of the DPM 2010*. LNCS, vol. 6514 (2011), pp. 1–7
480. V. Torra, Towards the formalization of re-identification for some data masking methods. Proceedings of the CCIA **2012**, 47–55 (2012)
481. V. Torra, Progress report on record linkage for risk assessment, DwB Project, Deliverable 11.3 (2014)
482. V. Torra, M. Carlson, *On the Hellinger distance for measuring information loss in microdata, UNECE/Eurostat Work Session on Statistical Confidentiality, 8th Work Session 2013* (Canada, Ottawa, 2013)

483. V. Torra, A fuzzy microaggregation algorithm using fuzzy c-means. Proceedings of the CCIA **2015**, 214–223 (2015)

484. V. Torra, *Data Privacy: Foundations, New Developments and the Big Data Challenge* (Springer, Berlin, 2017)

485. V. Torra, *Fuzzy microaggregation for the transparency principle* (J. Appl, Log, 2017). ((in press))

486. V. Torra, J.M. Abowd, J. Domingo-Ferrer, Using Mahalanobis distance-based record linkage for disclosure risk assessment. LNCS **4302**, 233–242 (2006)

487. V. Torra, J. Domingo-Ferrer, Record linkage methods for multidatabase data mining, in *Information Fusion in Data Mining*. ed. by V. Torra (Springer, Berlin, 2003), pp.101–132

488. V. Torra, Y. Endo, S. Miyamoto, On the comparison of some fuzzy clustering methods for privacy preserving data mining: towards the development of specific information loss measure. Kybernetika **45**(3), 548–560 (2009)

489. V. Torra, Y. Endo, S. Miyamoto, Computationally intensive parameter selection for clustering algorithms: the case of fuzzy c-means with tolerance. Int. J. Intell. Syst. **26**(4), 313–322 (2011)

490. V. Torra, S. Miyamoto, Evaluating fuzzy clustering algorithms for microdata protection, in *Proceedings of the PSD 2004*. LNCS, vol. 3050 (2004), pp. 175–186

491. V. Torra, Y. Narukawa, *Modeling Decisions: Information Fusion and Aggregation Operators* (Springer, Berlin, 2007)

492. V. Torra, G. Navarro-Arribas, Big data privacy and anonymization, in *Privacy and Identity Management – Facing Up to Next Steps*, ed. by A. Lehmann, D. Whitehouse, S. Fischer-Hübner, L. Fritsch (Springer, 2017), in press

493. V. Torra, G. Navarro-Arribas, D. Abril, Supervised learning for record linkage through weighted means and OWA operators. Control Cybern. **39**(4), 1011–1026 (2010)

494. V. Torra, G. Navarro-Arribas, Integral privacy, in *Proceedings of the CANS 2016*. LNCS, vol. 10052 (2016), pp. 661–669

495. V. Torra, G. Navarro-Arribas, E. Galván, Explaining recurrent machine learning models: integral privacy revisited. Proceedings of the PSD **2020**, 62–73 (2020)

496. V. Torra, J. Salas, Graph perturbation as noise graph addition: a new perspective for graph anonymization, in *Proceedings of the Data Privacy Management, Cryptocurrencies and Blockchain Technology* (2019), pp. 121–137

497. V. Torra, K. Stokes, A formalization of record linkage and its application to data protection. Int. J. Uncertain. Fuzziness Knowl. Based Syst. **20**, 907–919 (2012)

498. V. Torra, K. Stokes, A formalization of re-identification in terms of compatible probabilities. CoRR (2013), arXiv:1301.5022

499. M. Tromp, N. Méray, A.C.J. Ravelli, J.B. Reitsma, G.J. Bonsel, Ignoring dependency between linking variables and its impact on the outcome of probabilistic record linkage studies. J. Am. Med. Inform. Assoc. **15**(5), 654–660 (2008)

500. M. Trottini, Decision models for data disclosure limitation, Ph.D. dissertation, Carnegie Mellon University (2003)

501. T.M. Truta, A. Campan, K-anonymization incremental maintenance and optimization techniques, in *Proceedings of the 2007 ACM SAC* (2007), pp. 380–387

502. T.M. Truta, A. Campan, Avoiding attribute disclosure with the (extended) *p*-sensitive *k*-anonymity model, in *Data Mining*. ed. by R. Stahlbock, S. Crone, S. Lessmann (Springer, Berlin, 2010), pp.353–373

503. T.M. Truta, A. Campan, X. Sun, An overview of p-sensitive k-anonymity models for microdata anonymization. Int. J. Uncertain. Fuzziness Knowl.-Based Syst. **20**(6), 819–838 (2012)

504. T.M. Truta, B. Vinay, Privacy protection: p-sensitive k-anonymity property, in *Proceedings of the 2nd International Workshop on Privacy Data management (PDM 2006)*, p. 94

505. K. Uribe, *Bitartean heldu eskutik* (Susa, Zarautz, 2001)

506. J. Vaidya, C.W. Clifton, Y.M. Zhu, *Privacy Preserving Data Mining* (Springer, Berlin, 2006)

507. D. Vatsalan, P. Christen, V.S. Verykios, A taxonomy of privacy-preserving record linkage techniques. Inf. Syst. **38**, 946–969 (2013)
508. V.S. Verykios, Association rule hiding methods. WIREs Data Min. Knowl. Discov. **3**, 28–36 (2013). https://doi.org/10.1002/widm.1082
509. V.S. Verykios, M.L. Damiani, A. Gkoulalas-Divanis, Privacy and security in spatiotemporal data and trajectories, in *Mobility, Data Mining and Privacy: Geographic Knowledge Discovery*. ed. by F. Giannotti, D. Pedreschi (Springer, Berlin, 2008), pp.213–240
510. V.S. Verykios, A.K. Elmagarmid, E. Bertino, Y. Saygın, E. Dasseni, Association rule hiding. IEEE Trans. Knowl. Data Eng. **16**, 434–447 (2004)
511. V.S. Verykios, A.K. Elmagarmid, E. Bertino, Y. Saygın, E. Dasseni, Association rule hiding, version Jan. 7, 2003 of [509] (2003)
512. W. Wang, J. Li, C. Ai, Y. Li, Privacy protection on sliding window of data streams, in *Proceedings of the ICCC* (2007), pp. 213–221
513. Y. Wang, X. Wu, D. Hu, Using randomized response for differential privacy preserving data collection, in *Proceedings of the Workshops EDBT/ICDT 2016* (2016)
514. J. Wang, W.J. Zhong, J. Zhang, NNMF-based factorization techniques for high-accuracy privacy protection on non-negative-valued datasets, in *Proceedings of the PADM* (2006)
515. S.L. Warner, A survey technique for eliminating evasive answer bias. J. Am. Stat. Assoc. **60**(309), 63–69 (1965)
516. S.D. Warren, L. Brandeis, The right to privacy. Harv. Law Rev. **IV**(5) (1890), http://groups.csail.mit.edu/mac/classes/6.805/articles/privacy/Privacy_brand_warr2.html
517. L. Wasserman, S. Zhou, A statistical framework for differential privacy. J. Am. Stat. Assoc. **105**(489), 375–389 (2010)
518. P. Wayner, *Disappearing Cryptography. Information Hiding: Steganography & Watermarking*, 3rd edn. (Morgan Kaufmann Publishers, Amsterdam, 2009)
519. A. Westfeld, A. Pfitzman, Attacks on steganographic systems: breaking the steganographic utilities EzStego, Jsteg, Steganos, and S-Tools-and some lessons learned. LNCS **1768**, 61–76 (2000)
520. M. Willemsen, Anonymizing unstructured data to prevent privacy leaks during data mining, in *Proceedings of the 25th Twente Student Conference on IT* (2016)
521. L. Willenborg, T. de Waal, *Elements of Statistical Disclosure Control (Lecture Notes in Statistics* (Springer, Berlin, 2001)
522. W.E. Winkler, Improved decision rules in the Fellegi-Sunter model of record linkage, in *Proceedings of the Section on Survey Research Methods* (American Statistical Association, 1993), pp. 274–279
523. W.E. Winkler, Matching and record linkage, Statistical Research Division, U.S. Bureau of the Census (USA), RR93/08 (1993). Also in *Business Survey Methods*, ed. by B.G. Cox (Wiley, 1995), pp. 355–384
524. W.E. Winkler, Single ranking micro-aggregation and re-identification, Statistical Research Division report RR 2002/08 (2002)
525. W.E. Winkler, Methods for record linkage and Bayesian networks, Bureau of the Census (USA), RR2002/05 (2002)
526. W.E. Winkler, Re-identification methods for masked microdata, in *Proceedings of the PSD 2004*. LNCS, vol. 3050 (2004), pp. 216–230
527. W.E. Winkler, Overview of record linkage and current research directions, U.S. Census Bureau RR2006/02 (2006)
528. I.H. Witten, E. Frank, M.A. Hall, *Data Mining* (Elsevier, Amsterdam, 2011)
529. X. Xiao, G. Wang, J. Gehrke, Differential privacy via wavelet transforms. IEEE Trans. Knowl. Data Eng. **23**(8), 1200–1214 (2009)
530. S. Xu, J. Zhang, D. Han, J. Wang, Data distortion for privacy protection in a terrorist analysis system, in *Proceedings of the IEEE ICISI* (2005)

531. S. Xu, J. Zhang, D. Han, J. Wang, Singular value decomposition based data distortion strategy for privacy protection. Knowl. Inf. Syst. **10**(3), 383–397 (2006)
532. J. Yakowitz, Tragedy of the data commons. Harv. J. Law Technol. **25**(1), 1–67 (2011)
533. R.R. Yager, On ordered weighted averaging aggregation operators in multi-criteria decision making. IEEE Trans. Syst. Man Cybern. **18**, 183–190 (1988)
534. W.E. Yancey, W.E. Winkler, R.H. Creecy, Disclosure risk assessment in perturbative microdata protection, in *Inference Control in Statistical Databases*, ed. by J. Domingo-Ferrer. LNCS, vol. 2316 (2002), pp. 135–152
535. Q. Yang, Y. Liu, T. Chen, Y. Tong, Federated machine learning: concept and applications. ACM Trans. Intell. Syst. Technol. **10** (2019), arXiv:1902.04885
536. A.C. Yao, Protocols for secure computations, in *Proceedings of 23rd IEEE Symposium on Foundations of Computer Science, Chicago, Illinois* (1982), pp. 160–164
537. X. Yi, R. Paulet, E. Bertino, *Homomorphic Encryption and Applications* (Springer, Berlin, 2014)
538. L.A. Zadeh, Fuzzy sets. Inf. Control **8**, 338–353 (1965)
539. H. Zakerzadeh, S.L. Osborn, FAANST: fast anonymizing algorithm for numerical streaming DaTa, in *Proceedings of the DPM and SETOP* (2010), pp. 36–50
540. B. Zhou, Y. Han, J. Pei, B. Jiang, Y. Tao, Y. Jia, Continuous privacy preserving publishing of data streams, in *Proceedings of the 12th International Conference on EDBT* (2009), pp. 648–659
541. B. Zhou, J. Pei, Preserving privacy in social networks against neighborhood attacks, in *Proceedings of the ICDE 2008* (2008)
542. T. Zhu, G. Li, W. Zhou, P.S. Yu, *Differential Privacy and Applications* (Springer, Berlin, 2017)
543. L. Zhu, Z. Liu, S. Han, Deep leakage from gradients, in *Proceedings of the NeurIPS 2019* (2019)
544. http://arx.deidentifier.org/. Accessed June 2022
545. http://brenocon.com/blog/2008/12/statistics-vs-machine-learning-fight/. Accessed June 2022
546. https://ec.europa.eu/info/law/law-topic/data-protection_en. Accessed May 2022
547. https://desfontain.es/privacy/k-map.html. Accessed May 2022
548. http://www.who.int/classifications/icd/en/. Accessed May 2022. International Classification of Diseases (ICD), 10-th revision. Downloadable from
549. http://normaldeviate.wordpress.com/2012/06/12/statistics-versus-machine-learning-5-2/. Accessed June 2022
550. http://mixminion.net/. Accessed June 2022
551. http://stats.oecd.org/glossary/detail.asp?ID=6932 (version 2005). Glossary of Statistical terms, Inferential disclosure. Accessed June 2022. Also published as a glossary in [239]
552. http://stats.stackexchange.com/questions/1521/data-mining-and-statistical-analysis. Accessed June 2022
553. http://stats.stackexchange.com/questions/6/the-two-cultures-statistics-vs-machine-learning. Accessed June 2022
554. http://wordnet.princeton.edu. Princeton University "About WordNet." WordNet. Princeton University 2010. Accessed June 2022
555. http://www.census.gov. Accessed June 2022
556. https://www.bts.gov/content/motor-vehicle-safety-data
557. http://www.dssresources.com/newsletters/66.php. Accessed June 2022
558. http://www.echr.coe.int/Documents/Convention_ENG.pdf. Accessed June 2022
559. http://www.nytimes.com/2006/08/09/technology/09aol.html?_r=1&ex=1155787200&en=6c5dfa2a9c1be4ec&ei=5070&emc=eta1. Accessed June 2022
560. https://www.cs.cmu.edu/~wcohen/matching/. Accessed June 2022

561. The web page for the ODP, Open directory project was http://www.dmoz.org/, but it is not longer available. https://en.wikipedia.org/wiki/DMOZ. Accessed June 2022

562. http://www.un.org/en/documents/udhr/. Accessed June 2022

563. https://www.torproject.org/. Accessed June 2022

564. This code was in this web page, http://www.census.gov/geo/msb/stand/strcmp.c that is currently outdated. Code can be found at http://www.perlmonks.org/?node=659795. Accessed June 2022

Index

Printed in the United States
by Baker & Taylor Publisher Services